MacMillan

The American Grain Family

MacMillan

The American Grain Family

W. Duncan MacMillan

with Patricia Condon Johnston

Foreword and Epilogue
by John Steele Gordon

AFTON HISTORICAL SOCIETY PRESS
Afton, Minnesota

To all members of the next and future generations of
MacMillans in the hope that their lives will be enriched
and improved by a knowledge of our past

Half title page: A gathering of the clan at Craigbank in 1958. Standing, left to right,
are John Hugh MacMillan III and wife Susan Velie MacMillan, Cargill MacMillan, Jr. and
wife Martha Bacon MacMillan, Whitney MacMillan and wife Elizabeth Sutton MacMillan,
Sarah Stevens MacMillan, and W. Duncan MacMillan; seated, left to right, are Warren
Keinath, Jr. and wife Pauline MacMillan Keinath, Hubert Sontheim and wife Marion
MacMillan Sontheim, John H. MacMillan, Jr., Marion Dickson MacMillan, Cargill
MacMillan Sr., and Pauline Whitney MacMillan.

Frontispiece: MacMillan brothers Cargill and John, Jr.
with sprigs of lilacs in their buttonholes, 1904

Library of Congress Cataloging-in-Publication Data

MacMillan, W. Duncan (William Duncan), 1930-
    MacMillan: The American grain family/W. Duncan MacMillan, with Patricia Condon
Johnston; foreward and epilogue by John Steele Gordon.
    p. cm.
    Includes bibliographical references and index.
    ISBN 1-890434-04-3 (hardcover)
    1. Cargill, Inc.—History. 2. McMillan family. 3. Grain trade—United States—History.
I. Johnston, Patricia Condon. II. Gordon, John Steele. III. Title.
HD9039.C37M33 1998
380.1'4131'0973—dc21   98-10694
                                                                              CIP

Printed and bound in Canada

Afton Historical Society Press
P.O. Box 100
Afton, MN 55001
1-800-436-8443

CONTENTS

FOREWORD

This is a very American story, and the United States, like all other countries, is a creature of its history, its time, and its place.

In terms of place we are singularly fortunate. We are isolated from potential enemies, like an island power, and so, over most of our existence, have been able to pursue a maritime strategy, tying up few of our energies in a large military establishment. But we are also continental in size, like land-based powers, with the internal resources to match. By no means the least of those resources is the vast area between the Rocky Mountains and the Appalachians known as the Great Plains. No area of comparable size on earth—more than a million square miles—is so rich in agricultural potential.

We are equally fortunate in our time. The United States was born just as a profound economic—and therefore political—revolution was beginning in Europe. Adam Smith's *The Wealth of Nations* was published the very same year as the Declaration of Independence, and immediately began to transform the theoretical economic landscape. Before the peace treaty with England had been signed, James Watt's rotary steam engine had begun to transform the actual economic landscape. Because the United States was new and not yet set in its ways, it was able to weather the changes of the industrial revolution with far less difficulty than most of the old-world nations.

Just to give one example, in 1824, when the Supreme Court unanimously ruled, in the case of *Gibbons v. Ogden*, that the federal government had exclusive jurisdiction over interstate commerce, the United States established in one stroke a continent-spanning common market that Europe would not even attempt for more than a century and in which it has yet to fully succeed.

Finally, it is in our history that we have been most fortunate of all. It is not an accident that this country has always had an extraordinary can-do, get-up-and-go outlook on life. After all, the vast majority of our ancestors had to get up and come, often at great personal peril, in order to be here. And they were able to leave behind most of the ancient ethnic, religious, and political animosities that have so bedeviled the old world.

So while no one would call American politics tranquil, they have been—with the gigantic exception of the Civil War—largely peaceful. To get ahead and make their place in the world, Americans have needed to compete by means other than politics and its extension, war. James Gordon Bennett, who changed the world (and made a fortune for himself) by inventing modern journalism in the 1830s, noticed this as long ago as 1868. That year he wrote in the *New York Herald* that "Men no longer attempt to rule by the sword, but they find in money a weapon as sharp and more effective; and having lost none of the old lust for power they seek to establish over their fellows the despotism of dollars."

Bennett, as usual, was exaggerating, although the late 1860s was perhaps the most corrupt period in American history. But he was entirely correct in saying that Americans have sought advantage on the fields of capitalism more than any other nation. And while some have found advantage far beyond the average, we are all richer because of this individual quest for economic success.

This book is about one family's quest over the last century and a half to find economic success. To say they have found it would be understating the fact considerably as they are today the owners of the largest privately held company on the face of the earth. But while we usually think of American fortunes as coming from ever-newer technology, this one comes from America's oldest industry, agriculture.

When the MacMillan family arrived on this continent to stay, agriculture was still a highly fragmented enterprise. The primitive transportation then available limited how far produce could be economically shipped. But as steamboats and then the railroads penetrated ever farther into the heart of those bottomlessly fertile plains of the Midwest, the grain market was transformed. A myriad of local markets was transformed over the course of a few decades into one global market. During those decades the family faced an ever-changing economic situation as wars, depressions, booms, and busts made change the only constant.

Meanwhile, of course, the family had to live. And like all families, rich and poor, that was not always easy. Over the years of their saga, the MacMillans faced success and failure, love and loss. They even went broke once. But if they met with triumph and disaster, they learned, in Kipling's words, "to treat those two imposters just the same." They managed to retain the simple virtues that are so characteristic of their native land, the American Middle West.

The story of the MacMillan family is, then, a story of daring, luck, hard work, quick thinking, courage, and, of course, the occasional scoundrel. As I said, it is a very American story.

J. S. G.

PREFACE: MacMILLAN

There is more than one way to spell this ancient clan name. I am a MacMillan, but I have cousins who are McMillans. Long-ago Scottish Gaels wrote *MacGhillemhaoil* (Mock'-gheelia-vul). Springing from ecclesiastical roots, MacMillan means "son of the little tonsured one."

The progenitor of our clan was a twelfth-century monk named Gilchrist An Gille Maolan, a practitioner of the Culdee order of the Celtic Church. Unlike their Roman counterparts, Culdee clergy did not practice celibacy; they married, raised families, and passed on their church offices to their sons. To differentiate themselves from Roman clerics who shaved the crowns of their heads—and with whom they carried on a bitter, centuries-long feud over doctrine—Culdee churchmen shaved their hair in front of a line drawn over the top of the head from ear to ear. *An Gille Maolan* refers to this so-called St. John's tonsure.

Gilchrist was the third son of Cormac, the first bishop of Dunkeld about 1107, whose royal blood still flows in our veins. Descended from King Kenneth MacAlpin, who united the warring Picts and Scots in 844 and established his throne at Scone, Cormac was also the great-great-grandson of Macbeth. Shakespeare made mincemeat of the reputation of this wise and holy man, casting him as a usurper and bloodthirsty villain, but Macbeth was actually the earl of Moray with a three-fold claim to the Scottish throne; beloved by his Highland followers, he ruled Scotland for sixteen years with "right lawful" justice.

The first time our name appears in Latin, it is inscribed *mac Molini* in the Book of Deer, a record of land grants and offerings made to the Celtic Church between 1000 and 1150 A.D. During the next several centuries it is found in various English documents as *MacMolan* in 1263, *Macmolane* in 1452, *McMulane* in 1505, *McMillane* in 1632, and *Mcmillen* in 1641. By 1745, when Bonnie Prince Charlie landed in Scotland to lead his Jacobite clansmen in a last desperate attempt to regain the British throne for the Stuarts, the name was being spelled *McKmillan*, *McMilland*, *McMullan*, *MacMylan*, and *MacMyllan*.

Clinging to a long-established family pattern, my great-grandfather and his father and grandfather before him went by "McMillan." Sometime in the early 1890s, when he was twenty-three or twenty-four years old, my grandfather John H. MacMillan, Sr., born and bred in the American Midwest, adopted the spelling we use today. Whatever his personal reasons for doing so—some family members seemed to feel that "Mc," meaning "son of," was the abbreviated English version of the more authentic Scottish "Mac"—he also marked the beginning of a new era for our family.

The McMillan family fortunes did not survive the 1893 Depression and its aftermath. As a *MacMillan*, my grandfather John H. MacMillan, Sr. parented our present-day grain family. Credited with salvaging the foundering Cargill Elevator Company in the early 1900s, he delivered it from the jaws of its creditors and set the family on the course which continues to provide its livelihood.

John H. MacMillan, Sr. (center) with his brothers Will (left) and Dan on the front porch of John Sr.'s home at 317 Clifton Avenue in Minneapolis about 1914. Will was an astronomer who spent his entire career teaching at the University of Chicago. John, Sr. and Dan went to work each day at the Cargill Elevator Company in Minneapolis where John, Sr. was president.

MacMillan Genealogical Tree

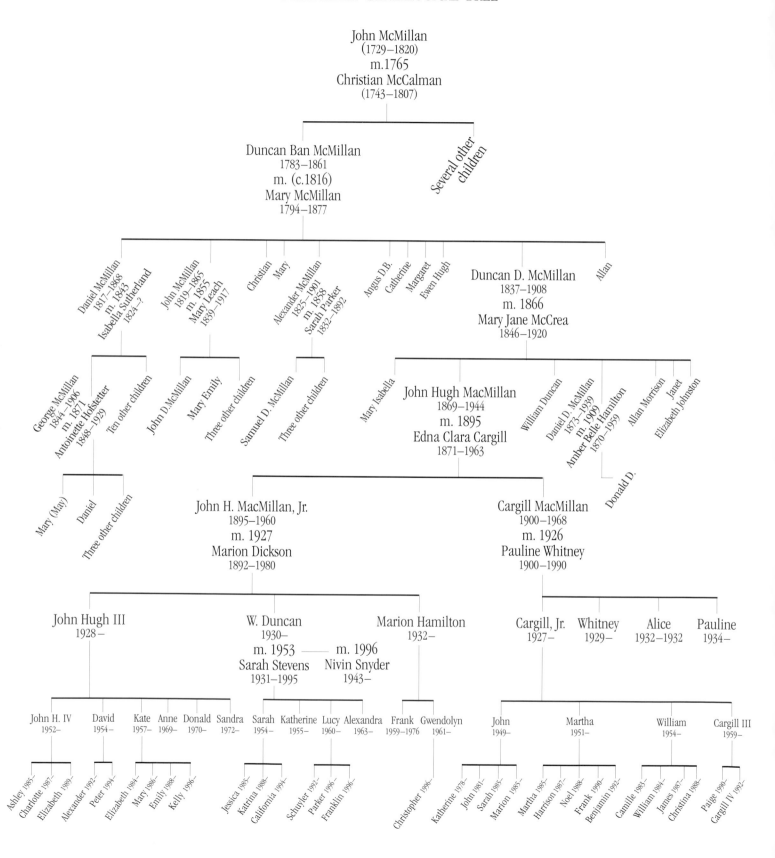

John McMillan
(1729–1820)
m.1765
Christian McCalman
(1743–1807)

Duncan Ban McMillan
1783–1861
m. (c.1816)
Mary McMillan
1794–1877

Several other children

Daniel McMillan
1817–1868
m. 1843
Isabella Sutherland
1824–?

John McMillan
1819–1865
m. 1855
Mary Leach
1839–1917

Christian

Mary

Alexander McMillan
1825–1901
m. 1858
Sarah Parker
1832–1892

Angus D.B.

Catherine

Margaret

Ewen Hugh

Duncan D. McMillan
1837–1908
m. 1866
Mary Jane McCrea
1846–1920

Allan

George McMillan
1844–1906
m. 1871
Antoinette Hofstetter
1848–1929

Ten other children

John D.McMillan

Mary Emily

Three other children

Samuel D. McMillan

Three other children

Mary Isabella

John Hugh MacMillan
1869–1944
m. 1895
Edna Clara Cargill
1871–1963

William Duncan

Daniel D. McMillan
1873–1939
m. 1909
Amber Belle Hamilton
1870–1959

Allan Morrison

Janet

Elizabeth Johnston

Mary (May)

Daniel

Three other children

John H. MacMillan, Jr.
1895–1960
m. 1927
Marion Dickson
1892–1980

Cargill MacMillan
1900–1968
m. 1926
Pauline Whitney
1900–1990

Donald D.

John Hugh III
1928–

W. Duncan
1930–
m. 1953
Sarah Stevens
1931–1995

m. 1996
Nivin Snyder
1943–

Marion Hamilton
1932–

Cargill, Jr.
1927–

Whitney
1929–

Alice
1932–1932

Pauline
1934–

John H. IV
1952–

David
1954–

Kate
1957–

Anne
1969–

Donald
1970–

Sandra
1972–

Sarah
1954–

Katherine
1955–

Lucy
1960–

Alexandra
1963–

Frank
1959–1976

Gwendolyn
1961–

John
1949–

Martha
1951–

William
1954–

Cargill III
1959–

Ashley 1985–
Charlotte 1987–
Elizabeth 1989–

Alexander 1992–
Peter 1994–

Elizabeth 1984–
Mary 1986–
Emily 1988–
Kelly 1996–

Jessica 1985–
Katrina 1988–
California 1994–

Schuyler 1992–
Parker 1996–
Franklin 1996–

Christopher 1996–

Katherine 1978–
John 1981–
Sarah 1985–
Marion 1985–

Martha 1985–
Harrison 1987–
Noel 1988–
Frank 1990–
Benjamin 1992–

Camille 1983–
William 1984–
James 1987–
Christina 1988–

Paige 1990–
Cargill IV 1992–

WITH WOLFE AT QUEBEC

Major General James Wolfe, a portrait made at Quebec, 1759

Our first MacMillan ancestor to set foot in North America was my great-great-great-grandfather John McMillan, who fought with the English hero James Wolfe at the Battle of Quebec in 1759.

A tenant farmer from Glen Nevis, a tiny green valley tucked deep in the steep, stony recesses of western Scotland, John McMillan was one of thousands of brave Highlanders, smart in their regimental tartans, who helped the British wrest control of the North American continent from the French during the Seven Years War—known in America as the French and Indian War.

By 1759 the auld Scotland of the ancient clans immortalized by Burns and Scott was already fading rapidly into myth; the old way of life had ended thirteen years earlier on a cold gray April morning at Culloden, where nine thousand veteran British redcoats had made quick slaughter of fewer than five thousand exhausted, disorganized, and ill-equipped Scottish clansmen. Settling forever the long brawl of Scottish history, the bloodbath at Culloden was the last battle fought on British soil.

English retribution in the wake of Prince Charles Edward Stuart's lost bid to regain the crown of his ancestors had been swift and terrible. Fugitives thought to have collaborated with the prince were hunted down and shot or hanged, and the countryside plundered. Parliament divested Scottish chiefs of their ancient estates, abolishing the hereditary jurisdictions that had given them the power of "pit and gallows" over their people; and newly installed managers on the forfeited estates introduced improved methods of agriculture

Answering Prince Charles Edward Stuart's call to arms, the Highland army by Loch Eil en route to Culloden in 1746. The last troops to fight for the Highland way of life, the Scottish clansmen were roundly defeated and dispersed by British soldiers under the Duke of Cumberland at Drummossie Moor.

that led to the dispersal and emigration of thousands upon thousands of destitute Highland families.

Stripped of his arms—Highlanders were forbidden under pain of death to possess any gun, sword, pistol, or arm whatsoever—the clansman was also stripped of his pride; the legislation most damaging to the Highland way of life was the insidious ban on traditional dress. By the time the government lifted the proscription against tartans in 1782, a new generation had forgotten the old passion for Highland dress. The wearing of the kilt had become an affectation of anglicized lairds, fancy dress for gentlemen, and the uniform of the King's Highland regiments.

John McMillan was twenty-eight when he signed on with Colonel Simon Fraser's 78th Highland Regiment of Foot in early 1757—the year English Minister of War William Pitt began recruiting wild *hielandmen* under their former chiefs to help build the British Empire. The 78th was a cross section of the clans that had fought at Culloden; most of the officers, Colonel Simon Fraser included, were Jacobite gentry who had been "out" under Prince Charlie, but there were also officers of Clan Campbell and other clans that had fought on the Hanoverian side for the king's fat son, the Duke of Cumberland.

Having vanquished the Scots at Culloden, England was soon fighting wars on both sides of the Atlantic, beginning with the French and Indian trouble in America in 1755. By the next year she was involved on a much larger scale in Europe, where it was Britain and Prussia against France, Austria, Sweden, a few small German states, and later, Spain. English men-of-war battled French and Spanish fleets in the Atlantic, the Mediterranean, the Caribbean, and the Indian Ocean; French and British armies warred in India; and hostilities reached as far as the Philippines, where the British captured Manila.

"This should really have been called the First World War," observed historian Samuel Eliot Morison, for "hostilities were waged over as large a portion of the globe as in 1914–1918."

On the eve of the contest for Quebec, the French Empire claimed the greater part of North America—from the Alleghenies, which hemmed in the English seaboard colonies, west to the Rocky Mountains, bounded by Rupert's Land surrounding Hudson's Bay to the north, and extending through the Mississippi River Valley to the Gulf of Mexico. All of this vast territory was governed from the Castle of St. Louis inside the walled city at Quebec, where the father of Canada, Samuel de Champlain, had established a fur trading post at the confluence of the St. Lawrence and the St. Charles Rivers in 1608.

John McMillan was one of more than a thousand Highland recruits who assembled in Inverness on Loch Ness in northern Scotland in late April 1757. Walking about the streets in their new red-and-green Fraser tartans, their black bonnets cocked jauntily over their right ears, "we were very proud of our looks,"

Private, 78th Fraser Highlanders, ca. 1758

wrote one volunteer. Issued Long Land muskets, pistols, and basket-hilted broadswords, the 78th Fraser Highlanders were shipped to Halifax in southern Nova Scotia. Under Brigadier James Wolfe they were part of an army of twelve thousand British troops that captured the French garrison at Louisbourg on Isle Royale (now Cape Breton) the next summer.

The fate of North America now hung in the balance, for the French still held the walled city of Quebec, the key to the continent that the British would need to unlock the American West. With fair weather and provisions in short supply, the Fraser Highlanders were shipped to winter quarters in New England, while James Wolfe sailed for England, where he lingered at Bath to nurse his poor health. The next year in June 1759, under the direction of Wolfe, whom Pitt had elevated to major general in charge of the expedition, an English fleet of two hundred ships, sloops, and transports with nine thousand men sailed out of Louisbourg harbor. So began the arduous thousand-mile voyage up the St. Lawrence to Quebec (named for an Algonquian word meaning "place where the river narrows"). English naval officer James Cook, who would later explore much of the Pacific Ocean, sailed ahead to buoy a safe passage though the tortuous channel separating Ile d'Orleans from the south shore. By the month's end, to the utter amazement of the French, who placidly assumed that none save a seasoned Canadian pilot could safely navigate the channel, the entire British fleet lay anchored at the foot of the Canadian citadel.

At thirty-two, James Wolfe was two years older than John McMillan. Audacious, courageous, and charismatic, he was a born leader who inspired fierce loyalty in his troops. An unlikely hero, on account of his slight build, frailty, and chronically ill health, he had gone into the army when he was fifteen and moved up quickly through the ranks. Before he was twenty, Captain Wolfe had led British troops against Scottish clansmen at Culloden. When he was afterwards stationed five years with his garrison at Inverness to keep the peace in that rough and dirty town, he gained the goodwill of the Highlanders for his fair dealings. A brilliant military strategist and student of warfare for whom death held no fear, this valiant, red-haired warrior has been called "the most Napoleonic soldier in English history."

Merely reaching Quebec and capturing it were two different matters, however. A natural fortress, Quebec was a rock-hewn stronghold of palaces, churches, houses, convents, and hospitals squatting solidly on top a precipitous two-hundred-foot bluff. Wolfe succeeded in seizing Point Levi, a thousand yards across the river on the south shore, then aimed his guns on the Lower Town beneath the cliff, reducing it to ashes. But the bastion itself appeared impregnable. Impervious to attack from the river, Quebec would also be nearly impossible to take by land, since a small number of men on the heights could readily destroy an army landing below. To be on the safe side, the French

View from the Citadel of Quebec from an engraving in W. H. Bartlett's Canadian Scenery, *published in London, 1840*

General, the Marquis de Montcalm, had concentrated sixteen thousand men including Canadian militia and Indians in and around Quebec.

Wolfe's health was deteriorating rapidly that summer, probably due to a flareup of tuberculosis. He ached for a pitched battle, but Montcalm refused to oblige him. The summer wore on with incessant artillery fights between British gunboats and frigates and French batteries on shore. Chaos reigned in Upper Town, where bursting shells half ruined the cathedral, tore up the streets, and demolished houses, burying part of the ramparts beneath the debris. But it did Wolfe no good to lay waste to the town if he could not defeat the French army defending it. Playing Fabius to Wolfe's Hannibal and avoiding a major encounter, Montcalm was protracting his defense and exhausting the supplies of his enemy, who would have to sail back to Europe before winter set in.

"My antagonist has wisely shut himself up in inaccessible intrenchments so that I can't get at him, without spilling a torrent of blood, and that perhaps to little purpose," agonized Wolfe in a last letter to his mother written on August 31. "The Marquis de Montcalm is at the head of a great number of bad soldiers and I am at the head of a small number of good ones, that wish for nothing so much as to fight him—but the wary old fellow avoids an action, doubtful of the behaviour of his army."

Wolfe, who had recently been confined ten days to his headquarters in a French farmhouse with a raging fever, believed himself to be dying, but he pleaded with his physician to "pray make me up so that I may be without pain for a few days, and able to do my duty: that is all I want." The lateness of the season demanded immediate action, and by early September Wolfe was implementing bold plans to land his army inside the enemy lines west of the city. From the south shore of the river above Quebec, he had discovered by telescope a steep, narrow path on the opposite bank, leading to the Plains of

Major General James Wolfe, in an engraving by R. Houston from a contemporary print

Abraham—a large, nearly level, grassy tract forming part of a high plateau. The place took its name from an early French colonist, Abraham Martin. There, in a small cluster of tents, Montcalm had posted a small picket guard, which, if taken by surprise, might be overcome. Wolfe had found his opponent's Achilles' heel.

On the moonless evening of September 12, his lank, diseased frame nervous with anticipation, Wolfe loaded seventeen hundred redcoats and Highlanders into large, flat-bottomed boats. At the stroke of two in the morning they began rowing silently down the St. Lawrence on the ebbing tide. The line of boats stretched out over half a mile. John McMillan was among the Fraser Highlanders who sat back to back on long benches in the packed boats, their muskets held upright between their knees, their broadswords tucked under their left armpits. Two Fraser Highlander officers rode in one of the foremost boats with General Wolfe and other staff officers. In later life, a young midshipman would tell how Wolfe had recited Gray's "Elegy Written in a Country Churchyard" with its famous line, "The paths of glory lead but to the grave."

The night's venture proceeded like clockwork. It was two minutes past four when the lead boat made a safe landing at a narrow strand known since as Wolfe's Cove. Spilling out of the boats, the agile Highlanders, their muskets slung across their shoulders, their broadswords in their teeth, picked their way up the steep ascent. Catching the enemy off guard, the first troops to reach the summit captured the small outpost. In the cove below, the van of Wolfe's army swarmed out of the flat-bottomed boats and clambered up the cliff. Larger vessels, bringing up the rear, emptied out additional troops. By daybreak, Wolfe had forty-five hundred British troops deployed on the Plains of Abraham. At the east end of the plains stood the city of Quebec.

Wolfe's Cove, from an engraving in Canadian Scenery

Montcalm had not slept that night. He was expecting the British to attack from a different quarter, but upon hearing the sound of cannon above the town at daybreak, he rode out from Quebec to see redcoats two miles away on the Plains of Abraham. Thinking he would find a detachment, he was stunned to discover an army.

> Full in sight before him stretched the lines of Wolfe [wrote Francis Parkman in his monumental *France and England in North America*]; the close ranks of the English infantry, a silent wall of red, and the wild array of the Highlanders, with their waving tartans, and bagpipes screaming defiance.

Forced now to do battle on Wolfe's terms, Montcalm prepared to attack. By ten o'clock, four thousand white-uniformed French troops had dashed on the double through the narrow Quebec streets to form up outside the city walls. Drums beating, banners flying, they began their advance. One young Canadian among them afterwards remembered how "very well" the Marquis de Montcalm looked astride "a black or dark bay horse along the front of our lines, brandishing his sword, as if to excite us to do our duty. He wore a coat with wide sleeves, which fell back as he raised his arm, and showed the white linen of the wristband."

Some of the advancing French troops began firing wildly, but the British held their fire, feigning composure and carrying away and replacing their dead. Not until the enemy was within forty paces did Wolfe, dressed in a new uniform for the occasion, raise his cane, giving the order to present and fire. It was all over in minutes. Musket fire rang out with the crash of a single terrible cannon shot, and a second equally horrendous volley followed. When the smoke rose, dead and wounded soldiers covered the ground. British infantrymen attacked the dazed survivors with fixed bayonets, and kilted Highlanders rushed after them with broadswords. Bagpipes shrieking regimental music drowned out the noise of the slaughter.

Both Wolfe and Montcalm sustained mortal wounds on the battlefield. Hit by musket balls in the wrist and in the groin during the French advance, Wolfe had remained in action, but a third lead ball shattered his right breast during the second volley, smashing his ribs and lung. Staggered, the fallen warrior slumped to the ground and was carried to the rear. There was no need for a surgeon, he told his aides, "It's all over with me." His spent body was carried down the steep path to the beach on a stretcher made from a Highlander's plaid and embalmed on board the frigate *Lowestoffe*.

The Marquis de Montcalm was hit during the French retreat by a round from the only fieldpiece the English had been able to pull up to the plain. Held up by a soldier on each side, he reentered the walled city on his horse. Learning from the surgeon that his wounds were fatal, Montcalm wrote to the English commandant: "Monsieur, the humanity of the English sets my mind at peace

General the Marquis de Montcalm

concerning the fate of the French prisoners and the Canadians. . . . Do not let them perceive that they have changed masters. Be their protector as I have been their father."

Five days later, with its garrison in utter confusion and men deserting hourly, Quebec ran up a white flag. Wolfe's troops, including the 78th Fraser Highlanders, ended up having to occupy the former capital of New France that desperately cold winter, taking shelter where they could find it in shelled and deserted houses.

> We had a stove, to-be-sure [wrote one English soldier], but our Highlanders . . . would not suffer the door to be closed, as they thought that if they could not actually see the fire, it was impossible that they could feel it. . . . Three or four would sit up close to the door of the stove, and when these were a little warm'd three or four others would relieve them and so on. Some days they were about frozen to death or suffocated by the smoke and to mend the matter they had nothing better than green wood!

In January, when the enemy began showing signs of activity, the Fraser Highlanders were ordered to stand guard in Lower Town after a severe sleet storm had glazed the streets with ice. Finding it impossible to march safely down slippery Mountain Street with loaded muskets, they sat down and slid down the hill, one after another, on their bare behinds. The nuns at the Ursuline Convent in Quebec knit long woolen hose for these breechless warriors.

Both food and fuel were scarce. As the winter wore on, the soldiers had no fresh meat or vegetables, and many wooden houses had to be torn down for firewood. Only 656 men in Wolfe's command had been killed in the battle for Quebec, but many more died of cold or scurvy in the months following. Out of a total garrison of 5,653 men at the end of September, 672 were dead and 2,312 sick or unfit for duty by late spring.

In the meantime, the war in America was not yet quite over. Despite the fall of Quebec, the French still possessed much of Canada, but they were fast losing their grip. During the summer of 1760, the 78th Fraser Highlanders helped quell an attempted French takeover of Quebec, then marched with General Murray and British armies under Generals Amherst and Haviland on Montreal, where the last French governor of Canada finally surrendered the colony to Great Britain in September.

Stationed during the next three years in Quebec, at St. John's in Newfoundland, and in Nova Scotia, the 78th Fraser Highlanders were disbanded following the Treaty of Paris in 1763, when France ceded all of eastern North America from the Arctic to Florida to Great Britain. Many of the Highlanders remained in Canada, accepting British land grants in Quebec offered to any soldier or officer wishing to settle there; but most of them, including John McMillan, chose to go home to Scotland. Ironically, more than fifty years later, John's son Duncan Ban McMillan, my great-great-grandfather, would emigrate from Scotland on a ship bound for Quebec and settle in Canada. The next generation of McMillans, Duncan Ban's children, emigrated from Canada to the United States.

In the 1950s, fresh out of college and beginning my career with the Cargill Company, I worked for a year in our Montreal office. On several occasions my wife Sally and I drove up to see the Plains of Abraham, and it always sent shivers up my spine. Canada's most celebrated battlefield is now a green-lawned public park, but it is easy to visualize the British holding steady on this great sweep of land in the face of the agonizingly slow French advance. And what about John McMillan? Little did this clannish Gael know that he was helping set the North American stage on which his descendants would play out their destinies.

Shipped back to Scotland and paid off in Inverness, John McMillan returned home to Glen Nevis, where generations of his family had tilled the same stony soil at Achintee Farm. The farm had been largely destroyed during Prince Charlie's failed rebellion, and the main house would not be rebuilt until 1813. This vine-covered two-story stone residence now caters to bed-and-breakfast guests. Behind it, crouching prettily at the foot of lofty Ben Nevis, Britain's highest hill at 4,406 feet, is the tiny, white-washed stone cottage that housed our McMillan forebears. The sole remaining example of several such tenants' dwellings once clustered at Achintee, our ancestral home is now a "self-catering cottage," updated and electrified to accommodate a growing influx of tourists.

In the 1880s Victorian meteorologists built and manned a squat, stone-walled observatory on Ben Nevis that was home year round, summer and winter, in foul weather and fair, to a team of brave scientists who sometimes risked their lives to keep hourly records of climatic conditions on the top of the mountain. Today thousands of people from all parts of the world come to Glen Nevis to climb the well-worn five-mile path to the mountain's summit. The path begins mere feet from the door of the former McMillan cottage.

Quickened by the clear and rapid trout and salmon waters of the river Nevis, Glen Nevis is a narrow, winding glacial valley rimmed by hunkering mountains. Ten miles long, it ascends four hundred feet above sea level to culminate in a breathtaking rocky gorge and rushing waterfall. Long-ago Pictish warriors built a stone-and-wood fort in Glen Nevis and raised their celebrated deerhounds on a grassy stretch of pasture near the river. In the year 790, emissaries of Emperor Charlemagne of the Holy Roman Empire and King Eoghan MacAodh of the Picts met near the entrance to Glen Nevis to sign a treaty that sent four thousand Pictish warriors overseas to fight in early French campaigns.

Ben Nevis, Olympus of Scotland, is not "a single mountain at all, but a colossal bundle of the hugest of Scotland's mountains rolled into one mighty mass," wrote local nineteenth-century historian Alexander Stewart, "on whose summit, if anywhere, all the hidden mysteries of ancient Celtic Baalism and Druidical worship may be supposed still to linger."

In more recent times, Cameron clansmen held sway in Glen Nevis. The Camerons had their seat at Glen Nevis House, now also rebuilt, which Alexander, 12th chief of the clan, and his family occupied during the 1745 Rising. Alexander ended up in Edinburgh Castle for his part in the intrigue, and his house was burned to the ground. With the redcoats approaching, Alexander's wife had hidden the family china and silver, wrapped her infant son Ewen in her plaid, and escaped to Samuel's Cave at the head of the glen. Legend has it that she was found there by Cumberland's human hounds, one of whom slit open her plaid with his sword. Expecting to find money or jewelry, he found instead that he had nicked, almost killed, baby Ewen.

The McMillans were tenants of the Camerons and relative newcomers to Glen Nevis, but the family had lived in the mountainous Lochaber region of the western Highlands since the twelfth century. During the English Civil War (1642-1649), when the Cameron of Lochiel (Lock-eel), chief of the Camerons, was recruiting manpower for the Royalists, the McMillans mustered over one hundred men for battle. Led by officers from the clan's principal families, their war cry was: *MacMhaolain Mor, MacMhaolain Mor!* (Great McMillan, Great McMillan!) Among the Lochiel's most trusted followers, McMillans were generally employed in any desperate enterprise that occurred.

The last hereditary chief of the Lochaber McMillans was John, 9th of Murlaggan, a staunch Protestant who had wanted nothing to do with Prince Charlie's rebellion. When asked by the Cameron of Lochiel to rally his men for the Catholic Pretender, John had replied that he would do so on the condition that the young chevalier publicly renounce his Roman faith at Kilmallie Church. This did not happen, but according to family tradition, Murlaggan's two sons were with Lochiel at Culloden, carrying him from the field after he was wounded in both ankles by grapeshot.

By a strange twist of fate, Prince Charlie made his last futile stand at John of Murlaggan's farm at Loch Arkaig. Prince Charlie and the Lochiel ultimately escaped to France, where Lochiel obtained a commission in the French army, but John of Murlaggan ended his days in penury. Stripped by marauding British troops of his livestock and household goods, he was forced to relinquish his hereditary Highland farm.

Called on to testify in a legal action in 1761, John of Murlaggan said in a sworn deposition that he was "Head of the tribe of McMillans or McIllywouls and he and his ancestors [had] been kindly tenants or possessors of Murlagan for more than 300 years past. That he himself possessed them for many years preceding the year 1745, when, falling low in circumstances, he was obliged to give up holding lands." For generation after generation, he stated, "the Lairds of Lochiell gave a cheap bargain of the Farm in order to secure the Attachment and personal Services of the Tribe of McMillan."

About 1765, two years after being mustered out of the 78th Fraser Highlanders, John McMillan married Christian (Christy-ann) McCalman. John was in his middle thirties, Christian, her early twenties. A daughter named Sarah, born in 1766, was likely their first child. Since there are no birth or christening records for the area prior to 1773, we first learn of her existence in later census records. Sarah never married; she was probably the daughter who stayed home to look after her aging parents. After their deaths, when she was in her late fifties, Sarah followed her much younger brother Duncan Ban McMillan to Canada, where she lived out her life on a farm he hewed from the wilderness in Finch, Ontario.

Christening records for John and Christian McMillan's children begin with Donald, born in 1774, followed by Ann in 1775, Ewen in 1777, an unnamed baby in 1779, Mary in 1780, Duncan Ban in 1783, and a second Ewen in 1784. (Although the first Ewen may have died by this time, Highland families sometimes gave a favorite first name to more than one child.) These are the children we know of, but there were likely more than these eight. During the eight years separating Sarah and Donald, it is reasonable to assume that earlier children arrived with the same regularity as later siblings.

Another reason for believing that there were additional children is revealed in their names. Scottish families traditionally named their firstborn son for the father's father, the second son for the mother's father, and the third son for the father. In the same manner, the first girl was named for the mother's mother, the second for the father's mother, and the third for the mother. None of the McMillan children are named for either John or Christian, so if they followed the traditional pattern, they already had six children by the time Donald was born, giving them a grand total of at least thirteen offspring.

Achintee Farm in Glen Nevis, 1989. The main house was rebuilt in 1813 after having been largely destroyed during the Jacobite rebellion. The barn behind it is a bunkhouse for climbers and is used for mountain rescues on Ben Nevis. To the left of the barn, not pictured here, is our ancestral McMillan cottage. The word Achintee derives from the Gaelic. One translation is "field of the stormy blast."

Our ancestral cottage in Glen Nevis, 1989. Home to several generations of our McMillan forebears, it is a typical eighteenth-century West Highland dwelling, built of mortared stone with chimney flues in both gable ends. The front doorway is only five feet, seven inches high.

Achintee Farm belonged to a Cameron who held other farms in the area and owned Ben Nevis as well. The joint tenants at Achintee included John McMillan and his brother Duncan. The McMillans were subsistence farmers who most likely grew potatoes along with some grain. They would have had a few black cattle, some goats, and several small Highland work horses for plowing, harrowing, carrying home peats, and hauling manure to the fields. Potatoes were the mainstay of the Highland diet, in some areas accounting for as much as seventy-five to ninety percent of the families' food. Very little livestock was killed for meat; herring from fisheries on the sea coast was served in its stead. Properly prepared, a savory dish of potatoes and herring was said to be food for a king.

Housewives made several varieties of bannocks—flat loaves of unleavened bread—and porridge from meal, and the families had milk, butter, and cheese from their livestock. The salmon in the river Nevis and the red deer in the forests belonged to the landlord, but no one faulted the Highlander who brought one or the other to his table from time to time. Apart from milk, the most common drink in the Highlands was whisky. The word *whisky*, in fact, derives from the Gaelic *Usque Beatha* meaning "water of life," and there was almost no part of the Highlands in which whisky was not distilled, much of it in illegal stills.

Life was simple in Glen Nevis, or it once had been, but tenant farmers like the McMillans were becoming redundant. John McMillan had arrived home from America just in time to see black-faced sheep introduced to the area in 1764. The arrival of the coarse-wooled animals in the Highlands led eventually to the sorry substitution of men by sheep, and the betrayal of their kinsmen by anglicized chiefs. In the Scotland of old, a Gaelic chieftain counted his prosperity by the number of fighting men he could put in the field; his broadswords were his

A page of the Kilmallie Church records listing the baptism of "Duncan, Son to John McMillan and Christian McCalman, Glenevis" on October 19, 1783

wealth, and his kinsmen his children. Suddenly, with the end of the warrior society in 1746 and the loss of their hereditary powers, the chiefs had found themselves poverty-stricken in an overpopulated and barren land. Wishing to live on a scale in keeping with that of their English counterparts and needing to pay their taxes, Scottish landlords began demanding money payments instead of rents in kind, and tenants were removed at will in favor of more profitable "four-footed clansmen."

We have no reason to believe that John and Christian McMillan were ever dispossessed, but their life in Glen Nevis was certainly becoming increasing difficult by the time my great-great-grandfather, Duncan Ban McMillan, the second youngest of their children, was born there in 1783. Duncan Ban was christened October 19 at Corpach in the present Kilmallie church, which grew out of an ancient Culdee shrine that Gilchrist An Gille Maolan, the first MacMillan, built on this site in the 1130s. Many of our ancestors and family members lie buried in the old walled churchyard at Kilmallie.

The year of Duncan Ban's birth was a poor one indeed for Scotland. Crop failures led to a devastating famine, prompting the Scottish government to institute an emergency food distribution program; but in order to receive rations, it was necessary to supply the local magistrate with a written request from someone of high standing who would guarantee repayment. Several years later, a list of people still owing money to the government included one Angus McMillan, drover, who had obligated himself for "three ferlets of potatoes" on behalf of a John Buie McMillan, who had fled bankrupt to America.

In America, where Duncan Ban's sons would become wealthy loggers, 1783 was a landmark year. The Peace of Paris ended the American Revolution, and the fledgling United States wound up the proud new owner of an immense chunk of the continent that extended west to the Mississippi, north to Canada, and south to the Floridas. Late in December General Washington resigned his commission as Commander in Chief of the American army; five years later he was sworn in as the first president of the United States in 1789.

Duncan Ban likely attended the parochial school at nearby Fort William, where Gaelic-speaking students learned English (the language of trade and good manners), reading, writing, arithmetic, bookkeeping, Latin, Greek, and geography. By the end of the eighteenth century, Scotland was preparing for a new age, in which the brightest and more ambitious of its children would make their lives elsewhere. While still in his teens, Duncan Ban left the Glen Nevis of his forefathers for the promise of Glasgow, where his mother's family, the McCalmans, were merchants, and his cousin Sammy Dow was becoming famous for his "Pigeon Blend" whisky.

Glasgow's Old Bridge with the steepled Merchants House in the background. from a drawing by John Fleming engraved by Joseph Swan in Select Views of Glasgow, *1828*

Seventy-five miles southeast of Glen Nevis as the crow flies, Glasgow (from the Gaelic *Glas Ghu* meaning "green glen") was a growing industrial center, soon to become the second city in Britain, when Duncan Ban McMillan first set foot there about 1800. Straddling both sides of the river Clyde, twenty miles from its mouth on the Atlantic coast, Glasgow occupies the site of a prehistoric Pictish settlement. About 550, St. Kentigern, an early Christian missionary also known as Mungo, went to Glasgow to convert the British tribes and stayed to found a religious community. The present cathedral, begun in the twelfth century on the site of his chapel, is dedicated to St. Mungo. Medieval Glasgow was a noted ecclesiastical center and seat of learning. Its world-renowned university dates to 1451.

Ideally situated between Highland and Lowland Scotland, and also between the western coast and Scotland's capital, Edinburgh, forty-five miles to the east, Glasgow prospered as a market hub. The city grew significantly after the union of the Scottish and English crowns in 1603, when the Stuart King James VI of Scotland acceded to the English throne and moved his court to London, becoming James I of England. Glasgow exported coal, plaid (wool cloth), and herring to Europe, and later dominated the world tobacco trade, importing tobacco from America and exporting it to European countries, especially France.

Tobacco accounted for by far the greater part of Scotland's foreign trade, and Glasgow's famed tobacco lords built huge fortunes. A caste unto themselves in their scarlet cloaks, cocked hats, and powdered wigs, the tobacco lords strutted the Plainstanes—Glasgow's one stretch of paving outside the new Exchange at the Cross—where no ordinary tradesmen dared approach them. When the

American colonies revolted in 1775, the tobacco trade came to an abrupt end and fortunes were lost, but Glasgow quickly recovered. Once tobacco imports were cut off from the New World, cotton manufacturing became the city's lifeblood.

A combination of fortuitous circumstances had suddenly enabled the city to produce the finest fabrics of their kind in the world. During the greater part of the eighteenth century, linen production had been Scotland's staple industry. Glasgow area weavers used silk and cotton thread as well, but they could not compete with Indian cotton until new methods of spinning finer threads were developed in England just before the American Revolution. The fine linens that had been shipped across the Atlantic to pay for tobacco had trained a generation of expert weavers, and rich investors who had survived the American crisis were seeking new uses for their money.

David Dale stands out as the best-remembered of Glasgow's early cotton mill owners, a group of able and enterprising men who quickly seized a place in Glasgow's new world of industry. A former weaver who supposedly inspired Sir Walter Scott's character Bailie Nicol Jarvie, Dale opened the first great cotton spinning mill at New Lanark in 1786. Like Glasgow's other early water-powered cotton mills, it was some distance outside the city, in this case, a day's ride by carriage through mountains and mists at the Falls of Clyde. Dale was not only an able entrepreneur but also a man of conscience who built houses for his workers and planned for their welfare. New Lanark became a showplace that drew visitors from around the world including Grand Duke Nicholas (later czar), who hoped to establish similar factories in Russia.

The new Glasgow area factories also attracted thousands of young Highlanders eager to find jobs in the burgeoning textile industry. Many of them were unskilled, but Duncan Ban McMillan came armed with a knowledge of weaving, an ancient craft in the Highlands, where housewives prepared the wool, washed it, dyed it with local plant materials, and spun it into yarn, often on hand-held spindles. Most of the Highland weavers who wove the yarn into cloth had been part-time farmers. Several of them lived close to the old Glen Nevis Bridge at the entrance to Glen Nevis, the focal point of community trade, where each summer noisy crowds of Gaelic-speaking people converged for a boisterous country fair. Weavers had been among Duncan Ban's Highland mentors, and he later passed on a love of weaving to his children.

In 1800 one Scotsman in five lived in Glasgow, and it was a strikingly handsome town. "Look through the town!" wrote one observer. "The houses here like noble palaces appear." Glasgow's New Town was a place of wide streets and public squares, its fanciful skyline embroidered by turrets and spires. The magnificent Trades House, designed by famed Scottish architect Robert Adam to give the city guilds a home worthy of their wealth and standing, was one of many new public buildings reminiscent of ancient Greece and Rome.

Long lines of gleaming, cream-colored stone tenements and terraces spread westward from the city center. In 1791 Glasgow had had 67,000 residents. Forty years later, the figure had swelled to 202,000.

Whether Duncan Ban went to Glasgow with any of his brothers and sisters or his parents, we don't know; possibly the whole family had been forced to give up farming in Glen Nevis and move to the city where they had relatives. According to the 1807 city directory, Duncan Ban's first cousin Samuel Dow was building a reputation in Glasgow as a spirit merchant. Sam was Duncan's mother's brother Ewen McCalman's son. Dow was an Anglicized form of McCalman—an old Irish name with Latin origins: columba, a dove. After Culloden, some family members adopted the surname Dow because the McCalmans were known Jacobites. McCalmans or Dows lived in and around the area of Banavie near Fort William, adjacent to Glen Nevis, for more than two hundred and fifty years. The name Dow was interchangeable with Dov, to which the "pigeon" in Sammy's Pigeon Blend whisky probably referred.

Did Duncan Ban ever work for Sammy Dow in Glasgow? Many years later, his son Alexander told a biographer in Canada that his father had been a merchant in Glasgow. If that was true, then Duncan Ban may have been employed by his cousin in the whisky trade. Yet Duncan Ban himself, when he emigrated to America, listed his occupation as "farmer and weaver." Formerly, he told emigration officials, he had been a farmer. Duncan Ban would have farmed in Glen Nevis, of course, and once he was living in Glasgow, he may have continued to farm on a small scale. Most Scottish handloom weavers in this period lived in rural or semi-rural communities, producing piece work in their homes or an attached shed for agents sent out by Paisley and Glasgow manufacturers.

The beginning years of the nineteenth century were golden ones for Scottish handloom weavers. "Then," wrote one of them, "was the daisy portion of weaving, the bright and midday period of all who pitched a shuttle." After steam-powered spinning machines were introduced in 1792, more and more weavers were needed to maintain the weaving side of the industry; in ten years, the number of cotton weavers increased six-fold, from eight to fifty thousand workers. Weaving employed more people than any other industry, and weavers made relatively high wages compared to those of other workers. More literate as a group than their peers, weavers were men of standing in their communities and intently religious, well-versed in Calvinism. Most of them, Duncan Ban included, adhered to the Established (Presbyterian) Church.

That they would soon become redundant, the weavers guessed not. But in the natural course of events, weaving attracted too many workers, and there were also cyclical slumps, due in part to the war with Napoleon, that caused many weavers to fall on hard times. To help ease their distress, weavers' societies sprang up in virtually every Scottish village, providing unemployment,

Scottish handloom typical of Duncan Ban's time at the Scottish Tartan Museum, Comrie, Perthshire, Scotland

sickness, and death benefits for members and their families. In 1812 a weavers' strike temporarily crippled the industry, but few weavers could afford to be out of work for long, and the strike foundered after twelve weeks. Where weavers had once lived in unaccustomed affluence, now their wages and status plummeted. Within a few years, with the advent of the power loom, handloom weavers would become obsolete.

For Duncan Ban, there was no going back to Glen Nevis, where a young and profligate Cameron of Lochiel was dispossessing his tenants in favor of Cheviot sheep. Since there was also no future for him in Glasgow, he, like many of his fellow weavers, decided to emigrate to America. The end of the handloom industry in Scotland would send another ambitious lad to the New World to seek his fortune, and find it, three decades hence, when twelve-year-old Andrew Carnegie would come with his unemployed father and determined mother to Pittsburgh in 1848.

Scots wishing to emigrate were encouraged to do so by the government. England in 1815, for the first time, offered free passage to Quebec for prospective settlers from Great Britain. In the New World, Duncan Ban could join his older brother Donald and his wife who had already settled in Finch Township in Upper Canada.

Scottish emigration to Crown lands in America had begun in earnest following the end of the Seven Years' War in 1763, when poverty, overpopulation, rising rents, and bad seasons all contributed to the outpouring of Scots from their homeland. Taking their cultural traditions with them, Scottish Highlanders transported an entire society to Canada, where they lived among their fellow clansmen in Gaelic-speaking settlements. At first, people choosing to emigrate faced considerable opposition from both Scottish landlords and the British government. Many lairds preferred increasing the rents on smaller, more efficiently run tracts of land to clearing them for sheep; and the outpouring of population and capital from Scotland threatened to thwart improvement efforts and create a labor shortage. Great Britain also feared the loss of military manpower for the British army, especially among a people noted for their martial capabilities.

Any hope of stemming the swelling tide of emigrants was unrealistic, however. The idea of emigration as a positive response to untenable conditions at home had caught on, and tens of thousands of proud Highlanders left Scotland for North America. Pamphlets and periodicals discussed the advantages of going overseas where families could make new and better lives for themselves, and Highlanders already established on farms of their own in Canada encouraged their relatives to join them. As the numbers of emigrants increased, clan ties worked in favor of emigration, since Highlanders were more willing to follow where friends and especially kinsmen had gone before them.

As early as 1773 James Boswell in his *Journal of a Tour to the Hebrides* described a lively dance inspired by emigration. "We again had a good dinner, and in the evening a great dance," he wrote.

> We made out five country squares without sitting down; and then we performed with much activity a dance [called] "America." A brisk reel is played. The first couple begin and each sets to one—then each to another—then as they set in the next couple, the second and third couples are setting; and so it goes on till all are set a-going, setting and wheeling round each other, while each is making the tour of all in the dance. It shows how emigration catches till all are set afloat.

Donald McMillan, Duncan Ban's older brother by nine years, and his wife had emigrated in 1802. They had been part of the so-called "MacMillan Emigration" to Canada, an epic journey led by two cousins, Archibald McMillan of Murlaggan and Allan McMillan of Glenpean. In early July, four hundred Highland emigrants bound for Montreal had set sail from Fort William on board three small sailing vessels—the *Friends*, the *Helen*, and the *Jane*. More than a hundred McMillans are named on the passenger lists along with lesser numbers of McDonells, Kennedys, Camerons, Grants, McPhees, Corbetts, and McDougalls. Many of them carried documents confirming their good character such as this one from the Reverend Alexander Fraser of Kilmallie parish:

> These do certify that the Bearer herof [*sic*], Duncan McMillan of Glendesary of Loch Arkaig, Ann McMillan, his wife, his sister and children, were all born and bred in this parish, have always behaved themselves as became decent, sober industrious people, are free from all scandal, and no cause appears to us, why they may not be received into any Christian Society, where it may please Providence to cast his lot.

This historical marker at St. Andrew's Presbyterian Church in Williamstown, Ontario, commemorates the MacMillan Emigration of 1802. Some of our first McMillan relatives to arrive in Canada lie buried in this churchyard.

Great hardship awaited these early pioneers in the New World. Upon reaching Montreal, Allan of Glenpean and many of the emigrants including the Donald McMillans had to row up the St. Lawrence in open boats to Lancaster, then trudge overland through wild scrub with their belongings to reach Gaelic-speaking settlements around Kirkhill and Laggan in eastern Ontario where they spent their first winter. Their final destination was Finch township, Stormont County, Ontario, where Allan had petitioned the Crown for grants for himself and more than a dozen settlers. As a leader of the expedition, Allan obtained twelve hundred acres; Donald McMillan and the others named with him, all of them McMillans, received two-hundred-acre allotments.

In 1804 four McMillans and four Camerons set out on foot from Kirkhill for Finch. After making a clearing and building small huts, they brought their families there the next year. In his history of Stormont, Dundas, and Glengarry

Explorer Alexander MacKenzie, the largest landholder in Finch, Ontario. The first European to cross the American continent, MacKenzie was a fur trader who headed the North West Company in Montreal.

Counties, John Graham Harkness writes that the lot of these settlers "was much harder than that of the settlers along the St. Lawrence, as they did not receive rations and supplies for three years and there were no half pay officers among them to scatter a little money. Their only sources of revenue were potash and oak barrel staves."

Located inland between the St. Lawrence and the Ottawa Rivers, Finch grew up on the banks of the Payne River, named for Glenpean which in Gaelic is *Gleann Peighinn* or pennyland glen—a pennyland being an old measure of land. The largest landholder in Finch was famed explorer Alexander MacKenzie with eighteen hundred acres, but the intrepid fur trader never lived there.

Born in the Scottish Highlands, MacKenzie lived in Canada from the age of ten. At twenty-five, he had charge of the North West Company's trade in the far Northwest with headquarters on Lake Athabaska. During the summer of 1789, after sending a flotilla of canoes east with the winter's harvest of pelts, MacKenzie set out to learn where the mighty waters of the Athabaska and Peace Rivers flowed. Traveling three thousand miles by canoe to the Arctic Ocean and back, he discovered one of the principal rivers of the world which is named for him—the Mackenzie River. Three years later, he was the first person to cross the American continent. Knighted by Queen Victoria for his discoveries—which ultimately saved British Columbia for the British Empire and Canada—MacKenzie later headed the North West Company's fur trade empire headquartered in Montreal.

Those emigrants who did come to live in Finch were plainer people, and most of them were named McMillan. Drawn there by his brother Donald, my great-great-grandfather Duncan Ban McMillan would put down deep roots in its virgin soil. Though now tumbledown and bleak, his deserted farmstead bears mute testimony to a once lively family enterprise.

In 1815, the year Duncan Ban went to Canada, the British government recast its emigration policy and launched its own program to promote settlement in North America. Any objections the King's ministers had nursed toward such relocation now seemed trivial, since this innovative approach would resolve Scotland's growing surplus population problem at the same time that it furthered British aims on this continent. In the eyes of colonial officials, Canada was a "country already too much inhabited by Aliens from the United States." Three-fifths of the seventy-five thousand sparsely scattered settlers in Upper Canada had their origins in either pre- or post-revolutionary America. An influx of Highlanders would redress this imbalance and provide a bulwark for the defense and economic development of Canada.

The first public notice of the emigration program appeared in Edinburgh and Glasgow newspapers in late February, and the Brits were indeed bending over backwards. With few strings attached, prospective settlers were offered free transportation to Quebec, one hundred acres of land in Upper or Lower Canada

(Lower Canada corresponding roughly to the present province of Quebec), free rations for six to eight months, and farm implements at cost. Friends and relatives who wished to settle together in the same neighborhood could apply for contiguous land grants, and the government would pay ministers' and teachers' salaries in the new communities. Aspiring emigrants were urged to forward their applications along with certificates testifying to their "general good character" from their local justice of the peace, clergyman, or "other respectable persons."

Duncan Ban McMillan's name is first on the surviving "General List of Settlers Inrolled [*sic*] for Canada" contained in government agent John Campbell's registry book at Canada's Public Archives in Ottawa. He was thirty-one years old when he set sail for North America from the Clydeside city of Greenock near Glasgow in July with seven hundred fellow emigrants on four government-chartered vessels, the *Atlas*, the *Dorothy*, the *Baltic Merchant*, and the *Eliza*. Besides the warm clothing and bedding they would need in Canada, the emigrants lugged their own oatmeal, cheese, butter, tea, sugar, potatoes, whisky, and meat for the journey. Duncan Ban no doubt also brought along some of the works for a loom. One man already living in Canada had written his brother, another weaver who was emigrating: "All iron work is very dear here; so you had better bring with you whatever your loom requires."

In September, the same issue of the *Montreal Herald* that announced the arrival in Quebec of the frigate *Atlas*—the ship we believe carried Duncan Ban—also reported the victory of the Duke of Wellington at Waterloo on June 18. This was Napoleon's final defeat, decisively ending twenty-three years of intermittent warfare between France and the other European powers. It must have reminded Duncan Ban of an earlier all-important contest between the French and English. How much John McMillan had told his son about the battle he had

The British frigate Atlas, *which brought Duncan Ban McMillan to Canada in 1815*

helped wage for a continent on the Plains of Abraham we can only surmise, but father and son must have had some serious talks before the latter set out for the New World. Did John, in fact, urge his son to emigrate, imploring him to take advantage of the opportunity for a new life in Canada that he himself had turned down fifty years earlier?

Quebec had actually changed little in the intervening half century since John McMillan had been there. Many of the well-made church and public edifices now greeting Duncan Ban dated to the old French regime. Though by then a flourishing British fur trade capital, Quebec still looked every inch a European city, with its narrow winding streets, neat public squares, and stately stone buildings. Visions of 78th Fraser Highlanders no doubt danced in Duncan Ban's head, and he surely paid his respects at the Plains of Abraham before setting off up the St. Lawrence and across country to Finch.

There was not much waiting for him in Finch, which in 1815 was still an embryo community with no homes of any size and no mills, merchants' shops, or storehouses. Only 182 acres of arable pasture and meadow had been cleared. The township's livestock amounted to forty-seven horses, fifty-one milk cows, and five young horned cattle. Only fifteen people were assessed in Finch, whereas an aggregate assessment for the Eastern District (Stormont, Dundas, and Glengarry Counties) showed the nearby communities of Roxborough, Lancaster, and Cornwall all prospering, with several hundred people assessed in each. Duncan Ban probably lived with his brother and his brother's wife in some sort of log dwelling at first, and within months he was a married man. Had his marriage been arranged before he set sail from Scotland? His bride was named Mary McMillan, and the two were almost certainly related. That McMillans married McMillans with some regularity in those years may account for a rare blood disorder that I and my descendants have inherited. I and all four of my daughters and my grandchildren have had to have our spleens removed to combat chronic hemolytic anemia.

Mary McMillan was born in 1794 on the shores of Loch Arkaig near Glen Nevis and came to America with her parents Angus and Margaret McMaster McMillan in 1802. Along with the Donald McMillans, they were part of the "MacMillan Emigration." Angus McMillan operated a small sawmill in Finch on the Payne River, cutting lumber for local customers, and Duncan Ban may have worked for him, at least for a time.

There are no records to prove it, but Duncan Ban and Mary McMillan would have been married at St. Andrew's Presbyterian Church in Williamstown, the site of the "MacMillan Emigration" commemorative marker. Before people in Finch had their own parish, they customarily traveled to St. Andrew's for their religious ceremonies. Founded in 1787 by the Reverend John Bethune, a Scottish Loyalist who emigrated to Canada from the Carolinas, St. Andrew's is the oldest

Presbyterian parish in Ontario. After Bethune died in 1815, parish records lapsed until his permanent replacement took charge. In the meantime, Duncan and Mary were probably married by an itinerant preacher whose records have disappeared.

The first of Duncan Ban and Mary McMillan's eleven children, a son they named Daniel—or Donald, the two names being interchangeable in Scottish Gaelic—was born in January 1817 (just sixteen months after Duncan Ban arrived in Canada), followed by John in 1819, Christian (known as Christy) about 1822, Mary about 1823, Alexander in 1825, Angus Duncan Ban in 1827, Catherine in 1829, Margaret in 1832, Ewen Hugh in 1834, Duncan D., June 20, 1837, and Allan, the last born child, date unknown. All of these children, with the exception of Allan who died at fourteen months, lived to maturity. Our branch of the family descends from Duncan D. (whom the family always referred to as a Victoria baby because he was born on the historic day that William IV died and his niece Victoria became queen of England). Duncan Ban's household ultimately also included his much older sister Sarah, who came to Canada in the early 1820s and lived out her life under his roof, helping care for his large brood.

After securing a crown patent on the south half of lot 23 in the third concession of Finch, a piece of land amounting to one hundred acres, Duncan Ban likely began clearing it to plant crops. This was tedious work for a man unaccustomed to an axe, but a few months' practice usually rendered a tenderfoot tolerably expert. Duncan Ban's lot was adjacent to his brother Donald's place and close to where his in-laws lived. The log house he built for his young family was probably about eighteen by sixteen feet with a bark or shingle roof and a stone fireplace. To protect their grain and livestock against the weather, farmers like Duncan Ban also built log barns which they replaced as soon as they could with large frame structures. Blessed with virgin soil that had been richening long centuries, they planted mostly wheat, followed by buckwheat, rye, and Indian corn. They also had some luck with potatoes, although these were inferior to those grown in Great Britain.

Emigrant families lived with some discomfort at first, but most of them were soon better off than they had been in Scotland. Once their gardens started producing and they had some livestock (pigs were popular because they multiplied quickly), they ate amazingly well. A visitor to Canada in the 1820s remarked that "the people live much better than persons of a similar class in Britain; . . . to have proof of this, it is only necessary to visit almost any hut in the back woods. The interior of it seldom fails to display many substantial comforts, such as immense loaves of beautiful bread, entire pigs hanging round the chimney, dried venison, trenchers of milk, and bags of Indian corn."

No photographs or paintings of Duncan Ban have come down through the family, but I imagine that he was probably a wiry, trimly built man, light-complected, with sandy-colored hair. Most of the MacMillans I have known are rather slight, small-boned people with small hands and small feet. As for his coloring, *Ban* is not really a second name, it is a Gaelic term meaning fair or fair-haired. Most of what we actually know about him has been pieced together from local church and government records that show him to be God-fearing, ambitious, industrious, conscientious, and civic-minded. Besides hewing a farm out of the wilderness and raising ten children (who grew up speaking both Gaelic and English) in a house he built with his own hands, he was a man of standing in his community who shouldered religious, educational, and social responsibilities.

In 1840 Duncan Ban helped set the local St. Luke's Presbyterian Church in Finch on its feet; founding records reveal that he was church treasurer, the person charged with collecting and disbursing funds. Lumber for the new frame church was supplied by Duncan's brother-in-law Alexander McMillan, his wife Mary's brother. St. Luke's first minister was the Reverend Donald Munroe who came to Finch that year from Scotland. Munroe preached in Gaelic, as did all the clergy in Canada's Scottish settlements. Parishioners traveled to services in wagons or walked from as far as fifteen miles away, dressed in their Sunday homespun and carrying their shoes.

His house full of school-age children, my great-great-grandfather was also a school commissioner in Finch. In a petition written in 1842 to the Eastern District Council, he asked that a new ruling that would tax communities to pay for their schools be rescinded. Finch was still too new a settlement to be able to afford such an arrangement, he argued, and the township wished to continue its practice of hiring its own teachers on its own terms. Finch was accustomed to "paying the greatest part of their salaries in produce which is a great advantage to us, as we are far from markets to make money out of our produce." Eighty townspeople including four teachers signed Duncan Ban's petition, and the new ruling was subsequently set aside.

In another petition to the Eastern District Council, Duncan Ban McMillan, this time as superintendent of area pathmasters (elected officials responsible for maintaining passable roads) voiced strong complaints about obstructions on the roadways, citing fences and timber felled in clearing that some settlers refused to move. What was needed, he wrote, was a law with fines and penalties that would require trespassers to remove impediments within a certain number of days.

It is safe to assume that times were generally tough on Duncan Ban's farm, and also that he tried his hand at logging. His father-in-law, after all, operated a sawmill, and his sons would later make their fortunes in the pine forests of Wisconsin. After farming, timbering was the chief source of cash income in Upper Canada, and many farmers worked winters in the logging camps. Having used up her own forests to keep the Royal Navy afloat, Britain increasingly depended upon the American colonies for timber. Parliament enacted protective tariffs encouraging Canadian farmers to take up their axes, sometimes to the detriment of their farms, and logging boomed in the counties fronting the St. Lawrence. Author Ralph Connor described the adventurous life of the lumberjacks in his best-selling novel, *The Man From Glengarry*, which is also an absorbing social history of the Highland settlements in eastern Canada.

Hard-working Scots—families named Fraser, MacLaren, Gilmour, and McDonald—dominated the Canadian timber industry, and thousands of sturdy, young men went yearly into the virgin pine forests above Ottawa. Using heavy broadaxes, they felled gigantic saw logs and hewed massive square-cut pine and oak timbers, hauling them to the frozen lakes and rivers with twelve to sixteen teams of horses or oxen. When the ice melted in the spring, they floated the logs and timbers out to the major tributaries of the Ottawa and St. Lawrence Rivers. Whole logs stamped with the owner's brand were sent to sawmills downriver. Squared timbers were made into rafts and steered to Quebec, often carrying cargoes of wheat, flour, and potash. In Quebec the rafts were broken up and the lumber loaded aboard timber ships for England.

Lured by the smell of adventure and the promise of cash money, the first of Duncan Ban's sons to go into the woods were the two eldest, Daniel and John. If they were employed by a sizeable logging firm, they would have worked as lumberjacks, teamsters, or raftsmen. If, on the other hand, they were working for themselves, perhaps with several cousins or other relatives, they would have performed all three jobs and marketed their lumber as well, riding it downstream all the way to Quebec. Whatever their involvement, the McMillan boys knew quite a bit about logging by the time they came to the United States.

For reasons unknown, once in 1834 and again in 1847, Duncan Ban put his farm up for sale. No price was given in either ad (which appeared in Cornwall papers), and we don't know why he wanted to relocate. The first listing appeared under the name of Simon Fraser. Was this the same Simon Fraser who discovered and explored Canada's Fraser River? Maybe. Barely recognized in his lifetime for his danger-fraught voyage down the great river that now bears his name, Simon Fraser lived out his life in relative obscurity in Cornwall, less than twenty-five miles from Finch.

A fur trader associated with Alexander MacKenzie in the North West Company, Simon Fraser was one of the wintering partners who looked after company posts in the West and the fundamental details of securing furs from the Indians. His voyage of discovery in 1808 was actually undertaken in the hope of finding a trade route from the Pacific Ocean to fur-rich Athabaska. In his early forties, by 1818, tiring of the hard life of a fur trader in the western wilderness, Fraser retired to live in Cornwall, where he raised a family of eight children and operated a sawmill, possibly also a grist mill, never very successfully. Interestingly enough, this Simon Fraser was also a kinsman of Simon Fraser of Lovat who in 1757 raised the 78th Fraser Highlanders, John McMillan's old regiment.

A lumber raft on the Ottawa River, in a watercolor by C.W. Jefferys

When Duncan Ban's property was advertised in the *Cornwall Observer* in 1847, it was described as having a "House and Barn and large clearance, situation very convenient." This time when his property still didn't sell, Duncan Ban improved it. In the 1850s, by then in his sixties, he built a stylish new story-and-a-half house from square-cut limestone quarried on the north end of his property. Reminiscent of his ancestral stone cottage in Glen Nevis, it was somewhat larger, with four bedrooms upstairs, and featured a fanlight over the front door. This was our first substantial family homestead on this continent.

The 1861 farm census for Finch township valued Duncan Ban's property including his new house at $4,200. Forty out of 100 acres were under cultivation. His harvest that year yielded 150 bushels of oats, 72 bushels of spring wheat, 20 bushels of buckwheat, 100 bushels of potatoes, 44 bushels of peas, and 6 tons of hay. The family also produced 150 pounds of butter, 100 pounds of cheese, 400 pounds of beef, 600 pounds of pork (both the beef and pork were put up in 200-pound barrels), 250 pounds of maple sugar, 27 pounds of wool, and 19 yards of cloth (he was still weaving!). Duncan Ban's livestock, valued at $272, included three horses, three sheep, four pigs, four milk cows, and three "steers or heifers under 3 years of age."

That same year, on August 10, 1861, Duncan Ban died in his stone farmhouse at the age of seventy-seven. Less than a month earlier, he had drawn up his will, which survives at the registry office in Cornwall, Ontario. Prepared on lined, light blue paper, it is signed in a graceful, flowing hand. Bequeathing his soul "to him who gave it in the certain hope of a glorious resurrection," Duncan handed down the farm to Angus, the only one of his six sons still at home, who would now be responsible for three dependent females under his roof: his mother Mary, his unmarried sister Catherine, and his aged aunt Sarah. Duncan Ban's widow Mary was to have "the use of all my stock of cattle and personal property;" Catherine was to have "two cows and one heifer and also Bed and Bedding" if she married; and Sarah, then ninety-five, "the use of the Room in which she now resides during her life with Comfortable Bed and Bedding and all other necessaries" and a "descent [sic] Funeral" after her death.

After learning the location of Duncan Ban's farm, I drove up to Finch from Montreal one spring in the late 1980s to see the property. My guide was Margaret Cameron, who is descended from Duncan Ban's daughter Margaret McMillan Sutherland. Then in her fifties and fiercely proud of her ancestry, Margaret was living in a large, rambling house a few miles outside Finch at Avonmore. The McMillans, Margaret told me, had been highly regarded as people of means. She wasn't talking about financial means, but means of education, and she said that they were a proud, proud family. They had a lot to be proud of, we agreed. Having migrated from one area of the world to another, where they had helped tame the wilderness, they enjoyed an above-average standard of living in Finch.

Duncan Ban's farmstead in Finch, Canada, built in the 1850s from stone quarried on the property. Three "belly" windows helped light and ventilate the second story. The porch is a later addition.

A barn in ruins on former Duncan Ban McMillan property in Finch, Canada, 1989

They were hardworking people, close to their church, leaders in the community, and they had an impact on the society of the times.

As it turned out, I missed seeing Duncan Ban's stone house by a mere few years. It had been taken down, Margaret told me, after its west wall had broken away from the other walls. Duncan Ban's house, made of hand-hewn rock, was no great shakes as houses today go, of course, but it represented a substantial frontier farmhouse for its time.

Except for the skeletal remains of several barns, at least one of which probably dated to Duncan Ban's time, the property when I saw it was vacant and the fields grown over with bramble. One look at the land, however, was enough to tell me that this was never prime farming property. The land is harsh, and to have farmed it without machines, as Duncan Ban did, would have taken a lot out of a man. In reality, the Ottawa Valley has never produced quantities of grain that leave the area; it does not have enough level land. Good soils are one thing, but the flatter the land, the better it is for farming. This is true throughout the world. It's no mystery to me why all but one of Duncan Ban's sons eventually moved out of the area.

All four of the daughters in the family remained in Canada, however. We don't know if Catherine married, but the other girls found husbands nearby and moved to farms within walking distance of the family homestead. At least two of them carried on the family tradition for weaving. Mary McMillan and her husband Allan Morrison produced both woven cloth and flannel yardage on their farm in Finch; and Margaret McMillan and her husband Joseph Sutherland in Roxborough also made flannel—a soft twilled wool or worsted fabric with a loose texture. Following my visit, Margaret Cameron sent me a woolen blanket made of undyed wool woven on the Duncan Ban farm that, despite having been used and washed through the years, is still serviceable.

In 1980, after changing hands several times in this century, Duncan Ban's original land grant farm sold to a man named Lynch for $225,000. The land was not being worked when I saw it, but the old quarry—once a popular swimming hole for McMillan youngsters—was still producing limestone used to make crushed rock for roadbeds.

Duncan Ban and Mary, we believe, are buried in the old McMillan Cemetery in Finch. There is a stone there for Mary's parents, Angus and Mary McMaster McMillan, but none for Duncan Ban or Mary. It is also possible that the two were interred in the old St. Luke's Cemetery, but there are no stones for them there either. Not being able to find headstones for Duncan Ban and Mary McMillan is disappointing but understandable because both graveyards suffered long years of neglect and old tombstones simply deteriorated. I found two broken pieces of stone inscribed with the letters "McM" in a pile of rubble along the fence at the McMillan Cemetery, all that was left of some early stones.

Flanked by the stones of other relatives, the tombstone in the foreground remembers my great-great-great-grandparents Angus and Margaret McMaster McMillan, who came to Canada in the MacMillan Emigration of 1802. Their daughter Mary married Duncan Ban McMillan.

In the present day, the McMillan Cemetery is a pretty, hillside oasis surrounded by prospering dairy farms. The grass grows rife with wild strawberries, and McMillans have been buried there as recently as the 1960s. Some people call it Laughing John's Cemetery, which one relative suggests is a corruption of the name Laughlin John. But there was indeed a man known as Laughing John McMillan in Finch. There was also a Roman John, so-called because he had converted to Catholicism, and a Tall John, Little John, Red John, and Black John, all of them McMillans. One of Duncan Ban's brothers-in-law was John Cnoc McMillan, *Cnoc* being Gaelic for hill, meaning that he lived on a hill. There were so many John McMillans in Finch that nicknames were needed to identify them.

This was one reason, my father told me, why some of the McMillans moved to La Crosse. There were just too many of them to be able to keep them straight in Finch.

LOGGERS AND LAWYERS

Duncan Ban had dabbled in trade in Glasgow, but his sons were the first real entrepreneurs in our family. Energetic, able, and ambitious, they became rich timbermen in Wisconsin, then branched out into other enterprises, everything from public utilities and real estate to banking and gold mining.

"There is probably no family whose various members have been more concerned with the development of the city [of La Crosse] than the McMillan family," wrote Benjamin Bryant in his *Memoirs of La Crosse County* in 1907. "Although they suffered reverses of fortune in later years they will always be accounted as among the men to whom La Crosse is indebted for her early prosperity." The McMillan brothers left Canada simply because it held no future for them as either farmers or loggers. As long as English tariffs had favored colonial timber, Canadian loggers had made good wages, but the Canadian timber industry peaked with the English railway boom in 1845—the most prosperous year in a generation—when more than twenty million cubic feet of timber came downriver to Quebec. The next year, two things happened.

Predictably, everybody and his brother went into the woods to cut timber. Loggers increased their output for Quebec to thirty-seven million feet, almost double what the English market could absorb, and prices fell sharply. Looking out for her own interests ahead of those of her colonies, England also removed preferential duties on colonial timber, giving Canada competition from rival Baltic timber ports.

In 1847 and 1848, overproduction for the British market plunged producers and merchants alike into bankruptcy. The collapse of the timber industry

Timbering settlement in Upper Canada, painted in 1838 by W.H. Bartlett

brought on a devastating depression in Canada that reached its nadir in 1848, the darkest year in a century in Canada. With most of the arable land in southern Ontario already settled, and few economic opportunities for them at home, the sons of Canada's foreign-born farmers began migrating in droves to the midwestern and northern United States where they could still take up prime agricultural and timber lands.

By 1848 two of Duncan Ban's sons, John, twenty-nine, and Alexander, twenty-three, were working in the Rossie area of upstate New York, still quite close to home. The brothers had boarded a ferry at Brockville, Ontario, less than fifty miles from Finch, and disembarked on the American side of the St. Lawrence River at Morristown, forty miles north of Rossie. What they were doing in Rossie we don't know, but the principal business in the region was iron. Possibly this was where Alexander learned the blacksmithing trade that later provided the underpinnings for the brothers' logging empire in La Crosse.

Two years later, in 1850, swept along on a tide of immigrants and Yankee entrepreneurs swarming westward to claim cheap land, John and Alexander headed for Wisconsin. The newest state in the Union (1848), Wisconsin contained some of the world's finest stands of white pine. Boarding a steamer at Clayton, New York (perhaps following a quick trip home to Canada to bid their aging parents goodbye), they crossed the Great Lakes to Detroit. From there they hopped an overland stage to Madison, Wisconsin's lively new capital city on beautiful Lake Mendota.

Centered in a large fertile area the size of Rhode Island, Madison could not help but prosper. After the village of Madison was incorporated in 1846, its population spiraled from 625 people to 9,000 in the next ten years. One thousand new buildings went up between 1847 and 1854. When the University of Wisconsin opened its doors in Madison in 1849, the city's future as a cultural mecca was assured.

Madison, 1851, King Street looking toward the state capitol, in a watercolor by Johann B. Wengler

John and Alexander McMillan lived with a German blacksmith named William Hosman and his family and five other boarders. Census records list John as a carpenter, and Alexander as a blacksmith. Hosman's other tenants included a well digger, a brick mason, and a wagon maker. We know from a brief biography of Alexander published during his lifetime that he also worked as a clerk in Madison and taught evening classes three nights a week. Since he had only a rudimentary education himself, he may have been teaching English. From his landlord Hosman, Alexander picked up a practical knowledge of German, a skill that would make it easier for him to do business with Wisconsin's large immigrant German population.

Madison was merely a stopping-off place for John and Alexander, however. The next year, continuing their odyssey, the brothers moved thirty miles north to Fort Winnebago, the former site of a frontier military post at the portage

between the Fox and Wisconsin Rivers. Later to become the city of Portage, Fort Winnebago was a bustling crossroads of more than two thousand people (including two families of McMillans and a large Dow family, some of whom may have been related to John and Alexander). Another ten thousand settlers and traders with their teams and stock plied the portage each year on their way west.

In July 1851, hitching their wagon to Wisconsin's rising star, Alexander and John McMillan purchased lot 1 of block 163, Webb & Bronson's Addition to Fort Winnebago, for $350. A prime chunk of real estate, a block and a half from the portage, it was the first piece of property owned by our family in the United States.

Ten years later, Portage would be the birthplace, in 1861, of historian Frederick Jackson Turner, whose frontier thesis revolutionized the way Americans thought about their past. Recognizing patterns of development in his hometown which he applied to the United States as whole, Turner explained how the fur trade had laid the groundwork for an agricultural and manufacturing society: "The Indian village became the trading post, the trading post became the city. The trails became our early roads." The fur trade closed its mission, he said, "by becoming the pathfinder for agriculture and manufacturing civilization."

Turner's frontier theory stressed the idea of an indigenous American character typified by perseverance, ingenuity, and self-reliance, traits he concluded had been engendered by the pioneer experience. Bringing these selfsame qualities with them from Canada, John and Alexander McMillan had a leg up on pioneering in this country. John filed his citizenship papers in 1851 in La Crosse (105 miles northwest of Fort Winnebago), and Alexander followed suit the next year in Fort Winnebago. By late 1852 they had sold their Fort Winnebago property (pocketing one hundred dollars profit) and moved to La Crosse, a small, crude settlement of log cabins and board-sided houses, still frequented by Indians who sometimes danced in the streets.

Situated on the east bank of the Mississippi at the confluence of the La Crosse River, about one mile below the mouth of the Black River, the town of La Crosse grew up on a sandy, almost treeless prairie that extended approximately seven miles along the Wisconsin shore and reached inland two and a half miles at its widest place. Millions of years ago, this prairie was the ancient bed of a much larger Mississippi River, contained by five-hundred-foot limestone bluffs that now stand four to five miles apart on both sides of the river. In historic times, this place was an Indian camping ground, frequented by fur traders and explorers who plied the river routes to the Northwest. French fur men called the area *Prairie La Crosse* for a ball game that the Winnebago and, before them, the Dakota, played at this place.

The first white settler in La Crosse was Nathan Myrick from New York, one of eight children, who came west as a teenager in 1841, purchased a small boatload of goods, and settled on a small island in the Mississippi opposite the present site of La Crosse to trade with the Indians. The next year he moved his trading post across the river to the mainland and built the first log house in La Crosse at the present corner of State and Front Streets (a few steps from where Alexander McMillan would set up his blacksmithing shop ten or eleven years hence).

Myrick's Indian trade in Wisconsin came to an abrupt end when the Winnebago were removed to a reservation on Long Prairie in central Minnesota in 1848, but by this time La Crosse was well on its way to becoming the supply center for logging operations in forty townships drained by the Black River. Some of the earliest lumbermen on the Black River were Mormons who came upriver in 1841 to cut timber for their great temple at Nauvoo, Illinois; by 1848, the year the Mormons were driven out of Nauvoo and made their epic trek to Utah, there were eleven small water-powered sawmills on the Black River and its tributaries, three of them owned by men from La Crosse.

After the town of La Crosse was named county seat of La Crosse County in 1851, settlers flocked to the area. The first of them, including John and Alexander, saw a village that was nothing more than a shabby jumble of several board and log structures. Front Street—the main street—was a dirt wagon road that ran along the crest of the river bank, and from Front Street, Indian trails led out to the bluffs and coulees in several directions, some of them taking a zigzag direction to avoid high sand hills. But some amazing changes took place in La Crosse in 1851: the town built its first courthouse (where John McMillan signed his citizenship papers), organized its first school (in the basement of the courthouse), published its first newspaper (*Spirit of the Times*), and held its first election (in which all thirty-six ballots were cast by men, women being still decades away from having the vote).

Joining the swelling ranks of pioneer businessmen in La Crosse, my great-great-uncles formed J. and A. McMillan, a logging partnership that ultimately

Nathan Myrick (far left) at his trading post, the first hewn-log cabin in La Crosse

paid huge dividends. Headquartered in La Crosse, the firm cut logs in the Black River pineries and rafted them to markets downriver as far as St. Louis. Like many of their fellow Black River loggers, most of whom came from the East where they had known similar immense pineries, John and Alexander built their empire slowly, enlarging their operations with their profits.

To help finance their logging activities, in 1852 Alexander opened the first blacksmith shop in Trempealeau, Wisconsin, a logging town about eighteen miles northwest of La Crosse. The following year he set up a second blacksmith shop in La Crosse, a half block from the steamboat landing at the foot of State Street. The *La Crosse Democrat* remarked on May 1, 1854, that "McMillan on Main Street is still shoeing horses and 'striking while the iron is hot.'" By that fall, according to an ad in the *La Crosse Independent Republican*, Alexander was also operating a livery stable a short distance away in the "Miller Barn":

Alex McMillan

> A. McMillan begs leave to say that he has procured a lot of GOOD HORSES AND CARRIAGES which he will keep to let on reasonable terms for ready pay. Passengers conveyed to any part of the country at short notice. . . . Good keeping by the day or week for cattle and Horses.

La Crosse, meantime, was growing at a good clip. Taking stock of the town's rapid development in *A Brief Sketch of La Crosse, Wisc,n.* (1853), Pastor Stephen Carr of the newly organized Baptist Church counted:

> 104 Dwelling Houses, 8 Fancy and Dry Goods Stores, 4 Groceries, 2 Drugs and Medicines, 2 Boots and Shoes, 2 Hardware, 2 Tin Shops, 2 Tailor Shops, 3 Shoe Shops, 1 Harness Shop, 4 Blacksmith Shops, 1 Gun Shop, 2 Bakeries, 1 Cabinet Shop, 3 Physician's Offices, 4 Law Offices, 1 Justice's Office, 5 Taverns, 1 Barber Shop, 1 Printing Office, 4 Joiner's Shops, 1 Steam Saw Mill, 1 Wagon Shop, 1 Jeweler and Silver Smith's Shop, 1 Mantuamaker [dressmaker] and Milliner Shop, 1 Office for sale of Government Lands, 1 Odd-Fellow's Hall, 1 Court House and Jail, 2 Meeting Houses.

Thirty percent of the 417 adult inhabitants Carr listed by name, birthplace, religion, and occupation had been born abroad—in Germany, Norway, Sweden, Britain, Ireland, Canada, and France. John and Alexander were two of only seven Canadians in town. John was listed as a millwright and Presbyterian; Alexander was a blacksmith with no religious preference. Both John and Alexander were Masons, members of Frontier Lodge No. 45 in La Crosse.

A gateway to Minnesota and beyond, the raw river town also attracted an ever-increasing tide of transients on their way west. In April 1853, 25 steamboats arrived at La Crosse, receiving and landing passengers and freight. Four years later, 1,560 steamers put into port. Adding to the waterfront congestion were scores of immigrant families traveling west by covered wagon and crossing the river by ferry. Once the railroad reached La Crosse in 1858—

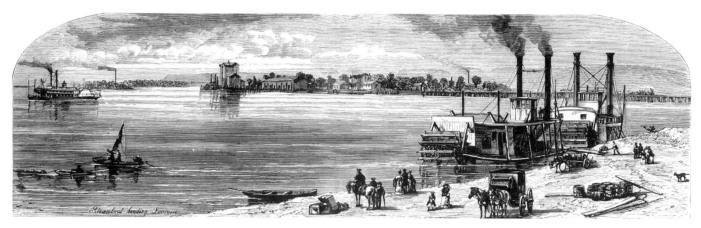

The steamboat landing at La Crosse

John McMillan, painted after his untimely death in 1865. John had the classic McMillan head, fairly large, with a high forehead and high cheekbones, a large nose, eyes almost too close together, straight brown or sandy-colored hair, and a small, insignificant chin (which he has disguised with a beard). This portrait bears a marked resemblance to my grandfather John Hugh MacMillan and his brothers.

tying the commercial life of the city to eastern markets by iron rails, bringing new settlers, and increasing the value of every area business, farm, and city lot—the town boomed.

John McMillan was the first of the McMillan brothers to marry, and he was already thirty-five when he wed a girl less than half his age, sixteen-year-old Mary Esther Leach, at her parents' home in La Crosse on August 7, 1855. That same year, Alexander quit blacksmithing; ready now to devote his full energies to lumbering, he sold his building to two men named Doll and Sundblad who operated a "plough factory" and shoed horses at "McMillan's old stand."

Mary Leach McMillan gave John five children at two-year intervals beginning with Allan (the first of our clan born in the United States) in 1856, followed by Esther in 1858, John Duncan (who would give my grandfather John H. MacMillan, Sr. his start in the grain business) in 1860, George in 1862, and Mary Emily (who got herself involved in a steamy scandal in her teens) in 1864. George died in infancy, but the other children survived to adulthood.

John McMillan became the first of the McMillan brothers to hold public office in La Crosse when he was elected alderman in the first ward in 1862. He and his family lived on the banks of the La Crosse River at the outskirts of town in a two-story white pine Gothic cottage laced with carpenter's gingerbread that John no doubt built with his own hands. At the time of the 1860 census, a third McMillan brother, Ewen Hugh, was living there with them, along with Mary's mother and eighteen-year-old sister Esther (Ettie) Leach, whom Ewen Hugh married the following year.

The fifth of Duncan Ban's sons, Ewen Hugh McMillan, called "Hugh," would become a stellar local attorney and his brothers' legal counsel. Twenty-two when he came to La Crosse in 1856, he had received the beginnings of a classical education in Canada, where he was tutored by St. Luke's Scottish minister Donald Munroe, and he entered the law office of W. H. Tucker and Edwin T. Flint who prepared him for the bar. Flint had been the first lawyer in La Crosse when he hung out his shingle in 1851.

Ewen Hugh would serve as city attorney, county attorney, and justice of the peace in La Crosse, and he was particularly well-versed in real estate, in which he and his brothers invested heavily. John and Alexander had begun buying property in La Crosse as early as 1854, when Alexander traded a span of horses that had outlived their usefulness in the pineries for two city lots near the river, and all three brothers bought numerous city lots and large rural parcels during the financial tailspin that sent land prices plunging in 1857.

Brought on by over-speculation in railway securities and real estate, the 1857 panic slowed business almost to a standstill in La Crosse. And in much of the rest of the country. The panic ended the boom brought on by the California gold strike of 1849, which had made the early 1850s very prosperous. Unlike the earlier panic of 1837, however, it did not lead to a period of protracted depression and business soon recovered. But the country's lack of a central bank for most of the nineteenth century would make the American economy prone to these periodic money crunches, because there was no mechanism to regulate the money supply or to provide liquidity in a financial crisis. The result, of course, was to make business in nineteenth-century America even more hazardous than it otherwise would have been.

The *National Democrat* reported that "parties below" owed La Crosse lumbermen $500,000, making it impossible for many loggers to meet their obligations to farmers, mechanics, and others. Scarce money caused a one-third drop in goods shipped to La Crosse, and the price of wheat dropped from one dollar a bushel in January 1856 to sixty cents in January 1858. Yet in spite of hard times, La Crosse continued to attract newcomers; between 1855 and 1860 the city's population more than doubled, increasing from 1,600 to 3,800 people.

In August 1861, quoting the *La Crosse Democrat*: "E. H. McMillan is now supplied with Land Warrants of all kinds which he will dispose of at the most reasonable rates. Emigrants and others who wish to locate lands will do well to call on 'Mack' and get a warrant. His office is next door to Uncle Sam's Land Office." Land in the pineries was selling at or near the government price of $1.25 an acre.

From everything I can gather, Ewen Hugh was an exceedingly colorful man, Scottish to the core, who helped keep alive Scottish traditions in La Crosse. Congenial and outgoing, he was a member of the St. Andrew's Society which on November 30, 1859, celebrated Scotland's patron saint's natal day at the Augusta House with well-laid tables of haggis, oysters, and "plenty of the fat things of the land [followed by] wines, champagne and other liquors [including] the good old Scotch Whiskey." Before finally calling it a night, Hugh and the others, dressed in their kilts, lifted their glasses to no fewer than twenty toasts. No teetotaler, Hugh would later die from the effects of alcoholism.

No wallflower either, it appears that Hugh could and did on occasion play the bagpipes. Tucked in the back of a music book handed down in our family are

Ewen Hugh MacMillan about 1865

a few loose pages of bagpipe music—songs named "Flowers of Edinburgh," "Miss Drummond of Perth," "Burns' Farewell," and "The Highland Petticoat." One of the pages is stamped, "Ewen McMillan, Finch"; another bears a handwritten inscription, "E. McMillan 3rd July 1855." My, what a pretty figure he must have cut!

In addition to lawyering and socializing, Ewen Hugh was especially interested in science and medicine, and he nursed high hopes of one day making La Crosse an important medical center. About 1860 he began promoting the formation of a medical college in La Crosse, but the Civil War seems to have interfered with the project. Finally, due largely to Hugh's persistence, the Wisconsin State Legislature granted a charter to the La Crosse Medical College in 1864. Hugh was thirty years old that year.

At its first meeting in April 1864, an optimistic seven-member board of trustees (comprised of five physicians, a chemist/druggist named William Wenzell, and Ewen Hugh McMillan) established chairs for Surgery; Anatomy and Physiology; Theory and Practice of Medicine; Materia Medica and Therapeutics; Chemistry and Pharmacy; Obstetrics and Diseases of Women and Children; and Medical Jurisprudence, all of them filled by the trustees. Ewen Hugh was named Professor of Medical Jurisprudence and also acted as secretary for the school, a job that had its macabre aspects. Once, in an attempt to procure cadavers for dissection by faculty members, Hugh wrote to the Rush Medical School in Chicago. That school's *janitor* replied:

"I can furnish you subjects without any injection at $15 delivered to the express office. I have no time to inject the subjects for you and I think it better to ship them before they are injected as the arteries break very easy when they are filled up. In regard to the embalming there is no danger that the subjects will spoil without it, as I should send you only fresh ones. If this suits you please send me your orders and I will fill them as quick as possible."

Believe it or not, in the two decades the college remained in existence, it never attracted a single student. Years after the college had died a slow death, the *La Crosse Tribune and Leader-Press* suggested that the sole purpose of the school had been to legalize dissections, but this accusation does not ring true. At most, only three dissections took place under the school's auspices. (Attendees paid five dollars each to cover expenses.) Until the college faded into obscurity, Ewen Hugh McMillan remained its faithful secretary, recording the trustees' annual meetings until 1881. There seems little doubt that he meant to keep the school's charter alive in the event the La Crosse Medical College might one day become operable.

Though it never issued a single diploma, the college *did* award three honorary degrees. One of these went to the chemistry professor, Wenzell, whom trustees felt should have the proper credentials; another was conferred on Ewen Hugh, probably for his legal efforts on behalf of the school; and the third was presented to an extraordinary man named Lafayette Houghton Bunnell.

The son of a physician and brother of a pharmacist from whom he had acquired considerable medical knowledge, Bunnell in 1849 had gone to California seeking gold and instead discovered and named Yosemite Valley while leading a battalion he helped organize against hostile Indians. (Yosemite derives from an Indian word meaning "grizzly bear.") During the Civil War, Bunnell served as a hospital steward and assistant surgeon in the Union Army. Shortly before he was mustered out, the newly organized La Crosse Medical College granted him a degree so that he could be promoted to surgeon.

Completing what became a formidable McMillan family foursome in La Crosse, my great-grandfather Duncan D. McMillan arrived in the city at age twenty-two in the fall of 1859. His naturalization papers filed in La Crosse stated that he came by way of Detroit. Reminiscing many years later, Duncan D. said that he had cast his ballot in the 1860 presidential election in La Crosse for Abraham Lincoln.

Educated like his brothers in Canada's common schools, Duncan D. had done some logging in Upper Canada, and he went to work at first in John's and Alex's lumbering business. These were heady times on the Black River. Logging was increasing rapidly and promised enormous profits in the years ahead. In 1860, together with other leading lumbermen, John and Alex McMillan formed the Black River Logging Association to oversee and police logging on the mighty stream, mainly during the annual spring drives. One of the largest member loggers was Cadwallader C. Washburn, later governor of Wisconsin, who used his lumber profits to finance a flour mill in Minneapolis that grew into General Mills.

A boom site for separating and storing logs on the Black River at La Crosse, looking north towards the Clinton Street bridge. The smokestacks of North La Crosse mills loom in the background.

After working only briefly for his brothers, Duncan quit lumbering temporarily to study law with Ewen Hugh. He was admitted to the Wisconsin bar in 1862, but that he ever practiced law is doubtful. The Civil War had broken out, and according to a biographical sketch published in 1892, Duncan D. served "in the ordnance department with Captain J. H. Burdick for several months after the fall of Vicksburg [1863]; and later he was in the Quartermaster's department at Memphis for a year with Captain A. R. Eddy." La Crosse largely met its army quotas during the war with volunteers (who were paid a $100 bounty by La Crosse businessmen—the idea being to keep leading citizens at home where they were needed to sustain the local economy).

Not everyone in La Crosse supported the war effort. Chief among its opponents was Marcus M. ("Brick") Pomeroy, the popular editor of the *La Crosse Democrat*. Pomeroy was one of a large number of Yankees known as Copperheads, mainly Democrats, who decried the war. Violently opposed to the draft, he professed "deep sympathy for those forced into this inhuman, murderous crusade," and he regularly denounced Lincoln in his paper as a despot, murderer, and traitor. Following Lincoln's assassination, when even almost every Confederate leader expressed regret, Pomeroy went down in history for printing the most vitriolic remarks about the slain president:

> The shameless tyrant, justly felled by an avenging hand, rots in his grave, while his soul is consumed by eternal fire at the bottom of the blackest hole in hell.

When he returned home after the war, despite any earlier misgivings he may have had about logging, Duncan D. purchased an interest in the family operation, which now became J. and A. and D. D. McMillan. There were fortunes being made in the Black River pineries, the McMillans' among them. Although he later involved himself in numerous city enterprises, Duncan D.'s primary source of revenue henceforth would come from timber. The McMillan brothers' three-way logging partnership was short-lived, however.

At the comparatively young age of forty-seven, John died of consumption (tuberculosis) while on a trip to Chicago in October 1865. Carrying the story on its front page, the *La Crosse Democrat* stated that "During his residence in this city [John McMillan] was principally engaged in the lumbering business, in which he had secured a competency." The McMillans thereafter did business as A. and D. D. McMillan, and by 1866 Duncan was secretary of the powerful Black River Logging Association. Moving up in town, he and Alex rented office space on the second floor of the three-story Juneau Block at Front and Main, where Ewen Hugh had been ensconced for several years.

John's widow Mary was twenty-six when she was left with four young children to raise. Alexander was appointed guardian to his nieces and nephews and oversaw John's property, much of which was real estate the two had purchased as partners. Some of the deeds also named Duncan D. McMillan as "special guardian" to the minor children. One such deed, ironically, was for the future site of the Cargill elevator on Front Street. Duncan sold this property to a La Crosse banker named Van Steenwyk in 1879, but it would end up back in family hands more than a half century later.

In their spare time, to keep fit, or just for the fun of it, Alexander and Duncan McMillan played the new game of baseball in La Crosse. Baseball, invented in New York City in the 1840s, had gained wide popularity in the army camps during the Civil War, as, indeed, it would nearly everywhere the American Army has gone since. La Crosse had numerous amateur baseball teams including the Butterfingers, Calicos, Castor Oils, Gateways, Long Stockings, Oakwoods, and Rough and Readys.

"The national game got loose on Saturday in La Crosse and made heaps of fun," reported the *La Crosse Democrat* on August 26, 1867. "Everyone in this city has the base ball [*sic*] fever fearfully, and to give all a taste of the noble sport a game was arranged between sides led by B. F. Montgomery and J. A. Kellogg." Alexander McMillan played third base with Montgomery's team; his much younger brother Duncan, "long-stop," with Kellogg and his gang. Each team had fourteen players including two shortstops, two center fielders, two right fielders, two left fielders, and a long-stop.

People worried some about the health dangers posed by baseball; in September 1866 the *Daily Democrat* stated that city physicians were concerned about the "probable effects of prolonged and violent muscular exercise, such as is necessary in playing base ball, cricket, etc., upon the health at the present season [and] they are unanimously of opinion it is dangerous, tending to the production of fevers and bowel disease particularly cholera and dysentery." The enthusiastic members of the La Crosse Base Ball Club should "take due notice and govern themselves accordingly," warned the paper. "We should hate to have any of the boys injured in their bow-wowels."

Besides playing baseball in his spare time, Duncan D. was also courting my great-grandmother. On Wednesday, September 5, 1866, when he was twenty-nine, Duncan D. McMillan married nineteen-year-old Mary Jane McCrea at the home of her brother, James McCrea, a carpenter and contractor in La Crosse. Mary Jane's family were Scots from Armagh in northern Ireland, and like many of the Scots-Irish people who settled in America, probably sprang from the thousands of Scottish Presbyterians whom England transplanted in Ulster beginning in 1607 to safeguard English rule in Ireland.

Mary Jane was born in Chateauguay, Quebec, near Montreal. Her father had already died in Canada when she emigrated to the United States eight months prior to her marriage with her mother, Elizabeth Johnston McCrea, and a brother, Stephen McCrea. Since then, she had been living with her brother James and his wife Ann in their neat little story-and-a-half frame cottage at 916 Cameron Avenue. Nineteen years hence, James and Ann's small son John, seven years old when his Aunt Mary Jane and Duncan D. said their vows in the midst of a small cluster of family, would be killed in a tragic accident at a new linseed oil mill owned and set into operation by Duncan D. McMillan. John McCrea's funeral would take place from this same house where Duncan and Mary Jane were married.

Duncan D. McMillan about 1866, the year he was married; Mary Jane McCrea McMillan about 1875

Mary Isabella McMillan, named for her paternal grandmother in Canada and seen here in a scottish sash

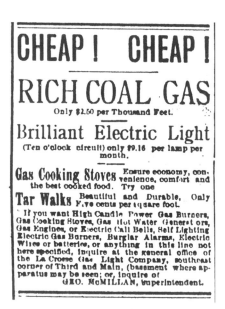

CHEAP! CHEAP!

RICH COAL GAS
Only $2.50 per Thousand Feet.

Brilliant Electric Light
(Ten o'clock circuit) only $9.16 per lamp per month.

Gas Cooking Stoves Ensure economy, convenience, comfort and the best cooked food. Try one

Tar Walks Beautiful and Durable, Only Five cents per square foot.

If you want High Candle Power Gas Burners, Gas Cooking Stoves, Gas Hot Water Generators, Gas Engines, or Electric Call Bells, Self Lighting Electric Gas Burners, Burglar Alarms, Electric Wires or batteries, or anything in this line not here specified, inquire at the general office of the La Crosse Gas Light Company, southeast corner of Third and Main, (basement where apparatus may be seen; or, inquire of GEO. McMILLAN, Superintendent.

An 1885 newspaper advertisement for George McMillan's La Crosse Gas Light Company

Duncan and Mary Jane's marriage was the first one recorded by the newly organized First Presbyterian Church in La Crosse. Both young people were devout church-goers who became deacons in the church. The couple set up housekeeping in a two-story frame house on the corner of Fifth and Division Streets, where their first child, Mary Isabella McMillan, was born in January 1868. Their second child, my grandfather John Hugh McMillan, arrived the following year on August 11, 1869. In the years ahead, five more children would arrive at regular intervals.

By this time, the close-knit McMillan clan in La Crosse also included the brothers' nephew George, who had emigrated to Wisconsin in 1863. George settled on a farm north of La Crosse, and his uncles Alexander and Duncan D. gave him his start in business. Plowing their lumber profits back into city improvements, the two bought controlling interest in the La Crosse Gas Works in 1869, rebuilt and extended its service to include street lights, and named George McMillan superintendent of the reorganized Gas Light Company. Gas lights were an innovation in the 1870s, replacing kerosene oil lamps on posts at street corners. Earlier, pioneer La Crosse residents had carried lanterns with candles or kerosene oil lights to guide them at night.

Adding still further to the McMillan presence in La Crosse, George's father Daniel McMillan, the eldest of Duncan Ban's sons, brought his wife Isabella Sutherland McMillan and their ten younger children to Wisconsin in 1867. Formerly a farmer and millwright in Canada, Daniel opened a farm in Campbell Township north of La Crosse, where the couple's twelfth child was born in 1868. That same year Daniel died in a tragic mishap.

No longer young at fifty-one, Daniel had been returning home from La Crosse on a freight train when he jumped off about a half mile from his farm and accidentally fell down an embankment into a shallow pool of water. Stunned by the fall, he drowned without regaining consciousness. Two physicians who examined the body found no evidence of violence or foul play. He still had his watch and pocketbook.

After burying Daniel near his brother John in Oak Grove Cemetery, his widow Isabella returned to Canada with their ten younger children. Their second oldest son, Allan, stayed behind in La Crosse to work for his brother George at the Gas Light Company. Daniel's children were the only ones to carry on Duncan Ban's surname in Canada. The La Crosse McMillans would continue to multiply with marked rapidity, however, and before losing everything they owned, reach high pinnacles of success during the town's glory years.

THE CARGILL CONNECTION

Twelve years older than my great-grandfather Duncan D. McMillan, his brother Alexander was the first really big success in our family. A prominent lumberman in a lumbermen's town, Uncle Alexander invested heavily in real estate and numerous local businesses. His influence also extended into politics. In 1866, beginning a career in public service that culminated with his election to the Wisconsin State Legislature, Alexander was elected city alderman from La Crosse's third ward.

A true renaissance man who lived life with as much gusto as a man brought up according to the strict tenets of the Presbyterian faith could probably muster, Alexander drove the "very prettiest, finest and best made cutter" in La Crosse (according to one news article) and fancied fast horses. Trotting races and fast horses had become the rage among affluent American men in the 1850s. In 1859 the *New York Herald* reported that "It would seem as if all New York had suddenly become owners of fast horses, and were all out on Bloomingdale Road [upper Broadway] on a grand trotting spree. This rushing to and fro of ship commodores, book and newspaper publishers, bankers, merchants, gamblers, and fast men generally, continues until the sun in its daily course has gone to visit the antipodes." It was no different in La Crosse and a hundred other Midwestern cities.

Proud to death of his prize mare, Lady Bashaw (who once turned up missing only to be returned to her stable days later in the dead of night by a thief who did not know what to do with so well-known a horse), Alexander helped organize and was the first president of the Oakwood Driving Park Association, which operated training stables and sponsored trotting races at Oakwood Park, "the best Half Mile Track in the West."

Trotting races in La Crosse County, Wisconsin

The fact that his own formal schooling had likely been brief did not hamper him. In 1869 Alexander was the founding president of the La Crosse Academy, a private school that, before La Crosse had a public high school, had its own newspaper, debating societies, and football. The La Crosse Academy held its first classes on Eighth Street in a building known as the Spiritual Temple, offering instruction in mathematics, languages, sciences, penmanship, bookkeeping, music, and painting and drawing. One advertisement stated that it taught "foreigners" to speak and write the English language.

Six hundred people turned out for the school's first commencement exercises in which both white and a few black children participated. John McMillan's oldest son, Allan, was enrolled at the school, and his daughter Esther performed a vocal solo. The next year, the academy built a small two-story structure at State and Sixth Streets and added teachers' training to its curriculum, only to be forced out of business in 1871 when La Crosse opened a new public high school. Few people in that time and place would pay to send their children to school when they could get free education for them.

Morally upright and straight-laced, Alexander was also president of the local temperance society which counted most of the La Crosse McMillans among its members (except probably for Ewen Hugh). Alcoholism has been a curse in our family down through the generations, and there were also many teetotalers like Alexander at the other end of the pendulum's swing. Alexander was married to a bright and talented amateur artist, the former Sarah Louise Parker, who helped keep him to the straight and narrow. She also would be the first woman in La Crosse to attempt to cast her ballot in a presidential election. Sarah and Alexander had four children, three girls and a boy, but the girls all died in childhood. Three small stones in the shadow of Alex's formidable McMillan monument, which is topped by a heroic-sized angel and cross, mark the graves of the little McMillan girls at Oak Grove Cemetery in La Crosse. Only their son Sam, who would wind up a notorious failure, lived to adulthood.

The 1870 census listed Alexander's assets at forty thousand dollars in real estate and an equal amount in personal property (more than $800,000 in 1990s dollars). That same year, Alexander and two men named Sill and Bliss shelled out twenty-five thousand dollars to build an eighty-by-fifty foot brick building on the corner of Main and Third Streets that would be the new Post Office Block. The pride of Main Street, with its tall rounded windows smartly eyebrowed with stone window caps, the Post Office Block provided much-needed office space for the McMillan brothers' expanding business interests—Alexander and Duncan's huge logging operation and Ewen Hugh's law practice.

For sixteen years, the McMillans had rooms on the second floor, cheek by jowl with prominent La Crosse physicians, dentists, and attorneys. Other tenants in the building included shops and saloons, a spiritualist church, a dance hall,

The McMillan brothers had their offices in the red brick Post Office Block built in downtown La Crosse by Alexander McMillan, W. R. Sill, and H. I. Bliss.

and the city's Masonic Hall. This La Crosse landmark would survive more than a hundred years—a major renovation transformed it briefly into a posh restaurant and night club called Valentino's in the 1970s—until it was judged structurally unsound and demolished in 1981.

Shortly after completing the Post Office Block and while still operating the La Crosse Academy, Alexander was elected to a one-year term as mayor of La Crosse on the Republican ticket in April 1871. Ordering up park improvements and new wagon roads leading from the city to outlying areas, while overseeing the construction of a local pound to detain hogs and cattle found running at large, the mayor also named a committee to persuade a railroad—any railroad—to build into La Crosse from the northwest. (By 1873, Chicago and North Western tracks would connect Madison to La Crosse.) The next year Alexander was elected to the Wisconsin State Legislature on a ticket that included U. S. Grant for president. His brothers Ewen Hugh and Duncan D. voted Republican that year as they always had, but after scandal rocked the Grant administration, they subsequently cast their ballots with the Democrats. Alexander always remained loyal to the Republicans.

At the state capitol in Madison, Assemblyman McMillan was appointed to standing committees on railroads and banking, both subjects he knew something about. Alexander sat on the board of the First National Bank in La Crosse beginning in 1871 and was elected president two years later. The year 1873 was generally a disastrous one for bankers, but not for Alexander. The financial panic precipitated by the failure of Jay Cooke and Company, which had financed the Northern Pacific Railroad, went relatively unfelt in La Crosse. No local banks failed, and lumber barons did business as usual.

As for railroading, in September 1872 Alex had been one of the incorporators of the La Crosse and Minnesota Bridge company, capitalized at $300,000 to build a railroad bridge between Wisconsin and Minnesota. Without this bridge, it is doubtful that Will Cargill would have moved his headquarters to La Crosse, and the paths of the two families might never have crossed. The actual building of the bridge was held up four years, however, while the Southern Minnesota Railroad and the Milwaukee Road wrangled over its location. In the interim, railroad cars continued to be ferried across the river on barges.

In the spring of 1874, Alexander, who loved to travel, took Sarah on a two-month trip east to sightsee and visit their former homes in Ohio and Canada. It is interesting to note that Sarah's hometown of Elryia is located on the Black River in Ohio and that Alexander was making his fortune on a river of the same name in Wisconsin. On Decoration Day (now called Memorial Day), Alex and Sarah attended ceremonies at the Tomb of the Unknown Dead at Arlington Cemetery, where they shared the grandstand with President Grant and members of his cabinet. The six-hundred-acre Arlington site had been the late General

This oil painting of Sarah Parker McMillan may be a self-portrait. Sarah was an accomplished amateur artist.

Mary McMillan McMillan in old age

Robert E. Lee's plantation, confiscated during the Civil War.

Reaching Canada, the couple found Alex's eighty-year-old mother Mary still living in the stone house Duncan Ban had built on the family farm, now owned by Angus. The single photograph of Mary passed down in our family shows her in old age, her face deeply lined. Alexander's three married sisters, Margaret, Christian, and Mary, would have been there to welcome him home as well, anxious to meet his wife of sixteen years. All three women lived with their families on farms of their own in the neighborhood. Now that Alexander was raising horses himself in La Crosse, he would have enjoyed tramping the fields he had helped work in his youth, comparing notes with Angus. Times were still tough on Duncan Ban's hardscrabble farm, and Alexander and his brothers in La Crosse may well have been contributing to its support; our family has a long tradition of brothers helping sisters, and sons helping their mothers.

The year 1875 marks an important milestone in McMillan family history. When he returned home from Canada, Alexander set in motion a small enterprise that would ultimately decide the family's destiny. With no notion of the family's future as grain merchants, Alexander and his brother Duncan, whom the *Republican and Leader* described as "wealthy and enterprising townsmen," purchased a half interest in a water-powered flour mill just north of La Crosse. Dating to the 1850s, when it had furnished feed and flour to area logging camps, the mill stood on three hundred sixty acres at Neshonoc on the La Crosse River, three-quarters of a mile north of the railroad station at West Salem.

The McMillans' partner in the mill was Alexander's brother-in-law Leonard Lottridge, a newspaperman whom President Lincoln had appointed postmaster at La Crosse in 1862. Lottridge was married to Sarah McMillan's sister Mary

The Lottridges' octagon house, built by Dr. Horace Palmer in nearby Neshonoc and moved to West Salem on log rollers

Elizabeth ("Libbie"), the widow of a physician. A tall, handsome, black-eyed woman, Libbie had gone to medical school herself following her first husband's death and was the first woman doctor in Wisconsin. She and Leonard Lottridge lived in West Salem in an octagon house now preserved by the West Salem Historical Society. Among its many amenities, the octagon house had an attached barn where Dr. Lottridge could hitch up her horse and get into her enclosed buggy before going out on calls in inclement weather. This was, no doubt, the first attached garage in West Salem.

The McMillan grist mill at Neshonoc about 1893. Neshonoc was founded in 1855 by Monroe Palmer who set up the mill as a saw mill, then planned the village around it.

"With this present organization [Alexander, Duncan, and Lottridge], the West Salem Mills will be in the hands of one of the strongest and most efficient business firms in the West," said the *Republican*.

Alex and Duncan were now in the grain business. "With ample capital," the paper declared, "the new firm will be able to take advantage of the grain markets; and also be independent enough to be out of the reach of panic-makers, and to carry a good stock of flour through 'tight times,' which often overtake a miller, and sometimes force him to yield temporarily to bad markets. The farmers of La Crosse Valley will soon have a strong and steady market for their wheat at the West Salem Mills. . . . Under the new management considerable enlargement of facilities, and improvement in machinery will be made. It is to be in truth, a first class establishment."

Coincidentally, the same 1875 La Crosse newspaper that reported the McMillans' purchase of the Neshonoc mill also announced the arrival in town of W. W. Cargill and his pioneer Cargill company:

> The firm of Hide [*sic*], Cargill & Co., of Albert Lea, Minnesota, controlling the wheat
> interest on the line of the Southern Minnesota Railroad, has rented the room in Levy's
> block opposite the International Hotel, formerly used by the Executive committee of
> the above mentioned railroad company, for an office, and will immediately enter

Captain William Dick Cargill

Edna Davis Cargill about 1885

upon business in this city, which will hereafter be the firm's headquarters. . . . La Crosse is always ready to extend the hand of welcome to men of pluck, brains, enterprise and capital, and is therefore glad to add to its business (and social) forces Messrs. Hide, Cargill & Co.

The McMillan and Cargill articles, seemingly unrelated, ran side by side on the front page of the *La Crosse Republican and Leader.* Their two names thus thrown together inadvertently by a newspaper compositor, the two families would find their lives forevermore entwined. The driving force behind the Hyde and Cargill operation was William Wallace (W. W. or Will) Cargill, and by moving his headquarters to La Crosse, the hub of a rail and water transportation network, he also set the stage for a family drama that ultimately took on epic proportions.

Born in 1844 on Long Island, New York, Will Cargill was the second son of a stouthearted sea captain, Captain William Dick Cargill, from Scotland's Orkney Islands. In 1839 Captain Cargill married Edna Davis at Setauket, Long Island. Edna was the cousin of famed American genre painter William Sidney Mount, and we still have in the family a portrait he drew of her as a young woman. Captain Cargill engaged in coastal shipping along the eastern seaboard, with occasional trips to South America and the Caribbean. Earlier he had sailed to China, and he also told his children that he had once sailed farther north than any previous captain of a merchant vessel.

Will and his four brothers grew up on the captain's stories of his adventures, but their mother did not want any of them to follow in his seafaring footsteps. Coming from a family of sailors herself, she had already lost one brother to drowning in a shipping accident, and another brother had returned home from the West Indies minus a leg. Wanting to bring up her boys as far away from tidewater as possible, she probably coaxed and pleaded until the captain agreed to give up shipping in favor of farming. If so, she also deserves the credit for helping preserve the family resources intact. In 1856, selling his business a year before the coming financial panic probably would have ruined him, Captain Cargill moved his family inland almost a thousand miles to Janesville, Wisconsin. There he purchased seventy acres of good wheat land and built a comfortable two-story frame house.

Still in his forties, Captain Cargill never became a serious farmer. The farm was for his boys, he said, and while Captain Cargill lived out his life as a retired mariner, young Will and his brothers spent their teenage years planting and harvesting wheat. By the late 1850s, Wisconsin was the nation's leading wheat-producing state, harvesting and selling fifteen million bushels of wheat annually; in 1860, the first of five years of bumper harvests, that figure jumped to twenty-eight million bushels. During the four years of the Civil War, Wisconsin produced nearly one hundred fifty million bushels of wheat, two-thirds of which was shipped east.

At the onset of the War Between the States, Will's parents tried to remain neutral and encouraged their sons to remain home on the farm, but their attitude softened when there was no speedy federal victory and the need for reinforcements increased. Will's older brother Thomas enlisted in the Union Army two days after McClellan stopped Lee at Antietam on September 17, 1862 (the single bloodiest day in the history of the United States Army; Union casualties totaled 12,410, Confederate, 13,724). Less than a month later, Thomas Cargill was dead of typhoid in a training camp just outside Janesville. Taking his place, perhaps, but in a civilian capacity, Will enlisted in the Quartermaster's department at Duval's Bluff, Arkansas.

At the war's end in 1865, twenty-one-year-old Will returned home briefly, maybe only to say goodbye again, then set out by train to seek his fortune in Conover, Iowa, a new boom town at the end of the McGregor Western line. The railroad was changing the way America did business; no longer would shipping

Captain W. D. Cargill residence and backyard in Janesville, Wisconsin, about 1865

Barn, windmill, and outbuildings at Cargill residence in Janesville

be confined to navigable rivers in the trans-Mississippi West. Pushing the frontier westward and inland, the railroads were expanding and multiplying, spreading through Missouri, Iowa, and Minnesota, and opening whole regions of rich farming lands to an influx of eager settlers.

Indeed, the railroad completely changed the nature of the grain business, transforming a myriad of local markets into a single international one. As early as 1886, Arthur T. Hadley, a distinguished economist and later president of Yale University, wrote in his book *Railroad Transportation* that "two generations ago the expense of cartage was such that wheat had to be consumed within two hundred miles of where it was grown. Today the wheat of Dakota, the wheat of Russia, and the wheat of India come into direct competition. The price at Odessa is an element in determining the price in Chicago."

Swarming with energetic ex-soldiers, Conover (named for an officer of the railroad) was barely a year old and promised agricultural and business opportunities galore. When Conover was incorporated on July 5, 1866, W. W. Cargill was one of the sixty-two incorporators. With twelve hundred inhabitants, two hundred houses, three hotels, a dozen stores, thirty-some saloons, and a full street of warehouses, Conover was growing by the minute. Will Cargill went into business with a man named H. C. Marsh running one of the grain warehouses or "flathouses"—storing, buying, and selling grain brought in at harvest time by area farmers. Most farmers planted hardy spring wheat on the Midwestern frontier. Prior to 1850 grain had been bagged and transported via wagon or water, but with the coming of the railroad, it would be shipped in bulk to the great trading centers of Chicago and Milwaukee. Warehousemen graded incoming grain and piled it (using handcarts) in the flathouse in bins, each of which typically held a carload. There were three grades of spring wheat plus a fourth classification—"rejected."

A farmer could simply store his grain in the flathouse and pay storage charges until deciding when and where to sell it, but most farmers needed ready cash at harvest time and sold their grain outright to the warehousemen. In turn, warehousemen like Marsh and Cargill established relationships with the railroads and commission merchants in Chicago and Milwaukee. Keeping abreast of up-to-date market information via the telegraph lines that had come west with the railroads, warehousemen used a hedging concept to sell grain in a market before the grain arrived. They were not speculators but rather saw themselves as middlemen. In Chicago and Milwaukee, the commission merchants minimized price risks by buying futures contracts which were later reversed by offsetting contracts when the actual grain was sold on arrival.

Will Cargill was started on the path that would lead to his success, but Conover quickly fizzled. In early 1866, just about the time the town was incorporated, the railroad dismantled its depot and moved it four miles south and east to Calmar, the second largest town in Winneshiek County, where a new railroad was building another road west to Charles City. Meanwhile the McGregor Western, laying rails west and north toward the Minnesota state line, reached Cresco, eighteen miles northwest of Conover, then Lime Springs, ten more miles to the northwest. Flocks of people packed up and left Conover for Calmar, Cresco, or Lime Springs, and local businesses failed.

In early 1867, former Conover resident H. C. Marsh built a warehouse in Cresco, probably in partnership with Will Cargill; that same year the two also built a warehouse in Lime Springs, where Will was a partner with a man named Clapp in a lumberyard. In Lime Springs, Will was joined by his younger brothers, Sam, twenty, and Sylvester, nineteen, whom he brought into his operations. All three were hard-working, frugal young men. As a later-generation family member wrote, "They didn't take rooms, but saved money by living in the flathouse, sleeping on cots in the room used as an office. They cooked there, on a pot-bellied heater with one stove lid. . . . One would handle the frying pan and do the cooking while the other held his hat over the open pan to protect the food from chaff and grain dust sifting down."

All summer the McGregor Western was laying track northward to Austin, Minnesota. At the same time the Minnesota Central Railway Company was building southward from St. Paul toward Austin. When they met amid much hoopla at Austin in October, they linked the Twin Cities of St. Paul and Minneapolis with Milwaukee, Chicago, and the East. Austin's potential was not lost on Will Cargill; crossing over into Minnesota, he with his partner Marsh built a grain warehouse there. His prospects were excellent, and on October 1, 1868, twenty-four-year-old Will Cargill married Ellen ("Ella") Theresa Stowell, fifteen, at Ossian, Iowa.

Ella's father, William Austen Stowell, was an insurance man, whom Will had likely met in Conover, where Stowell was a partner in a dry goods store. Described by the local R. G. Dun credit correspondent (usually a local lawyer) as "a regular rattling insurance man . . . a large business, good character," Stowell represented the Mississippi Valley Insurance Company. He kept a room above the dry goods store in Conover for his business visits, but he and his family lived in Ossian, about a dozen miles east of Conover.

Will and Ella Cargill set up housekeeping briefly in Austin, Minnesota, where their first son, William Samuel, was born in October 1869. Will's brothers continued to work in Iowa where Will built or acquired warehouses at Northwood, Kensett, and Sheffield. With his brother Sam, Will formed a partnership that would last a lifetime: "W. W. Cargill & Bro."; Sylvester Cargill later had his own mid-sized grain firm, the Victoria Elevator Company with headquarters in Minneapolis.

Pushing westward from LaCrescent, Minnesota (directly across the Mississippi River from La Crosse, Wisconsin), the Southern Minnesota railroad in

W. W. (Will) Cargill

Ellen Stowell Cargill about 1872

47

William Samuel ("Willie", later "Will S.") Cargill about 1875, the year the family moved to La Crosse

Edna Clara Cargill

1870 reached Albert Lea, Minnesota, twenty miles west of Austin. Following the future, Will Cargill moved his headquarters and young family to Albert Lea, bought two lots, and a constructed a small warehouse. When the warehouse collapsed a couple years later from overloading, Will replaced it with a larger, 18,000-bushel elevator that he equipped with an eight-horsepower engine for elevating the grain.

The plain but substantial home Will Cargill built for his family in Albert Lea stood on Grove Street, where a daughter, Edna, was born in September 1871. (Edna would marry my grandfather, John H. MacMillan, who would lead the Cargill Company through troubled times following W. W. Cargill's death in 1909.) That same year Will was elected Freeborn County coroner. In those days the coroner was a judicial official, not a physician, charged with conducting inquests into suspicious deaths. Apparently Will Cargill was highly thought of by his fellow townspeople.

An eternal optimist with his fingers in many pies, Will also had a way with bankers and financiers. Working out of a downtown office on Front Street in Albert Lea, Will bought land and built warehouses along the Southern Minnesota line at Alden, Wells, and Winnebago. His letterhead read, "Office of W. W. Cargill—Dealer in grain, pork, hides, wool, salt, etc." His most substantial of many business partners in the years 1870-1875 was Samuel Hyde, who had operated a grain trading firm in Lanesboro, Minnesota, before moving to Albert Lea. In 1875 the Dun correspondent for Albert Lea stated that the Hyde and Cargill combination owned forty-seven warehouses in twenty-seven places. Will Cargill, he said, was worth fifty thousand dollars.

Beginning in Albert Lea, Will Cargill forged lasting connections with pioneer financier Jason C. Easton, who had come to Minnesota from New York in 1856. Easton had his office at the Root River Bank in Chatfield, Minnesota, and by the early 1870s owned or held stock in at least eight southern Minnesota banks. Impressed by the confident young Cargill, Easton bankrolled him and frequently gave him business advice. In later years Will Cargill would also come to rely heavily for financing on prominent Milwaukee financier Robert Eliot. Eliot owned a large commission house through which he bought Cargill grain and extended a good deal of credit to Will's various partnerships. Quoting a brief internal Cargill history written in 1945:

> It is doubtful if there was ever in the grain trade any man with a greater capacity for inspiring confidence than W. W. Cargill. His spectacular early success was in large measure made possible by the friendship of a great Milwaukee banker, Mr. Robert Eliot, not once, but again and again, to their mutual profit.

Beginning in 1873 Will Cargill was also working as an agent for the National Life Insurance Company, a Minneapolis firm, selling life insurance and

Emma Cargill, 1879

This large brick residence with a round window in its center was the Will Cargills' first house in LaCrosse.

"endowment policies" in the Albert Lea area. How he found time for this enterprise and how long he continued at it is unknown. This was the year that economic chaos, brought on largely by overexpansion of the railroads on shaky financial ground, plunged the country into a widespread depression. But if Will Cargill was worried for his own financial future, he needn't have been.

While numerous country elevators failed during the 1873 panic, which paralyzed commercial credit throughout the country and forced the New York Stock Exchange to close for ten days, Will Cargill and his combines came out of that maelstrom in better shape than before it began. Between 1873 and 1878, by buying up cheap properties that would become profitable after the depression, Cargill companies increased their storage capacity by two hundred thousand bushels or four hundred percent.

Meanwhile, Will had moved his headquarters and family, now including a third child, Emma, born in 1874, yet again. This time, the destination was La Crosse, Wisconsin, some hundred miles east of Albert Lea. In August 1875 the *Liberal Democrat* reported that Hyde, Cargill and Company had upwards of sixty thousand pounds of wool in their brick warehouse on Front Street. The firm's primary business was grain, but it also dealt in other produce including wool, hogs, and chickens. "Ed Osborne, C. E. Page, and Sam Cargill are going out into the Minnesota chicken orchards next Monday," said the *Liberal Democrat*. "We give the notice thus early so that people who want to buy chickens by the car load will know who to order of."

When he first came to La Crosse, Will Cargill stayed at the International Hotel, traveling back and forth to his home in Albert Lea, Minnesota. But by fall, he had Ella and their three children with him in La Crosse, ensconced in an ostentatious, red-brick house with yellow limestone trim he rented on the northeast corner of Eighth and King Streets. W. W. Cargill was well on his way to his

Samuel Davis Cargill, Will Cargill's younger brother and lifelong partner

first million dollars. His brother Sam was his full partner, and their youngest brother, Jim, twenty-three in 1875, had also joined the firm.

In May 1876 the *Republican and Leader* reported: "Hyde, Cargill & Co.'s wheat receipts on the line of the Southern Minnesota are increasing. Tuesday they received 24,000 bushels, and probably as much yesterday. Their receipts here are increasing every day and they have a big pile now on hand." When they renovated their office, the paper asked, "A rise in wheat?" And their reviews only got better. The following spring, Will Cargill and his partners S. Y. Hyde and Major B. J. Van Valkenburgh took their wives to Chicago, causing the *Liberal Democrat* to crow: "They have been making so much money on wheat that they'll buy Chicago if they feel like it."

The McMillan mill at Neshonoc was also prospering. On March 15, 1876, the *Republican and Leader* reported that the grist mill was back "in running order [following] the terrible and unprecedented floods that swept almost everything before them. The Neshonoc water power has stood a severe test indeed, and is without doubt one of the best and safest in this county." The next week, according to the paper, the mill was "the busiest place in the county. Fifty teams at a time are seen these days in front of [it] waiting for an opportunity to unload their grists."

Alex and Sarah summered at one of the cottages on the mill property the next year, and Alex purchased his partner Lottridge's share in the mill and possibly his brother Duncan's as well. Their brother Ewen Hugh came to West Salem with his family in October to take charge of the mill, but this was only an interim arrangement. In December, Alexander offered the mill for sale, "the time of the owner being fully occupied with other business interests." When the mill didn't sell, Alexander expanded it into one of the largest in western Wisconsin.

Meantime, Hyde, Cargill and Company had moved to more commodious quarters in a brick block on the northwest corner of Second and Main Streets. After S. Y. Hyde left the firm in August 1877, it subsequently became Cargill and Van. Neither Will Cargill nor his now full partner B. J. Van Valkenburgh was the kind of man to let any grass grow under his feet, but sometimes they must have amazed even themselves as their empire grew in many different directions.

"Yesterday, Cargill & Van made a cable sale in Liverpool of 80,000 bushels of No. 1 Minnesota wheat, for prompt delivery," the *Liberal Democrat* reported in June 1878. "The wheat is now in the various elevators along the line of the Southern Minnesota Railroad, and in this city. This is one of the largest sales of actual wheat ever made in the northwest." Historian Henrietta Larson called it "the first important direct export of wheat from Minnesota."

Enlarging their operations to include production, Cargill and Van purchased more than six thousand acres of grain and grasslands from the Southern Minnesota Railway for a bonanza-type farm in Martin County, Minnesota. Will Cargill personally went to St. Louis to buy forty or fifty teams of mules to clear and plow the farm. Mainly, he planted wheat with some corn, potatoes, and root crops. By November 1879, Cargill and Van's Big Farm or Mule Farm, as it became known, contained buildings enough to make up a small village and employed several dozen men, two of them blacksmiths. "The cluster of buildings necessary to shelter 1000 head of cattle, 1000 sheep, 300 hogs and the necessary horses, mules and machinery, resembles a fort with barracks," said one source.

Will Cargill's interest in farming also extended to testing and experimenting with seed. In the spring of 1879, Cargill and Van tested two batches of number four wheat seed from the previous year's blighted crop in a dirt-filled box at their downtown office in La Crosse. One side of the box was planted with seeds picked at random, and the other with the most unfavorable looking seeds, some of them hardly larger than a pin. Both batches of seed sprouted, but the random seed produced more vigorous plants. The logical inference to be drawn from these experiments, said the *Chronicle*, "would be that by seeding a trifle heavier than usual, the desired results would be obtained at harvest time." But while the tests proved that the grain was still viable as seed, the paper pointed out that there remained grave doubts as to whether "shriveled and shrunken seed could bring forth a vigorous and virile fructification. . . . All experience has shown that the time-honored plan of securing the best seed, whether for the garden or the field, has paid well at harvest time, and there is no good reason why wheat should not be subject to the same natural laws."

Expanding and extending their grain business through Minnesota along newly laid track, Cargill and Van built wheat buying stations as far west as Flandreau, South Dakota. To the east, they opened new territory to Green Bay on the Green Bay and Minnesota Railroad. Sam Cargill went to Green Bay to take charge of the company's day-to-day operations at that end. In August 1879, the *La Crosse Chronicle* reported, "Cargill & Van are buying grain at 22 stations in Minnesota, 9 on the Green Bay and Minnesota, and 3 on the West Wisconsin [Railroad]." Without question, the paper said, they are the "heaviest produce dealers in this section of the country."

La Crosse was still a lumber town; but with direct rail connections both to Chicago and Milwaukee to the east and St. Paul to the north, it was fast becoming an important grain trading center. As fate would have it, La Crosse was also the place where my great-grandfathers and their families, the Cargills and McMillans, forged alliances that would survive through thick and thin to the present day. The two families have been exceptionally close, but their relationship has been strained on occasion. At one particularly glum time right after the turn of the century, Will Cargill's son, also named Will Cargill, took possession of and moved into the family mansion my great-grandfather Duncan D. McMillan built for his family in La Crosse and later lost in bankruptcy proceedings.

CENTENNIAL FEVER

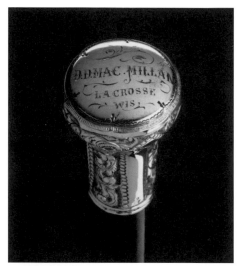

D. D. McMillan's gold-headed cane and pocket watch, the back of which opens to reveal a portrait of his wife Mary Jane

In 1876 the United States celebrated the one hundredth anniversary of the signing of the Declaration of Independence with the largest world's fair in history in Philadelphia. Among the nearly ten million visitors who flocked to the Centennial Exposition—roughly one-fifth of the country's entire population—were Alexander, Sarah, and Duncan D. McMillan.

Opened with great fanfare on May 10 by President Grant (who was criticized by a Polish journalist for wearing "just a business suit without gloves"), the World's Fair was a spectacular world within itself, set out in 249 buildings on 450 acres. It attracted thirty thousand exhibitors from fifty foreign countries and all thirty-eight states. Queen Victoria and her daughters sent embroidery made with their own royal hands; the French, the arm and hand of Bartholdi's Statue of Liberty (which would not be finished until 1884).

Organized into seven broad categories of exhibits: mining and metallurgy; manufactured products; science and education; machinery; agriculture; fine arts; and horticulture; the Centennial offered something for everyone.

> The farmer saw new machines, seeds, and processes [we read in James D. McCabe's huge *Illustrated History of the Centennial Exhibition* published in 1876]; the mechanic ingenious inventions and tools, and products of the finest workmanship; the teacher, the educational aids systems of the world; the man of science, the wonders of nature and the results of the investigations of the best brains of all lands. Thus each returned to his home with a store of information available in his own special trade or profession.

Several later brand-name successes including the Otis elevator and the Bissell carpet sweeper made their debut at the Centennial. The Remington Model 1 typewriter, produced by arms manufacturers E. Remington and Sons, was also new on the market in 1876, but not until Remington brought out its Model 2 with a shift key and both upper-case and lower-case letters several years later did the typewriter really catch on.

An unexpected sensation at the fair was twenty-nine-year-old Alexander Graham Bell's telephone, which the Scottish-born inventor demonstrated on a small out-of-the-way table amid exhibits of the Massachusetts Department of Education. Less than two years later in 1878, the first private telephone line in La Crosse would be installed between the homes of Ewen Hugh McMillan and W. P. Powers, a man who sold wooden water pumps.

I imagine that my great-grandfather Duncan D. McMillan, who was inclined toward mechanics, would have been particularly impressed by the gigantic 750-ton, 1,400-horsepower Corliss steam engine that was the showpiece of the Centennial. Rising loftily in the center of Machinery Hall, the Corliss engine was a great athlete of steel and iron that was supposed to bespeak the coming of age of industrial America. In fact it spoke to the past, as it was to be the largest reciprocating steam engine ever built. The future belonged to the steam turbine and electricity. Popular Centennial illustrations showed President Grant flipping the switch for the mammoth contraption on opening day, setting it and hundreds of smaller dependent machines in the building in clangorous motion.

Out in Montana, Centennial year celebrations were upstaged by a catastrophe that sent the nation into the kind of shock it had not known since Lincoln was assassinated eleven years earlier. On the afternoon of June 25, Lieutenant Colonel George Armstrong Custer led five companies of the famous Seventh Cavalry to annihilation and immortality on the treeless ridge rising from the east bank of the Little Bighorn River. When the smoke and dust of combat lifted, Custer and every one of his more than two hundred blue-shirted troopers lay dead at the hands of an estimated four thousand Indian warriors.

News of Custer's shocking and horrifying defeat did not become known in the rest of the country until July 6. Custer and his men had been dead more than a week when La Crosse, now twenty years old and boasting twelve thousand residents, celebrated the Fourth of July with hometown festivities. Former mayor Alexander McMillan chaired the executive committee sponsoring "The Northwestern Centennial Celebration," and he did a good job of it. Local Fourth of July festivities got off to a rousing start with a one-hundred-gun salute from booming cannon, followed by the ringing of bells, by shrill steam whistles, and by other rousing salutations. According to one reporter:

> The decorations of streets and buildings throughout the city were elaborate, tasteful, patriotic and appropriate. Flags, banners, and emblems, with evergreens and floral ornaments, garnished public edifices and private residences and business places. The in-coming crowds from the country, by boats, [railroad] cars, and [horse-drawn] private vehicles, came in great glee, and joined in the general demonstration of national gladness that pervaded the masses.

The mid-morning parade was "unquestionably the most attractive and brilliant display ever witnessed west of the Lakes." First came the La Crosse Drum Corp and the band from Wells, Minnesota, followed by veteran soldiers, local dignitaries, and the fire department. The Knight Templars in full uniform preceded the Norwegian Workingmen's Society, the Oakwood Base Ball Club, the Sons of Temperance, various German societies, a Bohemian society, and a company of Indian boys in war costume. Huge horse-drawn vehicles carried displays from various local manufacturing and business establishments, and citizens in all manner of carriages and wagons brought up the rear.

The Duncan D. McMillan residence in La Crosse

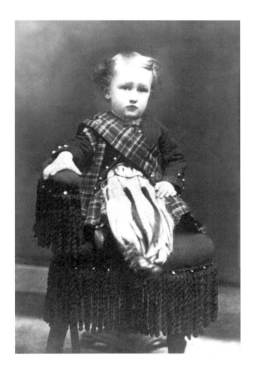

William Duncan McMillan in tartan with a sporran (pouch worn by Scottish Highlanders)

Celebrating the Centennial in a particularly personal way, Duncan D. McMillan was building a princely new residence at Cass and Twelfth Streets, which, when finished, would "eclipse any similar building as regards size and style in the city," crowed the *La Crosse Liberal Democrat*. Twelve blocks east from the banks of the Mississippi, Twelfth Street was on the outskirts of town in an area that was still mainly sandy, virgin prairie, and a brisk stretch of the legs from the increasing noise and congestion of the growing central business district. The launching pad for a dynasty, and a monument to enterprise and industry, Duncan D.'s stately red brick Victorian mansion with its arched windows and a four-story Campanile-like tower could also be construed as a clan castle.

Thirty-eight and self-made, Duncan D. McMillan—the D. stood for nothing, as is often the case with initials in Scottish names—was a leading lumberman and town father in a bright-eyed Mississippi River lumber town. A far cry from the small log house in which he had been born and reared with nine brothers and sisters in remote Upper Canada, his new abode, approached by a circular drive that enclosed a showy, three-tiered fountain, was huge; eighty-two feet deep by fifty-two feet wide, not including porches and verandas, it contained seven thousand square feet of floor space. Electric call bells summoned the help: two Irish servant girls, sisters in their twenties.

Duncan's large household in 1876 included his wife Mary Jane McCrea McMillan, twenty-nine; their eight-year-old daughter, Mary Isabella; four sons: John Hugh, six, William Duncan, four, Daniel, three, and Allan Morrison, a babe in arms, born in May while the house was under construction; Mary Jane's widowed mother Elizabeth Johnston McCrea, seventy-one; and Duncan's nineteen-year-old nephew Allan McMillan (his dead brother John's oldest son). During the next few years, rounding out the family circle, Mary Jane would give birth to two

Daniel D. McMillan at two years, eight months

more daughters, Janet in 1880, and Elizabeth Johnston (named for her grandmother) in 1884.

Following on the exultant heels of 1876, the next year was a sad one indeed for the Duncan McMillans. In April 1877, the *La Crosse Republican and Leader* reported the death of baby Allan Morrison McMillan from scarlet fever. His five-year-old brother Willie had also been confined to the house for four weeks with the disease, but was "improving" and "out of danger." Little Allan was buried from the new family residence. His family and a small entourage accompanied his tiny casket down the wide stone front stairs to a waiting horse and carriage for the cheerless trip to Oak Grove Cemetery.

An advertisement for wooden water pumps in the same day's paper as baby Allan's obituary attributed "the sickness in La Crosse" that year to "impure water":

> Think of this, you who are using water from open wells [warned pump salesman W. P. Powers]. You are drinking the distillation of rotten wood and all manner of animal and vegetable life, which goes in at the top, and also the drainings from the cess pools of the city, which sinks easily through this porous sand to the surface of the water, and then into your wells, as they take only the surface water. With a wooden Drive Pump you get the water pure as nature made it, from a depth of ten feet below the surface. . . . [These pumps] are cheaper . . . than a fit of sickness and less expensive than a funeral.

Scarlet fever, however, is not a water-borne disease, and this sorry picture of the general state of water sanitation in horse-and-buggy La Crosse did not apply to the McMillan residence in any case. It had its own windmill and a water tank on the roof. Duncan had borrowed the windmill idea from his brother Alexander, who had erected a similar apparatus at his own residence a few

The front entry of Duncan D. McMillan's house opened onto a full-blown Victorian interior. Note especially the tall gas light emerging from the newel post at the foot of the stairs. At the right rear of the main hall a hall tree blocks a doorway. This residence was razed in the early 1900s, but architectural elements salvaged from it were incorporated in the present prairie-style house on the site.

blocks away after seeing how popular windmills were on a trip to California. Thanks to an enormous heating plant in the basement (at a time when most houses were still heated with stoves), Duncan and his family also enjoyed hot and cold running water in their bathrooms and bedrooms.

Twenty years hence, Duncan would lose this magnificent house in his first big-time foray into the grain business, but in the 1870s it was every inch a stage-perfect backdrop for upper-class domesticity. Carved woodwork in the high-ceilinged rooms, filled with fussy fringed furniture and betassled swag draperies, was of solid black walnut from family-owned pineries. An artist from Milwaukee was brought in to fresco the walls, on which fine paintings hung by slender cords from high moldings.

Collecting art was becoming fashionable in La Crosse as it was elsewhere in America among business barons prospering in the burgeoning post-Civil War industrial economy. Both Duncan and his brother Alexander owned numerous paintings, etchings, and sculptures. Shortly before Christmas 1877, Duncan splurged on a painting titled *Rocky Mountain* by an artist named Herman, paying five hundred dollars for it to W. N. Fay and Company, a firm of auctioneers that sold 160 paintings in La Crosse that year.

About the artist Herman we know virtually nothing except that he worked in St. Paul in the 1860s. On the day after Christmas 1863, the year following the bloody Dakota War, Herman sketched the hanging of thirty-eight Indians in Mankato for *Harper's* magazine.

Opposite the Herman painting in the McMillan parlor hung a handsome oil portrait in a fancy gold frame of Duncan himself; a fine figure of a man, hardened in the pineries, he has a round face, brown hair, and a wavy chin beard.

Having learned to play the violin as a boy, in an age before television or radio, Duncan was a competent parlor musician. We read in the *Republican and Leader* that during a musical evening at the McMillan house sponsored by the "Bon Muse Society," Duncan and two friends performed Anton Rubinstein's "Trio in b flat for violin, cello and piano," which their appreciative audience "received with enthusiasm." He probably had a fine singing voice as well, for he was treasurer of a local choral group, the Mendelssohn Musical Society; and he also played the bagpipes. His small book of bagpipe music, "Strathspeys, Reels, Jigs & Quick-steps," published in Glasgow in 1848, with his name penned on the title page, has been passed down in his daughter Mary Isabella's family.

Although Duncan's musical talent seems to have dried up by my generation, it flowed in his children's veins. I don't think that my grandfather John Hugh McMillan was in any way musical, but his younger brothers Dan and Will were. Will played the violin, and Dan sang in a quartet much in demand for concerts and funerals in La Crosse. A younger sister, Janet, born in 1880, became an accomplished pianist and piano teacher. In the next generation, Duncan's grandson, his

Duncan's prized Rocky Mountain *painting hanging in the main parlor*

daughter Mary Isabella's son Malcolm Rowles, became a concert pianist.

Civic-minded like his father and brothers, Duncan began two years of service on the La Crosse County Board of Supervisors in 1873, and he was elected alderman for the third ward in 1877. Though lacking in formal education, he never let this hold him back; self-made, he was also apparently self-educated. In 1879 he was elected president of the La Crosse Board of Education.

The main parlor with Duncan D.'s portrait at the left

A letter Duncan wrote to the State Historical Society of Wisconsin on stationery identifying him as president of the Board of Education is one of only three surviving letters in his hand. Dated February 15, 1879, it concerns his donation of a prehistoric "copper instrument," which Historical Society annals described as "a copper implement six inches wide, hollowed out for a haft, sides turned up, with a cutting edge at one end—a fine specimen." Duncan wrote that the implement had been found by workmen about 1860 "within thirty or forty feet of the south bank of the La Crosse river while excavating and grading preparatory to erecting the La Crosse City Gas Works."

In 1880 Duncan invited the newly appointed pastor of the First Presbyterian Church, Reverend W. D. Thomas, to set up his personal library of twenty-two hundred volumes in his home. ("The new Presbyterian minister is a bachelor, a defect of which we confidently anticipate the invigorating climate of La Crosse will speedily cure him," chirped the *Chronicle*.) An erudite gentleman who became a close friend of the McMillans, marrying them and burying them, Thomas reportedly owned the largest library between Chicago and Minneapolis. Many of the books were theological tomes, but a majority of them concerned scientific and social questions of the day, and the library included standard authors and reference books as well.

My grandfather John Hugh McMillan, who would become president and chairman of the Cargill Elevator Company, was eleven when Rev. Thomas's library arrived, and his formal schooling would end four years later, but he prided himself on being a lifelong scholar. I have to believe that Rev. Thomas's library inspired John Hugh's love of reading. When my grandfather later built his first house in Arkansas as a young married man, he included a library that he stocked with fine books.

The music room behind the main front parlor, looking into the library. Is that Duncan's violin on top of the piano?

Lumbering remained the principal industry in La Crosse in 1880, accounting for sixty percent of the city's payroll, but it declined sharply after that as the northern pineries were depleted. Duncan was appointed general manager of the Black River Improvement Company in 1882, but he also spent part of that year prospecting for silver in southwest New Mexico as one of six partners in the Colossal Mine Company, incorporated in La Crosse. The New Mexico property was in the middle of desert ("where almost the only living thing to be seen is the cactus," wrote one visitor) and, after proving unproductive, was eventually forfeited for taxes.

The State Bank Building at 311 Main Street about 1890. Duncan was president of the bank for thirteen years.

The La Crosse Linseed Oil Company , organized with a capital stock of fifty thousand dollars in July 1884. Duncan D. McMillan was named secretary.

Duncan also had his eye on a less chancy business back home, however, and in 1883, shortly after celebrating his forty-sixth birthday, he was named president of the newly organized State Bank of La Crosse. Incorporated with a capital stock of fifty thousand dollars, the State Bank grew out of a private banking house established in 1879 by John M. Holley and Emil N. Borresen. Borresen was vice president at the State Bank under Duncan, and Holley, cashier. Both of these men would figure in Duncan's later financial downfall. When the State Bank quickly outgrew its first quarters, directors built a smart new two-story bank of red brick with white limestone and terra cotta trim at 311 Main Street. By 1888 the bank showed deposits amounting to $225,000.

Shortly after accepting the bank's presidency, at a time when area farmers needed to diversify their crops, Duncan, with his brother Alexander, helped establish the La Crosse Linseed Oil Mill in two four-story brick buildings on State Street between Front and Second. This was the approximate site of Alexander's pioneer blacksmith shop. One building was the mill proper, housing the grinders, presses, and engines; the other was a warehouse for barrels, flax seed, and manufactured stock. According to the *Republican and Leader*, the mill was "the best in the Northwest."

Massive hydraulic presses processed eight hundred bushels of seed in a twenty-four-hour period, producing seventy-five gallons of linseed oil hourly. Residual oil cake was sold as winter feed for livestock. The Chicago, Milwaukee and St. Paul Railway laid track between the twin buildings to facilitate shipping, and incoming seed was elevated from rail cars into the top floor of the mill. Farmers were invited to call at the mill to pick up seed and directions for planting, harvesting, and marketing their crops.

Ten months after the mill opened, tragedy struck; in October 1885 a horrible accident resulted in the death of Mary Jane McMillan's twenty-six-year-old nephew, John McCrea. McCrea was employed on the night crew, running one of the presses or formers for extracting the oil and making oil cakes. When the machine stopped for some reason, McCrea thought something must be out of gear, so he climbed into the area where the action of the machine normally pushed out a lever, leaving little space between it and the wall. Forgetting the danger, he told another man to start the machine, and the lever crushed him to death against the wall.

The funeral service for McCrea was held at his widowed mother's cottage on Cameron Street, where Duncan and Mary Jane had said their wedding vows nineteen years earlier. The Linseed Oil Company paid for his burial.

Will Cargill's Victorian mansion in La Crosse, its bay windows facing the Duncan D. McMillan residence across Cass Street

M ark Twain, when he made his famous trip up the Mississippi by steamer to St. Paul in 1882, marveled en route at the rapidity with which La Crosse had achieved an enlightened standard of living. "Here is a town of twelve or thirteen thousand population, with electric lighted streets, and blocks of buildings which are stately enough, and also architecturally fine enough to command respect in any city," he wrote.

Still under construction was grain dealer Will Cargill's gaudy red brick mansion, begun in July 1881, which would outshine even Duncan McMillan's abode. If Duncan McMillan had built a princely residence in which to house his family, Will Cargill was building one fit for a king directly across the street. During the year and a half that the Cargill house was under construction, Will and Ella and their three children, William Samuel, Edna, and Emma, lived in a red brick rental dwelling on one end of Duncan McMillan's property.

As the Cargill and McMillan children played together and watched from across the street, six teams of horses at a time hauled brick for the pretentious two-and-a-half story Cargill house rising from a cut limestone foundation. Confidently more elaborate than any neighboring mansion, the Will Cargill house epitomized regional Victorian architecture at its most flamboyant, combining every possible geometrical shape in a bracketed, gabled edifice run rampant with dormers and iron roof crestings. Before the family moved in, Will Cargill and Duncan McMillan macamadized Cass Street between their two homes for 250 feet from the corner of Twelfth Street. (Macadam was an early type of black-top paving named for Scottish civil engineer John Loudan McAdam.) These were still horse and buggy days, of course, but paved streets made for less dust filtering into the houses on hot, dry summer days.

William Wallace Cargill

The First Presbyterian Church in La Crosse where both Duncan D. and Mary Jane McMillan served as deacons

Close friends and confidants, Will Cargill and Duncan McMillan were birds of a feather. Self-made, civic-minded entrepreneurs who invested in some of the same La Crosse enterprises including the Edison Light Company and the Vote-Berger Telephone Manufacturing Company, they were both God-fearing Scotsmen, just one generation removed from the Old World; in 1882 they were both serving on the building committee for the new Presbyterian Church. When Duncan McMillan later got in over his head in a fledgling grain business in Texas, Will Cargill would do his best to bail him out, and there is no indication their friendship was ever compromised.

In the lives of the Cargill and McMillan children, growing up across the street from one another, however, far more complex relationships that would one day have worldwide implications were evolving. William Samuel (Will S.) Cargill and John Hugh McMillan, both thirteen in 1882, grew up to be lifelong antagonists. Will S. married May McMillan, the daughter of Duncan's nephew George McMillan; and my grandfather John Hugh married Will S.'s sister Edna Cargill. Ultimately, when Will S. turned out to be a bounder, after Will Cargill's death in 1909, it was John Hugh McMillan who took over the reins of the Cargill organization.

Will W. Cargill's businesses and fortune were growing dramatically in the 1880s. Gifted with an inventive, creative mind and endless, restless energy, he was continually striking out in new directions. Some of these ventures were closely tied to the grain business, while others were not. In 1881 Will formed a stock company in Albert Lea to prospect for coal in Freeborn County. He did so because he could merchandise coal through his country elevators, and he also had a retail outlet called the Cargill Coal Company in La Crosse. Similarly, when he purchased flour mills at Hokah and Houston, Minnesota, the connection to his primary business was obvious; the flour mills processed substantial quantities of Cargill wheat shipped from La Crosse. In November 1882 the *Chronicle* reported that "W. W. Cargill & Co.'s Hokah mill has lately made a shipment of 840 barrels of flour direct to London."

Perhaps egged on by Duncan McMillan, Will Cargill also flirted with silver mining, possibly with success. In March 1882, with former partner S. Y. Hyde and other La Crosse and Winona (Minnesota) capitalists, Will Cargill formed the Vienna Mining Company to prospect for silver ore in Idaho. The firm quickly struck it rich on Idaho's Pacific Slope at the headwaters of the Salmon River, but an 1883 news article did not list Will Cargill among the owners. Leaving us guessing about his actual exploits in Idaho, a newspaper article two years later mentioned a stock ranch owned there by the Cargill brothers and other La Crosse investors.

In 1880 the Cargill and Van partnership was dissolved and its business divided between a new firm (also named Cargill and Van) and W. W. Cargill and

Brother. According to the *Chronicle*, "All the business in Southern Minnesota and Iowa, and at this point, belongs to W. W. Cargill & Bro., while the Wisconsin business along the Green Bay and Minnesota road and the various cross lines is conducted by Cargill & Van." Almost immediately, W. W. Cargill and Brother began building a terminal elevator in La Crosse to collect and process grains from their line elevators for shipment to local mills, terminal markets at Milwaukee or Chicago, and downstream consuming centers including St. Louis.

The new Cargill elevator, located on the grounds of the Chicago, Milwaukee and St. Paul Railway, was an eighty-five-foot frame giant with a footprint measuring thirty by sixty feet. In January 1881, the *Chronicle* reported: "The new Corliss engine for the Cargill Brothers' elevator was received today [Will Cargill, too, had been to the Philadelphia World's Fair!], and will be placed in position at once and the necessary gearing property attached. . . . Two sets of steam shovels for unloading cars of grain are also to be added to the many conveniences of the elevator." This elevator proved too small within a year, however, and to meet increasing needs, W. W. Cargill and Brothers appended a sixty-foot addition to its south end.

In December 1881 a horrific accident at the mill took the life of a Janesville man whom the Cargills had known since boyhood. Henry Jones had been employed at the elevator only four months. According to newspaper reports, he turned a belt on the main shaft, then reached over to throw it on the tight pulley. Unfortunately, his right coat sleeve caught in the shaft and began winding up. As soon as the shaft wound up to his armpit, his body commenced revolving, at each turn his body and legs striking a heavy upright frame which supported the shaft. Eyewitnesses estimated that his body made at least 150 revolutions, and most of his clothing was torn away before the engine was shut down.

Fellow employees removed the unconscious man from the gearing and summoned Will Cargill and a local physician who came immediately and found the man lying in the engine room. The doctor gave Jones an injection of morphine, and the men took him by boxcar to the Vine Street depot and carried him to his room at the Central Hotel, where he died shortly afterwards. Jones was survived by a wife and three children in Janesville.

A second realignment of the Cargill grain firm took place in as many years when poor health forced Major B. J. Van Valkenburgh to retire from business in 1881. Van Valkenburgh sold his interest in Cargill and Van to Cargill Brothers, a second Cargill grain firm organized by Will, Sam, and their younger brother, Jim Cargill.

Jim (James Flett) Cargill had a burning desire to emulate his brother Will's success, and under Jim's aegis, Cargill Brothers entered the rapidly developing wheat country in the fertile Red River Valley. At the same time that wheat production was leveling off in southern Wisconsin and Minnesota, large-scale bonanza farming in the Northwest was proving spectacularly successful along the lines of the Northern Pacific, the Chicago and Northwestern, and the St. Paul, Minneapolis and Manitoba railroads.

By 1885 Jim Cargill had twenty-six elevators or warehouses in the northern part of Dakota Territory. He is also credited with having invented the "cribbed" type of elevator, which, during the many years that timber was cheap, became the standard in wooden elevators. In this type of construction, two by fours (or sixes or eights) were laid up flatwise and firmly spiked. This "log cabin" method of construction created a very strong building well able to resist the fluid-like pressures of grain on its sides.

Red River country wheat purchased at Cargill elevators traveled by rail to Minneapolis, which was fast becoming the largest flour milling center in the country. Minneapolis had been a minor milling city since the Civil War, but with the new wheat fields to the northwest, extended rail service, and the development of an improved method of milling called "New Process" that produced a "better, cleaner flour," its importance skyrocketed. Area grain dealers organized the Minneapolis Chamber of Commerce (later known as the Grain Exchange) in 1881, and Cargill Brothers moved its headquarters to Minneapolis three years later. The *La Crosse Chronicle* made the announcement on September 6, 1884:

> Cargill Bros. have located their general office for business on the Minneapolis and Manitoba Road at Minneapolis, No. 55 Chamber of Commerce. J. F. Cargill will be in charge. The firm has nineteen stations on that road and expect to handle 2,000,000 bushels.

This move split Cargill grain holdings into two distinct operations, one based in La Crosse (W. W. Cargill and Brother, comprised of Will and Sam) the other in Minneapolis (Cargill Brothers, owned by Will, Sam, and Jim). By 1885 the three Cargill brothers owned or controlled 102 structures in Minnesota and Dakota Territory, also a half dozen in Wisconsin (including the large La Crosse terminal and a leased terminal in Green Bay), and a couple of warehouses in Iowa. Probably from overwork, Jim Cargill suffered a nervous breakdown. Quoting a 1945 Cargill company history, "he was never again strong enough to assume heavy responsibility." Sam Cargill moved to Minneapolis to take his place in 1887, and Will and Sam bought Jim out, although Jim would still continue to work for the company, drawing a $5,000 annual salary. W. W. Cargill and Brother took over the operation of the Cargill Brothers firm.

In January 1889 a prepared statement listed unencumbered Cargill assets at La Crosse as

Samuel Davis Cargill

54 Elevators & Warehouses in Minn & Dakota	$147,597.16
16 Elevators & Warehouses in Wisc, G Bay RR	18,479.29
Houston Flour Mill & Water Power	40,128.54
Hokah Flour Mill & Water Power	29,384.51

Farm Lands in Minn & Dakota Cost Value	23,112.28
La Crosse City Property (Exclusive of Dwellings)	11,300.00
La Crosse Milling Co. Stock	4,500.00
La Crosse National Bank Stock	12,000.00
La Crosse Abittior [sic] Co. Stock	5,000.00
La Crosse Street Car Co. Stock	31,000.00
La Crosse Opera House Stock	2,000.00
Sault Ste. Marie Land Co. Stock	42,500.00
Sault Ste. Marie Water Power Co. Stock	44,000.00
Sault Ste. Marie Water Power Co. Bonds	14,000.00
Long Prairie Warehouse & Fixtures	<u>2,294.93</u>
	$427,296.71

This only reflected the La Crosse end of the business. Figures for Cargill operations in Minneapolis were probably comparable, although no records for that period survive. In addition, Will Cargill's personal investments included cattle, a coal mine, gold mine stocks, and many other non-grain enterprises. In his less than twenty-five years in the grain business, Will Cargill had done very well for himself, and he was only in his mid-forties.

During this period the McMillans had certainly not been idle. In 1885 Alexander had returned home to La Crosse from almost two years travel abroad (that included a sojourn at his family's birthplace in Glen Nevis, Scotland) to plunge headlong into the entertainment business. Rested and revitalized and full of pent-up energy and ideas, he purchased and refurbished the La Crosse Opera House on the corner of Fourth and Main. Renaming it the McMillan Opera House, he booked traveling troupes of actors and musicians.

Alexander's McMillan Opera House on the corner in the left foreground. This street scene looks west down Main Street from Fourth Street.

Interior of the McMillan Opera House

Playbills dated Friday evening, October 30, 1885, advertised the "most successful play, *THE WHITE SLAVE* with the New York Star Cast. Entirely New Magnificent Scenery! Startling Mechanical Effects! and the WONDERFUL RAINSTORM OF REAL WATER." The admission was seventy-five cents, fifty cents for gallery seats. At Christmastime the McMillan Opera House presented "Lilly Clay's Colossal Gaiety Co., 40 Handsomest Ladies in the World, culled from European Capitals, in a Grand Production of the Spectacular Burlesque, ROBINSON CRUSOE!"

The McMillan Opera House was a short-lived venture, however. Four years after acquiring the property, Alexander dismantled the third-floor theater and converted the entire building to office space. There were a couple of reasons for this. The third-floor exits were judged inadequate in case of fire, but it was also becoming more and more difficult to book modestly priced stage troupes, which were increasingly finding themselves entangled in litigation over stage and play rights. Up to this point, many traveling groups had simply neglected to pay stipulated royalties because their cheap rates could not stand the expense.

In 1889, his fascination with the entertainment business waning, Alex sold and shipped all the chairs, scenery, and other opera house effects to the proprietor of a similar establishment in Portage, Wisconsin. Several years later the McMillan Opera House building was destroyed by fire, and today the site is occupied by a McDonald's hamburger shop.

Glamorous though it may have been, the refurbishing of the Opera House had actually been a relatively minor project for Alexander during what was for him a very busy summer in 1885. In August, a scant month after purchasing the Opera House, Alexander called for bids to construct an elegant, five-story stone monument to the family name in La Crosse that became known as the "Scotch Castle." The architects were Frank B. Long and Frederick Kees, who were also drawing the plans for the grand Lumber Exchange Building in Minneapolis. Known for their masterful adaptations of Richardsonian Romanesque architecture, Long and Kees later designed several additional Minneapolis landmarks—the Masonic Temple, the City Hall and Hennepin County Courthouse, and the Flour Exchange, all of which are still standing.

Kitty-corner from the Opera House, the McMillan Block at Main and Fourth Streets was the most impressive office building in La Crosse. Stating clearly that the McMillans had arrived, it was the tallest and most substantial structure in the city. From the upper story, the Mississippi River was visible for several miles in both directions. The first-floor tenant was a dry goods store, and upstairs offices were rented to attorneys, physicians, insurance agents, an oculist, artists, and the School of Stenography, presided over by Miss Rose Keefe. Alexander and Duncan occupied rooms 212 and 214, and Alex's son Sam had space on the fourth floor, along with an architectural firm and an encyclopedia salesman. Some rooms were sleeping apartments. A barber named John Adams ran a tonsorial shop with three chairs in the basement.

Plans for the McMillan Block are preserved at the State Historical Society of Wisconsin, but although the eighty-room structure still stands on the same corner it has occupied more than one hundred years, few people in La Crosse today can identify it. Alexander's "Scotch Castle" has since become known as the State Bank Building for the State Bank of La Crosse, which has occupied the ground floor since 1913. A 1950s marble facing added to the first floor exterior hides both the original Romanesque arch and the words "McMillan Building" over the main entrance. The City of La Crosse has designated the building a historic preservation site.

If the McMillans were riding high in 1885, they were also at the center of a public scandal. In fact, workmen had hardly begun digging the basement for the grand new McMillan Building when the story broke in the papers. Shocking the community, Duncan's niece, twenty-one-year-old Mamie McMillan (his dead brother John's youngest daughter), had run away with Professor J. J. Cleveland, principal of the first ward school. Both Mamie and Cleveland sang in the Presbyterian Church choir, and the Cleveland, Duncan McMillan, and Will Cargill families were all friends. Cleveland left behind a wife and five children.

When the first facts were becoming known, it was only Cleveland who was thought to be missing. His wife reported that he had told her he had business in nearby Sparta and that he would be home the following day. He had given her thirty-five dollars, she said, and kissed his family goodbye. After five days went by without any word from Cleveland, however, with several friends disclosing that he had borrowed money from them, it became apparent that he had no intention of returning. In a front-page story, the *Republican and Leader* reported that "Mrs. Cleveland is very much broken down over the unaccountable disappearance of her husband."

Mamie, meanwhile, had gone to visit friends in Milwaukee. When it came time to leave, she said that she was going to Chicago before returning home. Evidently, that was where Cleveland had instructed her to meet him. When the appalling truth became known that Mamie McMillan was missing along with Cleveland, the school teacher was vilified in local papers. Calling him "the blackest of characters," the *Daily Republican and Leader* declared, "there is no longer a doubt that he has betrayed his best friends, and ruined the life of a young lady who has grown up in La Crosse and had the love and esteem of everyone."

After three months, during which her family must have been beside themselves with grief and worry, a contrite Mamie wrote home from Baltimore. She was alone and living in a boarding house; Cleveland had deserted her and taken her trunk and most of her money. Mamie's older brother John D. McMillan made

The McMillan Block at Main and Fourth Streets

a hasty trip east by train to retrieve her, and she was welcomed back into the bosom of her family.

Most people took pity on Mamie. Noting that "her punishment had been bitter," the *Chronicle* urged "all right-minded, kindly-disposed people" to receive her "as one so unfortunate, so sinned against and so penitent, should be received." Cleveland's whereabouts were unknown, and he never returned to his family.

Perhaps as a result of this episode, Mamie McMillan never married. Instead, inspired by Sarah McMillan's sister, Dr. Libbie Lottridge, Mamie went to medical school and became a practicing physician. For many years Dr. Mamie McMillan managed a private hospital on East 56th Street in New York. Family members loved her—she was a favorite aunt—and she returned frequently to La Crosse to visit and minister to ailing relatives.

While Alexander was busy in downtown La Crosse revamping the Opera House and constructing the McMillan Building, up on Seventh Street he was also redecorating his elegant residence top to bottom. The whirlwind of activity into which he flung himself that summer, at age sixty, would have taxed a man half his age. Visitors coming to the refurbished residence entered through carved double doors, each with a lion's head bearing Alex's monogram—"Alex" on the left door, "McM" on the right. A carved white pine staircase spilled into the foyer, and crystal chandeliers hung from twelve-foot ceilings, lighting parquet-floored rooms warmed by walnut-paneled fireplaces. Much of the extravagant Victorian furniture, including a floor-to-ceiling walnut and bird's-eye maple buffet in the dining room, had been custom-made to Alexander's specifications.

The redecorating took three months, but the results were phenomenal. Using newly developed techniques, craftsmen applied elaborate relief plaster decorations to the walls and ceilings—Renaissance-inspired scrollwork, leafy vine patterns, flowers, birds, and butterflies. In the library, plaster busts of famous authors peered down from the ceiling centerpiece. The ceiling in the conservatory, where Alex and Sarah nursed exotic plants from around the world, was painted blue with raised silver stars.

"The most characteristic room" reported the *Chronicle*, "is the Scotch or music room [where] natural and conventional forms of the Scotch thistle form the general ornamentation. . . . In each corner of the room upon a half circle is painted the McMillan plaid with the crest embossed thereon. The side wall frieze represents a music staff crossed by bars of flowers; rosettes and thistles are placed in no regular order upon the lines. This room is treated in warm green tints."

Putting her own considerable talents to work, Sarah painted wall murals, pictures, and china dinnerware for the house. One of her descendants has an entire dinner service decorated by Sarah, but none of her pictures or murals is known to survive. We do know, though, from period clippings, that Sarah habitually took first place prizes at the La Crosse County Fair for her oil paintings of

The Alexander McMillan residence as pictured in The Northwest Magazine *in the late 1880s*

flowers, animals, and landscapes.

Showplace that it was, Alex and Sarah's residence provided a splendid backdrop for many large gatherings. On one occasion when it was her turn to entertain the Nineteenth Century Club, a home study group that she and Alexander helped organize, Sarah spoke on the subject of "Christian Science." (Two decades later, my mother Marion Dickson MacMillan leaned toward the Christian Science religion and in her declining years kept Mary Baker Eddy's book and her bible by her bedside.)

In November 1880 Sarah McMillan had been the first woman to vote in a presidential election in La Crosse. It had been a spur-of-the-moment decision, she told a reporter for the *Chronicle*. She had simply "crossed Main Street near the City Building when a gentleman friend offered me a Garfield vote and invited me to go into the polls and deposit it." In the polling place, she said, "it was quite amusing to see the different expressions on the faces of the judges, which would have been worthy [of] the pencil of Nast [a political cartoonist].

> Seemingly, they did not know what to do or say. Finally, one came to the rescue and procured a tin box in which my ballot was deposited. . . . I did not insist on having my ballot put in the regular box and counted for I have been a married woman too long to insist on anything.

In West Salem, where Alexander was something of a country squire, he and his son Sam were operating a substantial stock farm, raising prize horses and cattle on part of the Neshonoc mill property. In April 1884 the *Republican and Leader* announced:

"Samuel McMillan has just added to his stock on his Neshonoc farm a Hambletonian stallion and the attention of farmers is called to this opportunity to improve their stock. The name of this horse, which was shipped from New York state is Abdalla Hambletonian, weight 1,050, color brown, age nine, pedigree, sired by Croton, he by Rysdyk's Hambletonian, dam by Snip (or Victor), he by Cassius M. Clay."

A view of the McMillan mill at Neshonoc showing the family residence, Buena Vista. The stone mill on the right was built in 1893 after fire destroyed Alexander's earlier frame structure. Partly visible on the extreme left is a covered bridge that led to the mill property.

The City Hall (and fire station) on Main Street that Alexander purchased and remodeled for Sam's men's furnishing business. Sam had his store on the left side; there was a second store on the right. Now minus its cupola, the building still stands next to the McMillan Building.

Samuel Duncan (Sam) McMillan in later life, looking every inch the charming rascal that family tradition purports him to have been

Taking his cues from Alexander, Sam helped revive the Oakwood Driving Park Association and took part in trotting races at the park. "These meetings are developing a wonderful degree of interest in turf sports and are the means of making fast horses known to the public," reported the *Republican and Leader*. In September 1889 Alexander was a daily visitor at the West Salem fair, looking over his horses. The next summer the *Daily Press* reported that he had shipped "a fine shire stallion to parties near Cedar Rapids, Iowa."

In May 1889 the *Republican and Leader* announced that "a $1,000 colt was dropped by Alex McMillan's standard-bred mare Minneapolis yesterday." Using West Salem as a country address, Alexander and Sarah now spent much of their time at the mill property, summer and winter. Their substantial two-and-a-half story brick and stone house at the river's edge was called "Buena Vista." Sometimes they came up from La Crosse by horse and buggy; other times, particularly if the road was muddy, they took the train. In La Crosse Alexander used spans of Cleveland Bays brought down from Neshonoc to keep his various buildings supplied with wood fuel hauled from the sawmills.

Alexander had great plans for his only son Sam, other than raising horseflesh and running the West Salem mill. As an only child, Sam had been given every advantage, finishing off his education at Oberlin and Yale. In 1886 Alexander purchased a house for Sam and his young family on Tenth Street in La Crosse, with the idea that his son would become a city businessman in his own right. The next year in October, right about the time Sam's third child was born, Alexander financed a retail men's clothing business for him and a partner named Frank Walker in the brick-fronted City Hall Building at 409-411 Main Street, which he had recently acquired next door to the McMillan Building for $17,500.

After ordering fixtures and installing custom shelving, Sam and Walker went to Chicago to purchase stock. The next summer McMillan and Walker advertised "Summer Underwear, Neckwear, Shirts, Gloves. Elegant Line of Furnishings, Hats and Caps." This business went under in almost record time, however. McMillan and Walker dissolved their partnership in less than a year, and Alexander was left to pick up the pieces. Beginning in July 1888, ads for the store identify the proprietors as "McMillan and Son." Later that year the firm folded and its remaining merchandise was sold at cost.

Sam would turn out to be a charming rascal, completely lacking in business ability, and "inordinately proud of his flaming red beard," my father remembered. Fairly early in life, he was penniless. At the end of the 1880s, Alexander, too, was facing trying times ahead. For several years following the men's furnishing store fiasco, Sam had charge of the Neshonoc Mill. Alexander rebuilt the mill in 1891 to include an elevator to store wheat and corn, but disaster was just around the corner.

First Sarah died in the summer of 1892 at the age of sixty on a trip to Hot Springs, South Dakota. Alexander brought her body home to La Crosse on the Chicago and Northwestern train and buried her beside their three little daughters in Oak Grove Cemetery. Then the Neshonoc mill burned after sparks from the chimney ignited the roof. (The previous week, the *West Salem Journal* had reported the mill on fire four times in one day when blazing cobs used for fuel were drawn up the chimney by strong drafts.)

Right about the time the mill burned, Alexander transferred its title to Sam, who rebuilt it to include a power plant to generate electricity for West Salem. Two days after Christmas 1893, Sam, with his uncle Duncan D. McMillan and two other men, incorporated the McMillan Mill and Power Company of Neshonoc. According to its charter, the firm intended to manufacture flour, corn meals, feed, and other articles from farm products, and to erect, put in, and maintain an electric light power system to furnish electric lights and power to West Salem.

It was a popular enterprise that boded well for West Salem, where the first electric lights were installed in 1895. Customers paid $1.25 per month for eight lights, $1.50 for ten lights, and $1.67 for fifteen lights, with service offered from sundown to sunrise each day. West Salem's population that year totaled 695 people; its residents owned 35 carriages and 19 farm wagons. There were 108 horses and mules, 11 colonies of bees, and 62 "milch" cows within the village limits.

West Salem's most famous resident was author Hamlin Garland, born there in 1860. The residence he later purchased in West Salem has been restored as a museum, and the street in front of it renamed Garland Street. In his book *Trailmakers of the Middle Border*, Garland described Neshonoc as it had presented itself to his father upon his arrival in the La Crosse River Valley in 1857:

> A little tavern . . . stood on the level ground above the bridge, a lovely spot for a village. To the east was the mill-pond. A trout-brook came in from the north, and a gristmill rose against a conical hill around whose base the river ran in a reedy curve. On the bottomlands to the west, scattered pines were growing, and in the edges of these groves and on the banks of the stream, a group of wigwams denoted the presence of redmen. Altogether it could have been used as an illustration for a poster. It had all the elements of pastoral beauty.

The gristmill Garland described was the one that Alexander later owned and operated, ending up as Sam's electric plant. And Sam's prospects were indeed looking up once he had the power company going, but by the next year the McMillan Mill and Power Plant was in receivership as a result, partially, of financial troubles in Texas for his father and Duncan D. McMillan and his sons. The mill was sold cheaply—three thousand dollars to the only bidder—and Sam filed for bankruptcy.

D. D. MCMILLAN & SONS

John Hugh MacMillan about the time he started work in his father's bank

M y grandfather John H. MacMillan, Sr. was fifteen years old when he started work as a messenger at his father's State Bank in La Crosse in 1884. Writing almost sixty years later to his grandson and namesake, my brother John Hugh MacMillan III, who was celebrating *his* fifteenth birthday, Grandfather gave him some kindly advice based on personal experience:

> You are getting along toward maturity now and will soon have all the ability you will ever have so it is up to you now to begin to show what you can do. I remember I was fifteen my last year in high school and I started to work in the State Bank of La Crosse when I was six or seven months older than you. I have been at work ever since. I had to give up school but I kept on studying and I think I had the equal to a college education finally.

That Duncan started his eldest off at the bank rather than in a logging camp is indeed interesting, because logging had become something of a family tradition and the means to the family fortune. MacMillans to this day are still involved in the timber industry, and my father John H. MacMillan, Jr. a generation later would begin his career in a logging camp in the Pacific Northwest. But in 1884 lumbermen had not yet turned their sights in that direction, and lumbering was in its last years in Wisconsin.

Although loggers once believed that Wisconsin's vast white pine forests were inexhaustible, they were learning differently. The *Republican and Leader* in July quoted "a well-informed lumberman" who calculated that "there is not over 600,000,000 feet of pine left standing on the Black River and the tributaries,

Looking east on Main Street from Third Street. The first building on the left is Alexander McMillan's Post Office Block. Next to it is the State Bank where John H. MacMillan started his business career. On the same side of the street, across Fourth, the McMillan Building is in the center background.

which if it is cut off at the rate it has been, will last four years, or five years at the outside." In the not too distant future, La Crosse would direct its energy and capital toward a broader range of manufacturing activities, some of them partially financed by MacMillans.

John H. spent four years at his father's bank, learning the basics of business. At age nineteen, ready to strike out on his own, he took a job with his first cousin, John D. McMillan, in the latter's newly formed grain business. On August 14, 1888, the *Republican and Leader* announced that "John McMillan who has been employed at the State Bank . . . has gone to Minneapolis, where he has accepted a position in the office of McMillan & Osborne." According to the *Chronicle*, "John McMillan gave a large party Monday evening, as a farewell to his friends before leaving for Minneapolis."

John D. McMillan, Mamie's brother, would become one of the most important grain dealers in the Northwest. While still in his teens, John D. had gone to work as a bookkeeper for W. W. Cargill in La Crosse in the 1870s, and he later was a partner with Jim Cargill in the Red River Valley. In 1887 he moved to Minneapolis to form Osborne and McMillan with another former Cargill employee, Edward Osborne, and it was this firm that gave my grandfather his start in the grain business. By 1917 the Osborne-McMillan Elevator Company, with John D. (whose branch of the family to this day to spells its name "McMillan") at its helm, owned the giant Shoreham elevator in Minneapolis; maintained a chain of well-equipped country elevators on the lines of the Great Northern and the Minneapolis, St. Paul and Sault Sainte Marie Railroads; and also had large holdings in the wheat-producing regions of the Canadian Northwest. John D. and my grandfather John H. would be lifelong friends and business associates, and John D. served on the Cargill Company's board of directors from 1910 to 1934.

John D. McMillan from Men of Minnesota, *1902*

John H. MacMillan, in right foreground, with friends in La Crosse

The Corn Exchange in Minneapolis where John H. MacMillan worked in the grain business owned by his cousin John D. McMillan and Edward Osborne

The Osborne McMillan elevator at 28th Avenue Northeast and Fifth Street in Minneapolis about 1910

His first two years in Minneapolis, my grandfather John H. lived with John D. McMillan, his wife Nellie, their two-year-old son John Russell, and John D.'s partner, Edward N. Osborne, in a rented side-by-side double house that has since been razed at 133 East Grant Street. (The Grant Street entrance to the new Minneapolis Convention Center now occupies this site.) Osborne and McMillan had an office in Room 55 at the new Corn Exchange Building on the corner of Fourth Avenue and South Third Street, one block from the Minneapolis City Hall.

One of the most treasured pieces of correspondence in our family archives is a letter John Hugh received from his father in La Crosse dated September 3, 1888:

Dear Son,

Your letter of August 31st is just rec'd. Yesterday was a real bright nice day and we had quite a good congregation out to Church morning and evening.

Jennie [John's eight-year-old sister] is having a splendid time with her tricycle. I fixed up Emma Cargills and Bessie [John's youngest sister, age four] is using it but is rather too small to make good use of it. Jennie starts to school this morning which will give her less time for riding and Bessie will be lonesome. Willie is getting ready for Lake Forest [University] and will start next week. I have no idea that you will have any trouble with your bookkeeping. Always keep in view to do your work rapidly and accurately. Both will come to you with practice. . . . It is like counting money in the bank. Your work will always be easier on you if you do it rapidly and when you are first starting in learn to work rapidly and accurately and you will give better satisfaction but above all let your work be thorough & accurate but that is not inconsistent with speed. Keep up your practice in writing and keep your book tidy and clean. I think if you use "Gillotts 303" pen your book will look nicer and cleaner than with any other pen I know of. It will lighten up your hand and your figures will be

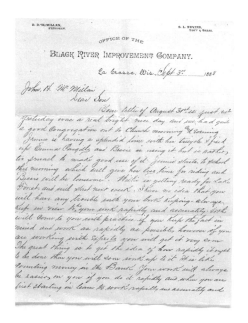

John's sister, Elizabeth Johnston (Bessie) McMillan, born in 1884

cleaner and plainer than if you use a soft pen and always have on your mind to have your work nicely done and if you get acquainted with a boy that is an extra good penman practice penmanship with him. You have no idea how quickly you will improve in that way. I write this letter with a 303 pen. . . .

I had a letter from Mr. Morton this morning and he kindly invited your mother and myself, during the State Fair to stay at his place. [W. S. Morton owned the three-story frame Morton House in North St. Paul, Minnesota, where Duncan and two other men had recently purchased thirty-five acres of property near the proposed Wisconsin Central Railroad shops. "The land is well located and will make fine building lots soon," said the *Republican and Leader.* Laid out in 1887, North St. Paul was a new manufacturing boom town, but if my great-grandfather intended to develop the North St. Paul lots, future circumstances prevented him from doing so.]

Your Aff. Father
D. D. McMillan

Duncan D. directed the activities of all three of his sons to an uncommon degree. My grandfather John H. occupied three years keeping books for his cousin John D. McMillan in Minneapolis, by which time his father felt John and his younger brothers Will and Dan were ready to launch their own grain enterprise in Texas. Will, at age twenty, had spent two years at Lake Forest University on Lake Michigan in Illinois, and another year working with the Union Pacific Railroad at Omaha; Will would eventually earn a Ph.D and become a famous astronomer, but as yet he had no idea of his future. Dan, eighteen, had left school three years earlier to work in W. W. Cargill's office in La Crosse and had spent the last year working in the grain business with a Cargill associate, J. B. Canterbury, in Norwalk, Wisconsin.

Leaving their jobs, John, Will, and Dan McMillan were full of high hopes and the vigor of youth when they packed their bags and set off for Fort Worth to undertake an exciting new family business venture that would either make or break them. Accompanied by their father, who was backing them financially, the McMillans planned to do in Texas what Will Cargill and his brothers had done in the Upper Midwest.

Announcing their arrival on June 11, 1891, the *Fort Worth Daily Gazette* stated that "Mr. McMillan is president of the state bank at La Crosse and comes to Fort Worth with his sons to establish the business of buying Panhandle wheat for export. Their headquarters will be located in Fort Worth. The gentlemen have strong financial backing, and will be able to handle the business. The young men will probably conduct the business here. All of the gentlemen are experienced wheat men [which stretched the truth a bit; at age twenty-two, John, of course, had worked in his cousin's grain business three years, and Dan had

Will McMillan

Dan McMillan

Wheat farming in 1890 in the Texas Panhandle

some experience in Will Cargill's office, but Will, in fact, appears to have had no experience in business whatsoever]."

The McMillans had come at an opportune time. The completion of the Fort Worth and Denver City Railroad in the late 1880s had produced an inpouring of wheat farmers to the Texas Panhandle, and this immense territory, totally undeveloped just a few years earlier, was being touted as the greatest wheat growing region in the country. The soil was deep loam, easily worked, and there was abundant water available by boring, sometimes at depths of as little as ten to twenty-five feet. In 1891 the Panhandle wheat crop was being estimated at eight million bushels, and Fort Worth banks were gearing up to handle vast sums of money. Fort Worth, a young city incorporated on the banks of the Trinity River in 1876, was already nearly the same size as La Crosse with twenty-some thousand residents.

Fort Worth papers followed the progress of D. D. McMillan & Sons. On June 17, the *Daily Gazette* reported that the fledgling firm had "appointed their wheat buyers and agents at points along the Denver, and will be ready to begin operations here as soon as wheat begins to move. They find that it is impossible to get adequate storage facilities anywhere in Texas, and they will have to ship their wheat to St. Louis or Chicago to the great elevators there until several ship loads have accumulated, when they will ship, but they will be buying continually."

It was a good year. The 1891 Texas wheat crop lived up to everyone's expectations, and wheat prices were high due to widespread crop failures in Europe. In October, in league with more than a dozen other grain men and millers, the McMillans helped organize the Texas Grain Dealers' and Millers' Association to promote the production of grain and other grain industries in the state. Fort Worth had visions of becoming a milling center equal to Minneapolis, and the McMillans were in on the ground floor.

In November, however, Duncan D. was forced to return home to La Crosse with Daniel who was suffering with a fever. Once recovered, Dan returned to Texas, but his illness seems to have been an early omen. As it turned out, the McMillans' Texas grain business never really had a chance. Two years hence the country would be mired in a nationwide depression, and the McMillans would be facing economic ruin.

No company records exist for D. D. McMillan & Sons, but a sparse outline of the firm's misfortunes can be pieced together from newspaper articles in the *Fort Worth Gazette*, the records of a La Crosse firm named Hixon and Warner that was helping D. D. McMillan & Sons with crop financing, and a handful of letters that John MacMillan wrote to Edna Cargill from Texas.

The future of the firm began going downhill in 1892 when drought and blighting hot winds ruined much of the crop, and the price of wheat declined.

The Hurley Building where D. D. McMillan
& Sons had its office in Fort Worth

Area farmers and D. D. McMillan & Sons took this setback in stride. Undaunted Panhandle planters, in fact, increased their wheat acreage. D. D. McMillan & Sons was operating country elevators and warehouses in at least a dozen rural communities strung along the Fort Worth and Denver City and the Wichita Valley Railroads in north central Texas near the Oklahoma border. They also leased space in the Mark Evans terminal elevator in Fort Worth, where they had an office in the Hurley Building.

Operating on a minuscule profit margin, usually two to three cents per bushel, the McMillans purchased grain—mostly wheat and oats, but also a small amount of corn—which they accumulated for sale to local millers and for shipment to central markets. Local farmers brought their grain to the elevators—much as they still do today, except that in those days they used horse-drawn wagons instead of trucks—where it was sampled, graded, unloaded, and weighed, then elevated into storage bins.

While his sons remained in Texas almost year-round, Duncan continued to spend much of his time in La Crosse where he still had his job at the State Bank. He also took time out in March to go with Mary Jane to Chicago, where the city was erecting the World's Columbian Exposition to celebrate the 400th anniversary of the discovery of America. In April, we read in the *La Crosse Daily Press*, John H. was home on a visit and had gone trouting with his cousin John D. McMillan.

No one was worried about the future of the family grain business. Even when the McMillan elevator at Seymour, Texas, burned in November, D. D. McMillan & Sons remained optimistic. Fires happened, and business would surely rebound the following year, thought the brothers when they returned to La Crosse for the Christmas holidays. A romance was also afoot. In January 1893, La Crosse newspapers announced the engagement of Miss Edna Cargill to Mr. John MacMillan. (This is the first recorded occasion on which my grandfather spelled his name "MacMillan." Texas newspapers reveal that his brothers Will and Dan also adopted this spelling in 1893.) Both families were delighted at the impending marriage, but the engagement would be a long one.

By March, John was on his way back to Texas. He planned to be gone about a year, and he had every reason to believe that this would be the best year to date for D. D. McMillan & Sons. Everyone expected a good wheat crop in the Texas Panhandle in 1893. Between November and March, forty-two thousand acres of new land had been broken. Half a million Panhandle acres were now in wheat. On March 19 the *Fort Worth Gazette* predicted that "if no untoward event occurs the expectation of a most bountiful crop will be realized."

The newspaper was particularly impressed by the "class of immigrants who are fast filling up the country." They were "not of the canvas-backed wagon variety," declared the *Gazette*, "but are people who understand farming in all its branches and have plenty of money to establish themselves in a new country. A large number [are] German farmers . . . from the vicinity of Des Moines, Ia." Where Panhandle fields had previously yielded fifteen bushels of wheat per acre (the national average was 12½ bushels), area farmers in 1893 expected to harvest twenty bushels an acre. Fort Worth mills were doubling their capacities to be ready for the bumper harvest.

In June harvesting was underway in Clay County, where the MacMillans had a new 25,000-bushel elevator at Henrietta. Twelve steam threshing machines were at work and county farmers that year purchased 230 binders. Dan had also established a branch office in Galveston, where it was "the intention of the firm to do an export business in large scale," reported the *Gazette*. But disaster was in the offing, not only for the MacMillans but for the country at large.

In 1893 the United States slid headlong into an unexpected and disastrous national depression. When gold reserves in the U.S. Treasury fell below the legal minimum of one hundred million dollars in late April, partly as a result of a financial panic in London that caused British investors to dump American securities, panic likewise ensued on this side of the ocean. In early May, the giant National Cordage Company entered receivership, causing securities to fall sharply on the New York Stock Exchange. A devastating crash followed in late June. The subsequent depression was comparable to the one that gripped this country in the 1930s; wages and prices plummeted, and every kind of business suffered.

By August there was a currency famine that shut down mills, factories, furnaces, and mines everywhere in large numbers, arresting commerce to an unprecedented degree. By September, 172 state banks had closed, along with 177 private banks and 47 savings and loan associations. By October, 158 national banks had folded, and by the end of the year 15,242 companies had failed.

The lack of money to pay farmers for their products delayed the usual heavy traffic in grain that autumn. Texas farmers raised a record five million bushels of wheat in 1893, but it enriched neither growers nor dealers. The price of wheat slid from 83 cents per bushel two years earlier to 53 cents. When Will MacMillan was interviewed at his office in mid-November, he told a reporter for the *Gazette* that the movement of wheat in the Panhandle was still encouraging:

"The finest wheat country in the Panhandle lies between Henrietta and Childress, and there is yet held by farmers of that section and stored three-fourths of a million bushels of wheat. This wheat will be moved between now and next June." During the previous month, Will said, D. D. McMillan & Sons had exported 100,000 bushels of wheat from Galveston. "Most of our consignments go to England, France and Germany, although shipments are also made to many other foreign countries."

Edna Clara Cargill

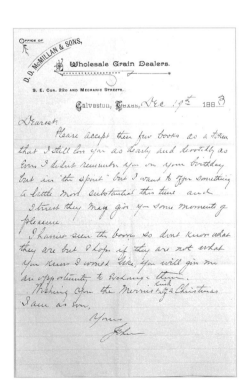

But conditions were fierce enough that my grandfather remained in Texas over Christmas. Scrambling to keep his fledgling business afloat, he wrote to Edna from Galveston on December 19:

Dearest:

Please accept these few books as a token that I still love you as dearly and devotedly as ever. I didn't remember you on your birthday [September 4] but in "the spirit," but I want to offer something a little more substantial this time and I trust they may give you some moments of pleasure.

I haven't seen the books so don't know what they are but I hope if they are not what you know I would like, you will give me an opportunity to exchange them. Wishing you the merriest kind of a Christmas, I am as ever,

Yours

John

It was late April 1894 when John finally went home to La Crosse, both on business and to see Edna. Financing was a perennial problem for D. D. McMillan & Sons, and the money always came through La Crosse connections. On June 1, Edna wrote in her diary, "Money came. Picnic on the Salem road." John remained in La Crosse six weeks, and this visit was the only substantial period of time that he and Edna spent together during their two-year engagement. Their courtship was mostly a long-distance affair.

The MacMillans were off to another fresh start in Texas in 1894. Will was elected to the board of directors of the Fort Worth Chamber of Commerce, which organized a grain inspection department to enable the mills of the state, as well as exporters and other buyers, to buy grain on official grades. A number of railroads were promising re-billing privileges—meaning that grain shipped through Fort Worth could be stopped there, graded, ground, and shipped out as flour at the same rate as if it were a through shipment from origin to destination. This, combined with the inspection department, would encourage commission houses to open offices in Fort Worth. It would also permit large elevators to be operated with a profit.

Will was also making a good showing for himself as a member of the Fort Worth tennis club. During a highly-publicized two-day tennis tournament in Fort Worth in September 1894, when the Fort Worth club played host to players from Dallas and Waco, Uncle Will won forty-two of the eighty-six games he played, making him the ninth-ranking tennis player in Texas.

"Tennis is strictly a gentle folks' game," intoned the *Fort Worth Gazette*, not requiring the "extreme training so necessary for football, [but] if you think it is a "sissy" game, which anyone can play, requiring no wind or endurance, you are mightily mistaken." The tournament in which Will participated was played on hot days, with "the wire netting [affording] about as much relief from the sun's rays as a barb wire fence does from a Texas norther," commented the paper. Still, "a man who enters a tennis tournament expecting to approach anywhere near the finals has no right to complain of hard work and heat."

In June, when Texas farmers were harvesting bumper crops, John wrote to Hixon and Warner that he expected grain to begin moving freely by the first of July. By mid-July, however, wheat was down to forty-some cents a bushel, and farmers weren't selling. John didn't think the farmers could hold out very long, because many of them were heavily in debt, but the farmers remained adamant. In August D. D. McMillans' traveling man reported that not over five percent of the Panhandle wheat crop had been marketed.

At the end of September Hixon and Warner wanted to funnel larger sums of money to the MacMillans, who normally borrowed in $5,000 increments, sometimes several times weekly. John didn't buy their offer, explaining:

> Grain seems to move in spurts and just now it is moving very slowly. We cannot afford as you can easily see to carry a big balance as well as to pay you a commission on all we buy. In fact the great advantage to a grain man in making this kind of an arrangement is to use money just as he may need it and you will find that we have been no different than any other grain firm would have been. We will draw Monday for another $5000 and trust that we may be able to use money more freely in the immediate future.

Remaining hopeful into October, John assured Hixon and Warner that conditions were bound to improve—that the present slow movement of grain could not continue. But most farmers *did* keep back their grain in 1894. The MacMillans finished the year with negligible grain handling profits, and their export business at Galveston was practically nil. In December, exacerbating their cash flow problem, the National Bank of Merrill, Wisconsin, asked them to pay up on at least one of their outstanding notes, using the excuse that they needed the money to meet "home demand."

Meanwhile, Edna Cargill had gone to Europe on a grand tour and to buy her trousseau, traveling with two of her aunts, Mrs. Samuel (Lydia) Cargill and Mrs. Sylvester (Libbie) Cargill, and two young McMillan women, Nellie (Mrs. John D.) and Mamie (John D.'s sister). On Tuesday, August 21, the women had taken the evening train from La Crosse to Chicago, where they changed trains for New York. After two days' sightseeing in New York, on Saturday at one o'clock in the afternoon, with one hundred fifty fellow first-class passengers plus hundreds more in second class and steerage, Edna and her companions sailed for Liverpool on the Cunard liner R.M.S. *Campania*.

The *Campania* and her sister ship, the *Lucania*, both launched just one year earlier, were the newest, largest (622 feet stem to stern) and most modern

The Campania's *passenger list naming Mrs. Samuel Cargill, Mrs. Sylvester Cargill, Miss Edna Cargill, Mrs. John [H.] McMillan, and Miss Mamie McMillan*

ships Cunard owned. Elegantly upholstered, carpeted and veneered, these luxury vessels catered to the wealthy while also offering budget accommodations to less affluent travelers. Passengers in steerage slept twenty to a compartment in bunks with straw mattresses and brought their own soap and towels.

Edna wrote in her diary that she carried a telescope and an alligator valise. Once the voyage got under way, she "took 15 grains of quinine, felt rather sick." The women's rooms were on the Saloon Deck, where they had two port holes, but it was very warm, and none of them slept during their first night at sea. The next day was calm with warm heavy fogs toward evening. Near the conclusion of the six-day, 3,100-mile crossing, Edna (always a woman of few words in her diary) wrote that it had been "calm all the way."

From Liverpool the women traveled by train to London for nine days before crossing the English Channel to France. Edna wrote that they saw Versailles and Fountainbleu. They also made the rounds of the couturiers. The women stayed ten days in Paris and returned later in the trip for another week, giving the dressmakers time to ready their purchases. During the intervening weeks, Edna and her companions toured Switzerland and Italy, taking in Geneva, Lucerne, Venice, Florence, Pisa, Naples, Rome, and the ruins at Pompeii. In Milan, Edna wrote that they had a good guide. The final days of the trip took them north from London to Edinburgh, where Edna would have felt right at home among her Scottish kinsmen.

Edna and her companions had been abroad two and a half fun-filled months when they reboarded the *Campania* for the return trip to New York from Liverpool on November 3. Two days after docking in New York, they were met in Chicago by Edna's mother Ellen and John H. MacMillan. John may have returned to La Crosse with them, but he was back in Texas attending to his nearly defunct business before the holidays. This was the second year since they became engaged that Edna spent Christmas without him. On December 20 John sent her holiday greetings and a gift of poetry books from Fort Worth.

It was only a matter of weeks before they would be married, joining, for better or worse, the fortunes of their two families. As he wrote Edna from Texas in mid-January, John was grateful for something pleasant to think about with the approach of the wedding date. He was glad to hear that the wedding cards had been ordered: "That seems to settle everything." So far he hadn't told anyone at the boarding house where he lived about his impending marriage, suspecting that life would be fairly miserable for him if he did. As it was, he was still able to escort single women to social affairs without being harassed.

Later that week, he told Edna, he planned to take a young woman named Maggie Wilson to see the play "Nominee" starring Nat Goodwin at Greenwall's Opera House. The play was adapted from a French farce, Goodwin was billed as "America's favorite actor," and it was Goodwin's first trip to Texas. This event would no doubt end his career as an "unmarried society man," John assured Edna. "I will probably have a few more games of cards but will not take any young lady to any more society affairs."

John was building a house for himself and Edna in Fort Worth at 105 Johnston Street (now Adams Avenue); it had been framed in, and the contractor promised to have it ready by February 15, John wrote. According to the architect, the arches would measure nine feet from the floor to the top of the molding, and John asked Edna if she thought they ought to have a door between the parlor and the hall. It seemed to him that they should because they would have to heat the house in the winter, but he wanted her opinion.

Edna and her mother had been buying furniture and accessories for the house, and her descriptions of their purchases in a previous letter obviously pleased him:

> Oh Edna, what an elegant home we will have. I had no idea things were going to be so beautiful as you described. . . . I am just simply speechless and that is all there is about it. It is quite amusing the way you speak about the few things I will have to buy. Here you and your mother furnish everything but a few things like tin pans etc., but you would quite make out I was doing it all. [Will and Ellen Cargill were furnishing the new house as a wedding gift to the couple.]

A homebody at heart, John was looking forward to the time when they would be married:

> Just think what happiness it is going to be for me to be with you all the time. I am afraid it will make me selfish. My own happiness will be so complete that I may not realize that you will require pleasures that I might rather prefer to keep away from. I may forget that you require social recreation to relieve [the] monotony of home duties and want to be at home always with you.

UTTER RUIN

John and Edna MacMillan in carriage by Cargill residence about 1895

William Samuel Cargill,
Mary Mac Millan,
Married

Wednesday, October twenty sixth,
Eighteen hundred and ninety two,
La Crosse, Wisconsin.

At Home
Tuesdays in December,
403 Orchard Place.

John Hugh MacMillan and Edna Clara Cargill were married on a wintry Wednesday evening, February 6, 1895, at the bride's parents' fashionable red brick Victorian residence in La Crosse. Precisely at half past eight, the orchestra struck up Wagner's wedding march from Lohengrin, and the bridal party started down the ornate wooden staircase, their footsteps muffled by the deep red persian rug stair carpeting. Leading the procession were two small ribbon bearers, Edna's younger brother, Austen Cargill, and John's nephew, Duncan Rowles (his older sister Mary Isabella McMillan Rowles's firstborn), dressed in white corduroy knickerbocker suits with ruffled shirts and white shoes. Following behind them came four-year-old maid of honor Mae Benedict in a floor-length white satin dress with huge, bouffant sleeves, her brown hair in finger curls. The bridesmaids were Edna's sister Emma Cargill and Grace Medary (a person about whom we know nothing); gowned in mauve satin, the two young women carried mixed bouquets of narcissus with English violets. Dan MacMillan was his brother's best man.

John was twenty-five and Edna twenty-three when they said their vows before two ministers under a bower-like canopy of roses and smilax vines in front of the curved bay windows of the flower-filled drawing room. Edna wore a high-waisted, pale ivory satin wedding dress with pearl embroidered lace and a full train that she had purchased in Paris. The ceremony was performed

81

John and Edna's wedding party included Duncan Rowles, Austen Cargill, and Mae Benedict.

by Reverend William Torrance, pastor of the First Presbyterian Church, to which both families belonged. He was assisted by Reverend W. D. Thomas, the church's former pastor and a longtime friend of the MacMillans.

According to a front-page story in the *La Crosse Daily Press*, the spacious Cargill residence was resplendent with roses throughout the entire lower floor, "the rich dark woods of the rooms being a fitting setting for the masses of American Beauties, Catherine Mermet and Bride roses that were gracefully bunched upon tables and mantles, and entwined with smilax that hung from doorways." In the room reserved for gifts were displayed sterling silver and cut glass pieces "the like of which has hardly ever been equaled in this city," gushed the *Morning Chronicle*. John's parents gave the couple a solid silver tea service.

"There was a deal of smart dressing," reported the *Daily Press*, with "all the late brides looking exceptionally handsome in their wedding frocks of white satins and brocades. The bride's mother Mrs. W. W. Cargill wore an elegant costume of pearl gray satin with bodice of turquoise blue brocade. Mrs. Duncan MacMillan was stately elegant in rich black satin with corsage trimmings of heliotrope velvet and black chiffon."

John was glad they were having a home wedding, he had written earlier to Edna. He didn't want "to have the whole town in a state of expectancy for years to come [waiting] to hear of some trouble between us or regarding us so they could say, 'Didn't I tell you—church weddings always turn out that way.'" In Texas, he said, he would have preferred a church wedding, "but La Crosse is so different." The *Chronicle* reported that John was well known in La Crosse as a "steadyheaded, reliable business man"; a second paper spoke of the line of grain elevators that he was operating "successfully" in Texas.

The wedding supper for two hundred guests was served at small tables set up in the dining room and library. None of the three city papers reporting

The Cargill house decorated for John and Edna's wedding. Doors salvaged from the mansion before it was razed in the 1970s now hang in the Family Room at Cargill headquarters in Wayzata.

the event described the menu other than to call it an "elegant collation." The bridal party was seated at a round table in the main reception room where places for eight were laid on a white satin tablecloth with wide insets of duchess lace. Shortly before midnight, their guests pelting them with rice, the newlyweds left by carriage for the depot where they boarded the train to Chicago.

John and Edna spent their honeymoon traveling to Fort Worth, with stops in Chicago, St. Louis, New Orleans, and Galveston. John was anxious to get back to work, and they settled into their new home about a mile south of Fort Worth's downtown business district. If Edna had envisioned a love nest in Texas with John, she was probably disappointed. All three MacMillan brothers had previously lived together in a boarding house, and now, with the new house, John invited Will and Dan to live with him and Edna. Likely, the three brothers spent many nights talking long hours about wheat. This would be the MacMillan brothers' fifth year in Texas, and they planned to finish it in the black.

John had made a deal with the Santa Fe railroad that he thought would do the trick. In mid-March he apprised Hixon and Warner: "We have one new feature which we are counting on for great results in the future. The Santa Fe Ry have granted to us personally and to no other firm in the state, the same re-consignment privileges that are allowed to Kansas City and which alone makes that city a great grain market. You can readily appreciate the importance of this to us as it will allow us to buy heavily from Kansas and Oklahoma grain dealers to supply the millers of the state."

That year, attacked by grasshoppers and drought, the crops failed in Texas. Farmers produced only half as much wheat in 1895 as they had in the past several years, and the price of wheat remained at rock bottom. Exactly how the MacMillans fared that year in Texas is largely unknown; the only extant business records are a handful of brief notes addressed to Hixon and Warner concerning monies borrowed and monies paid—the former amounting to more than the latter. Desperate to shore up the company's wobbly credit standing, Duncan persuaded his brother Alexander to join him in guaranteeing the indebtedness of D. D. McMillan & Sons.

On the bright side, John and Edna were expecting a baby. My father John Hugh MacMillan, Jr. was born in Fort Worth on Sunday morning, December 1, 1895. A bouncing baby boy weighing seven and a half pounds, he was delivered at home by Dr. John Todd, whose family and ours have remained longtime friends. It must have been a happy Christmas with a baby in residence that year, but any joy in the house was short-lived. In January, Edna took John, Jr. home to her parents' house in La Crosse, while John and his brothers stayed behind in Texas. The depression was bottoming out, and D. D. McMillan & Sons was in dire straits.

Their one last hope evaporated when the crops failed again in 1896. Three weeks before harvest time, hot, dry winds cut wheat yields to less than five

John Hugh MacMillan, Jr. Born in Texas, he spent most of his first year with his mother at the Cargill residence in La Crosse.

bushels per acre and completely destroyed the corn and oats crops. By summer the firm needed cash so badly that Duncan ended up borrowing twenty thousand dollars against his family home in La Crosse from Frank P. Hixon of Hixon and Warner; by autumn it appeared doubtful that D. D. McMillan & Sons could weather the crisis.

John wrote Edna that he didn't know whether he would be able to hold the firm together in Texas or not, but the idea of giving up appalled him. He also missed her terribly; she had been in La Crosse all year, and he wanted her with him now more than ever. These were his darkest hours; his usually stoic facade was cracking, and there are indications that my grandfather suffered one or more nervous breakdowns during this period.

A letter to Edna dated September 7 begins sharply: "My Dearest Wife: If it were not for our baby, I would begin to think our marriage a snare and a delusion. I don't see that I get a bit of good out of you now more than two years ago. I got your letters then. I get them now. . . . I may stand it until October 1st on account of Baby but not any later. The heat was terrific again today, 105 in our office, so of course I don't dare urge you to come now on his account, but surely by Oct 1st Baby will be well enough to travel. If necessary I will meet you in Kansas City, Chicago, or St. Louis, but you must come here then if there is the least show that we will stay here."

Will Cargill had offered John a position in Green Bay, and he was tempted to take it, he wrote Edna, but he was very reluctant to admit defeat in Texas. He had explained this in an earlier letter, but Edna had apparently misunderstood exactly what he was trying to say. "I don't think there is anything degrading in working for another," he now assured her.

> What hurt was the idea of failure—failure to make a success of what I managed and the idea that would almost necessarily follow—that I was unworthy of the position I had occupied and that henceforth I would find my level in carrying out what others directed instead of others carrying out what I directed. Don't for a moment think I think that of myself. Thank goodness I have too much conceit or self-respect—I don't know which—to rate myself in that class, but it is galling to have others feel that way and to feel that it will take years of hard work to again command the respect and confidence that I have or will have lost.

Business was dropping off day by day, and he dreaded the idea of having nothing to do. "We have quit running the elevator here at night and I suppose it is only a question of time until we will have to quit day times too. To see this all coming on and knowing so well what comes after makes one wish he had never seen Texas or never heard of finances and business, etc. I can see plainly enough why Will [his younger brother] wants to give up business life and become a student and a scholar. Very often I wish I could do the same. For five

John H. MacMillan, Sr. posing for a Texas photographer

years and over we have known nothing but failure. Never have we experienced the joys of independence but all the time this dark and dismal cloud has been hanging around us. Sometimes apparently retreating but all the time gaining steadily in power until once more it seems about to strike and to shatter and to level to earth all our fond hopes, all our proud desires, all our ambitions."

Like his brother Will, John wrote, he would like to be able to turn away from "such horrors and to contemplate a quiet and peaceful life away from the storms that crush and destroy," but he was different than Will. "I am conscious of or at least have a feeling that I have financial and business ability. I feel that my character is broadening and hardening under such as stress of experience. I believe my judgement is growing keener and my powers of observation and reason stronger and that the day will yet come when all I have suffered **will prove** a powerful lever to aid in ultimate success.

> Someone I believe [he continued] has said that the ultimate road to success is through failure and I am now ready to believe it. My former ideas were based on what I was taught and what I observed during periods of unbounded prosperity but they had not experienced the disasters of panics and financial depression. I see now the ideas were wrong. I see principles that I never dreamed of before, and moreover principles I never heard of in all that I have read and all that I have experienced before.

W. W. Cargill was having problems of his own that worried John as well. "It seems to me your father's actions in holding on to so much is really frightful. To me it indicates certain ruin in the end for I believe that one of these days . . . very shortly we are going to see another big slump. I may be wrong, I certainly hope so, but the market cannot stay just where it is. It will either advance or it will drop, and with the spring crop about to move, I cannot see how it can advance with money in such fearful shape. I don't want to preach pessimism, but I do want to preach safety."

In a second letter two days later, John's mood bordered on despondency. "I am almost getting afraid of myself. For the past ten days or two weeks it has just seemed as though I was standing all I could bear and a little more. . . . I have really lost for the time being the power of feeling any enjoyment and I am so nervous and irritable that I am ashamed of myself. . . . I think what worries me the most just now is that we have $10,000 due in Chicago the latter part of this month and first of next. I feel certainly they will demand payment and then we will have nothing."

Business was at a standstill. "We are buying no wheat and consequently making nothing and putting everything together grinds the very life out of one. Someway I have lost all hope. I can see nothing bright ahead. Everything has turned out as I predicted to Father a year ago unless he could then arrange for money and we not only got none but have had to continually pay up ever since."

Will Cargill hoeing corn in his back lot on Cass Street about 1895. The broad-brimmed hat protecting him from the sun also safeguarded his image; suntanned skin in his era was associated with people who did manual or farm labor, hence the term "redneck."

John's letter ends on a melancholy note with more unpleasantness: "You know I wrote you that we had two puppies. Well both of them are dead. One died yesterday, the other today. Don't know what was the cause but I rather think it was the change of food. They were little bits of things and I guess they still needed their mother. We felt quite badly about it as they were such nice, bright little puppies."

In a postscript added the next day, John informed Edna that a letter had come (probably from either Duncan McMillan or Will Cargill) telling him that he was to stay in Texas. He was sending her twenty-five dollars, he said, and she should begin getting ready to come down right away. It would probably be cooler by the time she was ready to leave, and he wanted her to bring a nurse or a cook along to help her.

Edna and little John, Jr. finally entrained for Texas in mid-October, but the young family was only together in Fort Worth for a few weeks before John sent his wife and son back to La Crosse. His worst fears had been realized: D. D. McMillan & Sons was bankrupt.

On December 1, 1896, John, Jr.'s first birthday, John, Sr. and his two brothers Will and Dan, their father Duncan D. McMillan, and their uncle Alexander McMillan were party to an agreement that transferred all of their assets to a trust controlled by W. W. Cargill, John M. Holley, and E. C. Warner. This included the entire property of D. D. McMillan & Sons, consisting of eight grain elevators at Iowa Park, Harrold, Chillicothe, Quanah, Childress, Henrietta, Vernon, and Seymour, Texas; six warehouses at Carlisle, Beaver, Oklaunion, Holliday, Dundee, and Abilene, Texas; eighty acres of land near Vernon in Wilbarger County, Texas; their office furniture and supplies in the Hurley Building in Fort Worth; machinery at Fort Worth in the Mark Evans elevator; and all bills and accounts receivable as well as grain and cash on hand.

Duncan and Alexander McMillan were utterly and completely ruined. Duncan was stripped of his real estate holdings including large timber acreage north of La Crosse and ninety newly platted city lots in North St. Paul, Minnesota. In addition he relinquished 154 shares of stock in the Black River Improvement Company, the logging corporation that John and Alexander had helped establish more than thirty years earlier. Capping his disgrace, he would also forfeit his family's fine residence of twenty years.

Alexander surrendered numerous commercial properties in La Crosse including the Post Office Block (which he had earlier purchased outright from his original partners) and the downtown McMillan Building where he and Duncan had their offices; sizeable timber tracts north of town; and 160 shares of Black River Improvement Company stock. Noting that he was only liable contingently, and that he had had no role in the Fort Worth business, the trustees allowed Alexander (who was a widower following Sarah's death four years ear-

John Hugh MacMillan, Jr.

86

lier) to keep his homestead. The agreement also provided for the possibility of payments from income derived from Alexander's rental properties, not to exceed two thousand dollars a year.

The trust agreement was an alternative to bankruptcy proceedings. Trustees Cargill, Holley, and Warner represented the McMillans' creditors, among them the National Bank of Illinois, the City Bank of Portage, Wisconsin, the German American Bank in La Crosse, and the State Bank of La Crosse. According to the terms of the trust, the creditors relinquished any and all claims against them in return for the takeover of McMillan assets. While the McMillans could not then meet their debts, the creditors believed that these could be discharged if their business could be continued with the free use of their property and resources.

The trustees were empowered to carry on the McMillans' business activities in their own names, with the profits to be divided pro rata among the creditors. They could sell or dispose of any of the property conveyed to them which they deemed superfluous to their purposes. The agreement would remain in effect until January 1, 1900, unless the debts were cleared up sooner, or unless the creditors, relying on the advice of the trustees, voted to liquidate the trust's assets earlier. If the debts were not paid by that date, the creditors could extend the agreement.

Duncan and Alexander McMillan never recovered from this monumental blow. Alexander soon afterwards suffered a paralyzing stroke that kept him largely confined to bed for the rest of his life. My great-grandfather was forced to surrender his stock in the State Bank of La Crosse and tender his resignation as president, the position he had held thirteen years. The new president of the bank would be George H. Ray, who had been a director since it was organized. Well thought of in La Crosse, Ray was connected with numerous city businesses

The Dr. John Rowles house in La Crosse. Duncan McMillan and his family lived here for six years.

Mary Isabella McMillan Rowles

Dr. John Alonzo Rowles

and served in the Wisconsin State Legislature, where he was elected speaker of the house in 1899. In 1913 Edna Cargill MacMillan's brother Austen would marry Ray's daughter Anne Louise.

Shortly after signing the trust agreement that gave him control of the McMillan assets, W. W. Cargill sent John MacMillan back to Texas to tie up loose ends and start a new business in cement that relied on potentially valuable limestone deposits on former McMillan property. Dan went along to help John and would remain his older brother's aide for the rest of his life. Edna and John, Jr. remained in La Crosse for the better part of the year before returning to Forth Worth in the fall. At Christmastime the John MacMillans had a full house in Fort Worth; both sets of parents—W. W. and Ellen Cargill and Duncan and Mary Jane McMillan—spent the holidays with them along with Will and Dan. For W. W. Cargill, this was more than a pleasure trip, of course; he needed to see and assess the Texas operation.

Returning home in January 1897, Duncan transferred the deed to his magnificent homestead, valued at $43,000, to the Cargill-Holley-Warner trust. The residence would remain empty several years; in December 1897 the property was surveyed and divided into seven single lots which were recorded as the "D. D. McMillan Addition." Now out in the cold, so to speak, Duncan and his family moved in with his daughter Mary Isabella and her family at 214 North Sixth Street. Duncan had purchased this Sixth Street property in the mid-1860s and transferred its title to Mary Isabella's husband, Dr. John Rowles, in 1896, perhaps to save it from his creditors. A much lesser house, it was still a sizeable three-story frame dwelling with enough room for all concerned.

At the time of the 1900 census, in addition to two live-in Norwegian servant girls, the Rowles house sheltered Duncan and Mary Jane McMillan and their children, Daniel, twenty-seven, Janet, nineteen, and Elizabeth, sixteen, as well as John and Mary Isabella Rowles and their two youngsters, Duncan and Malcolm, nine and one. Dr. Rowles carried on his medical practice in the McMillan Building.

In Canada, Duncan's brother Angus D. B. McMillan died in Finch on Christmas Day 1897, leaving no children. According to their father Duncan Ban's will, Duncan D. would have inherited the farm in this case, except that Angus had willed the property to his wife Margery shortly before he died. Duncan contested Angus's will, and a Canadian court split the property, giving half to the widow and half to Duncan. This was the last piece of property that Duncan ever owned. Several months later he sold his half of the farm to his sister Margaret McMillan Sutherland in Canada for nine hundred dollars.

The cement business in Texas was another lost cause. In April 1898, W. W. Cargill brought John and Dan MacMillan back to La Crosse. He put John in charge of a string of country elevators along the Great Western Railway, and Dan went to work for W. W. as a bookkeeper. John and Edna and John, Jr. lived with

Emma and Fred Hanchette in Switzerland. Both frequented European health spas; in April 1903, Emma wrote to her mother Ellen Cargill from Baden-Baden where she was taking mud bath treatments, "It's a good thing you have 'loads of money,' as John, Jr. says, "because you will need it to get me through Baden-Baden."

W. W. and Ellen Cargill before setting up housekeeping in a modest two-story frame home of their own at 112 North Tenth Street.

Their first summer back in La Crosse, John and Dan MacMillan took Edna and her younger sister Emma to the East Coast on a trip that was probably part vacation, part business. John, Jr. was left behind in the care of his doting grandmother Ellen Cargill. Emma had a crush on Dan and hoped to marry him, but Dan didn't propose, remaining a bachelor well into his thirties. (Years later, Emma's daughter revealed that a gift of candy from Dan still set her mother "all aflutter.") The Texas debacle had left Dan plagued by financial worries that seemingly drained him of any desire to take a bride.

In a letter to John dated March 22, 1899, Dan urged his brother to save everything he could for their future welfare: "I confess I am worried to know about what we can save each year between us. . . . Of course, it is our sacred duty to see that Jeanette [Janet] and Bess are in no way disregarded for we have a heavy obligation to discharge concerning their welfare. . . . I can save $600 and you ought to save . . . not less than another $600. . . . There is a duty that you owe Will and I and there is a duty that Will and I owe you.

"For myself, I never have a nickel from one end of the month to the other and I am strapped all of the time. I am willing to endure this for a season if we can but prosper. . . . If we lose what we have got I own that my business career is at an end. The grave will hold no terrors for me. To watch others stretch far into the lead is more than I care to endure. . . . My past life has embittered and made a melancholy man of me. A few more years like those that have passed over our heads would unfit me for any sort of companionship."

Emma didn't wait for Dan to come around. At age twenty-five, after a grand tour of Europe with her parents, she married an unhealthy young man named Fred Mark Hanchette at the Cargill residence on October 1, 1899. The *Chronicle* reported that "the beautiful drawing room with its walls hung with crimson brocaded silk formed an admirable background for the dazzling toilets and flashing jewels of the guests." Fred and Emma set up housekeeping on the mansion's third floor.

The Cargills had known the Hanchettes in Janesville, where the Hanchettes had a flour mill, and Fred's father G. M. Hanchette later opened a hardware store in Cresco, Iowa, when Will Cargill was there in 1867. Fred was a quiet, unassuming young man who, unlike Will's two sons and his son-in-law John MacMillan, never worked for Cargill enterprises. Three months after he and Emma were married, Fred was diagnosed with tuberculosis, and the couple spent long periods of time at sanatoriums and health spas in Europe. Fred and Emma were good correspondents, however, and a great deal of Cargill and MacMillan family history is contained in letters that they exchanged with John and Edna MacMillan through the years.

The D. D. McMillan house in the foreground, with the Cargill residence across Cass Street to the left

Daniel G. McMillan, who bought and razed the former D. D. McMillan house, which he considered a relic from an earlier, more flamboyant age. He had succeeded his father George McMillan as president of the La Crosse Gas and Electric Company.

The twentieth century began on a flat note for the MacMillans, who were still reeling from their terrible setback. On January 1, 1900, when the trust agreement they had been party to expired, W. W. Cargill, John M. Holley, and Joseph Boschert replaced it with a new corporation called the McMillan Company to manage the McMillan properties still owned by the trust.

One of the first things the new McMillan Company did was to sell the still empty Duncan McMillan house to W. W. Cargill's son Will S. Cargill for thirty thousand dollars. If the original plan had been to rent or sell the house to a disinterested party, no such person had materialized, and the house had been ransacked the previous summer and books and other articles stolen. In May the *Chronicle* reported that "substantial improvements" were being made to the exterior. Will S. was getting ready to move in with his wife, May McMillan Cargill, and their two little boys, William and George. May was the daughter of George McMillan, the nephew Alexander and Duncan had made superintendent of their Gas Light Company three decades earlier. Little William and George Cargill were close in age to their cousin John, Jr., and the three youngsters were constant companions during long periods when John, Jr. stayed at his Grandmother Cargill's across the street.

Will S. Cargill would prove himself a wastrel and philanderer who, after his father's death, lost his moorings. In 1913 May Cargill sold the former D. D. McMillan residence to her brother Daniel G. McMillan, who razed it to make room for a streamlined, brick and stucco prairie-style house that remains on the property today.

But the new century also brought with it new opportunities for the MacMillans. Down in Texas, John's brother Will had gone back to school and earned a bachelor's degree at Fort Worth University, where he was a member of two honor societies, Phi Beta Kappa and Sigma Xi. Cut from entirely different cloth than his brothers, Will would one day become a noted scientist, but for the time being, he had charge of the family ranch near Lubbock, an enterprise financed primarily by W. W. Cargill and John's wife Edna. Writing to John in March 1900, Will said that he was working harder than he had ever worked in his life.

> In fact, I have worked awful hard most of the time since I have been here, far harder than you would dream of, but Mr. Cable [the previous owner who had stayed on to help Will] and I are both imbued with the idea of keeping down expenses and we are going to make a good showing, I believe. I haven't even subscribed for a newspaper as yet as I want to see my way perfectly clear before I spend a cent on myself. I am working like the devil and saving at every possible turn. I am going to be successful if I can.

Will enclosed a Statement of Property; the ranch consisted of four sections of grassland with improvements including a house, two windmills, sheds, outhouses, pens, and ten miles of fences. Their stock included 110 cows, 1 registered bull, 2 grade bulls, and 6 horses. Will was raising red kaffir corn, sorghum, millet, and Johnson grass for feed. Twenty-four head of cattle had died that season, which "was too many and with more feed and better management will not occur again." He couldn't help it that the mule died, he said. "He ate too much green kaffir corn and busted."

Dan G. McMillan's modern prairie-style house where D. D. McMillan's Italianate mansion had stood

The ranch was easily worth $7,480, Will figured, and he was not unhappy in Texas; the country agreed with him. "Our pasture is as fine as there is in the county. We have three miles or more of the [Yellow House] canyon and it affords fine protection for the cattle, far better even than it looks. When the wind is a howling on the prairie it is scarcely blowing in the canyon. This is a fine thing in winter. . . . The weather has been fine except November and early December when there were cold rains, and the cattle got thin."

He could use some magazines and asked John especially to send him *Review of Reviews*:

> I am the most benighted individual you ever saw. I don't even know how the English are getting along in South Africa. I heard someone say that they had been

successful of late—I hope so. [The hard-fought Boer War, begun a year earlier in 1899, would go on into 1902 when the Boers finally accepted British sovereignty.] I have done almost no reading since I have been here. I have started Carlyle's *French Revolution* and read a little in Miss Clerke's *History of Astronomy*, but this is all. I play the violin more than usual and it is my sole companion. It makes me quite popular. Everyone likes it.

Will convinced his father to join him at the ranch the following winter in January, and the visit was good for both of them. In a letter to John in March 1901, Will said that having their father around "does much to keep me from being lonesome. He seems contented enough and I rather think he likes the place." Duncan, in fact, thrived in Texas. In May, Will wrote to John that Duncan was looking for better ways to water the ranch: "Father wants you to write him how the air compressor forces the water out of the artesian well so please find out and send him a diagram with explanation. . . . He thinks the same plan would work on our wells out here and be better than a pump 50 to 100 feet underground."

Duncan's inherent mechanical bent flourished, too, in Will. In another letter to John, Will described an invention he had in mind that sounded a lot like today's facsimile machine. "In a word the invention consists in making a mimeograph copy of any writing or printing by telegraph." This could be accomplished, he thought, by a complicated setup of tuning forks and electric magnets and electric circuits that he explained in great detail. "I am entirely satisfied it will work and father says it looks that way to him." Will hoped to interest Thomas Edison in the idea and share the patent with him, but this apparently never happened.

Duncan stayed on in Texas through the summer and planned to return to La Crosse in October. "I have advised him to do so," Will wrote John. "This is no place for him in winter as the house isn't very warm and father is aging very fast. He is quite slow and feeble and is bothered a good deal with rheumatism and his legs. His memory is very poor and on the whole I am rather afraid for him. I wouldn't have him get sick here for anything and I think he ought to be at home." Duncan was sixty-three years old.

All three MacMillan brothers had a stake in the ranch and were sending Will as much money as they could each month until it would become a paying proposition. "I have your letter stating you could send me 200 on the first of the month," Will wrote John in September 1900. "This I think will be enough for the time being." By the next May, however, acknowledging John's check for five hundred dollars, he wrote that he wanted to buy a section of land north of the house which was being offered to him for $650. "If you can send me Edna's $800 I will . . . have the deed made out to her if you wish."

For the next few years, Will coaxed every penny he could out of his brothers to put into the ranch. "I was kind of in hopes you would be able to add $50

Duncan D. McMillan. He was fifty-nine years old when D. D. McMillan & Sons failed. Will S. and May Cargill and their two little boys were living in his former residence when he spent the summer of 1901 with his son Will in Texas. The next year Duncan and Mary Jane McMillan and their two youngest daughters moved to Chicago.

a month out here which would have been a fine thing, particularly for two or three years when the calves will begin making returns," he wrote to John in January 1902. "Money put out here is a safe investment and for my part I want all you can possibly send." The stationery Will was using, six years after the firm had folded, said D. D. McMillan & Sons; Will simply crossed off the old Fort Worth address and penned in "Lubbock."

His thriftiness paid off. By spring 1903 he had increased the brothers' holdings to eight sections (5,120 acres). "We own 5 sections and lease 3," he wrote. "Of the 5 sections we own, 4 sections are school land for which the state has as yet issued no patent inasmuch as the purchase money to the state, 97½ cents per acre, has not been paid. This money is not due the state yet for 35 years and as it draws but 3% interest, it would not be profitable to pay it. . . . The other one section we own in fee simple."

Virtually all of the land was tillable, Will allowed, "and now that the country has learned that crops of sorghum and kaffir corn are sure every year there is a rapid development of farming on every ranch. . . . We have about 75 acres on the canyon which is suitable for alfalfa and . . . if it does as well as conditions indicate this land would certainly be worth $50 per acre." Will was running something over four hundred head of stock on the place—200 two-year-old Hereford heifers worth about fifty dollars each, and 200 less valuable grade Herefords and shorthorns, which he appraised at about seventeen dollars apiece. He had five Hereford bulls and eight horses.

Their land was worth $10,000, and the stock another $15,150, Will calculated. Against this, they owed $2,500 to the Stockmen's National Bank in Canyon, $2,500 to John's wife Edna Cargill MacMillan, and $5,000 to W. W. Cargill. So the ranch was humming along nicely, and Will now had help in the persons of a husband and wife who were working for him. "They are Kentucky people and are very nice. To have a good woman about the place makes it very much more pleasant."

Telling John that they would have some good sport when he came out, Will said that there was all kinds of game including deer, geese, ducks, turkeys, quail, wolves, and panthers at a place called Cap Rock, "50 miles east of here on the edge of the plains." He and a fellow rancher named Rob Cable particularly liked hunting rabbits and coyotes with a pair of greyhounds, he wrote, and he described how they had run down a coyote the previous Saturday:

> Rob and I espied the "critter" about a mile off. We were on our horses and we circled around the wolf drawing closer all the time. The dogs ran in between the horses. We got within about 100 yards of the coyote when we charged. Then the dogs lit out for the beast and we had the most exciting sport you ever saw. We fairly flew. The horses kept us right in the race, and we were right there when the dogs threw the wolf. He was a big one and fought viciously, but the dogs killed him in about 15 minutes. I have the skin hung up.

Today Cargill, Inc. has a large feedlot operation at Cap Rock. A portion of The MacMillan Farms, as the Lubbock ranch came to be known, remains in the family, owned by descendants of the MacMillan brothers' sisters, Mary Isabella McMillan Rowles and Elizabeth McMillan Wheeler. For as long as anyone now alive can remember, the ranch has raised cotton, not cattle, and in more recent times, wine grapes. Somewhere along the line, Will MacMillan sold about 1,500 acres of the ranch for a development, and other family members later sold off additional acreage. What remains today is about 1,400 acres. A few years ago, oil was discovered on the ranch.

All three MacMillan brothers learned valuable lessons from the Texas fiasco, a fact that became more apparent as their lives unfolded, but their father's last years were difficult ones. Five years after surrendering everything he had worked a lifetime to acquire, Duncan lost his sole surviving brother, Alexander, who had been his anchor in La Crosse. Alexander had never regained his strength following his stroke, and he sank gradually during his last year, passing away at his Seventh Street home in October 1901, two days after his seventy-sixth birthday. Alexander had been looked after in his declining years by his wife Sarah's sister, Hattie Baldwin, who had also been widowed. Alexander had very little money by then, and my grandfather John, Sr. was sending him a monthly stipend of $100, probably from the family as a whole.

In June 1900, thanking John profusely for his check, Hattie wrote:

> Your kindly expressed solicitude was very grateful to him, and brought the tears to his eyes. I think he will soon be quite as well, if not better, than he has been for some time. He is looking at life more hopefully, and with renewed courage.

Alexander was able to go out for daily carriage rides about town that summer, feeling much his old self, but with the onset of winter, he slipped into severe depression. In January 1901, Hattie wrote John that he was constantly worried about his taxes and had had two acute attacks of dementia.

> A week ago the girl came running to my room saying to come down quick, Mr. McMillan is going about the house in his night shirt. When I got down, he seemed not to know me, and would do nothing to help dress himself.

Alexander wanted to sell his house before the taxes were due again, Hattie told John, and he wondered if W. W. Cargill would be interested in purchasing it for Edna and her children. After Alexander died, his son Sam sold the family home to George McMillan, the new president of the La Crosse Gas and Electric Company (May McMillan Cargill's father). The *Republican and Leader* reported in October 1902 that Sam had closed the deal for $1,500, subject to a mortgage of $4,000 on the grand old place.

Alexander was survived by his son Sam and Sam's wife and their three boys; his brother Duncan; and three sisters in Canada. The Cornwall, Ontario, *Freeholder* carried the obituary of this native son made good, noting that Alexander and his wife Sarah had visited Canada when they went to Europe in 1883. "Mr. McMillan enjoyed this trip greatly and it was with pleasure that he would refer to it in his last days."

With his last brother gone, Duncan no longer wanted to live in La Crosse, where the reminders of their rise and fall were everywhere around him. Taking their daughters Janet and Bess with them, he and Mary Jane moved to Chicago, where they rented a brick townhouse on Kimbark Avenue in the Hyde Park neighborhood, one of the city's oldest and most fashionable suburbs. Named for a part of the old Westminster Abbey property that Henry VIII used for a deer preserve, the Hyde Park area in Chicago was an upper-middle-class neighborhood laid out on quiet, tree-lined streets several miles south of the loop.

By the turn of the century, electric streetcars and an elevated system connected Hyde Park with Chicago's bustling central business district, but it was family rather than commerce that drew Duncan there. The McMillan residence was within walking distance of where Ewen Hugh's widow Ettie lived with her four children, three of whom taught school. In 1907, the year before he died, Duncan moved his family to an apartment in the same neighborhood at 5407 Woodlawn Avenue, a cream-colored brick building with turned stone columns framing the entryway.

In the year 1900 John and Edna were making a fresh beginning in Pine Bluff, Arkansas, where her father had sent John to manage his newly acquired Sawyer and Austin Lumber Company. This was Will Cargill's first experience in the lumber business, but John would have his father's expertise to guide him. Sawyer and Austin had been one of the largest loggers in La Crosse until taking a nose dive the year before, due largely to bad luck. With Wisconsin forests nearly depleted, the company had purchased 100,000 acres of virgin pine forest near Pine Bluff, when co-owner David Austin died suddenly at his home in La Crosse, leaving his partner W. E. Sawyer with insufficient capital to finance planned construction of a mill and logging railroad at Pine Bluff.

Will Cargill saved the day by agreeing to invest in his friend Sawyer's business, so that on May 20, 1899, the *Pine Bluff Commercial* was able to announce that "Sawyer and Austin will build a three-band [three-saw] saw mill with the capacity of 100,000 to 125,000 [board] feet per day with a planing mill, dry kilns, sheds, etc. in the city of Pine Bluff and will make the city the terminus of its railroad."

W. E. Sawyer moved to Pine Bluff, employed fifty men to clear land and erect an office building, and entered into a contract with the state to obtain convict labor to build the mill and railroad. Using convict labor was a fairly common practice, and the men were "well treated," the *Commercial* assured readers. "They are not rushed, but are allowed to assume a slow and easy gait and

The Sawyer and Austin lumber mill on Rose Street in North La Crosse about 1887

Sawyer and Austin's office building in Pine Bluff, surrounded by tall pines

stroke at their work." The convicts were housed in a stockade made by driving twenty-foot logs into the ground next to each other.

Mr. Sawyer had only been in Arkansas a matter of months, however, when he died of typhoid fever at Pine Bluff in November 1899. At this point, as Cargill's 1945 history puts it: "Mr. Cargill was faced with the prospect of either kissing his investment goodbye or launching forth on a new enterprise. With characteristic courage, he decided to see it through, and put J. H. MacMillan in charge." Will Cargill was elected president, and John MacMillan, treasurer.

John and Edna with little John, Jr. and Edna's Aunt Tassie Stowell left La Crosse and its cold winter for the warmer climate of Pine Bluff in January 1900. Tassie, whose given name was Clara Stowell, was Ellen Cargill's sister, and she and her son Clarence had lived with the Cargills in La Crosse. Newspaper articles referred to Tassie as Mrs. Stowell, so she was either an unwed mother or a widow who chose to retain her maiden name. A prim woman who appears in family photographs wearing steel-rimmed glasses, Aunt Tassie had been a second mother to the Cargill children. Now she was helping look after John, Jr.

Sam McMillan and his sixteen-year-old son Clark were also working at the Sawyer and Austin sawmill in 1900; Sam was a foreman, Clark a machinist. Sam rented what must have been a modest house on West Twelfth Avenue for his family, before leaving the sawmill to start a small company of his own manufacturing "Brooders, Brood Coops, Roosting Coops, Portable Hen Houses, and Rabbit Hutches." By 1902 he moved his family to Lake Charles, Louisiana.

The John MacMillans took up residence in a large Victorian-era boarding house at 702 Second Avenue West in Pine Bluff with Charles Moore, his wife and two stepsons, and ten other boarders, among them three men who worked at the mill (a civil engineer, a lawyer, and a stenographer), a Russian nurse, and a man named Clifton Breckenridge and his wife and four children. Breckenridge was a commission merchant and president of the Sawyer-Austin Fishing Club, which worked at improving the bass fishing locally. Will Cargill was vice president of the fishing club, and John MacMillan was secretary.

John and Edna joined the First Presbyterian Church (to which they contributed fifty dollars annually) and changed their magazine subscriptions to Pine Bluff. An invoice from his news agent in New York reveals that my grandfather read *Bookman*, *Harper's*, and *Literary Digest*. If Edna had planned to remain in Pine Bluff with John, however, those plans didn't work out, and she and John, Jr. returned home to her parents' house in La Crosse in May. Edna was pregnant with a second child.

Now thirty-one years old, John MacMillan was an effective chief officer in Pine Bluff. He worked closely with his employees, but there was no question as to who was boss. Writing to Edna, he told her about a man named Russell from La Crosse who was determined to have a vacation the first year.

Cargill MacMillan, born in La Crosse in 1900

Sawyer and Austin company employees logging in Pine Bluff

Russell had given him every excuse in the book why he needed to get away—that he had business to attend to in La Crosse, that he was very nervous and owed it to himself to take care of his health, that Will Cargill had promised him a vacation.

"I simply told him 'We had to attend to business before pleasure'—that I had intended being away in August myself but when I found out business demanded that I stay, I gave up the idea," John wrote. "I was mild but determined with him and his effrontery did him no good. To most of his thinnest remarks, I made no answer, simply sat and looked at him and it embarrassed him considerably."

On October 10, 1900, my father's younger brother Cargill MacMillan came into the world, weighing a hefty ten pounds. For much of the next two years, Edna and the two children remained in La Crosse with her parents. Early in 1902, tired of boarding house living and wanting his family with him, John started construction of a fine, new residence in Pine Bluff that is extraordinary even to this day. The architect was Hugh Garden, a free-lance Chicago designer who had worked briefly for Frank Lloyd Wright and had offices in Chicago. Resembling Wright's innovative prairie house designs, John's new two-and-a-half-story house had wide overhanging eaves (that partially shielded the structure from sun, wind, and rain), leaded glass windows, and ample interior wood paneling. Watching costs carefully, John requested bids from multiple contractors, but he remained true to Garden's plans. "I am very glad to hear that you are going on with the house without changes," Garden wrote to him in July 1902, "because I think it nearly perfect as it is, and I would regret very much to have changes made."

John always pushed himself to the limit, and he accomplished a great deal in Pine Bluff, including the building of a railroad from Sheridan to Benton, Arkansas. In fact, he pushed himself too far, to the detriment of his health. In letters to Edna he mentioned being under a great deal of stress and having colds, while all the time assuring her that he was quite all right. "I am taking Bromo-quinine and no doubt will be well or rather cured by morning as of course I am not sick." When Edna took John, Jr. to Arkansas for a two-months' visit in mid-November 1902, however, she found her husband very sick indeed. The new house was still incomplete, and they spent Christmas at the boarding house.

Edna wrote in her diary that she attended the wedding of friends in Pine Bluff on November 17, and that John was "sick with typhoid from then on." Baby Cargill was being looked after in La Crosse by his grandmother Ellen Cargill, and the first letter we have written by my father is one he wrote from Pine Bluff to his brother (who would be his lifelong best friend and confidant) dated December 12, 1902. John, Jr. was seven and Cargill was two.

My Dear Brother,

I wish you were here. I was very glad to get your present. Thank you for the present. I will send you a Christmas present. I hope you are all right. Can you make mud pies yet. If you can you are a funny boy. Write to me. Make a mud pie and send it to me. I want you all right. Next time I write you it will be a funny letter. Tell Aunt Tassie to come down here and play with me. I have no one to play with me.

Your loving brother,

John, Jr.

John and Edna MacMillan's house on Martin Avenue in Pine Bluff in 1902, when Prairie School architecture was in its infancy

In late January 1903, accompanied by Will Cargill, John and Edna and John, Jr. took the train home to Wisconsin, where John recuperated. When the couple returned to Pine Bluff in March with their two boys, they moved into their newly completed house at 407 Martin Avenue. "Like new house," Edna wrote in her diary. A substantial house with a reception hall, living room, dining room, library, and kitchen on the first floor, it had four bedrooms, a nursery, and a bath on the second. The living room and nursery had tile fireplaces; ceilings in the first-floor rooms were almost twelve feet high with dark oak beams, and a brick and tile sideboard in the dining room held Edna's wedding crystal and silver.

The family would only live there a matter of months, but photographs of the house during that period show it filled with bric-a-brac, pictures on the walls, and matched sets of books on the library shelves, giving it a homey, lived-in look. Completed for a shade less than six thousand dollars, this Pine Bluff house is today the finest extant example of prairie-style architecture in Arkansas and in the 1970s was placed on the National Register of Historic Places.

John H. MacMillan's new library. Chicago booksellers A. C. McClurg and Company wrote to him in Pine Bluff: "We take pleasure in stating that all the books of your order were shipped by freight as requested, with one exception, the first volume of Massillion's Sermons *[which was out of print]."*

Samuel D. (Sam) Cargill in the Minneapolis office

John was fooling himself if he thought he had recovered his health when he returned with his family to Pine Bluff, however. In May he was convalescing at his brother Will's ranch in Texas when John, Jr. wrote to him from Pine Bluff. "My Dear father: Are you better or not? When will you be back? . . . Mother said for you not to come back till the first of June." John, Jr. had started school in Pine Bluff, and he told his father, "I was one hundred in my spelling today and finished my first third reader." His mother was putting up pictures, he said, and their garden had sprouted. "Our nasturtiums are up and have three leaves. We had some radishes yesterday. . . . Tell Uncle Will that I would like to see him."

Will Cargill had had every intention of keeping John in Pine Bluff, where he and Edna were just getting settled, but before the year was out, he suddenly needed him more in Minneapolis. The situation was this. In 1890 the Cargill Elevator Company had been formed to take over Cargill Brothers assets. Sam Cargill managed this Minneapolis based company with his brother Jim as his assistant. The La Crosse end of the business was still separate at this time, doing business as the W. W. Cargill Company.

In the spring of 1903, Sam Cargill was returning home from a vacation trip to the West Indies with his wife Lydia when he fell ill aboard a train and was taken to a hospital in West Baden, Indiana, where he died a few days later at age fifty-six. His death was indeed a staggering blow to the Cargill Elevator Company, and Jim Cargill subsequently took over full management of the firm. Jim had previously managed the country elevators, and that job went to Dan MacMillan, formerly employed by Will Cargill at La Crosse. Within months, however, the strain of his new position took its toll on Jim, and he suffered a complete breakdown in the fall. Something needed to be done immediately, and Will

Cargill decided that John MacMillan should take over management of the Minneapolis office with the title of vice president and general manager. Will Cargill was president of the Cargill Elevator Company; Jim Cargill, a second vice president; and John's brother Dan, secretary.

Following Sam's death, Will Cargill became the majority stockholder in Cargill Elevator; except for a few shares owned by brother Jim, he and Sam had owned the company jointly. Sam died without children, leaving an estate valued at $872,000, and his will provided that his shares in the company be divided equally among his four siblings—Will, Jim, Sylvester, and Margaret Cargill Barker—and his widow Lydia. Will also soon acquired Jim Cargill's shares through a transaction for which there is no documentation.

On November 5, 1903, the *Minneapolis Journal* announced that

> John H. McMillan [*sic*] and wife of Pine Bluff, Ark., have taken the Eugene Hay house on Clifton avenue for a permanent home. Mr. McMillan has been sent up to take charge of the Cargill Elevator company business. He has been managing the W. W. Cargill lumber business in Arkansas. Mr. McMillan was in the grain business in Minneapolis twelve years ago [it had actually been fifteen years since John had gone to work for his cousin John D. in Minneapolis] and later was at the home office in La Crosse, Wis., and also in the grain business in the panhandle of Texas.

Edna's diary reveals that their furniture arrived in Minneapolis on December 12. John, Jr. and his brother Cargill stayed with their Grandmother Cargill in La Crosse while she got the house settled. In a letter to Edna dated December 20, her mother wrote: "Baby is so sweet and cunning but John Jr. is the dearest boy that ever lived." John and Edna went to La Crosse for Christmas, and John and Will Cargill afterwards traveled to Pine Bluff for an inspection trip (John would continue to share management responsibilities in Pine Bluff with Will and his son Will S. until the firm was liquidated some years later), arriving back home in time to escort their wives to a Leap Year Ball on New Year's Day.

Returning to Minneapolis after the holidays with their two sons, John and Edna moved into their new house at 321 Clifton Avenue in early January 1904. This move marked the beginning of a new era for our family and the Cargill Company. If there was ever any doubt in Will Cargill's mind that John MacMillan was the right man for the job, he could have rested easy. As Ralph Nader once put it, my grandfather "established [at Cargill] a momentum toward expansion and profitability that continues to this day."

James Flett (Jim) Cargill

Snug and tight, the Cargill residence in La Crosse—a picture-perfect holiday house

LORING PARK

Loring Pond about 1905

John H. MacMillan rented the former Hay residence on Clifton Avenue in Minneapolis for his family in 1903.

The MacMillan family put down its first roots in Minnesota in the prestigious Loring Park neighborhood of Minneapolis. This section of Minneapolis had originally been part of the Fort Snelling military reservation, which was opened for white settlement in 1854. Within a few years, most of the Indians were gone from this rolling, partially wooded landscape except for Keg-o-ma-go-shieg, who set up his lodge each year at the southwest corner of the lake now called Loring Pond. His ancestors had lived there for generations, the Indian said, but he, too, soon disappeared.

In 1856 the United States government sold 160 acres to Joseph H. Johnson of Farmington, Maine. A second pioneer, Allen ("Deacon") Harmon, also from Maine, preempted 160 acres directly north of the Johnson tract. Johnson and Harmon and other early settlers, mostly New Englanders, cleared the trees, built neat white homesteads, and established so-called "garden farms," raising a few cows and growing vegetables to sell in the nearby city.

The future Loring Park district did not remain long in crops, however. As Minneapolis became a fast-growing financial, merchandising, and transportation center for a large agricultural area encompassing the entire Upper Midwest, well-to-do businessmen began migrating out of the sooty, central city in the direction of the Johnson and Harmon properties. Land values in the area soared, and pioneer farmers subdivided their property and sold lots. Central Park became Minneapolis's first park in 1883. Soon renamed for its champion, prominent miller Charles M. Loring, it was designed with meandering walkways and lush flower gardens by eminent landscape architect Horace W. S. Cleveland. The area around it became an exclusive sanctuary for affluent families connected with the city's prosperous lumber, grain, and milling industries.

Among the many elegant homes that sprang up around Loring Park's southern periphery was the large, two-story cedar-shingled residence with

Greek columns that my grandparents John and Edna MacMillan rented at 321 Clifton Avenue. Built during the previous decade for Eugene G. Hay, a Minneapolis lawyer who had been United States attorney for Minnesota, it was designed by Harry W. Jones, one of a small group of preeminent Minneapolis architects who helped define Loring Park's unique architectural heritage. John and Edna hired a French governess, a Swedish maid, and a Norwegian cook, and John's brother Dan, who had been living at the Vendome Hotel in Minneapolis after being named secretary of the Cargill Elevator Company the previous spring, also moved in with them.

Prior to moving to Minneapolis the previous April, Dan written John, asking him to forego sending their brother Will any money that month and instead "send mother my share of her allowance." (All three brothers were contributing to the support of their parents and sisters.) In preparation for his new position, Dan said, he had "spent just about $100 in clothes [for] a spring overcoat, shirts, gloves, shoes, and all sorts of things absolutely essential."

More than seven years after Texas, his credit was still no good, Dan informed John. He had gone to his father's old bank and asked John Holley to loan him $400 for three months, but the banker had turned him down cold. "Evidently we have no standing in that direction. Fifteen years ago I went to Mr. Holley and asked for a credit of $500 with which request he seemed glad to comply. I was then 15 years old, working on a salary of $25 per month, with no business experience and so far as was then visible no business prospect. At thirty years of age with an experience in the grain business surpassed by none, with a prospect of a salary of $2500 per year . . . he refuses even to consider me."

Dan was appalled at the man's lack of compassion. "He offered no word of congratulation, he spoke no word [of] encouragement. He glared at me with a banker's pitiless stare, he addressed me in a banker's heartless manner. He possesses a smooth voice, commands good English, and has acquired by experience a bland manner, an ideal man most people would say, but, to me, he lacks the first essential of this title, viz., a heart. The proof of this is that after having spent 20 years of close relations with father, as honorable a man as ever lived, to show some sign of pleasure and interest at our good prospects would be the most natural thing in the world for a man of generous impulses and refined sympathies. He dismissed me without a pleasant word of any kind."

In Minneapolis, although Dan always lived modestly, he finally found the financial security he so desperately craved, working side by side with my grandfather at Cargill. Each morning the brothers walked downtown to work together at the new Chamber of Commerce Building at 400 South Fourth Street where the Cargill Elevator Company had its offices on the fifth floor. More often than not, their cousin John D. McMillan walked with them. John D. and his wife Nellie and their three children lived a few doors away from

The Chamber of Commerce Building in Minneapolis. Cargill Elevator Company offices were on the fifth floor when John H. MacMillan was named general manager in 1903.

John Jr.'s cousins: Howard and Katherine McMillan

Emerson Grade School, where my father attended classes with his cousin Howard McMillan and Jean Paul Getty

ohn and Edna in a house at 239 Clifton designed by William Channing Whitney, the architect of the Horace Irvine mansion that is now the Minnesota Governor's Residence in St. Paul.

John D.'s son Howard Ives McMillan and my father John, Jr. grew up together, attended Emerson Grade School together, and remained close friends their entire lives. At Emerson, a brick structure on the corner of West Fourteenth Street and Spruce, five blocks from John, Jr.'s house, one of the boys' classmates was Jean Paul Getty, who lived with his parents in the Imperial Flats at 20 West Grant Street—another Harry Jones design.

Jean Paul's father George Getty was an insurance executive who struck it rich in the oil fields in Bartlesville, Oklahoma. Young Getty, later said to be the richest man in the world, kept a diary throughout his boyhood in which he several times mentioned Emerson School. After a tornado ripped through Minneapolis on August 4, 1904, Getty wrote: "Lots of trees down around our house. Windows broken. No church because the roof was stove in. *The Emerson is a complete wreck.*"

Friendships my grandparents formed on Clifton Avenue, which was peopled almost entirely by grain and lumber families, have survived to the present day, one example being the Charles Deere Velies at 225 Clifton (another massive brick and stone Tudor-style house by William Channing Whitney). Velie was the grandson of John Deere, who had founded the world-famous Deere and Company in Illinois with his son Charles and son-in-law Stephen Henry Velie, Charles Deere Velie's father.

Charles Deere Velie had come to Minneapolis following college to work in Deere and Company's branch office. In 1893 he was named secretary treasurer of the newly formed Deere and Webber Company, which became a giant in the industry, manufacturing and distributing farm machinery, vehicles, gasoline engines, and cream separators. Velie's partner in this enterprise was his neighbor at 411 Clifton, Charles C. Webber, another of John Deere's grandsons.

An able business executive, Velie was also a public-spirited philanthropist who in 1910, three years after Robert Baden-Powell founded the Boy Scouts in England, helped organize the movement in Minneapolis. My grandfather John MacMillan responded to Velie's first fund-raising letter that year with a check for ten dollars. The next year, when John, Jr. became a Boy Scout at age fifteen, he upped his contribution to twenty-five dollars. In the decades since its Loring Park beginnings, the relationship between the Velie family and ours took on renewed significance when my brother John Hugh MacMillan III married Charles Velie's granddaughter Susan Velie in 1951.

A few days after John and Edna moved into their new home, on Sunday, January 10, 1904, Will and Ellen Cargill came up to Minneapolis for a visit. The next morning Will Cargill suffered a stroke. The family called in a doctor, and

Cargill's wife and Will MacMillan (who was visiting from Texas) rushed him back to La Crosse by train that same evening. En route, at Hastings, Minnesota, they were joined by the Cargill family physician, Dr. Clinton Maine, whom they had reached by telegraph.

Ellen wrote Edna on Tuesday: "We got home on time last night. I was so sick I don't know what we would have done without Will. . . . Papa grew slowly worse all the way home . . . and today his side is not so good or his speech. He has been so blue and discouraged it has seemed as tho he could not stand it. Dr. Rowles (John MacMillan's brother-in-law) says he will be all right in a few days."

Two days later Ellen informed Edna: "Papa to me seems the same altho' Dr. [Rowles] says he is better. . . . There may be a slight better feeling in his leg but his hand and arm can't move a muscle—not a motion. . . . Will Mac stayed last night and Dr. Maine hasn't been in bed until this morning. . . . He has had a little sleep in his chair and lying beside Papa on the bed." Dr. Rowles didn't know the half of it, Ellen wrote, because "he sees him just a few minutes and Papa tries to brace up, but when he is gone he just seems to give up and thinks too much."

Brought on at least in part by business-related stress, Will's stroke was more serious than anybody thought, and he would remain partially paralyzed for the rest of his life. During his first few days at home, Ellen shielded him from everyone having anything to do with business including their son Will S. Some years before Will had invested in a new railroad between La Crosse and Viroqua, Wisconsin, a distance of twenty-four miles, and track was already being laid when the promoters ran out of money. Rather than lose his investment, Will had decided to complete the line and named Will S. president of the line's construction and operation corporation, which became known as the La Crosse and Southeastern Railroad. In June 1905 Will Cargill himself would drive its last-

golden spike, and from then on, as a railroading family, the Cargills would enjoy free passes on railroads throughout the United States.

By mid-February, accompanied by Dr. Maine, Will Cargill felt well enough to travel with Ellen and their sixteen-year-old son Austen to California. They spent the rest of the winter with Emma and Fred Hanchette in Pasadena. In a letter to Edna in late March, Ellen wrote, "The bonds were paid so Papa feels better over the R.R." Will had also bought a new Winton for Austen to drive in California. (The year before, the first automobile to travel coast to coast had made the trip from San Francisco to New York in fifty-two days.) After Austen was arrested for speeding within the city limits of Los Angeles and fined ten dollars in police court, Ellen complained to Edna that "it was a mean thing to do as he was out in the country." She also gave Austen money to buy a speedometer.

Beginning in March, Ellen's letters to her daughter were sent to a European address. After only a few months at the helm in Minneapolis, John was very ill with a stomach ailment which may have been related to earlier bouts of typhoid or malaria. Leaving John, Jr. and little Cargill at La Crosse with their French governess and Aunt Tassie, John and Edna sailed for Naples, where they stayed at the Hotel Britannique while planning an automobile trip to Paris. (Ellen had written to Edna, "I think [the auto trip] will be glorious if you dress right for it and wear a mask or glasses and a cap, but you could never go unless you did.") After getting themselves settled in Paris, John saw a Dr. Middleton who put him to bed and treated him with vapor baths and massage.

The Cargills with son Austen returned to La Crosse from California in April. They had left the Winton in California, Ellen wrote Edna, because it would have cost two hundred dollars to ship it home. Besides, she had her eye on a bigger, better automobile. "The Winton is perfect this year—has a fine canopy top on and a glass front so one is just fine—side curtains and all. We were going to get the Knox but have decided to get another Winton. Its the best looking machine I ever saw and Will Cargill is the agent for it here

Edna and John MacMillan, pictured on postcards datelined Nice that they sent home to their sons

William W. Cargill, John H. MacMillan, Jr., and George M. Cargill with Cargill MacMillan on tricycle

William Austen Stowell, Will Cargill's father-in-law, in his seventy-sixth year, 1899

and we save 250.00 on it. That's secret of course."

After eight weeks on the West Coast, Ellen was thrilled to be reunited with Edna's little boys in La Crosse. The French governess had become a problem, however, she informed Edna. Ellen felt that she favored Cargill and was "making a little parrot out of him"; worse still, baby Cargill was speaking better French than English. When she could no long stomach the French woman, Ellen fired her and set about finding a replacement. She had a chance to hire a new governess who spoke German and Spanish, she wrote Edna, but "I do not believe I shall take her as she sounds rather cranky to me. She wants the children to mind her and she teaches them to be neat, helpful, and a whole list of things that sounds rather suspicious to me."

John, Jr. finished out the school year in La Crosse, and he and Cargill played with their cousins William and George Cargill across the street in the former D. D. McMillan house. Sometimes their grandfather Will Cargill took all four of his grandsons to the farm he had purchased the year before to raise blooded cattle and sheep in Campbell County, about four miles from La Crosse on the road to West Salem. Will bought the championship herd at the 1904 World's Fair in St. Louis, and his cattle invariably took first place at all the leading state fairs and big stock shows.

Writing to his parents from La Crosse on July 3, John, Jr. said that he had "bearly got permoted into the fifth A grade," and asked them to bring him "a great many stamps of all the countries you go through." He had not been able to study French since Mademoiselle left, he said, "but I have read Baby some French stories. I like the French language very much now." With the Fourth of July coming up, his grandparents had bought him some number 2 firecrackers: "Grandma said I could shoot number 4's but I wouldn't do it for the world. . . . They are dangerous and could blow off my finger."

In August little Cargill, who was almost four, was seriously ill with typhoid fever when John and Edna returned from five months abroad. Edna remained at her parents' house with the boys until October, while John returned to the office to oversee details concerning the purchase of the Thorpe Elevator Company, which became a subsidiary of the Cargill Elevator Company and greatly enlarged Cargill's capacity. The Thorpe Elevator Company had been established in 1892 and owned more than fifty country elevators, mostly in Minnesota and North Dakota.

Early the next year, on February 13, 1905, La Crosse papers announced the death of Edna's maternal grandfather William Austen Stowell at her parents' residence. Born in New York, my great-great-grandfather Stowell had come to Wisconsin as a young man and was eighty-two years old at his demise. After his wife died eight years earlier, he had spent his declining years with his daughter Ellen and her family. At various times William Stowell had acted as Will Cargill's agent or representative, and at the time of his death, following a lengthy illness, the old gentleman was a member of the Minneapolis Grain Exchange.

Soon after the funeral, which was held from the Cargill residence, John and Edna took their two boys on the first of several family trips to California. Edna wrote in her diary that her parents and Fred and Emma Hanchette met them in Kansas City, and that they all stayed with the Hanchettes in Pasadena. My father treasured these trips west to visit his Aunt Emma. He loved her dearly and would later meet my mother Marion Dickson in California while visiting Aunt Emma.

Will Cargill apparently returned home hale and hearty from California that year. Local newspapers reported in the spring that he was taking a party of male friends from La Crosse, Green Bay, Chicago, and Boston down the Mississippi River to Hannibal on his pleasure steamer *Gallardo* (named for one of his father Captain William Dick Cargill's boats). Describing its upholstered furniture and well-supplied larder, the *La Crosse Chronicle* remarked, "Inside, the Gallardo has all the comforts of home." The *Gallardo* was one in a string of Cargill family boats that tied up at La Crosse. In 1908 Will's new boat, the *Ellen*, designed by his son Will S. and built at the Cargill docks on the Black River, would be the largest pleasure steamer on the Upper Mississippi.

While Will was out entertaining his stag party on the river, Ellen was making plans to remodel what one writer called "Will's chilly English castle," which she now found hopelessly out of date. In 1882 railroad tycoon Henry Villard had commissioned McKim, Mead and White to create an authentic Italian Renaissance palace for him on Madison Avenue in New York that spawned a plethora of lesser versions across the country. The revamped Cargill house would be one of them. Ellen was ready for her own Italian palace—a style especially suited to America's new breed of merchant princes.

Houseboat and pleasure barge belonging to Will Cargill

Cruisin' down the river: Ellen and Will Cargill on the right with their son Austen on the floor

Having made his mark as a grain dealer, lumberman, railroad owner, capitalist, and philanthropist, my great-grandfather Will Cargill was La Crosse's leading citizen. The *New York Almanac* for 1902 identified him as one of only four thousand millionaires in the country. On the grain side of things, he owned the W. W. Cargill Company in La Crosse, the Cargill Elevator Company in Minneapolis, and the Superior Terminal Elevator Company in Superior, Wisconsin. He also owned the La Crosse and Southeastern Railroad, and the Sawyer and Austin Lumber Company in Pine Bluff. In La Crosse, he held stock in all the public utilities and in many smaller corporations doing business in the city.

Ellen hired architect Hugh Garden, who had designed John and Edna's prairie-style house in Pine Bluff, for her remodeling and landscaping project. Anxious to get on with it, on December 14, she wrote Edna: "Emma has nearly emptied the house. . . . They are tearing it all down. The tower is off and bay window." Two days later, the Will Cargills moved across the street to their son Will S.'s house, the former D. D. McMillan mansion. "It's a queer Christmas for us," Ellen ruminated. Looking over at the old house, "everything" was white with snow. "It made Papa blue."

The remodeling would take nearly a year and a half, and the Cargills— Will and Ellen and Austen—went back to California after the holidays to wait out the winter. The three of them were motoring with Fred and Emma Hanchette and a chauffeur in the Santa Barbara area when they felt the earthquake that devastated San Francisco on April 18, 1906.

This was the most damaging earthquake in United States history. The first and heaviest early morning shocks were followed by three days of minor tremors. Buildings crumpled, streets buckled, gas and water mains erupted, and four square miles in the central business and residential districts burned.

Ellen Stowell Cargill

The ruins of San Francisco following three terrible days of earthquake and fire in April 1906

The catastrophe caused widespread damage in an area 450 miles long and 50 miles wide. Five hundred people were buried in the debris, and another 250,000 homeless flooded the streets and beaches. Among the thousands caught in the disaster was tenor Enrico Caruso, who vowed he would never return to a city "where disorders like that are permitted." And he never did.

To meet the emergency, the military commandeered all available automobiles to rush the injured to hospitals, deliver the imperiled to safety, haul dynamite being used to check the holocaust, and carry messages. "Hereafter the people of San Francisco will regard the automobile as a blessing, rather than a nuisance," wrote one newspaper editor. Leaving the Hanchettes and Will and Ellen Cargill behind, Austen and the chauffeur put their auto on a flat car and took the train to San Francisco, where they helped transport refugees and their belongings to safety.

Three days earlier John and Edna MacMillan and John, Jr. had lunched in California with the Hanchettes and Cargills on their way to Mexico. John was going down there to inspect several hundred acres of pine timberland that Will Cargill had purchased in Chihuahua for about seventy-five cents an acre for his Sawyer and Austin Lumber Company. Little Cargill had been left behind in La Crosse with a French governess, Mademoiselle de le Seighere. (Like the Rockefellers and many other wealthy families who employed French governesses at the turn of the century, the Cargills and MacMillans always called these women "Mademoiselle.")

After returning from Mexico, still without a home of their own in Minneapolis, the MacMillans took up residence in the newly completed Plaza

John H. MacMillan, Jr., at the left in the front row, with his class at Emerson School

The Plaza Hotel overlooked Loring Pond

Hotel; just west of Loring Park, the six-story Plaza was a fashionable, Italian Renaissance-style apartment hotel with maid service. Its guests often stayed years and even lifetimes. In a subsequent letter to his father-in-law Will Cargill, John remarked, "The children are both well, but I do not believe they like hotel life any too well."

John, Jr. graduated from Emerson Grade School on January 16, 1907, and John and Edna attended the afternoon exercises. "They had a combination of eight or nine of the ward schools—a total of 350 pupils graduating from these schools," John, Sr. wrote to his brother-in-law Will S. Cargill. "It was quite a sight to see so many children." Two weeks later, the MacMillans with their two boys departed Minneapolis for New York to sail to Europe.

"We left Minneapolis the 29th of January for Chicago arriving there the next morning," John, Jr. wrote in a boyish hand in the journal he kept of the trip. "We spent the day at Grandpa MacMillans. We barely caught the train for Albany [New York] which left the train station at Hyde Park at 5:45." In Albany, he and his family "walked up to the capitol [and] mother bought a few things. We then entered a hotel but mother did not like it so we went to another hotel and got dinner. We got on a train which went to Boston. It was then about 9 o'clock so we went to bed but the train did not leave till midnight."

The MacMillans stayed at the Hotel Touraine in Boston, where John took John, Jr. on a Cooke's tour that included Faneuil Hall, Old South Church, and Bunker Hill. At the Navy Yard, they saw the battleships *Michigan, Georgia,* and *Florida.* "A private on the Georgia told us that another private had stolen the captain's uniform and had been caught but got away," John, Jr. wrote. "The next morning we got a carriage and went to the boat."

D. D. McMillan in a wheelchair in his Chicago apartment with his wife Mary Jane, right, and his brother Ewen Hugh's widow, Esther McMillan

John H. MacMillan, Jr.

According to the ship's passenger list, Mr. and Mrs. J. H. MacMillan, Master John H. MacMillan, Master Cargill MacMillan, and their maid Elisa sailed for Naples from Boston on the White Star Line S.S *Republic* on Saturday, February 2, 1907. "By two o'clock all the visitors were ashore and the boat began to move," John, Jr. wrote. "As we got nearly off we suddenly saw about 200 people . . . all waving their handkerchiefs and hats and yelling. We watched them till they became an indistinct mass."

John, Jr. was a keen and observant traveler who delighted in foreign sights and local color: "The first day we saw land we were very glad and . . . we came to anchor in the harbor [at Ponta Delgada on the island of Sao Miguel in the Azores] and went ashore in small boats. When we landed we went to a flower battle where every one throws flowers. Several people from the boat took part in the battle. They hired carriages and got in the parade. The prize was won by a (carriage) wagon arranged with a birds nest made of sticks with children 5 or 6 years of age dressed up as birds."

Back on board the *Republic*, continuing his travelogue in engaging detail, my father described being seasick, eating his meals on deck, buying postal cards and stamps, being awakened at six one morning to see the lights on both the Spanish and African sides of the Straits of Gibraltar, and taking snapshots. On a side trip to Algiers (their maid Elisa had been born there, John, Jr. noted), he reported visiting a mosque, buying three Arab coins for a nickel from an Arab on the street, and looking in the stores. "The bread is so dirty that I would not touch it."

Fred and Emma Hanchette were waiting for them in Naples, which John, Jr. found "very large and poor and dirty." The Hanchettes now joined their tour through Europe. In Rome, Emma wrote: "In AM went to the forum with John, Jr., and he told us all about the place from his lecture he went to and did splendidly." Edna and Emma shopped for marble and shipped it back to La Crosse for the Cargill mansion.

Trooping through Venice, Florence, and Genoa, the MacMillans spent three months in Italy, until John, Sr. had to return in early May to the office in Minneapolis, where the first tremors of what would become the Panic of 1907 in the fall were beginning to be felt. Edna and the boys did not return home with him. John, Sr. was reluctant to leave them abroad, but Edna insisted; she wanted the boys to have French lessons, something both she and her husband considered important to their education. Elisa the maid remained behind with them, and Edna arranged lodging for the four of them in Geneva, Switzerland, where she enrolled John, Jr. at the Rosset School.

By the time John, Sr. reached Paris, he was already missing his family. "You don't know how crazy I am already to see you all," he wrote Edna from his room at the Grand Hotel. He had wanted to see Dr. Middleton, but the physician had moved to England, he said. At the Louvre, he didn't need a guide because "our training in Italy was all that was necessary." Prices were high in Paris, he felt, but he had purchased a combination aneroid thermometer and compass for his cousin John D. McMillan. He thought it would be nice for automobile trips because it would "show the height of any hill he goes up," barometric pressure, direction, and temperature. Telling Edna to cable him in Minneapolis, he said he hoped they would "all keep well and enjoy every minute of the time."

John never got used to the idea of Edna and the boys being in Europe by themselves. The boys caught whooping cough, and this worried him even more. In lengthy letters to Edna and "My Two Darling Boys," he included advice concerning their studies. "I think your idea of having Mlle. read to you every day is very good only I wouldn't overdo. . . . One should never get really tired at any kind of task and as soon as you feel that you are getting tired, you should stop at once or vary your exercise by doing the reading yourself or something of that kind."

When Edna sent him drawings the boys had made, he replied: "Tell John Jr. that his boat is very good but I should like him to draw something else. Have him draw from real life—trees, houses, or anything that strikes his fancy. . . . I don't want them to confine themselves to boats. Of course Cargill isn't interested in anything else and it may be harder to induce him to try other things, but John Jr. should be a little broader." (Boats remained my father's favorite subject, and he was still designing and drawing boats right up until the time he died.)

By early June, John, Sr. was wondering how long he could stand the separation. "I cannot enjoy a single thing. You know it worries me to have you having to associate with a lot of people that at home you wouldn't recognize in any way." If Edna would only come home, he wrote, he would arrange for French *and* German lessons for the boys. "You know the saving argument doesn't appeal to me anymore. . . . I would rather live *cheap* here with you than to have you live cheap over there."

While Edna and the boys remained abroad, Fred and Emma returned home from Europe in late May with astonishing news. Emma wanted to adopt a baby. John wrote to Edna that he and her mother didn't think it was a very good idea—that the Hanchettes were in no position to adopt a child, being "without a home, health or income." He also doubted that the Cargills could ever accept an adopted baby as their real grandchild. Emma persisted, however, and a few days later she and Ellen left for New York, where they checked in at the Waldorf.

Emma wrote in her diary that they saw a six-month-old baby girl the next day, who was "not pretty but very sweet and very fine family." They also went to Jersey City to see a nine-month-old baby. This second child was "very

Emma with her adopted daughter Ellen Cargill (Budley) Hanchette

"Plans calling for a lavish remodeling of the residence of W. W. Cargill at Twelfth and Cass streets have been completed and the work is well under way," reported the La Crosse Tribune *on January 12, 1906. "The big residence will be almost entirely reconstructed . . . and when completed Mr. Cargill will have the most palatial home in the city." Will Cargill is the man in the bowler in the right foreground.*

The large rented house at 410 Clifton Avenue, home to the John H. MacMillans for a year beginning in September 1907

beautiful," Emma wrote, "but I want the little six-month one." A few days later: "Went again to see the little baby and decided to take her and am very much satisfied with her. Very happy."

Emma and her mother picked up the baby just prior to the formal adoption proceedings on the morning of June 14. The judges kept them waiting more than two hours in court, but the baby was "good as gold," Emma wrote. She named the child Ellen Cargill Hanchette, but to the family she was always "Budley." (My father and his brother called her their little "buddy," which she grew up pronouncing "Budley.") In spite of John, Sr.'s misgivings, her grandparents worshiped her. In a letter to Edna in Europe, Ellen wrote: "She is a dear little darling and you will not wonder that Emma wanted her."

Ellen was still up to her ears remodeling the mansion. "The house is in such disorder, nothing is finished complete, only half done," she wrote to Edna in June. Her wrists were lame trying to make the elevator work, she was disgusted with a cheap-looking wooden mantel, and the garden fountain wouldn't be finished for two or three weeks. She thought that she should probably also sell the horses and build a garage with a gardener's cottage over it. It appeared that a garage was becoming a necessity. They had ordered a new black Stearns with red trim that Ellen had seen recently in New York, and also a limousine.

Edna and the boys had been on their own in Europe for more than two months when she finally gave in to my grandfather's pleas and returned home on the steamship *Teutonic* in mid-July. John, Jr. never became fluent in French—my father's French was always that of an eleven-year-old child—but he told me that he had liked Geneva so much that he later established Cargill's European headquarters there in the 1950s. Before returning to Minneapolis, Edna and the boys spent several weeks with her parents in La Crosse while John, Sr. looked for a house for them in Minneapolis.

In September the MacMillans moved to a two-and-a-half story colonial revival house designed by William Channing Whitney at 410 Clifton Avenue (rented for the grand sum of one hundred dollars a month), and John, Jr. enrolled in the first class at Blake School. Opened that year by William McKendree Blake, a graduate of De Pauw University in Greencastle, Indiana, Blake School was founded to prepare the sons of Minneapolis's new upper crust for prep school in the East. Schoolmaster Blake at first presided over classes in his white frame residence at 200 Ridgewood Avenue; in the spring of 1912, underwritten by prominent Minneapolis businessmen, work commenced on a new ninety-thousand-dollar school building on the Minnetonka trolley line. Blake School went on to become a MacMillan family tradition, and several of us have served on its board of trustees.

CHANGING OF THE GUARD

John H. MacMillan in his corner office on the fifth floor of the Chamber of Commerce Building about 1904. The window shades have been pulled for the photograph, hiding a generous view of downtown Minneapolis. Notice the oriental carpet, roll-top desk, two candlestick telephones, ink well, and spittoon.

Despite frequent bouts of poor health, John MacMillan made a respectable showing during his first few years in Minneapolis as chief executive of the Cargill Elevator Company. Esteemed and well-liked by his colleagues, he also turned good profits for the firm. Company earnings came in just under $300,000 his first three years, then jumped to over $400,000 for the 1906–07 crop year (July 1–June 30).

The widespread Panic of 1907 was squeezing even the Cargill Elevator Company by that fall, however, and John became particularly uneasy when the Pillsbury-Washburn Company in Minneapolis was forced into receivership. John blamed the Pillsbury problems on incompetent leadership and resolved to keep a strong hand at the tiller and expenses to a minimum. To the manager at Duluth, where Cargill was paying line employees 22½ cents an hour, he wrote: "There is no use of having any trouble with our men at this time of the year and if you have to pay them 25 cents an hour . . . you better do it and keep things working smoothly. Our entire profits will have to be made in the next two or three months, so we cannot afford to get tied up now. Then, after the first of January, if conditions are different, we can reduce wages."

Short-term financing needed to cover fall crop purchases that year was difficult to obtain, and John was shocked to be turned down by several money sources in Minneapolis. Will Cargill told him not to worry, that he could get all the money he wanted in La Crosse. The elder man proceeded to shake hands on some substantial loans in his hometown, but the Batavian National Bank in La Crosse later backed out of its agreement after the Knickerbocker Trust

114

Company in New York suspended operations on October 22, bringing the Panic to its nadir. Stunned into comprehension, Will wrote the next day to John, Sr., "This scare in New York may shut things up tighter than a clam."

In an unprecedented move, grain traders in Duluth including Cargill agreed among themselves to stop buying grain from farmers until the credit situation loosened up. John, Sr. explained to Will Cargill: "The salvation of the country depends on the movement of its crop and it seems a pity the movement should be interfered with, but at present it would seem . . . the farmers were better able to carry the load than anyone else . . . it is a necessity to force them to hold the grain until conditions become more settled."

Staying on top of business, John, Sr. also kept up with numerous friends and employees with whom he exchanged often lengthy, personal letters. During a two-month period at the depth of the depression, he wrote half a dozen times to a retired Pine Bluff employee, keeping him abreast of the latest news from Arkansas. The individual sent MacMillan and his family a shipment of apples from his farm in Michigan, for which John, Sr. thanked him on November 5: "I want to . . . tell you how very much we appreciate them. They are delicious and seem especially good coming, as they do, from your orchard."

In La Crosse, as 1907 wound down, Ellen Cargill, who had been suffering with a goiter since at least the previous Christmas, finally went to Rochester, Minnesota, for an operation at the end of October. She was wary of surgery, but John Sr.'s cousin Dr. Mamie McMillan assured her that doctors were experimenting on cases like hers with good results. Ellen, a heavy woman at two hundred pounds, suffered from heart trouble, but she came through the operation satisfactorily. She was still in the hospital and too uncomfortable to enjoy her fifty-second birthday on November 5 (when Edna and Emma gave her a string of diamonds and pearls); but she was back on her feet in her own unfinished home by December 15 to help organize a double birthday party for husband Will, turned sixty-three, and her darling adopted granddaughter Budley Hanchette, who was one.

"You should have seen her when she saw the doll [which John and Edna had sent Budley]," Ellen wrote Edna. "She pressed her little hands up to her heart [the way] she does when she loves you." Budley's other gifts, said Ellen, included a locket from her Cargill grandparents, a rocking horse from Fred Hanchette, a book From Will S. Cargill's wife May, a ball and blocks from George and William Cargill, and fur-lined mittens from Aunt Tassie. Budley would be the only girl among the Cargill grandchildren, and the family always made a great deal of her.

The day after the party calamity struck at the Cargill house in the shape of a fire that destroyed the family barn. Austen Cargill and his friend Myron Savage (who would be Austen's best man when Austen married Anne Ray in 1913) had

Ellen Cargill (Budley) Hanchette with her nurse, Bertha Husse

The W. W. Cargill family garage prior to the fire

been working in the garage portion of the barn when a light bulb burst into flames. It all happened so fast that the boys were unable to push out any of the family's three cars—the Stearns, a Packard, and an Apperson runabout. The carriages and horses and cattle were all rescued before the main part of the barn caught fire.

Austen sustained burns about the neck and face, and Myron on his arm, but neither boy was seriously injured. Damage to the cars and barn was estimated at fifteen thousand dollars, part of which was covered by insurance. According to an article in the *La Crosse Tribune*, the fire also destroyed more than thirty-five years of Will Cargill's early business records that he had stored in the barn. John MacMillan would have preferred to celebrate Christmas that year at his own home in Loring Park, but fire or no fire, he took his family as usual to La Crosse for the holidays. On December 30, Santa Claus addressed this typewritten letter to seven-year-old Cargill at 410 Clifton Avenue:

> My dear Cargill:
>
> I did not receive your letter in time to get the things for you before you went to La Crosse.
>
> I have not seen you since you left the Plaza Hotel. I always rode around in Loring Park, and could see you thru the windows, and I miss you from the Plaza.
>
> I wish next Christmas you would not go to La Crosse, but would stay at home, so I could bring the things you wanted Christmas night or Christmas Eve and might possibly get a chance to see you.
>
> You must have received a lot of nice presents from somewhere else, for certainly you have not asked very much from me. I left some presents at La Crosse which

Greycourt at La Crosse bore almost no resemblance to its first incarnation as a red brick Queen Anne house.

I think must have been for you, but I could not tell for sure, for there were so many people there.

I am sending you a pencil, tablet and some stamps, and if you want anything more, just send me another letter in care of Loring Park, for I shall be back again if we have any good sleighing. I rode around four or five nights trying to find out where you lived.

Santa Claus

Following the holidays and their annual winter trip to California, Will and Ellen Cargill returned in April 1908 to the comforts of a home touted as "the finest in the Northwest." The *La Crosse Tribune* estimated Will had spent $200,000 on the new palace Ellen dubbed "Greycourt." The marble for the front entrance hall was from Italy, the walnut for the reception hall from England, and the mahogany for the library from Africa. Hand-cut velvet, silk brocades, and hand-tooled leather covered the walls; the floors were parquet, spread with specially loomed carpets; the chandeliers, Waterford crystal. There were six fire-places and seven tiled bathrooms, each with an oversize tub. Ensconced in an alcove with a stained-glass window at the top of the grand staircase was a pipe organ that no one in the family could play.

The formal dining room with its massive carved furniture and bas-relief friezes of native wildfowl, flowers, and fruits was the work of German wood-carvers from the famed Hackner Studio in La Crosse. (Austen Cargill always said that he had been sent out to shoot the ducks they used for models.) The ceiling in the library was gold leaf, and the glassed-in parlor at the room's north end looked out over formal Italian gardens with red tile walks and a goldfish pool bordered by lilies.

Over the years, stories about the Cargill mansion and its lavish garden became the stuff of legend. Looking back in 1959, the *La Crosse Tribune* described the large ornamental fountain that had stood in the garden "with three lions' heads at the top where the water came out." These heads, reported the paper, "had real rubies for eyes, the jewels being taken out each evening and replaced each morning." In fact, the fountain was real, but the rubies were a figment of someone's imagination. Surrounding and enclosing the Cargill grounds was a wrought iron fence mounted on a low concrete wall. Gossips said that Ellen had wanted a high privacy wall, but since Will was of a more open frame of mind, they compromised on this combination wall and fence, the only remnant of the house and garden that remains on the property today.

Greycourt was the Cargills' last hurrah, a grand gesture marking the close of an age. None of the family lived there very long. More and less than a house, the residence became the final, fitting stage for the last act of an epic drama. Ellen's grand parties there were but brief, concluding moments of gaiety

The backyard garden at Greycourt

that rang down the curtain on Will Cargill's generation. Ironically, the completion of Greycourt signaled a changing of the guard. One after another, Tassie Stowell, Duncan McMillan, Will Cargill, and Ellen Cargill all died within a two-year period.

Aunt Tassie (Clara Stowell) was the first to go, and her death was completely unexpected. Only months after moving into Greycourt, in late summer, Tassie took the train to Minneapolis to undergo surgery for an unspecified ailment at Northwestern Hospital. Writing to her on new stationery engraved "Greycourt," Ellen reassured her: "Remember all I said now and don't *worry* or be *afraid of anything*. You will just be mad at yourself when its all over that you worried so. Now please do as I say and be just as unconcerned as you would to take a dose of castor oil. I am telling you the truth."

Tassie came through the surgery, but she died suddenly when her heart failed several days later on August 6, 1908. She was fifty-nine years old and had lived with Will and Ellen Cargill from the time they were married. "She was regarded by the children of the family with almost the same affection as their parents and had been devoted to them throughout their whole lives," said the *La Crosse Chronicle*. Known in La Crosse as Mrs. C. E. Stowell, although Stowell was her maiden name, Tassie was survived by her son Clarence Stowell, who was working for Cargill interests at Pine Bluff.

In Chicago, Duncan D. McMillan died at his Woodlawn Avenue home two months later on October 15, 1908. Having lived long enough to see his son Will earn his Ph.D. in mathematics and astronomy from the University of Chicago in August, Duncan was seventy-one. The cause of death was listed as apoplexy. The *La Crosse Leader-Press* stated that the former La Crosse lumberman and banker had been incapacitated since suffering a paralyzing stroke "some time ago."

Alongside Duncan D.'s obituary in the *Milwaukee Sentinel* on October 16, an article in the adjacent column stated that Will S. Cargill had been chosen president of the new American Herford (*sic*) Cattle Breeders Association in Kansas City, Missouri. It was only an ironic coincidence that the two articles ran side by side, but it was, of course, the same Will S. Cargill who was living in the mansion D. D. McMillan had built and forfeited in La Crosse.

Duncan's family accompanied his body to La Crosse, where the funeral, conducted by longtime family friend Reverend W. D. Thomas, took place from his daughter Mary Isabella Rowles's residence. Pallbearers included Duncan's nephew Jim Taylor (his widow Mary Jane's sister Elizabeth McCrea Taylor's son), Fred Hanchette, and Will S. Cargill. He was buried alongside his infant son Allan Morrison and Mary Jane's mother Elizabeth McCrea in the family plot at Oak Grove Cemetery. The family never erected a monument; only a simple, flat stone marks my great-grandfather's grave.

One year to the day that Duncan McMillan was buried, his closest friend Will Cargill died in La Crosse on October 17, 1909. His death at age sixty-four shocked the community. Insiders might have predicted it.

For the past couple of years Will had been spreading himself thin with outside projects, investing in a copper mine that failed, the La Crosse and Southeastern Railroad, timberlands in Mexico and British Columbia, and a massive land development and irrigation project in Montana that was by far the most costly. Will S. had talked his father into becoming the principal financier for this last; begun under different management (like so many of Will Cargill's enterprises), it was a gigantic undertaking that appealed to Will Cargill's idealistic vision. The "Valier project," as the several companies connected with it came to be known collectively, was organized to purchase a vast area of unwatered land in northwestern Montana, build dams, reservoirs, and canals to water it, and then sell or rent the land to potential farmers and ranchers. In the process, it almost brought down the house of Cargill.

In Minneapolis, credit was still tight in 1908 when John MacMillan apprised Will Cargill that his needs would be substantial for that fall, writing, "I feel a little bit anxious to extend our financial arrangements in the East." Always the optimist, Will Cargill replied: "Received your letter this morning in regard to credit, etc., which of course I knew and would like to have a reserve on hand and if [the Valier, Montana project] comes out half the way I think it will, we will have it, and if I could sell off the Railroad or the Mexican property, we would not have to question it. I am not going into anything new on any account."

Cargill Elevator Company profits had dropped to $332,000 for the 1907–1908 crop year; the next year would see them decline to $208,000. Needing cash, Will considered selling some of his Sawyer and Austin lands, but John MacMillan dissuaded him, reminding Will that he had potentially valuable bauxite deposits on the property: "As I have told you a good many times I think it is one of the most valuable things you own, if not the most valuable [and] the only way to get the real value out of it is to . . . wait for a few years until the use of aluminum becomes more general and the effects of this panic are worn away."

It was full speed ahead in Montana, however, where Will Cargill and Peter Valier, the former superintendent of the La Crosse and Southeastern Railroad, were beginning construction of a new railroad to bring in and serve settlers. The Montana Western Railroad would connect Conrad, Montana, and the new town of Valier, Montana, twenty-seven miles to the northwest. Valier was wholly owned by a syndicate of La Crosse men headed by Will Cargill.

In April 1909 a gleeful Will Cargill informed his brother Jim that "if we sell 26,000 acres this Summer we pay for the whole shooting match and the rest is all velvet." Later in a letter to John, Sr., he wrote: "the Montana proposition . . . is a great big proposition. They have 105 teams at work and about 250 men and Will [S., the onsite manager on whom most of the blame would be laid for the project's many difficulties] is starting the Railroad. . . . After the dam is complete the teams on the dam will go on to the ditching work and get that so they can furnish water in July to all the deeded land."

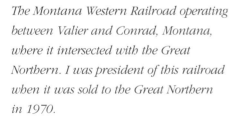

The Montana Western Railroad operating between Valier and Conrad, Montana, where it intersected with the Great Northern. I was president of this railroad when it was sold to the Great Northern in 1970.

John H. MacMillan, Sr. inspecting corn for silage in Valier, Montana

Anticipating that the territory between Conrad and Billings, Montana, would soon become a great grain producing territory, Will had made application to the Billings and Northern Railway for sidetracks and elevator sites at several points along the road including Conrad, Splonkop, Stanford, Judith Gap, and Broadview. "This is, perhaps, the most important improvement made in the history of the territory now covered by the Billings & Northern railway," observed the *La Crosse Tribune*. "The elevators for the storage of grain are an indicator of what the new country is to be within the few years to come."

John, Sr. was himself enthusiastic about the project and went to Montana to hire contractors to build the country elevators and establish implement houses at the towns. Back in Minneapolis, he and his brother Dan and Will Cargill filed incorporation papers for the Montana Central Elevator Company on September 9, 1909. Capitalized at fifty thousand dollars, the firm planned to build five or six country elevators that year and gradually extend into the developing grain producing territory.

Early in October, Will Cargill and Peter Valier took the train to Conrad, Montana, to be present for land drawings in the town and to inspect the Montana properties; Will could no longer ignore the enormous and costly engineering problems that were plaguing the project. In August he had written to one of his lenders in Chicago that "it has taken considerable more money than we expected," and his bankers in Boston were expressing concern about the large liabilities he was incurring.

What actually happened upon Will Cargill's arrival in Montana is unclear. Met by his son Will S., the elder Cargill had examined only part of the properties when he was taken suddenly ill by what was variously described as indigestion, a stomach ailment, or an acute gastrointestinal attack. Perhaps what he saw and heard was just too much for him. Starting for home immediately, he arrived by train in St. Paul where Ellen and Dr. Maine were waiting to take him back to La Crosse on the steamer *Ellen*.

The next day Ellen wrote Edna from Greycourt that they had tied up at Wabasha, Minnesota, in a severe storm. By the time they reached La Crosse a day later, both she and Dr. Maine were sick with the flu. The Cargills' chauffeur met them at the levee with their automobile, and Ellen conferred with a second doctor named Christiansen, reporting to Edna: "Papa is better but has some fever, but his mind is more clear. Christiansen looked pretty sober and I know he fears his kidneys."

Dreading the worst, the family gathered at Greycourt. Edna arrived from Minneapolis, and Austen returned home from Ithaca, New York, where he was attending Cornell University. Emma, however, was in Davos-Dorf, Switzerland, where Fred was confined to a sanatorium. Will seemed to improve over the next few days, but on Saturday, October 16, he became delirious, and he died the

W. W. Cargill with his five grandchildren. The two boys standing are my father John Hugh MacMillan, Jr., and his cousin William W. Cargill. In the foreground, left to right, are George Cargill, Ellen (Budley) Hanchette, and Cargill MacMillan. William and George Cargill were the sons of Will S. and May McMillan Cargill.

next morning at three o'clock. The doctors said that he had been recovering from an infection of the digestive organs when pneumonia set in, causing his death. The *Leader-Press* reported that the cable notifying Emma of her father's death had arrived in record time, taking only about thirty minutes.

John, Jr. and Cargill MacMillan were in Minneapolis with their father when they were all awakened by a phone call from La Crosse. Jim Taylor told John, Sr. that Will Cargill had died an hour earlier. "I shall never forget the time from then till daybreak," John, Jr. wrote in his diary. "I went to bed again but I did not sleep. I heard Father walking up and down in his room. At 6 I got up and we tried to eat breakfast but I could eat nothing."

John, Sr. hurried the boys to La Crosse by train. On the ride down, the three of them had to sit in the smoking part of the car, John, Jr. wrote. "When we got to the house Mother and Grandma were all in. We met Mother in the guest chamber. As she saw us she suddenly broke down. I have never seen her so cut up. We ate at Uncle Will's that noon [Will S. Cargill's house across the street]. It was terrible. Everybody was so silent and grave and the very air seemed to say that Grandpa was dead."

Hundreds of people attended the simple afternoon funeral rites conducted at the Cargill home by Reverend D. C. Jones, pastor of the First Presbyterian Church. There was no music. Banks and businesses closed during the services, and members of the La Crosse Board of Trade attended as a group. A great cortege followed Will's coffin to Oak Grove Cemetery where it was placed temporarily in his brother Sam's granite mausoleum until a new mausoleum could be built to receive it.

Ellen Cargill faded quickly following her husband's death and died less than six months later on Good Friday, March 25, 1910. Edna had gone to La Crosse to help take care of her mother in late January, and John brought the two boys down in March. John, Jr. wrote that the sight of his grandmother shocked him: "She seemed so white. She was raving most of the time from the morphine."

"While I was there," wrote fourteen-year-old John, Jr., "I rarely went into Grandma's room because I somehow felt that I wasn't wanted. . . . All of Friday morning I played with a cart we made. And in the afternoon I went to Joe Coleman's and I read *Under the Sea to the South Pole* and part of Mark Twain's *Tom Sawyer Abroad*. I then came home and sat in the library. In a few minutes Father and Cousin Jim Taylor and Uncle Fred came in and they had barely been seated when we heard some one running down the front stairs and Miss Rhuman, the nurse, came to the large door and said out of breath and with a rather scared look on her face, 'She's going.'

"Father and Uncle Fred jumped up and ran upstairs to Grandma's room. Cousin Jim set to pacing the floor and I found myself reading altho I didn't know a word of what I read. . . . It was seven minutes to six when Miss Rhuman came in and at six or about two minutes to, George [his cousin from across the street] came in and said, 'Don't read.' Those five minutes seemed like five hours. At two minutes past six Father came in and said, 'She is all over.'

"It was horrible. I thought I should break down. Father in a few minutes told me to go up to Mother which I did. In the meantime he and Cousin Jim telephoned and made out lists. I can remember very little of the time following Father's return to the library and Dinner which we had at eight. I seemed dazed."

The grand mausoleum planned for Will Cargill was never built. After Ellen died, his coffin was removed from Sam's mausoleum, and he and Ellen were buried together at Oak Grove Cemetery in a Cargill family plot near many of their McMillan neighbors. With Will and Ellen Cargill died an era. Amidst the complexity of Will's far-flung business enterprise, the pendulum of fortune had already begun to swing toward a MacMillan hegemony.

Ellen Stowell Cargill

COUNTING PENNIES

*"Father and Cargill in the living room,
Dec. 31, 1911," one of several snapshots
John, Jr. took while he was home for
Christmas vacation and pasted in his
Andover album*

On Christmas Eve 1909, the *Minneapolis Journal* reported that Northwestern National Life had issued the Cargill Elevator Company a half-million-dollar policy on the life of Cargill vice president and manager John H. MacMillan. "The MacMillan policy just issued is the fourth big deal of its kind in this city," the insurance company said. "A few weeks ago the Northwestern placed a like amount on the life of A. C. Loring, president of the Pillsbury Flour Mills Company." A. C. was the only child of Minneapolis miller and parks enthusiast Charles M. Loring.

In ordinary times, the publicity surrounding John's life insurance would have been good public relations for the Cargill Elevator Company, pointing up prudent financial planning. The idea of protecting business interests by insuring chief officials was an excellent one that was gaining ground in the Northwest. In 1900 Minneapolis grain man Frank Peavey had taken out a million-dollar "key man" policy naming his company as beneficiary. Peavey died a year later, after paying only one $48,000 premium. Coming when it did, however, shortly after Will Cargill's death, news of the MacMillan policy underscored the firm's present predicament.

Will Cargill's death in 1909 wreaked havoc in his grain business. He had died a wealthy man, but his estate inherited business debts large enough to threaten the dismantling of his life's work. He had also died intestate. Under Wisconsin law, his entire estate passed to his widow. When Ellen died, the estate was divided equally among the four Cargill children, William Samuel Cargill, Edna Cargill MacMillan, Emma Cargill Hanchette, and Austen Stowell Cargill.

W. W. Cargill was still conducting his business from the second floor of the building in the right foreground—the La Crosse National Bank Building on the corner of Main and Third Streets—at the time of his death. Directly across Main Street, in the left foreground, is the Post Office Block where the McMillans once conducted their logging business.

Clive Talbot (C. T.) Jaffray, one of the Northwest's leading financiers, began his career as a messenger in a Canadian bank. After moving to this country, he took a job in 1895 as a cashier at the First National Bank of Minneapolis and soon worked his way up to president. Jaffray was an avid golfer and helped found the Minikahda Country Club to which John MacMillan belonged.

Outside accountants in November 1909 placed a value of $6.7 million on the total assets of all the W. W. Cargill enterprises. In addition, his personal estate was valued at $1 million. With the exception of the Cargill Elevator Company, however, which had a net worth of more than $2 million and operating capital of $1.5 million, most of the Cargill assets were producing niggardly returns. These included the La Crosse and Southeastern Railway and the Sawyer and Austin Lumber Company. The immense Montana project was still under construction, and Will's own W. W. Cargill Company in La Crosse, which had absorbed much of the costs connected with his outside projects, was in acute trouble.

Sometimes without even bothering to enter it in his books, Will Cargill had borrowed heavily through brokers and banks to finance one enterprise after another. The mountain of debts that surfaced flabbergasted John MacMillan. "I knew nothing about the finances of La Crosse until about two weeks after Mr. Cargill's death," he wrote to a friend. "[He] used those companies as though they were personal matters." More than one analyst has concluded that these debts would no doubt have been easily liquidated in the normal course of business, but once Will Cargill died, his creditors began calling their notes as they became due.

Playing for time, Will S. Cargill, now in charge at La Crosse, tried to siphon funds from the Minneapolis end of the business to keep the creditors at bay, but John MacMillan refused to let him raid the Elevator Company's treasury. With the Cargill Elevator Company itself at stake, my grandfather called in the banks, and a creditors' committee headed by First National Bank president C. T. Jaffray was formed. Other members of the committee were Thomas Baxter of the brokerage firm of Bond and Goodwin in Boston and La Crosse lumberman Frank P. Hixon. Hixon was also one of the executors of Will Cargill's estate, along with Will S. Cargill and John MacMillan.

The Security Bank Building at Second Avenue South and Fourth Street in Minneapolis about 1908

Most of the assets of the W. W. Cargill Company would have to be liquidated, but John MacMillan convinced the creditors' committee that the Cargill Elevator Company in Minneapolis was sound and should not be sacrificed. Will Cargill had always intended that his son Will S. would succeed him, but the Valier morass had cast the son's business acumen and even his honesty into question. Instead, the creditors turned to John MacMillan who assumed control of all Cargill interests.

On November 18, 1909, a scant month after Will Cargill's death, the *Minneapolis Journal* announced that the Cargill Company was moving its headquarters to the Security Bank building in Minneapolis. Despite extensive business that necessitated maintaining offices at Green Bay, Minneapolis, Duluth, Little Rock, St. Louis, Kansas City, and other points, the Cargill headquarters had always remained at La Crosse. The financial business was handled there, the paper stated, but "hereafter this will be done in Minneapolis."

To facilitate the reorganization of the Cargill Company in Minneapolis, John MacMillan helped form the Cargill Securities Company (later Waycrosse, Inc.) to take over the indebtedness of the W. W. Cargill Company in La Crosse as well as its assets, which included more than thirty elevators and several warehouses. The incorporators besides John, Sr. were C. T. Jaffray of Minneapolis and John's cousin James B. Taylor of La Crosse. Cargill Securities' principal asset was Will Cargill's Elevator Company stock (he owned eighty-three percent of the company), against which it issued $2,500,000 in bonds to the creditors. These gold notes carried a maturity date of January 1, 1917. Only when they were paid in full would the crisis be over and the future of the Cargill Elevator Company assured.

Now began the sale of expendable Cargill-held assets. Chief among them was the Sawyer and Austin Lumber Company in Pine Bluff, which the Long-Bell Lumber Company acquired in 1911 at a sacrifice price of something over $1 million, with Cargill retaining the mineral rights to certain portions of the Arkansas property and the firm's timber holdings in British Columbia and Mexico. This was a shrewd piece of business on John MacMillan's part. In 1912 Cargill entered into a lucrative lease agreement with the Aluminum Company of America to mine huge bauxite deposits on the Pine Bluff property, eventually netting royalties amounting to more than $2 million. After most of the bauxite was mined off, the Aluminum Company bought the remaining tailings for a lump sum of $500,000.

Up in British Columbia, timberlands on the mainland and Vancouver Island, comprising ninety so-called "limits" of 640 acres, brought more than $1.5 million. In Mexico, where political unrest made Cargill's timberlands in the State of Chihuahua unsaleable at the time, the government later confiscated Cargill's more than 240,000 acres of pine timberlands in the 1920s, only to repay the company for them more than two decades later. With the passage of the

Work at Valier Is Shut Down

Financial difficulties has caused a complete suspension of the irrigation works west of town. All work was suspended this week and it is given out that a receiver will be appointed to take charge of the affairs of the Conrad Land and water Company.

There was a meeting in Valier this week of those interested and from what can be learned Messrs. Cargill and Withee have withdrawn from the enterprise and on the appointment of a receiver the work will be again started up and completed by the Cargill estate.

J. H. McMillian, administrator of the Cargill estate and John Harrington were here looking after the interests of the Cargill estate and Mr. Conrad's interests was looked after by Jas. T. Stanford at the meeting.

Conrad Observer, *July 21, 1910*

Mexican Claims Act of 1941, designed mainly to reimburse the owners of confiscated American oil fields, Cargill attorney James Dorsey filed a claim for the Cargill holdings and was awarded $300,000, Cargill's cost plus interest.

The Valier project was too involved to be sold off easily or quickly. When it was finally liquidated some four decades later, the venture would prove very profitable to Will Cargill's heirs, but in the 1910s the scheme appeared a grand failure. No great rush of settlers had developed, and only about half of the available lands had been sold, most of it at prices far less than expected. There had also been some dishonesty and fraud connected with the enterprise. While he was at Yale, my father wrote a term paper using company records in which he alleged that Will S. Cargill had deliberately misled his father Will Cargill as to its particulars—that Will S. and his partner W. W. Withee had made contracts that they couldn't live up to, and that no satisfactory accounting was ever made for large sums of money. "The elimination of these two gentlemen was imperative, once the true state of affairs had been uncovered," John, Jr. wrote.

All of this regrouping came about at the cost of considerable family discord. Following one meeting that Will S. Cargill had avoided, John H. saw him outside the hotel and went out to speak with him. "At first he turned his head but I stuck my hand directly in front of him and he finally very gingerly shook it," John wrote Edna. "He would only answer in monosyllables and fortunately Frank Hixon came along and relieved the tension."

Because of his financial double-dealing, and also because he had gotten himself involved with the wife of his partner Withee in Montana, Will S. was cast in the role of black sheep in the family. His relationship with Mrs. Withee did not last, but neither did he return to his wife May in La Crosse. The three remaining Cargill heirs—Edna, Emma, and Austen—accepted and wholeheartedly supported John MacMillan in his new role as family patriarch and head of Cargill operations.

At the Cargill Elevator Company, an entirely different stance was adopted. Heretofore, the company had succeeded by pursuing an aggressive policy of expansion, adding to its holdings year by year. Guided now by the creditors' committee, it was forced to assume a conservative posture. Every outlay had to be approved by the banks; there was no margin for risk-taking. The 1945 Cargill history characterizes these years as ones of "hard work and hardships, with difficulties which could only be overcome by a firm hand and a strong heart."

Acting in concert, the whole family tightened its belts, holding the line on unnecessary expenditures. My grandfather actually counted every penny, both at home and at the office, sometimes writing creditors concerning errors or discrepancies that amounted to less than a dollar. The net result was that Cargill came through these trying years very successfully. John MacMillan had been right about

127

keeping the grain side of the business unimpaired: Cargill posted dividends during the years 1911 through 1915 of 20, 25, 30, 16, and 15 percent respectively. Due to my grandfather's ceaseless efforts, the creditors were paid in full in 1916.

My father John, Jr. was in his last year at Blake School when his grandparents Will and Ellen Cargill died. Judging by his diary, John, Jr. was a well-adjusted, reasonably healthy, exuberant teenager, crazy for outdoor sports, conscientious about his studies (which that year included French, German, Latin, rhetoric, and history), and a budding young scientist—although he sometimes carried things too far to suit his father. "This evening I arranged a wire on the door knob with my coil so that when I pressed my key one would get a shock," he wrote late one night in January 1910. "We gave father one and he declared that if we did anymore things like that he would take away my electrical stuff."

In an era before radio and television, John, Jr. collected stamps, played baseball and football at Blake, skated and skied in winter, took an interest in the family business ("Uncle Daniel [said] that Cargill elevator has three hundred fifty elevators that average 25,000 bushels each"), and chummed around with Paul Clifford, his cousin Howard McMillan, Dave and Charlie Winton, Lewis Barbour, Jack Sprague, and Martin Bovey. The latter had "the cutest little sister named Ruth. She told me that Mademoiselle taught her French and Fraulein taught her German. They were the same person." Paul Clifford was later my father's best man when he married my mother at Aunt Emma's in California.

George Bishop Lane came to Minneapolis from Vermont after beginning his career as a bank clerk. Like John MacMillan, Lane golfed at the Minikahda Club.

Penning many of his diary entries in cipher, Dick Tracy fashion, John, Jr. randomly converted both routine and what could be deemed classified information to code. Shortly after Will Cargill died: "I learned that the amount of grandfather's debt was three million nine hundred thousand dollars." On January 21, 1910: "Yesterday Lewis [Barbour] agreed with his mother to be home at half past five and he was home at six. The Lanes made him eat bread and milk for dinner and go to bed right afterwards while they had company for dinner."

George and Nellie Lane were my grandparents' best friends on Clifton Avenue. Lewis Barbour was Nellie's son by an earlier marriage. George Lane was a founder of Lane, Piper and Jaffray investment brokers, which later became Piper Jaffray and Hopwood. In 1909 he built a mansion designed by William Channing Whitney at 309 Clifton Avenue for $109,000, a sum that bought quite a lot of house at the time. In 1971 newswoman Barbara Flanagan interviewed the Lanes' former chauffeur Walter J. Upgren for an article in the *Minneapolis Star*. Upgren told her about his first New Year's Eve on the job, when the Lanes were going to a party at the Eugene Carpenters' across the street. "I backed out our driveway, backed to the Carpenters' front door, let them out and then drove back into our driveway," Upgren said. "Nobody walked to parties on Clifton."

Besides Upgren, the Lanes employed a caretaker, a cook, and three maids, all of whom helped with parties at the house. "In those days," Upgren continued, "the invitation said 7:00 P.M. and every guest was there. One cocktail was served and everybody sat down to dinner—usually five or six courses—at 7:15 P.M. After dinner, the men went to the billiard room for cigars, brandy and coffee. The ladies went to the living room. Later, they all played bridge or whist."

In the early months of 1910, when Edna was spending weeks at a time in La Crosse with her dying mother, John, Jr. sometimes stayed with his Uncle Dan

The MacMillans' chauffeur Alvin in the family's Apperson limousine, 1911

John, Jr.'s 1909–1910 journal, portions of which he penned in cipher

MacMillan. Less than a year earlier, Dan had married a woman named Amber Belle Hamilton, with whom he was very much in love. The two were renting a house on South Colfax Avenue in Minneapolis, but Amber Belle had departed for Europe. It would eventually come out that Amber Belle was a clever con woman who had married several wealthy men in succession. Dan knew when he married her that she was involved in a bigamy scandal, but he believed her to be the injured party. John, Jr. wrote that Dan had "a red cockerel spaniel," which he described as "the finest dog of his kind west of Chicago."

Uncle Dan prided himself on being a thinker, and he and my father sat up evenings discussing a wide variety of subjects. "[Uncle Dan] spoke to me seriously about . . . the corruption and the money grabbing that is going on," John, Jr. wrote in February. "I agree with him in that most of the large fortunes are made by dishonesty and luck. (I don't think that luck plays as large a part as he thinks.) He spoke enthusiastically about married life [which turned out very badly for Dan]. I think as he does that the country is the only place. The farmer is a producer and he gets away from the vices of the city of which even I see. The quiet of the country is the only thing and our modern conveniences bring one in close touch with the city."

One night they discussed mental telepathy: "Uncle Dan thought that as in ancient times art and war were the things striven after and that as now and in the past the physical sciences are being developed so in the future the telepathic world will be developed. He thinks that if the foremost scientists in Europe believe in it there must be something in it. I firmly believe that one mind can affect another at a distance. Friday night, January 28, when Mother came home from LaX [La Crosse] I couldn't sleep and so got awfully restless about 11 o'clock. I then got up and walked to the window, a thing I never do and saw a carriage. I knew instantly that it was Mother altho she had not wired or written or telephoned and I went down and let her in. I have had similar experiences with Father."

Austen Cargill was now living with the John MacMillans on Clifton Avenue. After losing both his parents within the year, Austen had left Cornell and moved to Minneapolis, eager to begin work in the family business. "Uncle Austen . . . is working in the office as a bookkeeper," John, Jr. wrote in his diary. "He has his car here too." The next year, when he was twenty-three, Austen Cargill became the Cargill Elevator Company's youngest director. Dan MacMillan was voted a director in 1913, and until Dan's death more than a quarter century later, John MacMillan, Dan MacMillan, and Austen Cargill were the official tripartite hierarchy at Cargill.

Austen took my father to see his first aeroplane and dirigible at the highly publicized Twin City Aviation Meet held June 22–25, 1910, at the Minnesota state fairgrounds. Billed as a historic event, it was described by the *Minneapolis Sunday Tribune* as "the first opportunity of actually witnessing man's conquest of the air" in the Northwest. Its star attraction was Glenn Curtiss, who "does not look upon flight merely as a sport, but as a means of passenger transit, a means of commercial utility and a possible element in war."

"I shall never forget the sensation I had when I saw Curtiss rise off the ground," John, Jr. wrote. "We had barely gotten in our seats when a low black thing at the north end of the field began to sputter and a propeller began to revolve. The sputter increased to a roar and the black thing leapt forward at the same instant the cryer cried 'He's off.' The aeroplane ran for perhaps a hundred to two hundred feet and then suddenly slanted upwards and went up at an angle of perhaps 20 degrees [until it reached an altitude of] about 300 feet high and then it flew over for about a half mile and then returned and passed over the grandstand at about a hundred feet high.

"None of the other aviators rose more than ten or 12 feet. Curtiss had an 8 cylinder motor so he got up but the other men having only 4 cylinder motors failed to fly well. . . . I also saw Barney Oldfield in his lightning Benz go 4 miles [on a circular dirt track in] 3.32 [minutes] flat. He beat the world's record by 10 seconds." Oldfield had been the first man to drive a mile in less than a minute in 1902. Interviewed at the fairgrounds, he told a reporter for the *Minneapolis Morning Tribune* that he felt that a 40-second mile (90 m.p.h.) would one day be possible. At the time of the meet, the paper stated, his machine was "the fastest of all moving things," surpassing trains, birds, and aeroplanes. Curtiss was averaging slightly under 60 m.p.h. in his aeroplane.

In the fall John, Jr. went east to Phillips Academy in Andover, Massachusetts. Pushing himself beyond everyone's expectations, he had graduated from Blake at age fourteen after finishing his last year and a half in six months. Edna hoped that he would be accepted at Hotchkiss, where Lewis Barbour was going. She hired tutors who drilled him all summer in algebra, geometry, English, and Latin, but he apparently applied too late to Hotchkiss. His mother accompanied him to Andover on the train and helped him settle into his private room on the third floor in Williams Hall.

Making friends easily, my father pasted photographs of his classmates in his diary—boys named Dudley C. Brandenburg, William Reed Rodgers, Willard Wright, Frank Trevor Hogg, and Stuart Baker Emerson. "Nearly all the boys here use words like H___ and d___, but I haven't heard anyone but Emerson use any worse language," he wrote. His first-year classes included arithmetic, algebra, Latin, German, French, and English, in which he made decent but not outstanding grades.

His first year at boarding school, John, Jr. kept careful track of his income and expenses in a ledger titled "My Year's Expense." John, Sr. sent him monthly checks for $100 to cover his board and books and incidentals (John, Jr. listed football pants, chapel, tennis shoes, tennis balls, shoe blacking, tooth

This advertisement for the Twin City Aviation Meet appeared in the Minneapolis Sunday Tribune, *June 19, 1910.*

John, Jr. "studying hard (?) with 'Titusville John' in background."

John, Jr.'s meal ticket at Andover. On the back of it he noted: "Bought Thursday, September 28, 1910. Last punch taken Friday noon, Oct. 14, 1910."

brush, moving pictures, hot chocolate, garters, collars, handkerchiefs, and *Saturday Evening Post*). Once when my father purchased a raffle ticket for twenty-five cents, he recorded winning five dollars. Nonetheless, he was usually short of cash.

This, of course, annoyed my grandfather, who was a stickler when it came to careful money management. "You know what you are allowed and you should live within your allowance and always keep enough ahead to pay your requirements," he chided John, Jr. "That should be both a matter of principle and honor and you will always be in trouble all through life if you do not observe it."

"Don't ever get thinking that I am rich for I am not," he told him. "It is all I can do to educate you boys and live in comfort ourselves and any calamity like my health breaking down, business reverses and the like might make it necessary at any time for you to earn your own living."

While my father was away at school, his family moved to 317 Clifton Avenue in March 1911. (This ended their peregrinations in Loring Park until 1929, when they lived briefly at 510 Groveland before moving to the Minneapolis suburb of Orono.) When he came home on spring break, John, Jr. wrote in his diary: "We have moved across the street into the Sikes house where the Wintons lived. It is such a change but I am not sure but what I like our old house, Mrs. Hall's, better because it is so small. This is the fourth house we've been in on Clifton Ave., the Hay [at 321] Mrs. Passmore's [410], Mrs. Hall's [326], and the Sikes now."

The frame and timbers Sikes house had something of a Swiss chalet look to it. Topped by a third-floor ballroom, it had been built in 1896 for leather belting manufacturer Simeon R. Sikes at a cost of ten thousand dollars. This house remains standing in the 1990s, although it was damaged by

"The house in Mpls. –20 degrees. Dec. 30" from John, Jr.'s Andover album. The MacMillans had moved to this house at 317 Clifton Avenue in March 1911 while John, Jr. was away at school.

fires in 1948 and 1961. Following the last fire, it was converted into eleven small apartments.

John MacMillan was an attentive parent and good correspondent who kept in close touch with John, Jr. at Andover and later at Yale, writing him weekly epistles that sometimes ran to a dozen pages. "I got your letter," John, Jr. wrote to his father on September 16, 1910, shortly after arriving at Andover. "It was the finest letter that I ever got. I will try to do always as you would want me to do. I shall always keep it." This particular letter is now lost, but there is considerable correspondence between these two from this period in our family papers.

John, Sr.'s letters kept John, Jr. current on family activities, but they went far beyond that, often digressing into lectures about business, politics, world affairs, and later, after the United States entered World War I, patriotism. In October 1912, when Theodore Roosevelt was running for president on the Bull Moose Progressive party ticket, John, Sr. wrote: "There is no doubt in my mind that he is much the greatest man in political life at the present time, and I feel grateful . . . that he has been spared to his country in spite of that attempt on his life. Frankly, I haven't fully determined how I shall vote but you rest assured that no mere sentiment of business life will ever determine my vote. If I do not vote for what I think is the best interests of our country, then I am not a patriotic citizen."

It would be a three-way presidential election that year. The Republicans renominated incumbent President William Howard Taft, and Woodrow Wilson was the Democratic candidate. John, Sr. was leaning toward the latter. "I have always been a free trader," he told his son. "I always voted the Democratic ticket until Bryan secured control and I think that most of the evils of today are because the high tariff has made industrial life more profitable and agreeable than farm life and therefore the consuming population has increased out of all proportion to the producing population. . . . Now I do not think it right or possible to at once do away with the tariff but I do think the theory of protection is all wrong. So you see from this point of view I would naturally support Wilson." That November, Wilson carried the election with an electoral vote of 435 to 88 for Roosevelt and 8 for Taft.

John, Jr. was not always a model of decorum. In December of his senior year at Andover, he was party to some horseplay that resulted in his breaking down a door. His companions had assured him they would foot the bill for the damage, but the school suspended John, Jr. and his friends from the building in which they were living.

My grandfather was furious. "Your letter of the 10th has just come in and it grieves me more than I can tell you," he wrote back immediately. "I do not object to fun but I do object to rowdyism, vandalism, etc. It is not the right

spirit to think you can break things because you can pay the bill and I do not wonder that Mr. Forbes got angry nor do *I blame them in the slightest particular for expelling you from the building. I could not even blame them if they had expelled you from the school.*"

It was imperative that John, Jr. retain the respect of his teachers and classmates, my grandfather wrote, and he did not like the cavalier tone of his son's letter. "Now the manly thing for you to do is to accept your punishment cheerfully, to admit it is just and to go to both Mr. Freeman and Mr. Forbes and apologize, tell them frankly it was purely a spirit of boyish pranks, that you intended no disrespect and that you regret the whole incident and will accept your punishment as just. . . . The spirit you show in your letter is beneath you. It is the spirit of the boy who says 'I won't play' because he cannot have his own way."

As the time of his graduation approached, my father wrote home that he was thinking about taking up engineering. This came as quite a revelation to my grandfather. "[Your letter] took me so by surprise that I hardly know what to say," he replied. "If you feel sure that you are better fitted to become an engineer than a businessman, then I want you to become one," but it was not a decision he wanted him to make hastily, he wrote. Had John, Jr. considered that at least until he worked his way up to consulting engineer, he could expect to lead a camp life?

There were also other considerations John, Sr. wanted his son to think about. "Engineering does not afford much opportunity to mix with men of affairs in early life," my grandfather explained. "To get on in the world from a financial sense at any rate, it is quite essential to be able to mix with [the leading men in] business. . . . Now of course money is not the big thing in life but it is a power that one must always reckon with and it is well to think clearly and not allow yourself to be influenced by any fleeting sentiments."

If, on the other hand, John, Jr. planned to go into business, his father continued, then a college education would be "a fine thing because it trains the mind in the culture and knowledge of all ages. It broadens one, gives a big view point of life, and . . . the friends you make there will be a powerful factor in your later life. . . . From the point of pure business success, it is not important but it gives one a bigger field in life, keeps him in touch with all sorts of conditions and keeps his interest in things much more important than money."

By the end of his senior year, John, Jr. was complaining of feeling less than fit, and his father recommended that he spend the summer working out-of-doors. "I can send you down to the ranch in Texas or I could probably get you some kind of work . . . in the engineering department, out at Valier, Montana. . . . The engineering might give you a taste of what you seem anxious for. The ranch on the other hand would give you a little of real farm life, but either should keep you busy out of doors and put you back in fine shape for fall."

Experimenting with his camera, John, Jr. took this double exposure of himself with an unidentified classmate at Andover.

My father chose the ranch, where he ended up liking the cowboying life so much that he returned the next summer as well. Writing to his mother at the Sea View Inn, Biddeford Pool, Maine, where she and his brother Cargill were vacationing, he described how he had helped brand calves: "They drive the calves into a lot and then two men will catch a calf and then throw it and hold it down while they brand it. Guy Vaughn and I worked together and managed quite a number of them. We'd pick out the smaller ones and only once ran into one which we couldn't handle without roping. You'd be surprised at their strength. It's very exhausting work."

In the fall, at age seventeen, my father entered Yale to pursue a liberal arts education, but he ended up devoting a great deal of his life to engineering, mostly civil, as well as some mechanical and electrical. He had an especially keen interest in all phases of transportation, and as a result, Cargill effected great advances in the handling and storage of grain. Under his direction, the company also made giant strides in water transportation, designing, building, and operating its own cargo carriers on the Erie Canal and the inland waterways.

In John, Jr.'s immediate future loomed World War I, which almost nobody in this country expected.

WAR IN EUROPE

One of my grandparents' friends snapped this picture of John and Edna on a picnic.

The year 1913 was one of heady optimism in America. If storm clouds were gathering in Europe, they were almost totally ignored in the United States, where progress was reaching intoxicating new heights. New Yorkers built the world's tallest skyscraper, the sixty-story Woolworth Building designed by Cass Gilbert. Henry Ford in Detroit had introduced the assembly line to massproduce his Model T (and the next year would pay his workers a revolutionary high wage of five dollars a day). In March, a wireless message sent from Arlington, Maryland, was received at the Eiffel Tower in Paris. In October, President Woodrow Wilson pressed an electric button at the White House to blow up the Gamboa Dike, making ship travel possible through the new ocean-to-ocean Panama Canal.

For the MacMillans, it was the bittersweet year that John, Jr. graduated from Phillips Academy at Andover and entered Yale; the year the State Bank began doing business in the forfeited downtown McMillan Building in La Crosse (the bank is still there in the 1990s); and the year Mrs. Will S. (May McMillan) Cargill sold the former Duncan D. McMillan residence on West Avenue (formerly Twelfth Street) in La Crosse to her brother Dan G. MacMillan. At age thirty-nine, Dan G. was the retiring president of the La Crosse Gas and Electric company. Earlier in the year, running for mayor as a non-partisan who would operate city affairs according to "modern business principals," Dan G. was eliminated in the primaries. Before the year was out, he razed Duncan D.'s mansion and replaced it with an up-to-date prairie-style house.

There were two family weddings in the fall. On September 6, Austen Stowell Cargill married Anne Louise Ray in a religious ceremony at her mother's residence at 928 King Street in La Crosse. Myron Savage of Kansas City was his best man; the ushers were my father John H. MacMillan, Jr. and his cousin William W. Cargill, Jr., who carried ribbons from the foot of the stairs to a flower-banked bower in the bay window of the living room, forming an aisle for the bridal party. Seven-year-old Ellen (Budley) Hanchette carried the ring, concealed in the heart of a lily.

The bride was the daughter of the late George H. Ray, who had replaced Duncan D. McMillan as president of the State Bank of La Crosse in 1896. Austen's wedding gift to Anne was a stunning diamond and ruby ring that been belonged to his mother. The Cargill mansion, closed since Ellen's death three years earlier, came to brief life for the newlyweds' reception. Following a short wedding trip to Chicago, the couple set up housekeeping in Green Bay, where Austen was working for Cargill as an assistant to office manager Charley Quackenbush.

Three weeks later on October 1, my grandfather John H. MacMillan's youngest sister Bess (Elizabeth Johnston MacMillan) married Arthur Wheeler at

136

her mother's apartment at 5407 Woodlawn Avenue in Chicago. The bride and groom had met several years earlier on a trip up the inside passage to Alaska in 1908. Bess and her recently widowed mother had been in Portland visiting relatives after Duncan D. died, when they decided to splurge on the Alaskan cruise. Arthur, a traveling salesman for a manufacturing company that made rain slickers in Boston, was calling on the canneries in the Northwest and decided to use his vacation the same way. His state room on board ship was next to the one occupied by Bess and Mary Jane MacMillan.

Bess and Arthur had a prolonged engagement while he helped put his sister through Radcliffe and the New England Conservatory of Music. Tragically, this sister would die in the flu epidemic that followed World War I. The wedding in Bess's aging mother's apartment was a small family affair. Janet MacMillan, herself a musician and piano teacher, was her sister's maid of honor. After their marriage Bess and Arthur Wheeler lived in Boston.

In May 1914, Mary Jane MacMillan rented out her Woodlawn Avenue apartment in Chicago for a year, visited friends and relatives in La Crosse, and went to Boston to stay with Bess and Arthur. On June 18 her son Will and daughter Janet sailed from New York for Europe aboard the *President Grant*,

Arthur Loring Wheeler, a Harvard graduate who worked as a traveling salesman when he married my great-aunt Bess in 1913

Elizabeth (Bess) Johnston MacMillan with her sister Janet MacMillan. Bess's wedding announcement indicates that she and Janet as well as their mother Mary Jane were now spelling their name "MacMillan."

Will MacMillan with his sisters Janet and Bess in 1915

planning to tour the continent before settling down in Germany in September. Ten days later, Archduke Ferdinand was assassinated in Sarajevo. World War I broke out, and Will and Janet were stranded in Europe.

Three days before my grandfather John MacMillan's forty-fifth birthday on August 11, he returned from a trip to the ranch in Texas to find an anxious letter from Mary Jane in Boston. "I do not wonder that you are worried about Will and Janet," he replied, "but on the other hand, I have the utmost confidence in their ability to look out for themselves, and am sure there is nothing that can be done from this side." Every large European city had an American consulate, he told her, that had been issued special instructions for assisting tourists, but it would probably be some time before mail got through. "I presume mails in Switzerland [where Will and Janet had last been heard from] will have to get through by way of Italy, and then by boat from Italy to America, and if so it will take probably at least three weeks for a letter to reach its destination. Of course, it is possible that France is taking care of this mail, but I think it entirely unlikely as the railroads are all taken over for military purposes."

John and Edna finally received a letter several weeks later dated August 18 from Will and Janet saying that they had managed to get through by way of Holland. They had been in Hamburg for about two weeks, they said, and expected to start home as soon as they could get passage from Holland. In the meantime, they were staying in Hamburg because it was impossible to get into any of the hotels in Holland. Relaying this news to Fred Hanchette on September 15, my grandfather wrote, "I notice by the papers that every English line is booked ahead up to Oct. 4, but I am hoping every day to hear that they have landed on this side."

The whole family breathed easier when Will wired from New York on October 2 that he and Janet had arrived on the Holland American steamship

The Holland American liner Noordam *on which Will and Janet secured passage back to the States. Will returned without his field glasses which had been confiscated in Germany on the chance that they were war materiel. The American ambassador at Berlin took the matter up with the German government, writing Will in Chicago on October 10, 1914: "I have to inform you that the Embassy has received the pair of field glasses belonging to you. They will be forwarded to your address in the United States through the Department of State by our next Embassy pouch."*

Noordam. After spending a few days in Boston with his mother and Bess and Arthur, Will traveled to Minneapolis to see John and Edna before going down to the ranch in Texas. Writing to Fred Hanchette, my grandfather said: "We have enjoyed very much hearing about their experiences in Europe after the war broke out. Fortunately they had no very trying experiences. Of course, they are very glad to be back on this side. Will put in a half day with John, Jr. at New Haven last Saturday; went to a foot-ball game with him."

My father was in his second year at Yale where, according to the *History of the Class of Nineteen Seventeen*, his nicknames were "Mac" and "Woogie." He had roomed alone at 576 Pierson as a freshman; this year his roommates at 272 Durfee were Rufus Hodges Clapp, John Landon Davis, Arleigh Dygert Richardson, Jr., and Maurice Robert Smith. Davis, Smith, and Richardson had been at Andover with him, and the four of them would room together their junior and senior years at 356-357 White and 7-8 Vanderbilt. All four pledged Beta Theta Pi.

Twenty-five years later, my father would be president and director of Cargill, Inc. in Minneapolis; John Landon Davis, a vice president and general manager of the Central Oil Paper Company in Indianapolis; Smith, a supervisor at the Kansas City Life Insurance Company; and Richardson, vice president of the Ironsides Company in Columbus, Ohio. Rufus Hodges Clapp died suddenly after completing his junior year at Yale in 1916.

On October 2, the same day Will and Janet reached New York, my father wrote his parents: "I had the surprise of my life today when Arthur Wheeler walked in and announced that Aunt Bess and Grandma were downstairs in a car. I had an awfully pleasant visit and they took me to the Taft for dinner. They were on their way back from N.Y. and Atlantic City and stopped over for one train. It seems that it's Grandma's first visit to N.Y. and to hear her talk you'd believe that she enjoyed it. They went to a show every night."

John, Jr. was glad to be back at school. "Our rooms are perfectly wonderful," he enthused. "We are using one of our three bedrooms as a sort of training room. Whoever is in strict training gets it. At present Maurice, who is out for football has it. Rufe and I are in the best other bedroom while Budge Richardson and Landon have the other. . . . Our room in particular is going to be a regular hangout which is quite what we want it to be. . . . We certainly are the luckiest bunch that ever came to Yale. . . .

"I've gotten a flying start in my lessons. Got a perfect paper in economics and all right in everything else. I had some little trouble with dropping German and taking History . . . but appealed the case to the Dean who promised to fix me out tomorrow. I like my studies ever so much more than those I had last year. . . . No languages seems too much like heaven to be true. . . . I am taking Economics, Advanced Physics, Advanced Calculus, American History & Geology. Two Geology books cost me $6.20 by the way."

Ivy-covered Vanderbilt Hall at Yale where John, Jr. roomed during his senior year in 1916–1917

John, Jr. would be nineteen that year. A few days before his birthday on December 1, he wrote to his father, thanking him for a gift of money: "Your birthday present was most pleasing and acceptable and will not only enable me to go up to Boston but will enable me to pay for the suit which I ordered the other day."

In February John, Jr. wrote that he was "heeling" for the position of assistant swimming manager. "To be perfectly frank with you I haven't a chance in the world. I started it just the other day but I've already learned that like most other things here pull counts nine-tenths and work and ability one-tenth." John, Jr. had learned to swim at the YMCA his grandfather Will Cargill had built in La Crosse. A later undated letter to his parents talks about his experience as a "plunger" on Yale's swimming team:

> The prime requisite of a plunger is great weight. Accordingly I have special food, consisting of just about everything that the other members of the team are not allowed to eat. I get milk and cream galore, as much butter as I can get, and in general everything that could tend to make me fat.

It's little wonder he later developed serious cholesterol problems!

Yale suited my father perfectly. He was a natural leader who came into his own at the school. Prior to final exams in June, in a typed five-page letter to his parents, he apologized for being lax about writing, explaining: "Work on our new house has just been piling up and I as usual have had to attend to everything. The Committee of the Covington Trust Association (our alumni) was going to put up a place that didn't in the least come up to our ideas as to what the house ought to be like so I had to scurry around and see what I could do about raising more money." Working with alumni and fathers of members, John, Jr. arranged the financing for a colonial-style brick addition—it was actually a second house—to the front of his fraternity house.

Though strong-willed, John, Jr. also had a distinct streak of the Good Samaritan in him. Right at the moment, his letter continued, he was concerned about a down-on-his-luck Irishman named Patrick Ambrose, whom he had met wandering about the campus selling portraits of U.S. presidents for twenty-five cents. "I have just run into the most pitiful case of genuine hard luck that I have ever seen." Nobody was buying the pictures, and the man hadn't eaten for two days, so John, Jr. and his friends had taken Ambrose up to their room and persuaded some of the other men to buy $3.25 worth of pictures, which to the Irishman "seemed like a million dollars."

Ambrose was a graduate of the Royal University of Ireland and had been a teacher until his health broke down five years earlier, John, Jr. wrote. A doctor told him that the only thing that could save him was a sea voyage "so the crazy fool came to this country and landed in N.Y. three months ago with $100." After trying to find work in New York, Boston, and Philadelphia, he had spent

"Johnny MacMillan with his latest Packard,"
a photo appearing in a Yale publication

John H. MacMillan, Jr.

his last ten dollars on the pictures, hoping to peddle them to patriotic Americans. He spoke flawless English with an Irish accent, but "he seems to be on the verge of a breakdown, with his eyes all shot to pieces."

John, Jr. had helped him get work tutoring some of the men in Latin for fifty cents an hour, but he thought that Ambrose would be better off if he could work his way west, where his chances of finding permanent employment would improve. "I am very much interested in the man and would like to help him out. If I could have him on the ranch for about two months no one would know him for the same man," he told his father. Taking John, Jr.'s advice, Ambrose headed west as a book salesman, but he was unable to sell a single volume. In July my grandfather wrote to his brother Will in Chicago that Ambrose had appealed to John, Jr. for a temporary loan to get him back to Ireland, but he personally was opposed to this plan. "He says that this man is so physically broken down that what he needs is complete rest and freedom from care and worry for a few months, so as to get back his health and his nerve. He is very anxious to send him to the ranch."

Ambrose would be arriving in Chicago, my grandfather informed Will, and he should buy the Irishman a ticket to Texas and see that he reached the ranch. Possibly, Ambrose could do some light work such as gardening or driving the horses, but he didn't want him to feel under any obligation. "I have never heard of a case that has [so] aroused my sympathy . . . as this man is plainly not a grafter, but is on the contrary a thorough gentleman of high standards and attainments."

Patrick Ambrose showed up on Will's doorstep in Chicago as my grandfather had said he would, but he didn't want to go to Texas. Uncle Will gave him twenty-five dollars to help him get back to the old country where he had a brother. If our family ever heard from him again, there is no record of it.

America had so far remained neutral in the war in Europe. In May 1915 German U-boats torpedoed and sank the Cunard liner *Lusitania* off the Irish coast with the loss of more than 1,100 civilians, 128 of them Americans, but President Wilson still turned a deaf ear to the press and leaders like Theodore Roosevelt, who clamored for war. While Wilson refused to be stampeded into war, there arose a public ground swell of support for military "preparedness," especially among those who believed that America would eventually intervene on the side of England and France.

British veterans including Ian Hay, whom John, Sr. heard speak in Minneapolis, addressed pro-Ally meetings; American college students organized an ambulance corps to aid the Allies; and the Navy League and other societies pleaded with Congress to prepare for war—if only to preserve neutrality. During the summer of 1915, at the behest of New York business and professional men, General Leonard Wood and the War Department organized the first Plattsburg training camp to instruct twelve hundred volunteers in modern warfare. These

The Tenth Field Artillery, Connecticut National Guard, also known as the Yale Battalion. John, Jr. is circled.

men paid for their own food, uniforms, and travel expenses. The idea spread, and the next summer, a number of "Plattsburgs" trained sixteen thousand men to serve as officers of a new army.

When he returned to Yale in the fall of 1915, my father enlisted in the Tenth Field Artillery, Connecticut National Guard. Known as the Yale Battalion, the outfit drilled on campus under regular army officers. In February, much to his delight, John, Jr. was chosen for an aeroplane corps—which did not have the use of any aeroplanes. "We are devoting ourselves to the study of co-ordination of artillery and aviation," he wrote home. The men were selected on the strength of their experience in fields connected with aeronautics, my father explained, and he had listed his qualifications as follows:

1. Thoroughly conversant with gasoline engines, including 8 years experience driving cars of all makes.
2. Thorough knowledge of telephones.
3. Knowledge of wireless gained from experience as an amateur.
4. Had numerous advanced courses in chemistry, mathematics, physics, and geology.
5. Understand use of contour maps.

"It was 1, 4, and 5 which put me through," he wrote with obvious pride. "We go up to Hartford . . . for purposes of instruction and are to study later the plant of the Connecticut Aircraft Co. located in New Haven. The whole thing should be quite interesting and would be of infinitely more value in time of need than being merely a gunner in a battery.

"The only thing that I dislike about the whole thing is that on our frequent trips to Hartford and other points we have to go in uniform. These uniforms are horribly conspicuous, and when you are going around alone evoke all sorts of comments. The other night I had to go out to dinner in one because I wouldn't have time to dress afterwards and I would infinitely rather have worn a bathing suit."

By the spring of 1916, America was also on the brink of war with Mexico. After Mexican revolutionary Pancho Villa seized a train at Santa Ysabel and murdered eighteen American mining engineers, two months later raiding the town of Columbus, New Mexico, and killing sixteen citizens, President Wilson ordered a large part of the regular army and the national guard to the border. General "Black Jack" Pershing with a column of six thousand men pursued Villa three hundred miles into Mexico, and Congress passed legislation enabling the president to draft the militia into federal service. In July the Yale Battalion was ordered to Camp Summerall at Tobyhanna, Pennsylvania, for artillery instruction.

Situated midway between the Delaware Water Gap and Scranton on a flat ridge in the Pocono Mountains, Camp Summerall was a scenic, well-arranged camp, spread out over eighteen thousand acres of rocky terrain. The band played reveille each morning at 5:15, beginning a strenuous day's work, but no one complained. The food was good, and the men were fired with patriotism. My father was appointed corporal and battery agent.

At present, putting my grandparents somewhat at ease, there was no danger that the Yale Battalion would be ordered to the Mexican border. "We are, of course, tremendously pleased over the more peaceful aspect of affairs," his father wrote John, Jr., "and I am in hopes . . . you will be able to get back into college this fall just as you planned. . . . I think you are indeed fortunate to be detailed as orderly to the First Sergeant, and I hope you can continue to hold that until you get some promotion."

In Minneapolis, marking a milestone in company history, this was the summer that Cargill Elevator paid off its remaining creditors. The wheat market was particularly volatile in 1915. Crops were at record levels in many of the world's wheat growing areas, but at the same time World War I prevented the wheat crop of Russia—one of the world's foremost grain exporters prior to the advent of communism—from reaching the world market. The loss of Russia's export earnings would play no small part in the outcome of the war on the eastern front. But Cargill had enjoyed five profitable years since Will Cargill's untimely death. In a letter to John, Jr. dated July 5, 1916, John, Sr. wrote: "We cleaned up the estate on Saturday exactly as per the plan which I showed you when you were home. . . . Everyone is exceedingly pleased over the outcome and I am having a good many hearty congratulations."

According to John, Sr.'s plan, the Cargill Elevator Company declared a dividend of 240 percent, virtually its entire working capital, amounting to $2,400,000. Cargill Securities Company's eighty-three percent share of this, together with a small loan, provided enough cash to redeem the collateral trust notes due to mature in January 1917. Cargill stockholders received $800,000 of

W. W. Cargill's older sister Margaret Cargill ("Aunt Maggie") Barker, the only daughter of Captain William Dick Cargill. She lived out her life in Janesville, Wisconsin, where her husband George Barker was a gentleman farmer.

Austen Cargill about 1916

preferred stock and $800,000 of common stock to cover property and assets remaining after the dividend. To provide working capital, Cargill sold 8,000 shares of common stock for $100 each to employees and a few friends. The employees' common stock purchase (4,400 shares) was largely financed by loans from Margaret Cargill Barker and Mrs. Sam D. (Lydia) Cargill; the former was Will Cargill's sister, the latter his brother's widow.

At this point, with the Cargill Securities Company stock back in the hands of Will and Ellen Cargill's four children, Austen Cargill bought out his older brother Will's one quarter share in the estate for five hundred thousand dollars, thus taking his elder brother out of any further dealings with the company, to the great relief of the other heirs. The creditors' committee was disbanded, and from this time forward, Cargill management could conduct company business with a free hand, which it has continued to do with measurable success.

As my father began his senior year at Yale, Pershing was on a wild goose chase in Mexico, missing his catch and about to be recalled. In Washington, President Wilson was continuing his isolationist stance, declining to believe that war against Germany and its allies was inevitable. John, Jr. was mustered out of the federal service in September and discharged from the National Guard on November 30. The next day was his twenty-first birthday, which his father commemorated with a six-page letter. "It is hard to realize that you have become a man and from now on are responsible for your own destiny," John, Sr. began.

> Your days from now on will be filled with care, with sorrow and I hope, also of joy. Whether your life will be a failure or a glorious success depends entirely upon your own efforts. If you show dogged perseverance and determination and rugged honesty, there can be no question of the outcome. You might have periods of discouragement, even of failure for a time but in the end the result will be sure. The greatest thing in the world to my mind is character and that is attained only by rigid self-analysis as well as honesty, courage and determination and hard work. However all these things are joyous in themselves and make for the very best and happiest kind of a time. The happiest are those who do their full share of hard work. A little play is necessary for relaxation and good health and I hope you will never forget how to play. That will keep you youthful but that should be only an incident of life—not the main purpose.

He and Edna had counted on being able to celebrate John, Jr.'s birthday with him, he wrote, but "it has not been possible this year. I am sending you a check for $50 . . . and we are increasing your stock in the Cargill Elevator Co. to $1000. . . . I hope this will be an incentive to you to begin saving as soon as you begin work. . . . You want to make it an infallible rule to save at least 1/3 of your income to add to your capital each year. No matter how small it seems, the discipline and training are worth many times the money saved."

Cooking out: John and Edna MacMillan

Keeping news of the family for last, John, Sr. wrote that Austen and Anne Cargill were coming for the Thanksgiving weekend. The previous Sunday, he and Edna had gone picnicking with their friends, the Lees, the Lanes, and the Hulls. "We built a big bonfire, cooked bacon and sausage and had a wonderful dinner." My grandfather never tired of the out-of-doors, and although that it was the end of November, he was still enjoying weekly hikes:

> We had a fine tramp last Saturday with the usual crowd—excepting Judge Jelley. We walked from the Oxboro Heath to the Minnesota River bottoms at the foot of Lyndale Ave. and then along the bluff to the Long Meadow Gun Club where we had dinner. There is a big fireplace there and it is most enjoyable to sit around the fire while we are resting and enjoy the good fellowship that results. We started for Fort Snelling about 9 p.m. and took the street car home arriving home about 11 p.m.

Much to John, Sr.'s chagrin, Woodrow Wilson, whom he now considered weak and vacillating, had been reelected by a narrow margin over Associate Supreme Court Justice Charles Evans Hughes in November. "I presume you are displeased with the outcome of the election," he wrote John, Jr. (In a straw vote at Yale, Justice Hughes had polled 1,326 votes to Wilson's 599.) President Wilson hoped to mediate a "peace without victory" in Europe, but neither the Allies nor the Central Powers were willing to come away empty-handed from the sacrifices they had endured. Then on January 31, the German government announced that its U-boats would sink any ship that entered the German-declared war zone around the British Isles or the Mediterranean. Confronted with this unwarranted threat to American merchant shipping, President Wilson severed diplomatic relations with Germany.

My grandfather wrote to John, Jr. that he approved wholeheartedly of Wilson's action. "The President did the right thing." Whether or not this break

The Long Meadow Gun Club in Bloomington is the oldest hunting club in Minnesota, dating to 1883. Grandfather MacMillan never belonged to it, but Austen Cargill's name appears several times on club tallies of birds shot by members. On October 6, 1928, Austen bagged five mallards, one gadwell, and one ringbill; on October 1, 1939, he wound up with five mallards and one widgeon.

Cargill MacMillan in his first year at Andover in 1916

President Woodrow Wilson with his second wife, the former Edith Galt, whom he courted and married during his presidency

would result in war remained to be seen, John, Sr. said, but he cautioned his son not to "be rushed off your feet by any temporary excitement of the moment." If possible, he wanted John, Jr. to finish out his last year at Yale. Should the president ask for volunteers, he advised his son not to enlist again as a private. "With your education and military training . . . you at least would be entitled to a commission."

John, Sr. and Edna spent their usual extended winter vacation in early 1917 sightseeing in Nashville, Chattanooga, Atlanta, and Jacksonville before settling in for several weeks at the Hotel Clarendon at Seabreeze, Florida. Writing to John, Jr. at Yale, his father advised him that they would be arriving at The Homestead in Hot Springs, Virginia, on March 24; they were looking forward to having John, Jr. and Cargill join them there for Easter.

"Did you order a tuxedo coat and vest?" his father asked. "If not be sure and do so and you can send the bill to me. You will have to have it at The Homestead. You will also want golf clubs. I bought a new bag so I have two but you can either pick out a set of clubs in New Haven or New York or get them through the professional golf man at Hot Springs just as you prefer. These will be an Easter present from me."

Fifteen months earlier, President Wilson and his bride Edith Galt had honeymooned at The Homestead. This year John, Jr. and Cargill were there with their parents when the President addressed a special session of Congress on April 2. Wilson's special day of reckoning had arrived. Earlier, the British had intercepted and decoded the infamous "Zimmermann Note" addressed to President Carranza of Mexico, in which Germany proposed a German-Mexican alliance against the United States. Mexico's share of the booty was to be New Mexico, Arizona, and Texas. Then on March 18, German U-boats had sunk three unarmed American merchantmen with heavy loss of life. The United States could no longer remain neutral.

"It is a fearful thing to lead this great peaceful people into war, into the most terrible and disastrous of all wars, civilization itself seeming to be in the balance," President Wilson told Congress.

> But the right is more precious than peace, and we shall fight for the things which we have always carried nearest our hearts,—for democracy, for the right of those who submit to authority to have a voice in their own government, for the rights and liberties of small nations, for a universal dominion of right by such a concert of free peoples as shall bring peace and safety to all nations and make the world itself at last free.

The United States Senate on April 4 voted 82 to 6 to declare war on the German Empire. The House of Representatives concurred, 373 to 50. Two days later on April 6, a deeply grieved President Wilson signed the declaration of war. That it was Good Friday added to his anguish.

CAPTAIN JOHN H. MACMILLAN, JR.

Artillery instruction at Fort Snelling

Wilson's words raised fresh hopes for victory and a lasting peace in Europe. With America preparing to mobilize, John, Jr. rushed to reenlist in the army at Yale. Wild horses couldn't have stopped him. Every red-blooded American college man wanted to help rout the Germans, and Yale, in particular, was a hotbed of patriotism.

America had been caught unprepared for war. On April 1, 1917, the United States Army numbered only two hundred thousand officers and men, one third of whom were National Guard. Before the month was out, Secretary of War Newton D. Baker ordered camps established to train ten thousand new officers. Writing to his father from New Haven, John, Jr. asked him to see what he could do about getting him assigned to the officers' training camp being fitted out at Fort Snelling near the Twin Cities. My grandfather replied that he would talk to one of his friends who might have some influence with the commanding officer, but "I have no doubt that these army officers know about the Yale Battalion who were at Tobyhanna last summer and I do not believe you will . . . be overlooked."

Proud of his son's initiative, John MacMillan, Sr. never doubted that it was every man's responsibility to defend his country. In a letter to Minnesota Congressman C. B. Miller in Washington, D.C., on April 26, John, Sr. congratulated him for "the very able speech which you made in the House in support of the President's stand, asking for universal liability to service:

> I must confess that I do not see how any thinking person can look at this subject in any other way than you do. It seems to me that it is self evident that the situation is as follows:

147

First, that it is either the duty of every man to serve, or second, that it is a privilege. In the first case, it is the equal duty of every man and it is extremely contemptible to attempt to evade this duty by crowding it on those who are willing to shed their blood for their country.

In the second case, it would mean the formation of a privileged class, who could very rightfully demand of their country, when the war is over, some compensation for the risks put forth and I think in a democracy, a privileged class is entirely out of place. We have seen what it can do, in Europe.

My father was one of twenty-five hundred candidates chosen from among six thousand applicants from Minnesota, Iowa, North Dakota, South Dakota, and Nebraska for the First Officers' Training Camp at Fort Snelling. He arrived home in Minneapolis the first week in May. Like many of his classmates at Yale who enlisted in the service, John, Jr. would miss June graduation exercises at New Haven and receive his diploma by mail. Following a three-day outing with his father and Uncle Austen at the family fishing camp at Spooner, Wisconsin, John, Jr. reported for camp, suitcase in hand, on May 11. It was a warm day, hot by noon, and the long line of candidates waiting to be processed stretched out of the door of the administration building, down the steps, and across the lawn. After being checked in and routed to the hospital for a physical examination, the men were assigned to barracks, then marched to the quartermaster's supply depot to pick up equipment and the olive drab uniforms they would wear for the next several months.

Once the country's northwesternmost outpost, the oldest part of Fort Snelling was built in 1820 on steep limestone bluffs overlooking the confluence of the Mississippi and Minnesota Rivers. Its dual purpose was to block British infiltration of the Northwest and protect the newly established fur trade by maintaining peace among the Indians. During the thirteen-week crash program in which John, Jr. was enrolled, candidates put in eighteen-hour days filled with drill

Officer candidates pitch horseshoes outside the YMCA building at Fort Snelling. Wholesome recreation combated vice conditions in and around military training camps, greatly increasing military effectiveness during World War I.

Following graduation from Fort Snelling Officers' Training Camp in August 1917, Captain John H. MacMillan was assigned to General Stephen Foote's 163rd Field Artillery Brigade at Camp Dodge near Des Moines, Iowa.

periods in the morning and afternoon; lectures, recitations, and written examinations; physical exercise; and evening study periods. Reveille sounded each morning at a quarter past five, and lights remained on in the study halls until eleven in the evening. "Seldom have men been subjected to such short, intensive and terrific training as in the effort to turn them into capable officers in 90 days," commanding officer General Gage told a reporter.

The Young Men's Christian Association and similar organizations provided religious services and recreational activities—sports, dances, and musical and dramatic programs. During half-hour periods of football each afternoon, coach Dr. Henry L. Williams from the University of Minnesota taught the men how to organize athletics in the units they would soon command. At the end of each week's strenuous training, candidates were granted a leave of absence from Saturday noon until Sunday night. Those who lived near the post like John, Jr. were able to visit their families.

During their first five weeks in camp, officer candidates studied the fundamentals of military science, including the use and care of rifles and pistols. Particular emphasis was placed on skills such as bayoneting, grenade-throwing, and "mopping up" after a bomb attack, all of which would be needed for the kind of trench warfare being waged in Europe. Many of the original twenty-five hundred candidates were weeded out at the end of this period. Those who remained were divided into infantry companies and field artillery batteries. My father trained in field artillery, but under much the same conditions as at Yale. At both places, the lack of an artillery range made it necessary for the men to study range-finding, observation of fire, fire control, and similar problems under simulated conditions.

The following eight weeks were given over to practicing the American open or skirmish type of warfare and trench warfare, using picks and shovels to dig a complete trench system south of the post. Near the end of their training, with muscles hardened and hands calloused, the candidates frequently participated in stirring military ceremonies with music furnished by the 36th United States Infantry, which was brigaded nearby. On August 10, the whole camp took part in a huge military pageant portraying the infantry attacking the "enemy" in trenches on the western front. Drawing thousands of visitors from the Twin Cities, this served as a finale to their course of training and commencement exercises. Official visitors included the governors of North and South Dakota and Iowa. Former Minnesota Governor Samuel R. Van Sant represented Minnesota Governor Joseph A. A. Burnquist, who was ill.

Ninety percent of the men remaining in camp received commissions. Out of 1,551 successful candidates, more than two-thirds became second lieutenants, about two hundred, first lieutenants, and a smaller number, captains. John H. MacMillan, Jr. graduated as a captain of field artillery.

In Minneapolis the 1916–1917 crop year had started out an especially difficult one for the Cargill Elevator Company. Writing to Fred and Emma Hanchette in California in September, my grandfather told them: "We have got absolutely the most complete crop failure that the Northwest has ever known. . . . We have never been up against a situation as bad as this one." Things seemed to go from bad to worse, and by November, he was worried as well about a possible grain embargo or a railroad strike. "All of these things of course, are extremely wearing and make us very anxious as we cannot foresee what complications may arise or what losses may be incurred if either of these two calamities should happen to strike."

In December, when Fred and Emma suggested that he and Edna visit them in California, he thanked them but declined their invitation. "This is one of those wild years that I do not want to get any great distance away from home at any time until we get cleaned up and can feel easy about the future. Everything so far has worked along better than I could have hoped for at the beginning but it is a dangerous situation and probably will continue so right through the crop year. I hope that we will be able to get cleaned up though before navigation opens next spring as you have no idea the strain of a year such as this one is."

Then the unexpected happened. Even before the United States entered the war, grain prices had begun to escalate during the first six months of 1917. Three years of intensive warfare had seriously reduced the wheat crops in the Allied countries of England, France, Italy, and Belgium, inducing foreign governments to buy up as much wheat and flour as they could in American markets. Frequently they ended up bidding against each other, and they also purchased heavily in May futures on the Chicago Board of Trade. The price of wheat rose from about $1.80 per bushel in December 1916, to over $2.40 in April. It was the first time wheat surpassed $2.00 in a normal market. When May came and buyers demanded delivery, grain prices skyrocketed. Before the Chicago Board of Trade suspended operations on May 12, forcing the settlement of outstanding contracts at agreed-upon prices, No. 2 Red Winter wheat sold for $3.45.

The MacMillans did "clean up" all right, as John, Sr. had put it, and in more ways than he had expected. On June 30, six weeks into John, Jr.'s training at Fort Snelling, Cargill Elevator Company books showed a profit for the crop year of more than one million dollars. It had been the firm's best year ever.

Writing to Fred Hanchette in California, my grandfather said that the company had decided to pay a forty-five percent dividend on its common stock. Emma's share, he said, would amount to something over seventy-five thousand dollars. Emma was "tickled to death" to hear such grand news, she wrote back. "I can't believe we have all that money." She and Fred used it to buy a big house and expensive car.

This windfall should not be regarded as an indicator of things to come, however, John, Sr. warned Fred. "I presume you understand that this is an abnormal year, something that we have never had anything like before, and probably never will have again. We do know that the Government is going to interfere in the handling of the grain crop. . . . I do not believe that the Government is going to force us to do business for nothing or at a loss, but they might put us on a basis where it will not be possible to pay over somewhere between 5 and 6%."

My grandfather knew whereof he spoke. In May 1917, he and other leading grain men had met in Washington with United States Food Administrator Herbert Hoover to discuss ways and means of regulating the grain trade. Hoover's job, which he performed admirably, involved increasing production and decreasing consumption of wheat and other basic commodities at home to ensure that overseas armies and civilians were adequately supplied. To prevent a repetition of recent runaway prices, he fixed the price of grain at $2.20 and established a grain corporation to buy and sell it. He also urged Americans to observe wheatless Mondays. In January 1918, as a result of his continuing work with Hoover and the Food Administration, John H. MacMillan, Sr. would be elected national president of the Council of Grain Exchanges, the central governing body for this country's fifteen major grain exchanges.

In La Crosse, where Will and Ellen Cargill's house had been closed for several years following their deaths, the family home was reopened during the summer of 1917. My grandfather called in plumbers to repair some pipes, and a La Crosse newspaper announced in July, "It is understood that for the rest of the summer the house will be occupied at various times by either the [John H.] MacMillan family or Mrs. MacMillan's sister, Mrs. Hanchette of California." Earlier, my grandfather had written Fred Hanchette saying he hoped "we can all put in a little time down there, especially so if John should happen to be assigned to the artillery camp at Sparta, Wisconsin."

Both John, Sr. and Edna and the Hanchettes enjoyed being back in La Crosse among old friends and relatives, but John, Jr. never wound up at Sparta. Instead, along with more than half the graduates of the First Officers' Training Camp at Fort Snelling, he reported to Camp Dodge in central Iowa. Named for Civil War General Grenville M. Dodge, the camp was one of sixteen huge cantonments the federal

Easily the biggest facility in Iowa, Camp Dodge was constructed in five months at a cost of eight million dollars to house forty thousand soldiers training to fight for a new world order in European trenches. To impress upon workmen the urgency of the vast undertaking, construction engineers posted a placard in prominent places about the camp that read:

TIME IS PRECIOUS NOW; OUR COUNTRY IS AT WAR.

We are building for men who will leave their families, homes and business and offer their lives to fight for our country.

It is our job to build this cantonment within the next two weeks. One day's delay might cost precious lives, a week's delay might lose the war.

An old brick farmhouse serving as the first division headquarters at Camp Dodge

Captain Wheelock Whitney, who was a year ahead of John H. MacMillan, Jr. at Andover and Yale

government built with great haste to train the new national army.

Still under construction when the first troops began arriving, Camp Dodge occupied more than five thousand acres of former cropland about ten miles northwest of Des Moines. As many as six thousand civilian employees worked seven-day weeks from July through December, erecting fourteen hundred flimsy structures, including administration buildings, officers' quarters, and three hundred company barracks to house forty thousand men. Several localities, including Fort Snelling, had been in the running for the camp site, but Des Moines had two things in its favor: Iowa was "dry" (meaning no alcoholic beverages), and Des Moines boasted three thousand more hours of sunshine than any rival site.

My father was assigned to General Stephen Foote's 163rd Field Artillery Brigade. Before he left Minneapolis, his parents gave him a new Dodge convertible—an early birthday and Christmas present—that he drove to camp. Writing home on September 20, he told them the car was proving "invaluable." Now that he had moved up to headquarters, he said, "they are continually calling on me for all kinds of odd jobs at the other end of camp. . . . I figure that the car means a saving to me of at least two hours daily that would otherwise be taken up in walking." Already the first draftees were pouring in from Iowa, Minnesota, North Dakota, and part of central Illinois. "Today our Brigade gets some 3000 men . . . and I can see long streams of men filing by outside in double file."

More Minnesotans (including John, Jr.'s friend Wheelock Whitney, whose sister Pauline would marry John's brother Cargill) were assigned to Camp Dodge than any other cantonment. My grandfather visited John, Jr. there in October and afterwards reported to his Boston banker friend Tom Baxter (who had earlier been part of the Cargill creditors' committee): "There seems to be a wonderful spirit of enthusiasm everywhere and the very best of feeling between the officers and the men. It cheered me up very greatly to notice this as I had rather expected to find more or less gloom and dissatisfaction among the men on account of being taken away from their usual work."

My father was less enthusiastic about some of the recruits, many of whom had never made it through grade school. "Altogether it is most discouraging, particularly when you are trying to get men for specialists as we are," he wrote in one letter home. "The 338th is made up of men from North Dakota, and while they might make an excellent lot of mule skinners it's quite out of the question to make artillery men out of them let alone wireless operators. I will admit though that there are a surprising number of gas engine experts among them and it is quite pitiful how they all claim to have operated farm tractors and then when you ask them what make they can't even name it to you. They all have an idea that a knowledge of the use of tractors will in some mysterious way keep them back of the lines, so although they really may know a lot about automobiles they one and all claim to have an intimate knowledge of tractors."

In October John, Jr. applied and was accepted for three months advanced artillery training at the School of Fire at Fort Sill. His father reported in a letter to Edna's cousin Mary Cargill Barker in Janesville, Wisconsin, "This will give him the very best artillery education that can be obtained anywhere, as this is the Government Artillery School and is post graduate work after West Point for those who are making artillery a specialty."

Before leaving for Fort Sill in November, my father drove his car home to Minneapolis one night in fifteen-degree weather. He had come "through two feet of snow, with the top down," he wrote to his brother Cargill, now a senior at Andover. "Besides that, I had to change two tires, and take it from me it was cold work."

In weekly letters from Camps Dodge and Sill, John, Jr. kept his younger brother (fondly called "Gee") abreast of his activities, praised Cargill for having the gumption to try out for the *Phillippian*, and sent him ideas for articles. "Our work here is mostly a rehash of truck that I have already had, but I have hopes that we will soon be able to start firing," he wrote on November 8. "They have an allowance of 250 rounds of ammunition per officer (each round costing anywhere from $10 to $50) and am crazy to fire my first problem. You know they say that you aren't an artillery officer until you have fired a problem."

Thanking Cargill for copies of the *Phillippian*, John, Jr. wrote that "all the Andover boys here took quite an interest in them," and filled him in on what some of his classmates were doing. His former roommate J. Landon Davis, '13, was a second lieutenant of field artillery at Chillicothe, Ohio; Davis had run the quarter mile on both the Andover and Yale teams. Another roommate, Maurice Robert Smith, '13, who had played on Andover's football, baseball, and wrestling teams, and been prominent in all forms of athletics at Yale, was a first lieutenant in the Balloon Section of the Signal Corps at Fort Omaha, Nebraska. Russell H.

Fort Sill in winter

John, Jr.'s birthday and Christmas present from his parents in 1917, a new Dodge convertible

John, Jr. in his sheepskin coat at Fort Sill

Bennett from Minneapolis, '15, (who would soon join John, Jr. back at Camp Dodge) was a student at the Second Officers' Training Camp at Fort Snelling. William Howard Bovey, '15, also from Minneapolis, was in the Mosquito Fleet as a non-commissioned officer.

At Fort Sill, in addition to his studies, my father instructed the officers of his old regiment in panoramic sketching, occupation of position, and reconnaissance work. On top of this, he drew the job of teaching French to the brigade's officers. He didn't fancy himself a language instructor, but he had been unable to hunt up a French professor in nearby Lawton, so "I guess we'll have to instruct ourselves," he wrote his parents. "I rather think we'll establish tables at mess where only French will be spoken." John, Jr. turned twenty-two on December 1 at Fort Sill, where he spent his first Christmas away from home. Over and above the gift of the Dodge convertible, his father sent him a fifty-dollar Liberty Loan bond for each occasion. He was also sending him a new overcoat, he wrote, although "I may have to let it go until after Christmas on account of the crowds doing their Christmas shopping." Government regulations required officers to wear either the regular issue overcoat or a sheepskin-lined jacket.

My grandfather selected a warm sheepskin that arrived at Fort Sill just as the temperature plummeted to thirteen degrees below zero. "I never anticipated receiving any such magnificent affair as that," my father wrote home thanking him on December 31. "It is quite the best one I have seen yet, and although not quite regulation for our division can easily be made over so that it is." The closing date for his class had been postponed until January 18, he informed his parents, "which means that I won't get home until the 20th."

Edna was busy through the holidays that year with Red Cross work. In the year beginning June 1, 1917, Minneapolis women sent to the front nearly 2,500,000 surgical dressings, along with other supplies and books and magazines. John, Sr. spent two weeks in early December with his brother Will at the ranch in Texas and upon his return wrote to the ranch manager, H. L. Zollers: "Mrs. MacMillan selected a few little things for me for your children for Christmas. . . . This is the only kind of a Christmas any of us are doing up here this year as Red Cross and other charities are taking up all the surplus time of everyone and also incidentally the surplus money as well."

My father had ten days' leave with his family in January. Reporting back to Camp Dodge on February 1, 1918, he wrote home the same evening, "I am nicely settled in the chateau [where] we have two orderlies to look after us." Earlier in the day, his cousin Katherine McMillan (John D.'s daughter who lived with her parents at 239 Clifton Avenue in Minneapolis) had "brought out her gang and they all watched fire and then came over to our quarters for a while, where the General did his best to entertain them." Everyone was very interested

Katherine McMillan, born in 1895, was the same age as her cousin John, Jr. In October 1919, in what one paper called "the most fashionable wedding of the year," she married Captain Frank P. Shepard who had been with John, Jr. at Yale, graduated with him from Fort Snelling Officers' Training Camp, and served at Camp Dodge.

Captain John H. MacMillan, Jr. signed these receipts for gear including a .45 caliber revolver, a gas mask, and eating utensils at Camp Dodge.

in his "invention," he said, and the general was having one made up by an engraver from St. Paul, a first lieutenant named McWhorter.

My father's invention was a sighting device that he tested successfully a few days later. "The guns were fired and the correction found to be 140.7 yards. . . . Using my little machine I got exactly 140 yards, much to everyone's amazement. The General is very much pleased with it. The error of .7 yards is of course about $1/20$ of the error which we can allow and still have the machine at maximum value. . . . The whole thing is $3\frac{1}{2}$ inches across, and is small enough so that you can slip it in your shirt pocket and never know that it is there."

He had left his car in Minneapolis, and he could easily wait a couple of weeks for it until someone could drive it down for him, he wrote. As for his laundry, he would "much prefer to send it home, and if Mother could send me some kind of boxes which I could use to send it back and forth it could easily be arranged." Did his mother have an old rug or piece of carpet that he could use in his bedroom? he inquired. She did, and she sent him two rugs.

John, Jr. was appointed acting brigade adjutant in March, and the big question was when he would be sent overseas. In the interim, he wrote his parents, he was kept so busy with routine paperwork that he hardly had time to sleep. Detachments came and detachments went. Their training was short-term, and many of the men were transferred to the National Guard, which irked him terribly. "They are simply stripping the division . . . and I am inclined to believe that some 23000 men are to be transferred," he complained at the end of the month. "What I can't understand is why they don't call out more men, unless it is that they are afraid of dislocating industry."

In April there was a regimental dance which my father described as "by far the best [party] I have been to since I've been here. I went in with Gen. and Mrs. Foote. They are both very good dancers." Katherine McMillan and her crowd from Minneapolis were there, and it was three in the morning when he finally got to bed. Two hours later, fire broke out in the base hospital. "I hustled around, ordered all the infirmaries to prepare their stretchers in case they wanted to use our hospitals for any of the sick, and then dashed over myself." The blaze, it turned out, was confined to the nurses' quarters, and although the patients had a good scare, no one was hurt.

Spring that year at Camp Dodge brought with it an unusually high incidence of sickness. "This recent dust seems to have carried the germ of a very virulent type of pneumonia," my father informed his parents. Twenty-five men had died, and the dust grew worse in May, whipped up by abnormal winds. So much of it filtered into the dining room that the dishes and food could not be put out before the men sat down, and outdoor drills were impossible. "A five minute walk out doors and you need a bath the worst way and then its awfully hard to get out the dirt." (Fifty-seven thousand American enlisted men died

Newly arrived recruits filling their mattresses with straw at Camp Dodge. Much to the dismay of its officers, who feared that the cantonment might never send a division overseas, Camp Dodge saw a continual turnover of enlisted men. The overriding national task of bringing to full strength units being prepared for early transportation abroad resulted in a steady outflow of trained and partially trained troops from Camp Dodge to various camps throughout the United States.

Colonel Frank C. Todd, commanding officer at the base hospital at Camp Dodge

from disease during World War I, outnumbering those who died in combat.)

The commanding officer at the base hospital was Dr. Frank Todd, a close friend of the MacMillans from Minneapolis, and the same physician who had brought my father into the world in Texas. Born in Minneapolis, the son of a prominent lumberman, Dr. Todd would himself become a casualty of the war at age forty-eight. President of the Minnesota Academy of Medicine when war broke out in Europe, Dr. Todd died July 4, 1918, at the Presbyterian Hospital in Chicago after contracting a severe cold that developed into pneumonia.

At Andover in the spring of 1918, seventeen-year-old Cargill MacMillan was also preparing for war. The entire school of several hundred boys had been organized into an infantry regiment instructed by two Canadian officers with experience at the front. "We are taking up musketry and bayonet drill now, and it all seems very interesting work," Cargill wrote his parents in January. "We have to wear our uniforms all the time [and] our rooms are now open to inspection at any time that any officer wishes." The faculty was considering operating a military camp at Andover during the summer months, he said, and he hoped to be allowed to attend.

"It is becoming more and more obvious that the war is going to last until I am of age," Cargill explained to his parents, and he wanted to be sure of getting a commission. "It is also becoming more and more obvious and evident that school life, not only at Andover, but also at Yale, is becoming based on success in military lines. . . . I know that you are happy and proud to have a son of Junior's caliber, but you would be so much more so if you had two of them."

My grandparents attended Cargill's graduation exercises in late June, and Edna afterwards took him to the Hotel Thorwald at Bass Rocks, Gloucester, Massachusetts, for a short vacation. Cargill entered Andover's summer military camp on July 3. My grandfather joined Edna at Bass Rocks, and they stayed on for several weeks, going over to visit Cargill frequently at Andover. When John, Sr. returned to Minneapolis, he wrote to Fred Hanchette: "Cargill went thru his camp at Andover with a fine record. They made him a permanent second lieutenant and he was the only permanent officer that was appointed during the summer camp." In the fall, Cargill entered Yale, where he joined the Reserve Officers Training Corp, serving until 1922 when he was commissioned a second lieutenant.

In Chicago, my father's Uncle Will was summoned to Washington at the end of June 1918. Will had earned a Ph.D. in mathematics and astronomy at the University of Chicago, graduating *summa cum laude* in 1908, and was back teaching at the school where he would spend his entire career. Will had been called up because the government was considering sending a scientific commission of mathematical experts to England and France to compile data and theoretical information related to artillery and aeroplane work, including bombing.

Major William D. MacMillan was recruited at the University of Chicago where he was one of this country's leading astronomers. "I took dinner with Capt. Kinsky, formerly prof. of physics at Chgo. the other night at the Cosmos Club which is a club mainly of scientific men [and] saw there a number of men I knew," he wrote John, Jr. from Washington. "I met Prof. Pegram who is one of the Deans at Columbia and who will be one of the members of this commission. . . . Prof. Hull of the Department of Physics at Dartmouth is another member." The men present generally felt that the army was more inclined "to cooperate with and enlist the services of our scientific men than a few months ago," Will said. "There is no doubt but that the scientific men of the country are hard at work on problems that have already been presented to them, and quite likely they will be drawn in more and more as time goes along."

While still waiting in Washington to see if the commission would materialize, Will wrote to John, Jr. at Camp Dodge:

"I have your letter of July 10th in which you ask for my impression of things here. I have the feeling that the organization here is so vast that it is impossible for anyone to properly estimate it through direct contact. . . . There have been literally acres of buildings put up here and many offices are scattered throughout the city still. The Ordnance Dept alone has five or six enormous buildings and any one man seems utterly insignificant in such a swarm of people.

"Our artillery has over forty different types of guns and over 100 varieties of ammunition requiring over 100 range tables. . . . Pershing [who had been named commander of the American Expeditionary Forces] is calling for guns which will outrange the German guns so we shall soon have some new guns and ammunition to fill that bill. . . . At present, I am 'mathematician' in the Ordnance Dept at $200 per month." (As an army captain, John, Jr.'s pay was also $200 monthly.)

For his part, John, Jr. was anxious to be in the thick of things. Speculating on the possibility of his being shipped overseas anytime soon, he wrote to his parents at Bass Rocks on July 17, "It seems pretty well substantiated that our departure for abroad has been delayed, but some 17,000 recruits are due here the latter part of this month so that someone will have to get out." In the meantime, he was "leading a rather hectic existence" that included a full social calendar.

"On Friday night we had regimental reviews . . . and after them Wheelock [Whitney] gave a dinner party at the Hyperion Club. . . . Saturday night there was another party at the Country Club. . . . Then last night I had to go to town to see one of the Generals daughters off [to California]."

Suddenly in mid-August, while his parents were still vacationing at Bass Rocks, John, Jr. wired them that his outfit was preparing to leave Camp Dodge for France. They should come to New York where he would be at Camp Mills near Garden City, Long Island, before shipping out, he advised. Following his instructions, John, Sr. and Edna arrived in New York the same day John, Jr. reached Camp Mills on Thursday, August 15. The three said their goodbyes that evening in a Garden City hotel, along with General Foote and other officers and their families. "John appeared about 9:30 and was with us until nearly midnight. . . . Of course, we had to put in more or less time visiting with others, so we did not have any too much of John to ourselves," John, Sr. wrote Fred Hanchette.

Early the next morning, Captain John MacMillan, Jr. called for General Foote at the hotel in a car at 7:20 A.M. and they motored down to the docks at Hoboken, New Jersey. "We do not know the name of the boat he is on, nor when it sailed," John, Sr. told Fred. "I found that the names have been taken off the ships and they are known only by numbers. We went down to the harbor to see the transports. They are weird looking sights the way they are camouflaged."

My father's ship lay off Staten Island for more than a week before embarking for France. Writing to his parents from "An Atlantic Port," the date inked out by the ship's censor, John, Jr. informed his parents: "You may be interested to know that a recommendation was forwarded to Washington last Sunday that I be made major [as permanent adjutant to General Foote]. . . . However, I must impress upon you the necessity of not telling anyone about it. I will cable you as soon as I do get promoted if at all."

The latest war news he had was encouraging: "I see by the *Times* that the French have staged another splendid attack and netted some 8,000 prisoners. The situation certainly looks promising and I have hopes that by the time we get into it that the Allies will have regained all the ground lost since last March 21st and then some."

On March 21, German Field Marshall Ludendorff had launched a massive assault on the British lines from Arras to La Fere. Within a week the Germans advanced twenty-five to forty miles, and they were within cannon shot of Paris by late May. This great spring offensive faltered when U.S. Second Division troops recaptured Belleau Wood near Chateau-Thierry on July 6. Ludendorff attacked both sides of Rheims in the Second Battle of the Marne on July 15, but the assault broke down against French defenses. On July 18, turning the tables on the Germans, the Allies counterattacked at Soissons, forcing them to retreat across the Marne.

Ten days after boarding ship and still in port, John, Jr. and his outfit were hardly happy and contented on shipboard, but "we are at least comfortable," he wrote his parents. "The men are carefully exercised each day, and are . . . quite as well cared for here as they would be on shore." In all probability this would be his last letter before sailing, "as the ships censor has declared that he [has] no

John, Jr. carried these photos of his parents and brother Cargill to France in a pocket wallet. After the war, the unfolded wallet stood on his bedroom dresser for the rest of his life.

intention of taking any more mail ashore before our arrival overseas. . . . While I think of it you might mail to me (not parcel post) two of those unbreakable watch crystals and two of the khaki straps for my wrist watch. It is a small Waltham. You know it was so hot at Dodge that it melted my other unbreakable one." John, Jr. had started to number his letters home; this was No. 3.

Writing to his brother Cargill at the summer military training camp at Andover, John urged Gee: "When you get back to New Haven work like a dog on *everything* . . . because it will eventually get you where you want to be. Every single thing I have ever studied has been of value to me in the year that I have been out of college, and I only wish that I had studied more thoroughly when I was there, and not put in so much time at bridge, Maury's [his friend Maurice Smith's room] and the Taft Bar."

He also advised Cargill to keep up his language studies. "During the past week I have managed to make myself invaluable because of my scanty knowledge. I have had occasion to converse [with crewmen on board the transport] in French, German, Spanish, Italian and Portuguese. To be quite frank . . . I know that we would have been severely handicapped without them [his languages]. I have a hunch that it was because of them that the General finally put in his recommendation for my promotion."

John, Jr.'s family learned of his promotion, which came through on August 22, before he did. John, Sr. wrote from his office: "Cargill just called me up from the house and tells me that in looking thru the war orders in the *New York Times* he found notice of your appointment as major. . . . "I am sure it is needless to tell you *how very proud we are*. I have an idea that this makes you the youngest major in the army."

The war news being printed in Minneapolis was "so very cheerful that we are getting quite optimistic and I am afraid too much so for our own good,"

John, Sr. continued. "While the Germans have been driven back to the Hindenburg line, yet I have no doubt there is a very strong defensive position there. . . . Next month will be a very interesting time and will probably determine whether or not they will be able to hold that line the balance of this year. I imagine if they are driven further it will be a comparatively easy matter to keep them going."

Everyone at the office was "quite exercised" over the new draft regulations (which required all men between the ages of eighteen and forty-five to register for the draft), he remarked. "It seems that everyone has to claim exemption and I find the temper of our office force here is that they will not claim it, so I presume I will have to do it for them. We simply could not run the organization if these men between 31 and 45 are drafted, as that takes in practically the entire organization from Uncle Dan down." (Several Cargill employees did, however, join the armed services.)

John, Jr.'s first letter to his parents from overseas was datelined September 10, the Ritz Hotel, Piccadilly, London. "By a rare stroke of luck I managed to get in to London for an afternoon and evening," he wrote. "I have not been to bed for the last two nights and have not had my clothes off for seventeen nights. Sheets will feel good to me. I was to have met the General here today, but somehow we missed connections, so I will return to camp in the morning. We are located in an English rest camp, more I cannot say, except that it is not for long.

He was surprised, he wrote, to find that the lid on liquor had been removed. "Of course when we debarked all the officers made a bee line for the bar, but somehow or other a year of absolute abstinence did not seem to improve the taste for the stuff, and two glasses of beer was absolutely all I could swallow. Tonight we had dinner at the Savoy and I ordered a bronx cocktail. Would you believe it I couldn't finish it."

His outfit had experienced "a most interesting and anything but uneventful voyage which I hope to be able to tell you about some day," he said. "At present it is of course, out of the question, although you have undoubtedly read of some of our adventures in the newspapers. They were really corking." On September 17, upon reaching his unit's training camp "after almost continuous travelling since August 12th," John, Jr. described his new surroundings in a nine-page letter home:

"We are located at a most picturesque town in the very heart of France. It is called Clermont-Ferrand and is in the department of Puy-de-Dome. You, of course, are familiar with the region. It is an old volcanic region, and is filled with low mountains, very much eroded, but still quite angular. They are called Puys, and the highest of them is the Puy-de-Dome, about 1000 ft. high, just west of the town.

"Clermont is a town of about 20,000, and is exceedingly picturesque but like all French towns very dirty, and with narrow winding streets. It is built about a long hill, and consequently has very steep hills, so steep in fact that our big cars have difficulty in navigating. We have a large Winton limousine for the use of the General, and it is so long that we cannot turn many of the corners without backing. . . . The country is magnificent, still green as can be, and on every hand are magnificent views, in fact we have very few like them at home, chiefly because our mountains are in wild or arid regions, whereas these are covered with orchards and cultivated fields."

Brigade headquarters was located in a building that had formerly housed ecclesiastical students on one of the dirtiest, narrowest, darkest, and poorest streets of the town, and "our detachment has not arrived yet so we are without trunks, sheets, bedrolls, etc." The former residents had left behind an excellent library, and the building had electric lights, but "I have been unable to find any running water for bathing. Personally I don't believe that the brothers believed in it."

The regiments were scattered in villages as many as twenty or thirty kilometers away, he explained. "Last night and today we inspected the men in their billets. My conclusion is that billeting is one of the last things to be sought. The men have to sleep in bare rooms, six to 20 in a room, on the floor with only bedsacks filled with straw beneath them. . . . Vermin and flies are inevitable. The only bathing facilities are usually the village fountains, and it is quite a problem to keep the men from drinking from them. . . . The water is invariably contaminated."

While in Paris he and fellow officers had stayed at the Continental "where we received excellent treatment. A larger limousine was put at our disposal, and we took in Paris in 36 hours. . . . That evening we had a rather amusing incident. Someone said that we must have dinner at Ciro's, but we thought we would check up by asking our driver. He replied: 'Why it must be some place, 'cause I take any number of General officers there.' It was some place, as you doubtless know."

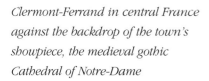

Clermont-Ferrand in central France against the backdrop of the town's showpiece, the medieval gothic Cathedral of Notre-Dame

Captain John H. MacMillan, Jr. in flight or driving gear

By September 20, John, Jr. was "beginning to get well organized. My office is already running very smoothly, although I lost my Sergeant Major and two stenographers just before leaving the U.S., all having been exposed to measles.

"This afternoon we inspected Col. Vestal's outfit, which is located in a string of villages spread all along a beautiful little valley. Bob Paine's battalion is . . . located in a magnificent chateau . . . at the top of a squalid, filthy little village. . . One wing of the castle was inhabited, in fact the officers had their quarters with the family who lived there, and they told me that it was quite modern.

"The rest of the castle was entirely abandoned and . . . it was in this part that the men were quartered. The woodwork and any wooden flooring that there may have been was gone, and nothing remained but masonry and a few beams, all of very dark smoke stained oak. The rooms were at least 20 feet high . . . The kitchens were most interesting, and were being used by our men without any . . . alterations, except that they had to provide metal sheeting for tops to the stone stoves. The huge cauldrons made of iron and stone were merely cleaned out and fires built beneath them. . . . The cooks told me that they were of just the right size for 500 men."

On John, Jr.'s first Sunday in Clermont-Ferrand, General Foote and his adjutant were invited to dine with a baron and baroness. "It was a most elaborate luncheon with several kinds of wine which we all had to drink because of the Baron's pride in his wine cellar," John, Jr. wrote. "His champagne was particularly fine, while his cognac (80 years old) nearly choked me." The baroness, a woman in her forties, had just returned from sixteen months at the front with several decorations for bravery under fire, "the last one having been conferred by Gen. Pershing . . . at Chateau-Thierry."

Later that day, joined by other officers, General Foote and John, Jr. had tea at a chateau near Rhions, "which was by far the most magnificent of any we had seen yet. . . . We had in our party a famous portrait painter, a Red Cross Capt., and he declared that there were many [portraits] there of great age (saved from the Revolution) and of great value as well as beauty. The library, a huge sunlit series of rooms opening on to the terrace, contained more than 60,000 volumes. It would have delighted Father."

Following tea ("The linen and silver were quite the finest I have ever seen, and made a most profound impression on the General"), they were still at the table when into the room "burst about a dozen of the handsomest children you ever saw ranging from 4 to 8. The oldest carried a wreath of oak leaves and made a very pretty little speech to the general in which he stated that the leaves came from a tree which his great grandfather had planted from acorns brought from America 130 years before. Then all the rest recited English nursery rhymes which reminded me of when I used to recite 'Maitre corbeau sur un arbre perche.'"

Weekdays back at brigade headquarters, it was business as usual. "Yesterday was undoubtedly the busiest I have had since joining the army," John, Jr. wrote home on Monday, September 24. "When I came in at 9 A.M. I found [correspondence] piled a foot high on my desk, and I kept four stenographers busy all day. . . . This morning [General Foote] approved in its entirety my scheme for the organization of our headquarters. . . . After more discussion with people who have been to the front I find that we are to be vastly more important and are to have far more responsibility than we ever imagined.

"If I go into the field as adjutant I shall most certainly have a tremendous job on my hands. It is really quite staggering, but I have enough of the MacMillan conceit against which Aunt Emma once warned me to feel confident of my ability to handle it."

When or even if he would actually get to the front remained to be seen, however. The German line was staggering under a succession of Allied onslaughts that had turned the tide of the war. On September 26, the American First Army launched the Meuse-Argonne offensive with Sedan as its objective. This was the greatest battle mounted by U.S. troops prior to 1944; 896,000 American soldiers with 135,000 French troops took part in the advance. In four days, struggling through forest against German machine guns and artillery, the attackers took the commanding height of Montfaucon and 18,000 prisoners.

"We are all quite thrilled by the big push that is going on, [but] frightfully anxious for news," my father wrote his parents on September 27. "Practically all we get are the official communiques and they are so . . . unsatisfactory. The United States is the real place from which to get the war news. . . . The newspapers here are not allowed to print any comment, few maps, and poor ones at that."

He had been to a bridge party the day before at a French home, where "running true to family traditions, I won a prize, a very beautiful little silver ash tray. . . . To-night the General & I are having dinner with a Miss Oglesby, who is described by the Frenchmen as being the heiress of the former Grand Duke of Illinois [whom this might have been, I have no idea; there is no place in France named Illinois]. . . . Mother will rejoice I am sure, to hear that I am wearing heavy woolen underwear for the first time in eight years. I could buy no other kind, and I had to have clean clothes. However, the buildings are not heated and it is rather cool so that I do not suffer as I thought I would."

In Minneapolis my grandparents were becoming worried when they still had not heard from John, Jr. by September 25. Overseas mail was taking weeks to get through, but "I have heard of several cablegrams being received from Minneapolis boys . . . from England so of course, I am sure that you are there also but we have been somewhat disappointed not to hear from you direct," John, Sr. wrote.

"Cousin Jim [Taylor] and [his wife] Ella, Mother, Cargill and I motored

A poster urging Americans at home to support the war by investing in war bonds

A U.S. Food Administration plea for Americans to "save the wheat for our soldiers"

down to La Crosse last week and had a very pleasant trip of it. . . . They have the most wonderful crops in that region and the farmers I think are more prosperous than ever before known. They are getting 40 to 45 cents per lb. for tobacco so that they will make from $800.00 to $1000.00 per acre on that. Then they are getting 60 cents per lb. for butter fat so that their dairy products are also more profitable than ever before known.

"I suppose you know something about the new tax bill which has just passed the House to raise eight billion. On top of it comes the 4th Liberty Loan issue of six billion. They are staggering amounts and I am wondering if it is going to be possible for the country to meet them. . . . If some means can be devised to get at the farmer and the laboring classes, who are getting the biggest pay also ever known, to do their full share, then it could be made a great success." (Cargill Elevator Company had paid its annual dividend that summer—on net profits that barely reached $125,000—in four-percent Liberty Bonds.)

John, Jr.'s first three letters home reached my grandparents on October 1. My grandfather immediately replied: "We have been frightfully worried about you. [It] seemed as though it was possible that your ship had been submarined and sunk. We are most exceedingly anxious to know what the experience was that you . . . refer to.

"There was an article in the newspapers here which stated that on the 8th an English ship transporting American troops had been torpedoed off the coast of England but that they were able to beach the ship and that all the troops had been rescued by destroyers, and that there was not a life lost. It went on to say this ship had something wrong with its machinery and that it dropped behind the convoy and we are all wondering if it is possible that this was your ship.

"You do not refer to your promotion so I take it that you have not heard of it. . . . I was very much interested in your remarks about the removal of the lid on liquor. I do not understand that for . . . if there was ever a time that a man needs to be in command of all of his faculties, it is when the lives of other men are in his charge. . . . We are all very much interested on this side in the prohibition that goes into effect next July as a war measure. The maltsters have already been stopped in making any new malt and the brewers will not be allowed to make any beer after Dec. 1st."

In a handwritten postscript to this typed letter, he added: "Think the name of that torpedoed ship was Persic. I am now quite of the opinion that your outfit were aboard."

John, Sr. forwarded John, Jr.'s three letters to Cargill at Yale, who wrote to his brother on October 5: "I am certainly glad to hear from you." Yale was a changed school, he informed him. "We are in the army now. . . . Today we all had to have the military hair cut and it really is a funny sight. Another rather amusing sight was when we all appeared in issue clothes for the first time, but we are settling down and will all be in over seas hats by next week. Of the 150,000 that are in the Students Army Training Corps we are the only detachment that does not have to wear the S.A.T.C. hat cord. We wear the artillery hat cord. . . . It has gotten around that we are to go across before June, but I think that that will only include the fellows that are twenty or over. Yet it does not seem that the government should spend so much money on us if they are not going to use us. We are getting thirty dollars a month, have issue clothes and everything else. This is no R.O.T.C."

On October 8, when his parents had heard nothing further from John, Jr., my grandfather wrote him: "I understand from those who have had sons abroad for a long time that [letters] come in rather irregularly—on the average of about once in three weeks, so I suppose we have no right to expect anything from you so soon, but just the same we should like very much to know where you are and what you are doing.

"It is needless to tell you how tremendously interested we are in the fighting that is going on and the efforts of the Germans now to get peace so they will not have to admit that they are whipped. . . . I am hoping that France and the Allies are going to break thru on the Southern battle line so they will be able to cut across the lines of retreat of the troops further North and that the Germans will meet with such an overwhelming disaster that it will force them to come to terms."

Business was as lively as ever that fall, he reported, "and we are getting filled up everywhere. Ships that were intended to be loaded with grain have been diverted for use of the army on account of this big offensive so that grain has been backing up from the seaboard until I am afraid another ten days or two weeks will see the elevators all over the Northwest filled to the roof. We have never required such an enormous amount of money to handle the business. Everyone is rushed to death and we are all quite happy. . . . I think we can rest assured that [our profits] will be reasonable and that is all one can expect during war times."

Peace appeared to be in the offing. During the first week in October, Allied troops from Australia, New Zealand, Canada, and the United Kingdom successfully breached Germany's formidable Hindenburg Line, a ten-mile deep defense zone, belted with barbed wire. With the German army crumbling and dangerously close to final defeat, newly appointed Imperial Chancellor Prince Max of Baden sent a message to President Wilson, asking for an armistice.

"We are fast rounding into shape, but are just a bit worried over these peace offers," my father wrote home on October 6. "It may be that we never will get to the front except for border patrol service. Of course we are anxious for the war to be over, but I would like to get one good crack at the Germans with our brigade before that time. It really does look dubious though.

"We have had lots of social activity lately with more to come. Our schedule for next week looks something like this:"

Sunday afternoon:	Tea at the Chateau Villeneuve
Sunday evening:	Theatre with Madame Dumont
Monday afternoon:	Tea with the Countess de Choiseul
Tuesday evening:	Dinner & theatre with Miss Oglesby
Wednesday afternoon:	Official visit to Nevers
Thursday afternoon:	Bridge at Mme. Chaffraud's
Friday evening:	Dinner with Mme. de Villetre
Saturday, 3 P.M.:	Dedication of a cemetery followed by tea with a French general

Later that day after fulfilling his first engagement, he added: "This afternoon we went out to the Chateau de Villeneuve and found it perfectly delightful. Their library . . . was a little gem, a trifle dark perhaps but marvelous nevertheless. Their gardens were also perfect. . . . They had a very marvelous tennis court, one of the best that I have ever seen. It seems that the old gentleman is president of some very famous Paris tennis club, and is in fact considered the father of French tennis. . . . His daughter not only speaks perfect English but plays a marvelous game.

"But I must close. It's time for the theatre. Isn't war hell."

Within the week, however, the war became infinitely more real to my father. "We have just had a magnificent drive across France, the General, George Brooke [their chauffeur], and myself in the General's Cadillac," he wrote to his parents from Dijon on October 11. "We are on our way to the front for 10 days of observation. . . . We are of course immensely pleased with the opportunity, and expect to bring back with us much that will be of value. . . . Where we are going or to what units we will be attached we do not know, and if I did I could hardly tell you.

Bunkers on the infamous Hindenburg line, named for German Chief of Staff General Paul von Hindenburg, who withdrew his army to the more defensible line east of Bapaume and north of Soissons in France in March 1917

"Last night I had a most interesting thing happen to me. I had become quite lost just before dinner and enquired of a Frenchman the way home. He exclaimed 'You speak French! Come with me.' He grabbed me by the arm, hustled me through dark alleys and I finally found myself in the editorial room of one of the papers. It seemed that Mr. Wilson's reply to the German Chancellor had just come in and they wished it translated so that it could be read to the soldiers at the theatre (an American vaudeville was to be given). I did so and later had the privilege of hearing it read at the theatre. My translation was also printed in the morning paper."

The press in America almost unanimously decried the German peace offer as a maneuver or trap, and my grandfather and his friends in Minneapolis worried that President Wilson would begin negotiations with Germany. "None of us felt their word had any value," he wrote John, Jr. on October 15. "Our Chamber of Commerce yesterday wired the President as follows: 'Members of this Exchange believe that the civilized world will be satisfied with nothing but unconditional surrender from the central powers and punishment for those guilty of the atrocities.' I have no doubt that the president received thousands of such messages. I merely give this as an illustration of the almost universal feeling."

News from the front continued as good as could be hoped for, John, Sr. continued. "It looks to me very much as though we will be in position to force a surrender of the German armies before next spring, provided that the weather remains good until Jan. 1st. I do not believe Germany can stand the fearful pounding they are getting all along the front. It is quite evident that they are short of ammunition and manpower as they do not seem to be holding anywhere excepting in the American sector."

The Germans, as well as the Allies, were also battling a world pandemic of Spanish influenza, which in four months claimed more lives than were lost in the four years of the World War. In the United States alone, where the flu closed schools, churches, and theaters, estimates of the death toll reached 500,000. Many war plants shut down, telephone service was cut in half, and the draft call was suspended in several cities. Citizens scanned long lists of the dead in newspapers, published side-by-side with rules for preventive hygiene.

Following an influenza outbreak at Yale, Cargill was in quarantine at the school. At the Great Lakes Naval Training Station, Aunt Mary's son Malcolm Rowles was seriously ill with the disease. In Madison, Wisconsin, according to articles in La Crosse newspapers, Will S. Cargill was caring for seven convalescent soldiers in his home; two years later, the flu would take his own life.

On October 18 my grandparents finally received John, Jr.'s first letters from Clermont-Farrand. "It would almost seem you were having a delightful pleasure trip," my grandfather replied. "The French people are surely most hospitable if all of them are as courteous as those [you mentioned]." Uncle Will had received his uniform and was waiting to sail for Europe in about ten days, he told John, Jr.

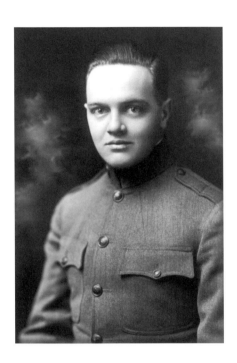

Austen Cargill described his World War I service record thus: "Enlisted U.S. Navy as machinist mate, 2nd class, December 13, 1917. After two weeks training in submarine chaser work, was transferred to work on aviation motors. Sailed on May 14, 1918, and was stationed thirty miles down Gironde River from Bordeaux, where along with F. [Frank] L. Neilson, was in charge of maintenance of Navy aviation motors patrolling the French Coast against submarines. In October, we both secured transfer to the Northern Bombing Group engaged in bombing operations near Calais as part of the Royal Air Force. Remained with the group until returned to States in February, 1919."

In California, Fred Hanchette had passed his physical and worried my grandfather by hoping to go to France with the Red Cross. "Even if he has gotten entirely over that lung trouble, the cold damp weather of France in winter without sufficient heat will be very hard on him, and I do not feel any too easy about it."

In France, my father returned from the front on October 24 to find a two-week-old telegram announcing his promotion to major along with a sheaf of congratulatory letters from his family. "I am proud as punch to know a major," wrote Chief Machinist's Mate Austen Cargill, who had joined the navy at the tail end of 1917. "We gobs aren't used to associating with officers of such a high rank and I don't lose a single opportunity of bragging about it."

Austen was supervising a large repair operation for Liberty Motors at the U.S. naval air base in France at Pauillac, Gironde. "I have become as enthusiastic over aviation as I used to be over automobiles," he wrote. "It certainly is great sport and not half as difficult or dangerous as one would think. When I get my home on [Lake] Minnetonka, I certainly will have a boat to go to work in each day."

"We are all bursting with pride," Uncle Dan MacMillan had written: "It is a funny thing how titles and rank dazzle the imagination . . . but I want to say to you, John, as between man and man and good American citizens, the best title that you will ever possess in my estimation, is plain John H. MacMillan, Junior, citizen of the U.S.A. . . . One good, solid conversation with you would prove to any man that you have not spent your time idly over the frivolities of life."

Responding to Dan's six-week-old letter, John, Jr. replied: "Your congratulations on my promotion certainly arrived at an opportune time in fact the very day on which I received notification of it myself. . . . The fact that I was promoted . . . did not mean that I was to assume any new duties. It merely meant that the General was satisfied in the way in which things ran, and I can quite truthfully say that I owe it to the efforts and ability of the other officers on the staff, more than to any unusual demonstration of ability on my part."

His trip to the front had been "most interesting," he wrote, and he had even had a couple of rather narrow escapes: "One wet muddy afternoon (it is always wet, and always muddy at the front) we were going forward in the General's car to visit an advanced battery (it was on a magnificent macadam road in territory just vacated by the Germans so still in perfect shape) when without the usual warning, which consists in a preliminary noise like the ripping of a huge sheet of silk, a 150mm (about 6 inch) shell burst not fifteen yards in front of us and just off the road. [Luckily the muddy ground] rather smothered it, and our car was merely covered with mud, not a splinter hitting it.

"[On the second occasion] we were going through . . . what had formerly been a village, but was now as flat as the rest of the country, when a couple of 77s fell about 200 meters to our right. The Corporal, our chauffeur, showed a tendency to slow up to watch them, and I was later joshed about my request to him to make haste, but it was fortunate I did so for the next two landed right where we had been not five seconds before. As it was . . . they merely took the paint off the rear fenders."

Before leaving the area, John, Jr. and his party had also been "fortunate" enough to witness the bombardment of a road by German 380mm guns. "This time though we were about a kilometer away and as the road was quite deserted could watch it with the same enjoyment with which you would a fourth of July celebration. . . . This particular bombardment lasted for some 30 minutes, and was amazingly accurate, as hardly a shot was more than 100 feet away from the road and two were right in it. The craters are tremendous, big enough to swallow up several of our largest trucks."

Writing to his parents, John, Jr. said that his ten days at the front had coincided with "the exchange of all these peace notes, and I am proud to be able to state that the general sentiment among officers and men was to the effect that they one and all hoped that the war would not end until we were able to carry it into Germany proper. To let the Germans off as easily as to stop the war now would be nothing short of criminal, horrible as the war is.

"I met the Commander in Chief [General John Pershing], three Corps Commanders, and innumerable division and brigade commanders, of course, through General Foote, who was a personal friend of all. They all addressed him as Stephen and then explained that part of the operation in which they were interested quite as father would explain the grain situation in Minneapolis to a grain man from New York. George Brooke [the chauffeur] and I drank it all in. . . . It was the opportunity of a lifetime and I treated it as such except that I kept no notes out of regard to regulations.

"I learned more about my own duties and those of our staff than I would

General Pershing's General Headquarters of the American Army at the provincial town of Chaumont, on the rail line from Troyes to Nance and at the headwaters of the Marne. General Pershing went to such lengths to keep its whereabouts secret that Americans at home knew only that it was "somewhere in France."

in a year at school. I visited everything from G.H.Q. to the front line trenches, and experienced everything from being shelled to being machine gunned. Fortunately in spite of being exposed more than I would in a year of normal life at the front, I am quite unharmed, except for having to go without a bath for some two weeks.

"The letters of congratulation were most certainly appreciated and by the time I got through reading them I began to think that I was some pumpkin. You asked what I wanted for Christmas. I sent you a Christmas slip. You may enclose in the box four pairs of major's leaves, regulation size. . . . Don't under any circumstances get any solid gold, they are not necessary, and the best thing is gold plated silver ones. . . . I can think of nothing else except a couple of those khaki straps for my wrist watch, and a pair of unbreakable goggles giving as wide a field of view as possible and the maximum of protection to the eyes."

Four days later on October 28, John, Jr. received his father's October 1 letter mentioning the *Persic*. "Father's surmises . . . were quite correct," he replied. "Since the details have already been published I see no harm in stating that we were in the same convoy as the Persic. . . . It was all very thrilling and I can make a most interesting story out of it." The French around Clermont continued to be more than kind to them, he said. "We are overwhelmed with invitations; at this very moment I ought to be out at one with the General but I begged off on the plea of . . . too much work to be done. My days are filled with visits to the various regiments, and I have to catch up with the paper work in the evening. True I have an assistant, but there are a certain number of things which I must see. In fact I try to read everything that goes on the General's desk, so that when he refers to anything I know what it is."

There was a rumor floating around that evening, John, Jr. continued, "that Austrian and German replies to our President's last note are on the way and that they are most favorable for peace. We are all very much worried for fear our Brigade will never get into action, although our training is really progressing very favorably. . . . [The war] can't be over too soon to please me . . . once we get our brigade up at the front, but we do want to get up as a unit before it is all over." By the end of October, however, Germany and its allies were collapsing on every front. An Allied offensive at Vittorio Veneto in Italy routed the Austrian army, and with British troops in Damascus and Aleppo, Turkey signed an armistice. Austria-Hungary signed an armistice on November 3, the day before the British captured twenty thousand prisoners and 450 guns at Valenciennes, and French and American forces swept through to Sedan.

A general armistice was imminent when John, Jr. wrote home on November 8: "We are quite excited by a rumor . . . that the armistice has been signed. . . . If the end should come today it would be a remarkable historic coincidence that it should follow upon the taking of Sedan." Actually, at the very time John, Jr. wrote, a German delegation was meeting with Allied representatives led by General Foch

at his headquarters in a railroad restaurant car on a siding in the Forest of Compiegne. Three days later, at five o'clock on the morning of November 11, 1918, they signed the armistice that ended the war. The firing stopped at 11 A.M.

Once the news was out, pandemonium ensued on both sides of the Atlantic as overjoyed citizens celebrated in the streets. John, Sr. was in Chicago on his way east on the morning the armistice was signed, and he described the scene in a letter to Fred Hanchette (who had never made it to France):

"It was a wild city. It looked as though the entire town was down on the streets and there was more noise and confusion and hilarity than I ever saw before in my life. Every conceivable kind of a vehicle was on the street packed with people to a point of breaking down, and they had every conceivable kind of thing for making noise from tin pans and horns up. New York I understand had even a wilder time than Chicago, and in all cities it was more or less the same thing."

John, Jr. reported from France: "The celebration here at Clermont was really pathetic in its enthusiasm. One of our bands came in and played . . . before the statue of Vercingetorix [the heroic Celt who united the Gauls against Caesar in 52 B.C.]. The square and all its approaches were jammed, and when they had finished by playing the Marseillaise, they were picked up by the crowd and carried around and around the square. Then the ban on dancing was of course removed, and even old men and women danced in the streets to music furnished by any old instrument. At the cafes in the evening no American could possibly buy a drink. At least a dozen Frenchmen fought for the check."

Beneath the gaiety there was of course a sobering sadness to the celebration, he concluded. "All France is thinking of its dead."

The Vercingetorix monument in Clermont-Ferrand

The S.S. Persic *was torpedoed off the English coast on September 8, 1918.*

Three months after the armistice, while he was waiting to be shipped home from France in St. Eulalie, Gironde, John, Jr. was at last able to discuss the *Persic* incident. "Mother wanted to know all about our submarine attack," he wrote home, "so here goes:"

> We crossed on the SS Tras Os Montes, a Portuguese boat, formerly the German VonBelow, a ship on the Japan run from Hamburg. She was of about 10,000 tons, and a beautiful boat, but unfortunately had been . . . taken over by the Portuguese. . . . The boat had been running between Algeria and Marseilles carrying 4,000 negroes at a clip, and as they had not the least idea of sanitation she was in unspeakable condition even when the General and I came aboard on Friday morning, August 17.

The troops boarded the next day, and they set sail on the 19th, but within hours the boat blew a boiler, so they returned to port for ten days of overhauling. Everything went wrong from the very start, what with

> our American troops (2,200 of them), our English signal boys, our Italian stewards, not to mention the Portuguese crew. No one could understand anyone else, and the Portuguese refused to listen to any of the Americans who could really have run the ship, as we had several naval officers as passengers.

After ten days at sea in a convoy of thirteen ships, John, Jr.'s troopship was about halfway between Ireland and England "on a bright sunny afternoon without a ripple on the water," when the *Persic* was attacked. "I was playing bridge in the smoking room when the whistle began to blow," he wrote. "I got to deck just in time to see the torpedo hit the Persic which was about a hundred yards behind us, *occupying our rightful position*. It seems that by mistake the Portuguese had gotten too much steam up and had crowded the Persic out. We had just received orders from the flagship to get back into position when the attack came."

Through his field glasses, my father could see the men forming on deck and the lifeboats being lowered. Several of the destroyers accompanying the convoy "turned in at full speed and dropped depth bombs at the place from which the submarine was supposed to have fired the torpedo [but without hitting their target]. They each made a tremendous rattle, far louder than the torpedo, and made our steel rails rumble in a very curious manner."

Troops on the *Tras Os Montes* learned that evening that the *Persic* "had been beached and the 2,800 men taken off in the four destroyers which had accompanied her."

Major John H. MacMillan, Jr. arrived home on the S.S. *Koeningen der Nederlander*, which docked five days late at Newport News, Virginia, on January 9, 1919. "These are very happy times for us," his father wrote to him at Camp Dodge, where he would be discharged from the army on January 21. "Just to know you are safely back on this side is an enormous relief."

He urged John, Jr. not to try to hurry through his discharge in any "irregular" way. "The papers of late have had some very disquieting articles on the breakdown in morale of our army officers since the armistice. I want you to see the thing through in the same brilliant way that you commenced your career— leaving a record without the slightest blemish. This is one of the most prominent milestones in your life's history."

He and Edna had not put anything of much value in his birthday or Christmas box, John, Sr. reminded him; now that he was home, his belated present would be new civilian clothes. "You can order whatever you want and send me the bills." His brother Cargill had taken John, Jr. at his word, his father said, and cleaned out his closet. "However, I do not believe that any of your old clothes would fit you now so [you are not] any the worse off because they are gone."

It would be a "nice and complimentary" gesture, John, Sr. suggested, if John, Jr. and his fellow brigade staff officers made "some kind of a valuable parting gift to General Foote. He has been exceedingly kind to all of you and a remembrance of this kind will always do a great deal to bind you all together." He also hoped that John, Jr. would sign up for the reserves. "The leadership of this country must necessarily come from its young men and there is no way that I know that you can continue your influence and your leadership better than you can by sticking by the colors." John, Jr. apparently agreed with his father, for he remained a major in the Reserve Officers Training Corps for about ten years.

My father returned to a changed nation following the World War. With more than half its 105 million citizens living in cities, America for the first time

Major John H. MacMillan, Jr., far left, and fellow officers with General Stephen Foote, seated in the center. The other men are, standing left to right: First Lieutenant George Brookes, Captain Donald Leslie, First Lieutenant Russell Bennett, First Lieutenant Walter Lewis, Second Lieutenant Drew, and Second Lieutenant Stanton; seated, left to right: Lieutenant Gambier, Colonel Kimmel, Major Gaul, and Lieutenant Bertin. In the rear is Second Lieutenant Timmons.

Thanks to trees planted before the turn of the century, Clifton Avenue presented an inviting vista when "Johnny" came marching home again in 1919.

had become a predominately urban society. Twenty years earlier, fewer than one third of the people lived in communities of more than 2,500; now New York boasted more than five million residents, and Chicago, almost three million. Increasing by leaps and bounds, the population, already swelled by thirty million since 1900, would grow another seventeen million before the end of the decade. Moreover, the average American could expect to live fifty-four years—five years longer than at the turn of the century.

Better and happier times were ahead, of that everyone was certain. Having dramatically increased production in their fields and factories to help win the war, Americans had a new sense of accomplishment. Thousands of new jobs had been created, and an expanded peacetime economy would mean more employment opportunities, better wages, and a higher standard of living. By the end of the decade, with Wall Street busier than ever and stocks climbing, business would be the ultimate expression of the American ideal and the successful businessman, an American hero.

Back in his civvies, John, Jr. was anxious to begin his career with the Cargill Elevator Company, but he was in no shape to do so. My father had come home from France suffering from nervous exhaustion; emotionally scarred and physically ill, he badly needed several months rest. John, Sr. was troubled with recurring headaches himself and presumed he, too, needed a vacation, so he and Edna made plans to take John, Jr. to California in February. Due to an influenza outbreak in the Los Angeles area, the three stayed at the Hotel Del Coronado in Coronado, California, before going to visit Fred and Emma Hanchette in Pasadena; both Senior and Junior played golf as Fred's guests at the Midwick Club.

The MacMillans returned home to 317 Clifton Avenue in Minneapolis in late April, and John, Jr. started work for the Cargill Elevator Company on the

Emma Cargill Hanchette

Emma and Fred Hanchette's residence at 1289 Oak Knoll in Pasadena where John, Jr. recuperated from nervous exhaustion in early 1919

trading floor of the Chamber of Commerce. His entire life had been leading up to this time, and he plunged into the work wholeheartedly, immersing himself in learning to be a good trader. In June, however, on a motor trip east with former Yale roommate Maurice Smith to attend a forty-six-class reunion, he picked up a fierce case of food poisoning. Complicated by a bad cold, it put him out of commission once again. John, Sr. disclosed to Fred Hanchette that he had reached home "a complete wreck."

John, Jr. spent the rest of that summer taking it easy and recovering, with his parents looking after him. In September, by now more than eager to return to work, he was assigned to the Duluth office, where he trained under Frank E. Lindahl, working as a cash grain buyer and pit trader on the exchange floor of the Duluth Board of Trade.

Frank Lindahl was becoming a legend at Cargill, having begun his career as a country elevator manager at Hope, North Dakota, for James F. Cargill in 1884. After the Cargill Elevator Company was organized in 1891, Lindahl opened the firm's Duluth office, which operated largely as a separate organization. Taking my father under his wing and treating him like a son, Lindahl supervised his work at the office and invited him to Thanksgiving dinner with his family.

When John, Jr. returned home for the Christmas holidays, he came down with another bad cold. He went back up to Duluth in January but was soon back home again, seriously ill with the life-threatening flu that his parents had tried to protect him from in California. Several weeks later, John, Sr. wrote to his brother-in-law Dr. John Rowles in La Crosse, "Dr. Staples insists that we must send [John, Jr.] to California as he is altogether too weak to stand the rigorous spring weather that we get in this climate."

John, Jr. was not strong enough to travel, however. Except for a few rides in the family limousine, he remained confined to the house. "He seems to collapse upon making any effort of any kind," John, Sr. wrote his brother Will, and February turned into March before John, Jr. started for California on the train. Emma reported that he arrived safely but very badly tired out, which was to be expected, and he stayed with the Hanchettes until mid-June. "We . . . had no idea when he left home that he was in anything like as serious condition as he was or we never would have passed on so much responsibility to you and Emma," John, Sr. wrote Fred Hanchette.

Both his father and Frank Lindahl kept John, Jr. up-to-date on business matters while he convalesced in California. "There has not been much change in the grain situation since you left, excepting that Elevator 'T' has sold considerable rye," John, Sr. wrote on March 17. "They have outstanding sales now of about 800 M bu. The car situation however, is worse if anything, than it has been at any time. I do not know when we will be able to get this rye shipped."

Panoramic view of Duluth and Lake Superior in 1920

Frank E. Lindahl always held a special place in John, Jr.'s affections. He helped shape the destiny of the Cargill Company and my father's career as well. In 1940 John, Jr. held an eightieth birthday and retirement party for Lindahl at our home in Orono. Amazingly enough, Lindahl learned to drive a car after he was eighty. He died in 1945 at St. Petersburg, Florida.

About that time Frank Lindahl in Duluth chartered the steamer *Emory L. Ford* to carry 500,000 bushels of rye to Buffalo, but Lake Superior was still frozen solid. It would probably be a week or ten days before a tug could break up the ice. "That ice bill will probably cost us from $75.00 to $100.00, but we are glad to do it to get the Steamer Ford in there." Lindahl also described for John, Jr. the house he was building on a hill overlooking the lake in Duluth:

"We are going to have two spare rooms, and the one on the lake side has the most marvelous view, and the next time you get sick, I am going to put you into that room and it would soon straighten you out, as it is tremendously exhilarating. I expect to have so much pep when I get up on that windy knoll, that I will certainly need you here to hold me down."

As a key employee, Lindahl had been allowed to purchase a large block of Cargill stock when the company was reorganized in 1916, but he later decided to sell it back to the company. "I must confess I cannot understand him at all," John, Sr. wrote Austen Cargill in August 1922, explaining that Lindahl considered the stock a complete failure. "I feel rather hurt over his lack of appreciation for what has been done for him [but] I am inclined to think that it is going to work out very much better this way. . . . I believe that this will entirely remove any anxieties he may have had in connection with the ownership of this stock and that . . . he will work very much better with the others than he has." Lindahl stayed on the job until retiring after fifty-five years of service at the venerable age of eighty in 1940.

On June 1, 1920, while my father remained with the Hanchettes in Pasadena, his grandmother Mary Jane McCrea MacMillan died at her daughter Mary Isabella Rowles's home in La Crosse. John, Sr. and Edna had driven down from Minneapolis to be with her, and Will MacMillan arrived from Chicago the next day for the funeral, as did his brother Dan from Minneapolis. Earlier that year doctors at Presbyterian Hospital in Chicago had confirmed that she had a bad heart; she had appeared to rally after going home to the Rowleses, but she was very frail and, despite various ups and downs, never recovered. Widowed twelve years, she was seventy-three years old. Following services at the Rowles residence, my great-grandmother was buried beside her husband Duncan D. McMillan at Oak Grove Cemetery. John, Sr. arranged for perpetual care of the family plot, paying $120 to the Oak Grove Cemetery Association.

Shortly after Mary Jane's funeral, John, Sr. sent my father up to Canada where the company had a logging operation near Victoria on Vancouver Island. This would be the first of several summers that John, Jr. spent working out-of-doors in British Columbia in an effort to combat his poor health and harden himself, but he arrived tired and depressed. "He said he did not feel able to call up his friends and was taking his meals in his room," John, Sr. wrote to Fred Hanchette. John, Sr. and Edna, along with Austen and Anne Cargill, were planning to join him there when word arrived from May Cargill that her husband Will S. was dying in Madison.

Putting their travel plans aside, John, Sr. took Edna to see her older brother. Senior's diary entry for June 23 reads: "George [Cargill] met us at train. Will quite a bit better. Seemed very glad to see us. Spent day with the family and went to Park Hotel for the night." More than two weeks later, while Will S. lingered between life and death, John, Sr. left Edna behind and made the trip to British Columbia with his son Cargill. "Cargill and I arrived 8 a.m. Vancouver," he wrote on July 16. "Mr. Johnston [the on-site manager] met us at train. Johnston, Cargill and I left for Victoria on night boat Princess Adelaide 11 p.m." Three days later, John, Sr. received a telegram from Austen stating that Will S. had died.

Mary Jane MacMillan with her daughter Mary Isabella Rowles in La Crosse. On November 14, 1918, three days after the armistice, Mary Jane wrote to Mary from Chicago: "Dr. [Rowles] was right about the war being over before Xmas. You never heard such bedlam as there has been here. I hope the kaiser will get all that is coming to him."

Will S. Cargill, who was survived by his wife Mary ("May") MacMillan Cargill, their two sons William and George, his brother Austen, and his two sisters Edna Cargill MacMillan and Emma Cargill Hanchette

Will S. was only fifty years old, but having forfeited his birthright by his double-dealing in Montana and other shenanigans, he was a broken man. After Will Cargill's death in 1909, Will S. had stayed on in Montana (where he was romantically involved with his partner's wife) until new management was appointed. These were very difficult years for his family, his son William Wallace later told author John Work for *Cargill Beginnings*.

William was in high school at the time, and he remembered that there had been no money for his mother and him and his brother George in La Crosse. "To help find money to live on, I set to work mowing lawns and, in the wintertime, shoveled four blocks of snow and fired the furnaces of four nearby houses. At our house (the former D. D. McMillan mansion), we lived entirely in the dining room to save heat." May's brother Dan G. McMillan, who had succeeded his father George as president of the local gas company, helped provide for the family.

When Will S. returned to La Crosse in the spring of 1912, he found nothing left for him there. After Dan G. McMillan purchased and moved into the former D. D. McMillan house, Will moved his family to Michigan, where he bought a chicken farm. He wasn't lazy, and he didn't want to be idle, his son said, but the chicken farm didn't prosper. The family was living on a thin income in 1915 when Austen Cargill came down from Minneapolis with an offer from Cargill Elevator to buy his brother's one-quarter share in the company. Will S. sold out for $25,000 cash and $225,000 in gold bonds on the La Crosse and Southeastern Railway.

The *La Crosse Tribune* reported that "Mr. Cargill succumbed to illness following the flu, complicated by pneumonia, contracted while in St. Petersburg, Fla., last winter, from which he never recovered." Upon the death of his parents, Will had moved to Madison in order to be with his sons William and George during their university years. Funeral services were held there, and the body was taken to La Crosse and buried in the family plot at Oak Grove.

John, Sr. did not return from Canada for the funeral; instead he stayed with John, Jr. and Cargill to oversee the logging activities until August. So many millions of board of feet of lumber had gone into building trenches during the World War that lumber prices had risen tremendously, and he was anxious to maximize the potential of the Cargill Securities property in British Columbia. Austen Cargill joined them there with Anne after his brother Will's death, and for the next several years, Austen would manage the Canadian venture, coming in for a great deal of criticism in the process from John, Jr. My father went home to Minneapolis for a few days' visit in October, but he remained in Canada over the Christmas holidays that year. Writing to him on December 23, John, Sr. remarked:

"I am very much interested in the good shooting you have and the fact that you have gotten such a taste for it. I have always had an idea you did not

John Jr.'s snapshots of lumberjacks (top) and loggers' housing surrounded by downed timber (below) at a Cargill lumber camp

care for anything of this sort. I think it is a splendid thing for you to cultivate, for anything that will keep you out in the open to give you fresh air and exercise will be a fine thing." He hoped that by the following spring, John, Jr. would be feeling quite himself. "Just as long as you are a little fearful of your condition, you can be rather sure that you are not entirely well, but I should think that perhaps a little later you will begin to crave seeing people and that will be a pretty good symptom that your system will stand it."

My father's health remained precarious for the next several years, but he persevered in building himself up by logging each spring and summer in British Columbia. In the fall of 1921 he put in several months in the Duluth office under Frank Lindahl; in subsequent years, he worked the balance of the year in the Minneapolis office, gaining increased experience as a grain merchandiser. His

This picture just about says it all: John H. MacMillan, Jr. loved the outdoor life in the Canadian timberlands.

brother Cargill spent summer vacations with him in British Columbia, and their father sometimes went up for a month at a time.

These were also perilous years for the Cargill Elevator Company. After a half dozen relatively prosperous years, the bottom began to fall out of the national economy in late 1920. Thousands of businesses failed, rapid deflation drove thousands of farmers into bankruptcy, and for the first time crop acreage in the United States began to decline. The principle cause of the decline is seldom recognized, but it had a profound effect upon the American economy in the next twenty years. Just as Henry Ford revolutionized transportation with the Model T, the Model T revolutionized the market for agricultural products. Before the automobile, the nation needed one-third of its cropland to produce fodder for draft animals. But with the Model T (and the export of hundreds of thousands of horses for use on the western front during the war), the demand for hay and oats rapidly diminished. When Ford introduced an affordable tractor, farm animals also were rapidly replaced. As the demand for land for fodder crops declined it became available for human food crops, and the profits for the latter declined. The result was a depression in American agriculture that began in the early 1920s, many years before the worldwide depression of the 1930s.

For the first time in its history, Cargill Elevator posted a loss (in excess of $116,000) for the crop year 1920–1921. "The Banks are very much alarmed over the bad losses the grain trade have sustained this year," John, Sr. wrote to Fred Hanchette in July 1921. A national railroad strike in 1921 added to the grain traders' problems.

Cargill pulled out of the decline to post reasonable profits of $420,000 the following year, but the company was not out of the woods. Writing to Fred Hanchette in October 1922, John, Sr. confided: "Matters in our own business are the worst I have ever seen at this time of year . . . so bad I really do not know which way to turn, as we are so peculiarly helpless. The enormous crop in Canada has simply flooded all the Eastern ports with grain, so it is impossible for Duluth to get boats unless they can guarantee prompt unloading in Buffalo and that we cannot do." Cargill Elevator barely wound up in the black that year, with a minimal profit of $34,000.

By spring John, Sr. was worrying that he might not be able to keep the company afloat. "Ever since the close of navigation we have found it impossible to sell our wheat," he wrote in April to Austen Cargill in British Columbia. "We have two cargoes still unsold in Buffalo and we have all the winter's accumulation in Duluth and do not seem to be able to get any bids at all. It is a most peculiar situation and I cannot figure it out." Cargill MacMillan, who was doing postgraduate work in statistics at Cambridge University after graduating from Yale, wrote to his father from England: "I was scared to death that I have been spending too much money."

The 1945 Cargill company history attributed the firm's sluggish sales and general malaise to the "revolution [that] was . . . taking place in the method of sales into the eastern consuming market."

> Up to this time Northwesterners offered their grain through brokers in Buffalo and New York basis c.i.f. [cost, insurance, plus freight] Eastern lake ports. They chartered the vessels, insured the grain, and drew on the buyers with documents (invoices, bills of lading, insurance certificates) attached. Not a single firm in this neighborhood made a practice of carrying grain in Buffalo or offering direct to Eastern consuming clientele. Nor did the Eastern concerns carry any grain stored in the West prior to 1919.

Following World War I, however, the largest Buffalo wheat broker had leased space in Duluth and begun buying wheat in the Minneapolis and Duluth exchanges. Once the beachhead had been breached, the invasion continued. Two important New York exporters began buying spot grain in the Northwest, and the large European importers—Dreyfus, Continental, Mooney—opened offices in the American interior to buy their grain direct. John, Jr. would later recall: "Overnight you suddenly discovered that . . . you didn't know of any business. You never had a bid. The grain just went right on by. It didn't take any genius to figure out that either we set ourselves up to compete with that or they would just take us over piecemeal."

As if on cue at that critical point for the company, opportunity came calling. In the spring of 1923 Cargill was offered the chance to take over an important Milwaukee grain firm, Taylor & Bournique Co., which had not weathered the depression and was being forced to liquidate. T & B had branch offices in New York, Boston, Philadelphia, Pittsburgh, and most importantly, in Buffalo. The latter was exactly what Cargill needed, wrote John, Sr. to an associate, "so that we can move grain freely through that port at all times and not be in a position where the Canadian grain can absorb all the facilities there at the expense of the Northwest."

The deal was consummated in June and cost Cargill Elevator Company very little. In exchange for purchasing the office furniture and equipment and taking over the leases on the offices, Cargill acquired the T & B organizations in Milwaukee, Buffalo, and New York. The lease on a large T & B terminal in Milwaukee belonging to the Chicago, Milwaukee & St. Paul Railroad was transferred to Cargill, as was the lease on a small terminal at Ogdensburg, New York. Also part of the bargain was T & B's private wire system, which gave Cargill a real boast in the area of communications. "The wire service is a wonderful thing; it keeps us posted in a way that we never have been posted in the past," John, Sr. wrote to Austen Cargill.

The acquisition of Taylor & Bournique was truly a giant step forward for the Cargill Elevator Company, which in one fell swoop was transformed from a regional into a national organization. Quoting Wayne Broehl in *Cargill: Trading the World's Grain,* "It would not be an exaggeration to say that one can trace the modern Cargill's world focus directly to this single management decision."

Cargill MacMillan returned from Cambridge in the fall and set up a statistical department at the Cargill Elevator Company. John, Jr. was also back from British Columbia. "I have both John Jr. and Cargill in the business with me now," John, Sr. wrote to his banker friend Tom Baxter in October 1923. You could hear the pride in his voice. If John, Sr. played favorites, and he tried hard not to, he was particularly captivated by John, Jr. and took a special delight in his elder son's wide-ranging new ideas, unbounded enthusiasm, and bright intellect. John, Sr. had learned through adversity to be cautious, but John, Jr. was always more willing to take risks, and his father was coming to rely more and more on his judgement.

In early 1924, instead of going to California and the Hanchettes' for their usual midwinter break, John, Sr. and Edna took a Mediterranean cruise aboard the S.S. *Rotterdam,* sailing from New York on February 6. In their absence John, Jr., who was showing signs of strain at the office, returned to the Cargill logging operation in British Columbia. Despite Austen Cargill's best efforts, the logging business was deteriorating, but John, Sr. did not want to abandon it for reasons he had explained in a letter to Frank Hixon:

> Austen has taken an intense interest in the problem. . . . His tastes are entirely along mechanical lines. I do not think that he ever will fit well into the grain business or ever be happy in it. The business was well organized . . . but when the slump in log prices came, Austen fully realized that the methods which he was using could not possibly succeed, so he got further back from the water's edge. . . . I am very anxious to see him make a success. . . . Austen has an excellent knowledge of accounting. He does not fool himself in the slightest as to his operating costs, so that all told I feel it would be a grave mistake not to give him this . . . chance.

John, Sr. soon had a change of heart, however. He was no sooner home after ten stimulating weeks in Madeira, Portugal, Spain, Gibraltar, Algiers, Athens, Constantinople, the Holy Land, Egypt, Italy, and the Riviera than he received an alarming five page letter from John, Jr. in Call Creek, British Columbia. In it my father outlined what he felt to be wrong with the way Austen was going about logging. "You will remember the essence of our scheme was to do nothing that was not already standard," John, Jr. wrote. Austen evidently had ideas of his own, and John, Jr. was pretty sure he would bungle the job. "You can't drive Austen to make a decision relating to things more than a few days distant, and when he does decide everything must be done right off the bat, a very expensive and nerve racking process."

Keeping Fred and Emma in California abreast of the situation, John, Sr. wrote on May 6: "I am sorry we allowed Austen to go on with that logging operation, for unfortunately he has not seemed to grasp the essentials and is tying up a lot of money." John, Jr. was home from Canada with a bad ax cut on his

Anne and Austen Cargill in British Columbia with the first of their two adopted children, Anne Louise (who later changed her name to Margaret Anne Cargill), born in 1920. Their son James Ray Cargill was born in 1923.

182

George Cargill with sailfish. George and John, Jr. vacationed together in Florida and Cuba over the Christmas holidays in 1924. The next year they traveled together to Panama. George had grown up in the former D. D. McMillan house in La Crosse, across the street from the Cargill residence where John, Jr. was a frequent visitor. George was only thirty-one when he died in 1927 after being operated on at Rochester for a stricture of the colon resulting from colitis.

hand, but he planned to return to camp as soon as possible, and John, Sr. proposed that he and Fred go up there as well on an inspection trip.

"I have been tremendously worried about that problem ever since I found out Austen's plan of operating, for it is not at all what I had laid out for him, and I do not believe it can succeed," John, Sr. continued. "We will have to determine some very vital policies . . . and I am sure we will all feel better about it, you and Emma and Austen and I if we work out our decisions together."

John, Sr. made the trip to British Columbia with John, Jr. in June—it doesn't appear that Fred was with them—in an attempt to lay out a profitable course for the logging operation. Whatever was decided resulted in strained feelings because Austen resented my father's interference in what he considered his bailiwick. In a letter to Austen in September, John, Sr. stated: "Hope you are getting things running more smoothly up at camp for I am very much afraid we will have to give up that problem as soon as you have finished up there this fall. There is no point in continuing to log at a continued loss." While he customarily signed letters to Austen "Yours affectionately," this one ended with a succinct "Sincerely."

John, Jr. came home to Minneapolis in late August that year laid up with first one cold and then another. "He is none too robust as yet, and I am afraid will always have to be rather careful of his health," John, Sr. wrote to a business associate in October. In December, hoping that his son might thrive in a sunnier climate, he sent him on holiday to Florida and Havana, Cuba, with his cousin George Cargill for two months. The two fished and visited George's mother May McMillan Cargill and her brother Dan G. McMillan in Miami. My grandfather was glad indeed when John, Jr. returned home in seemingly better shape than he had been in since leaving the army.

My father's good health turned out to be an illusion, however, as he was unable to eat solid food. John, Sr. sent him to Chicago to consult with a noted authority on stomach trouble, a Dr. Brown, and once there, Dr. Brown put him in Presbyterian Hospital for two weeks' observation. "I do not know what to think of Dr. Brown finding the same trouble that Dr. Fulton found five years ago, but it seems to me there is something more, although possibly this would account for all of your trouble," his father wrote him in February 1925. But no amount of doctoring could entirely cure my father's squeamish stomach. He lived much of his life on the verge of nausea, vomiting if he became angry or upset and always prone to seasickness.

After John, Jr. arrived home from the Chicago hospital, John and Edna embarked on another European vacation. "I have been feeling pretty seedy lately and Dr. Bell is quite insistent that I must . . . get far enough away so that I will forget business entirely, so we are sailing on the S.S. Minnetonka Saturday and leave here tonight," John, Sr. wrote to his brother Will on March 25. He and Edna stayed abroad until July, and my grandfather's weekly travel letters to "My dear Sons" inevitably included some bit of business advice.

Meanwhile, unbeknownst to my grandfather, an insurrection was brewing in his absence. Austen Cargill and Cargill treasurer James B. Taylor were plotting a takeover of the Cargill Elevator Company. Something had to be done, they had decided, to curtail John, Jr.'s influence with his father. Either John, Jr. would have to work directly for Austen on Austen's terms, or he would be out of a job, they agreed. If my grandfather had other thoughts, he, too, was dispensable. Given a chance at the presidency, Jim Taylor thought he could do a better job of running the company.

This mutiny, now ingrained in our collective family memory, was fortunately short-lived. As I understand the story, my grandfather learned of it when he landed in New York from his son Cargill. John, Jr. and Cargill had tossed a coin to see which one of them would break the news, and Cargill had lost. Going home to Minneapolis, my grandfather shut himself up in his house and called together his banker friends. Explaining the situation to them, he asked them if they wanted to loan money to a company whose directors were on the outs? Or to a giant elevator firm under new, inexperienced management? The answer was apparent given my grandfather's twenty-year record at the Elevator Company, and John, Jr.'s ascendancy was assured in the bargain.

Writing to Fred Hanchette in August, John, Sr. said he was sorry Fred had not been able to attend the recent annual stockholders' meeting. "The curious feature of the situation is that everything evaporated as soon as it was known that I was home. . . . I think I can say beyond any question or doubt, that if the plan that was attempted had been put over, you, nor I, nor any of us would have had any income for a considerable period ahead . . . this business could not have gone on. This business is absolutely dependent on borrowing vast sums of money, and no bank will loan money where there is known to be a fight for control within the organization.

"I was sorry, more sorry than I can tell you, that Austen was so misled. Having been out of the business for five years [in British Columbia], I can see how he might have listened to gossip originating from jealousy and similar motives, not realizing the real situation. However, I am sure that you will be glad to know that he is quite straightened out, and he and Anne, and Edna and I had a very delightful time up at Spooner last week and the first of this week."

Soon afterwards, however, Austen resigned from the Cargill Elevator Company. In January 1926, writing to Frank Hixon, he said that John, Sr. had asked him to come back into the organization, and before giving him a definite refusal, he wanted the lumberman's advice. Hixon replied immediately:

"I do not know just what John's proposition is, but, unless you wish to keep yourself free from business duties and responsibilities, I wish you could see your way clear to accept it and at least give it a trial. You could thus keep in touch with the business, and what is just as important, meet John part way in what I believe to be an earnest effort on his part to establish and maintain pleasant relations."

Austen and John, Sr. ended up working together amicably for another two decades, but my grandfather found it more difficult to forgive his cousin Jim Taylor. From all the evidence, Taylor had been the brains behind the scheme.

John, Sr. had known and trusted Jim Taylor his entire life. Their mothers, Mary Jane and Elizabeth McCrea, were sisters. Taylor had begun his grain career in La Crosse working for Will Cargill. In 1912, the year he moved to Minneapolis, he was one of the incorporators, with John H. MacMillan and C. T. Jaffray, of the Cargill Securities Company. Five years later he became a director of the Cargill Elevator Company. Following the attempted coup, my grandfather asked for his resignation.

The balance of power at the Cargill Elevator Company also shifted during this period. Sometime in the fall of 1925 Fred and Emma Hanchette sold their 5,000 shares in the Cargill Securities Company to John MacMillan, Sr. for $410,000. Having overextended themselves for an expensive house and car, they were now sick and had medical bills to pay. John, Sr. made a gift of 2,500 shares of the Hanchette stock to each of his two sons. The MacMillans now owned 12,500 out of 20,000 shares of the Cargill Securities Company, with Austen Cargill holding most of the remaining shares. In May 1927 the Cargill Securities Company purchased the Hanchettes' common stock in the Cargill Elevator Company (tired of relying on uncertain dividends, Fred and Emma simply wanted to be out of the business altogether), giving the John H. MacMillan family majority control.

Through the Cargill Elevator Company, my grandfather supported a number of local and national organizations that came to the firm for donations. Most local groups received fairly small checks, with the exception of the YMCA and the Minneapolis Society of Fine Arts. In 1911 John MacMillan pledged $1,000 to help build the present Minneapolis Institute of Arts edifice. In 1917 the American Red Cross "War Fund" received $5,000, and in 1920 the European Relief Fund, $500. When the company was approached in 1928 by the Mount Rushmore Foundation, however, Senior had no time for the new scheme to carve the likenesses of four presidents on the face of the mountain. Blunt and to-the-point, he replied, "I am entirely out of sympathy . . . a desecration of the natural scenic beauty of the Black Hills."

In January 1927 John, Sr., Edna, and Austen Cargill presented Greycourt, the former Will and Ellen Cargill house, to the First Presbyterian Church in La Crosse. The gray stucco mansion had become a white elephant. No one in the family wanted to live there, and nobody appeared eager to buy it. Several years earlier the family had refused an offer from a party wanting to convert it to a maternity hospital, and a deal with the president of the First National Bank of Viroqua for the ridiculously low sum of forty thousand dollars fell

John H. MacMillan, Sr. on the side yard of his house in Minneapolis at 317 Clifton Avenue

Dan G. McMillan, his daughter Mary, and his wife Mary Belle (Samuels) in Cuba, 1938

through. With upkeep on the house costing five thousand dollars a year, "we would have been money ahead to date if we had given the property away ten years ago," John, Sr. wrote Fred Hanchette in August 1921. The place had become a "nightmare" for him.

The First Presbyterian Church made overtures about acquiring the house as early as 1922, and John, Sr. would have been glad to let the parish have it, but neither Austen Cargill nor Edna was enthusiastic about the idea. Edna was more inclined to tear down the house and sell the building site. Was the rumor true, wrote Dan G. McMillan from across the street in his new prairie-style house, that the Cargill residence was being offered very cheaply—for nothing, in fact—to anyone who would wreck it and remove it from the property?

No, that wasn't the case, replied John, Sr. in Minneapolis. The price was still forty thousand dollars; there was at least that much salvage value in the property.

Dan G. McMillan subsequently sold his La Crosse house in January 1924 to move to Florida, where he already lived part of each year. Writing again to John, Sr., he inquired about renting the Cargill garage to store some furniture and his cars, and he also asked if he could purchase hall fixtures in the Cargill house for his Florida home. My grandfather wrote back that Dan was free to place his belongings in the garage at his own risk, but that the family didn't want to rent the garage as they were anxious to dispose of the property. They also wanted to hang on to the electrical fixtures for the time being. And so it went.

Then in April 1926, men professing to be federal law enforcement agents, saying they were acting on a tip that liquor was being made or stored on the premises, entered and searched the Cargill house, leaving greasy stains on the expensive rug in the parlor. Reporting the incident to John, Sr., La Crosse attorney George Gordon wrote that caretaker Albert Wicks had let the men in after they showed him their government cards. A carpet and rug man estimated that the cost to clean the carpet (and he could not guarantee that it would afterwards be the same color) would be about five hundred dollars. John, Sr. believed the men to be imposters, and he was angry with Wicks for allowing them to enter the premises without a search warrant. He also knew that something had to be done about the house.

John, Sr., Edna, and Austen Cargill owned the property jointly, and all three agreed to make a gift of it to the church in which they had been raised. Only two conditions were attached to the gift: first, that the family could remove articles it wanted to retain (Austen wanted the organ), and second, that Albert Wicks would stay on as caretaker and janitor at his same rate of pay, one hundred dollars per month. Six months later, when the church held formal dedication services on June 21, crowds of curious visitors thronged the home throughout the afternoon and evening.

In the decades that followed, the church used the Cargill house for various social functions and religious education. In 1928, for instance, the *La Crosse Tribune* reported that members of the congregation and their friends were invited to a "covered dish supper and frolic" on February 1. Moving pictures featuring Charles Lindbergh (who had recently flown the Atlantic) would be shown continuously in the first floor drawing room; the fish pond, bean bag contest, and homemade candy sale were slated for the library; a golf putting exhibition and contest would take place in the south room of the second floor; a curiosity shop and art museum was being set up in the southwest room on the third floor; and there would be bowling and horseshoe pitching in the billiard room in the basement.

As the church's congregation swelled in the 1950s, every available room in the house was used for Sunday school classes, and the coach house out in back was remodeled to accommodate the overflow. But time eventually caught up with the house, and, sad to say, I eventually helped dismantle it. By the 1970s the house had been placed on the National Register of Historic Places, but the church could no longer afford to maintain it, let alone upgrade it to meet modern building codes and fire standards. While a church committee wrestled with the question of whether to repair, refurbish, or raze the house in the spring of 1974, vandals broke into the house, which had not been used for two years, doing several thousand dollars worth of damage.

Apprised of the problem, I convinced my cousin Jim Cargill (Austen's son) to join me in asking the church to allow us to buy the house, disassemble it, and return the site to its natural state. The congregation was split on whether or not the property should be sold. Finally, the church was convinced by an insurance representative that continuing to own the building in its current state was tantamount to disaster. Jim Cargill and I hired the firm of Kraus Anderson to carefully dismantle the old house, returning one room with a fireplace to the church for its parish center. The majority of the woodwork and carved paneling was incorporated into various rooms at the Cargill Office Center, and several key pieces have been placed on our family boats, the *Carmac VI* and *Carmac VII*.

With the benefit of hindsight, I now believe that the house should have been restored to serve as a focal point for Will Cargill's descendants. At the time, however, I was unable to gather any support for this project from other family members. Those were the end of the olden days and the beginning of new days. It was felt that the past should be let go; building on the future was the prevailing theme. We are at least fortunate to have preserved something, rather than to have left this reminder of our family history to be scattered in the wind.

"Razing of Cargill House Under Way" reported the La Crosse Tribune *on January 31, 1975. "Wrecking crews have begun the demolition of historic Cargill house . . . and the house is to be completely dismantled by the middle of next week. . . . The site, owned by First Presbyterian Church, is to be made into a lawn and garden area. Destruction of the house was ordered when church officials decided they could not afford to maintain the building."*

Cargill and Pauline MacMillan's wedding party, May 1926. Standing left to right, Paul Ferris Clifford (who would be John, Jr.'s best man in 1927), Richard Pillsbury Gale, Wheelock Whitney, Clara Elizabeth Baldwin, John H. MacMillan, Jr., Pauline Whitney MacMillan, Cargill MacMillan, Lois Whitney Perry, John E. Hawley, Jr., and an unidentified man. Elizabeth Sims is seated on the left, Ruth Hull, right.

Although they were five years apart, my father and his brother Cargill were as close as brothers could be. They worked their whole lives together at Cargill, and they always lived next door to each other, first in Minneapolis and later in the Minneapolis suburb of Orono. In Minneapolis, they rented homes within walking distance of their parents on Clifton Avenue. Later, after John, Sr. purchased property and built a new home in Orono, the two brothers built homes side by side on part of the property.

When it came time for them to marry, John, Jr. and Cargill did so within a year of each other. On May 1, 1926, Cargill MacMillan married Pauline Wakefield Whitney at her elegant family home in St. Cloud, Minnesota. Both the bride and groom were twenty-six that year. The Whitneys, a leading St. Cloud family, were longtime friends of the MacMillans. Pauline's late father Albert Gideon Whitney had died four years earlier while in Maine for his son Wheelock's wedding.

Owner and president of St. Cloud's public utilities, active in the real estate, loan, and insurance businesses, and prominent in the city's civic affairs, A. G. Whitney was to St. Cloud what Will Cargill had been to La Crosse.

Pauline's mother Alice Wheelock Whitney came from a distinguished family in upstate New York and would donate the property for Whitney Memorial Airport in St. Cloud. In 1941 she entertained Eleanor Roosevelt at her St. Cloud home. (The family still has Mrs. Roosevelt's bread-and-butter note from the White House, in which she thanks Alice Whitney for returning her eyeglasses.) Pauline was the youngest of three children and a graduate of Smith College in Northampton, Massachusetts, where her sorority was Alpha Phi. Her sister Lois, married to Donald I. Perry, lived in Newburyport, Massachusetts. Her brother Wheelock had attended Phillips Academy at Andover and studied electrical engineering at Yale; graduating a year ahead of John, Jr. in 1916, he served with the 339th Field Artillery in France.

Delighted with Cargill's choice, John, Sr. and Edna entertained Pauline and her mother at their Clifton Avenue address in March. On April 23, John, Sr. wrote to Fred Hanchette: "About all we can think of right now are the various doings in connection with the wedding—more luncheons, dinners, and teas than any two young people have a right to take part in, say nothing of the older members of the family. I figure that by May 1st all of us will be complete wrecks."

The spacious colonial-style Whitney house at 524 First Avenue South in St. Cloud sat high on wide lawns overlooking the Mississippi River, but the outdoor wedding that had been planned was moved inside by sudden rain. It was

Pauline Wakefield Whitney on Mediterranean cruise, 1925

The Whitney house in St. Cloud, built in 1917 for A.G. and Alice Wheelock Whitney and their three children, Wheelock, Pauline, and Lois. In 1955 the property was acquired by St. Cloud State College.

the first precipitation that season, and "everyone was so happy over the rain that it did not mar the affair in the least," John, Sr. wrote afterwards to Hanchette. "I am only sorry that you and Emma could not have been here to see the beautiful genuine Sheraton table which you gave jointly with Austen and Ann." Dan, Will, and Janet MacMillan gave the young couple six antique mahogany dining chairs.

Minneapolis society turned out en masse for the wedding—Pillsburys, Crosbys, Bells, and Boveys. A string quartet played the bridal chorus from Lohengrin for the processional, and Dr. John E. Bushnell, pastor of Westminster Presbyterian Church, to which the MacMillans belonged in Minneapolis, performed the afternoon ceremony. Pauline's brother Wheelock walked her down the aisle and gave her away. Her sister Lois was her matron of honor, and John, Jr. was Cargill's best man. Pauline wore her sister Lois's ivory white satin wedding gown and carried lilies of the valley.

For her going-away outfit, Pauline chose a green crepe dress with a matching felt hat and a green bengaline (a crosswise-ribbed fabric) coat trimmed with gazelle fur. After saying their goodbyes following the ceremony and reception, Cargill and Pauline motored to Minneapolis in a roadster belonging to one of her attendants to catch the train for Chicago and New York; another car trailed behind in case of trouble. On May 5, the newlyweds sailed for Italy, spending their spare time on board the French Mediterranean liner S. S. *Providence* writing thank-you notes for more than three hundred wedding gifts.

In the first of weekly letters to his parents, Cargill told them that the trip to New York had been hot and dirty, and that thanks to John, Jr. and usher Paul Clifford, his clothes were disheveled. "You know that while I was dressing Paul & Jr. packed my bag. First Jr. tried and couldn't get everything in so Paul had to do it and after heroic efforts they managed to close it. You may be sure that is the last time I ever let either of them pack my bag. When we got to Mpls all of my clothes were ruined."

Pauline's letter in the same envelope bubbled: "We are so awfully happy. This beautiful trip is hard to believe. . . . We have only done one awfully stupid thing." Finding themselves with a two-hour layover in Chicago, she said, they had decided to go on a shopping spree at Marshall Fields. "We hailed a taxi, told him to take [us] up to M. F.'s, paid him, and tried three doors of the store all of which were *locked* before it came to us it was *Sunday* morning. We simply roared when it came upon us."

After landing in Sicily, Cargill and Pauline worked their way northward for a month in the Italian lakes region, and afterwards toured Switzerland and France before returning to New York on July 12. In Minneapolis, while they readied their new apartment at 2205 Pleasant Avenue, less than a mile away from his parents' Clifton Avenue home, Cargill and Pauline stayed with the senior MacMillans. Cargill was secretary of the Cargill Elevator Company and its

A sketch of John H. MacMillan, Sr. with his string of elevators, appearing in a portfolio of cartoons published in Minneapolis in 1915

First National Soo Line Building at Fifth and Marquette in Minneapolis, where the Cargill Elevator Company had its offices on the eleventh floor from 1915 to 1927

youngest officer.

The July 3, 1926, issue of *The Cargill Co Mission* (Vol. 1 No. 9) contained a brief history of the Cargill Elevator Company written by John H. MacMillan, Sr., in which he noted that the firm had grown considerably in the thirty years since 1896. The company now owned 136 country elevators in Minnesota, Iowa, South Dakota, North Dakota, and Montana; terminal elevators at Superior, Minneapolis, Green Bay, and Gladstone, Michigan; and was leasing elevator facilities in Buffalo, La Crosse, and Manitowoc, Wisconsin.

Officers of the company were:
> J. H. MacMillan, president
> F. P. Hixon, vice president
> F. E. Lindahl, vice president
> D. D. MacMillan, vice president
> A. S. Cargill, vice president
> Cargill MacMillan, secretary
> R. N. Hoople, assistant secretary
> E. S. Mooers, treasurer

Vice president F. P. (Frank) Hixon, a giant in the lumber industry, had been a lifelong friend of Will Cargill's and one of the administrators of his estate. Though not active in company management, he was available for consultation and advice. Dan (D. D.) MacMillan had charge of the country elevators; E. S. Mooers had been company treasurer for thirty-five years; and R. N. Hoople headed the accounting department. John H. MacMillan, Jr. was a director of the Cargill Elevator Company and vice president of its subsidiary Cargill Grain Company, handling spring wheat sales to the eastern trade.

The periodical also stated that the *Mission's* founding editor John Todd had left the Cargill Elevator Company to try his hand at insurance. The son of Dr. Frank Todd (who had delivered John, Jr. and served with him in the army at Camp Dodge), John Todd had come to work for Cargill after graduating from Cornell a year earlier in 1925. When he decided to sell insurance, John, Sr. made it possible for him to set up a payroll deduction plan for employees at Cargill. "This did more to carry me as a beginning agent than any other single thing," Todd confided in an autobiography he wrote in the 1980s. As he matured in his profession, Todd became a trusted advisor and later wrote numerous business and personal policies on the lives of MacMillan family members.

The next issue of *The Cargill Co Mission* (Vol. 1 No. 10), which came out August 11, 1926, was dedicated to John H. MacMillan, Sr. on the occasion of his fifty-seventh birthday, and new editor Thomas Totushek printed an up-to-date sketch of the company. As president of the Cargill Elevator Company, a Minnesota corporation, John, Sr. headed its five subsidiary companies: the Montana Central

Elevator Company, the Cargill Elevator Company of North Dakota, the Cargill Commission Company, the Minneapolis Seed Company, and the Cargill Grain Company.

The Cargill Securities Company, of which he was also president, held the following subsidiaries: the La Crosse and Southeastern Railway Company, the Willow River and Stony Lake Timber Company, Ltd., the Cargill Company of Canada, Ltd., and the Cargill Lumber Company. Outside the Cargill companies, John, Sr. sat on the boards of the First National Bank of Minneapolis, the Millers National Insurance Company in Chicago, and the Valier-Montana Land and Water Company in Montana. The next year, Cargill's board of directors voted to increase his annual salary to fifty thousand dollars.

In February 1927 my grandparents sailed for Italy on the steamer *Comte Biancanamo* with their next-door neighbors, the George Lanes. Fred and Emma Hanchette were in Europe for their daughter Budley's wedding and met them when they landed in Naples on February 22. Five days earlier Ellen Cargill (Budley) Hanchette had married Walden Elbert Trimble in Florence. Later in their stay in Italy, my grandparents and the Lanes had dinner in Florence with the newly-weds. John, Sr. noted in his diary on March 28, "We liked [Trimble] very much."

On this side of the ocean, romance was blooming closer to home. When my grandparents arrived back in New York on April 27, John, Jr. met them at the dock with the surprising news that he was to be married in less than a month to Marion Dickson Ehrhorn, whom he had met in Pasadena while they were abroad.

Marion Ehrhorn, who would be my mother, was a stunning thirty-four-year-old widow and tennis devotee, red-haired, brought up Catholic in Belvedere, California, and educated in convent schools. Twelve years earlier when she was twenty-two, she had married an insurance executive, Adolph E. Ehrhorn, age twenty-six and also Catholic, in her parish church. Born in South America and schooled at Stanford University, Ehrhorn was the son of a Californian of German descent, Oscar A. Ehrhorn. His mother, Teresa Pachieri, was an Italian woman, born in South America, whose brother was the Italian ambassador to Argentina. (I have a sword cane that belonged to him.) The Ehrhorns had tin mining interests in Bolivia, where young Adolph was raised in a religious household in Cochabamba, cocooned in European-style comfort.

Following their marriage, Adolph and Marion lived in Pasadena. In 1920, possibly after the onset of the unnamed illness which would claim Adolph's life, the couple took a six-months' trip to South America on the S. S. *Santa Luisa* to visit his family and childhood home in the Andean highlands. Sailing south from New York, through the Windward Passage separating Cuba and Haiti and the newly completed Panama Canal to the Pacific Ocean, they stopped to sightsee in several ports along the Peruvian and Chilean coasts.

Budley Hanchette in her teens

April 1915: Marion Hamilton Dickson
and Adolph Ehrhorn were married in
a Catholic ceremony in Belvedere,
California.

My mother's carefully annotated photo album from this trip contains the
only pictures we have of her during her marriage to Ehrhorn. On board ship
after crossing the Equator, she is shown being duly initiated with other passengers into the playful ORDER of the DEEP by Father Neptune and his cohorts. In
Peru she and Adolph posed for the camera while touring the Botanical Gardens
with friends in Lima. AE, as Marion called her husband, was a tall, slightly
built man in a rumpled suit coat, dark tie, and rakish cap. Marion wore a broad-
brimmed picture hat with a fussy ankle-length dress and jacket.

The photographs from Cochabamba reveal an upper-class family with
more than a half dozen mixed-blood and Indian servants. Their two-story,
tile-roofed villa was tastefully decorated with crystal and silver chandeliers, plush
Victorian furniture, and patterned carpets. Adolph's father Oscar was a retiring,
mustachioed man in spectacles, a flat Panama hat, and a tight bow tie. Photographed "after church," Teresa Ehrhorn, black-haired and matronly, peered
intently from the past in a severe, dark-colored suit, her purse clutched in her
hand. Beside her, Marion appeared almost nun-like with a veil covering her hair.

Outside the family apartments in a main part of town, Marion photographed peasants praying on their knees in front of elaborate street altars

The Adolph Ehrhorn residence (left) in Cochabamba, indicated by an arrow

The Ehrhorn living room (right) with Victorian furniture and family portraits in Cochabamba

Marion Dickson Ehrhorn on the right, with her mother-in-law Teresa Pachieri Ehrhorn after church in Valparaiso

crowded with statues, candles, and flowers. Further afield, in scrub-covered mountains near Colcha, Bolivia, we glimpse the family's primitively run Berenguela Tin Mines: Indian workers in peasant dress carrying machinery up to the mine, installing a ski-lift-like ropeway to haul buckets of tin ore down the mountainside, and loading llama pack trains. A panorama of the Berenguela village, tucked in a stony cleft, shows natives living in thatched-roofed mud brick huts, tilling the poor soil with wooden plows and oxen.

Five years later, when Ehrhorn lay dying in California, Marion took him back to Cochabamba in an oxygen tent. After his death, the young widow found herself confined to the house in Cochabamba until, tired of thinking up ways to escape the family's close scrutiny, she returned home to California. Adolph had been dead a month when the San Francisco Social Register for 1926 was published; both he and Marion and Marion's parents, Francis W. (Frank) and Minerva Dickson, were listed in it. The Ehrhorns' address was given as 727 La Loma Road in Pasadena. The Dicksons still lived in fashionable Belvedere, north of San Francisco across the Golden Gate Bridge in Marin County.

My grandfather Francis Dickson was born in 1861 in Campbeltown, Scotland, and became prominent in the insurance business in California. His father William Dickson was a merchant and his mother Marion, descended from gentry. The two were married in 1842 at The Orchard in Lanarkshire. The Dickson family appears in Sir Walter Scott's novel *Castle Dangerous*. Frank Dickson was eleven years old when he came to this country with his parents. He later settled in San Francisco where his brother Robert managed a prosperous insurance business for the Royal Exchange Assurance Company of London.

My grandmother Minerva Barry Dickson came from Catholic stock and, although her husband was a staunch Presbyterian, raised her daughters in the Roman religion. Marion had two younger sisters, both of whom died in

Marion, on the right, with her mother Minerva Barry Dickson and younger sisters

childhood, so she was essentially an only child for most of her life. The Dicksons were fairly prosperous during my mother's growing up years and enjoyed an upper-middle-class life with summers at the seashore.

John, Jr. was thirty-one when he became captivated by Marion. After knowing her just one week in Pasadena, where he was visiting Fred and Emma Hanchette, he had asked her to marry him and she accepted. His first letter to Marion after leaving California, which was penned on board the *Gold Coast Limited* train en route to Montana on March 28, 1927, is written in the form of a newspaper, *The MacMillan Daily*, Vol. I, No. 1. "In this issue," it announced, "by John H. MacMillan, Jr., 'I Love You, I Love You, I Love You.'"

During the next six weeks, he bombarded her with daily letters addressed to Mrs. Marion Ehrhorn at 692 S. Grand Avenue in Pasadena, numbering them

My grandfather Frank Dickson in a rowboat

Cargill MacMillan with Cargill, Jr. at three weeks. The proud father sent this photo to New York with John, Jr. who was meeting their parents' boat (with incredible news of his own) upon their return from Europe in April 1927.

Cargill, Jr. was John, Sr. and Edna's first grandchild, and once back in Minneapolis, my grandfather confided to a family friend: "It is needless to say we are greatly enjoying our grandson, and I know we are going to enjoy him more and more as time goes on. He is so tiny as yet that I have not had a chance at him; so far I have only been privileged to look at him."

sequentially—Vol. I, No. 2, and so on. As much in love with my father as he was with her, Marion responded with affectionate letters of her own, but while she saved his, hers to him have been lost. They planned to be married as soon as possible, but first, John, Jr. wanted to break the news of their engagement in person to his parents when they returned from Europe.

Right from the start, however, he made Marion a partner in every aspect of his life, sharing both business and personal confidences with her. From the Hotel Rainbow in Great Falls, Montana, on March 31, he wrote: "The resident head of our project [The Valier-Montana Land and Water Company] met me here today, and we spent the entire day in conference with our attorney. I had a terrible time concentrating on the problems under discussion and I heard one of them ask the other what the devil was the matter with me anyway. I didn't tell them—but I felt rather foolish."

On April 4, still on hand in Montana to "assure the settlers that we really are not wolves in sheeps' clothing," he reported: "The meeting today was a great success. We put over our program right according to schedule, the old steam roller functioning perfectly. The attendance astonished us all, about 125 being present representing 57,000 out of 73,000 outstanding shares of stock. I had to make a speech, which was very well received—in fact they applauded rather enthusiastically when I got through, which astonished me not a little, as all I told them was a lot of well worn platitudes."

Once back in Minneapolis, after a hectic first day at the office "with everyone laying for me, and with so much to be decided," he picked out a ring for Marion. He couldn't find a setting he liked, but she could have the stone reset when she came to Minnesota. That evening he went to his brother Cargill's for dinner and to see his new nephew, Cargill, Jr., who had been born while John, Jr. was in Montana.

"This is the first time that I've become an honest to God Uncle and I'm thrilled to death," he wrote Marion. "For one week old he is singularly good looking, and will probably grow up to be homely as can be. . . . I was very good looking as a baby, a fact which all the family bring out as proof, or rather to account for me now."

Cargill's wife Pauline had wanted to know all about her, he told Marion, "and by 'all,' I mean all. Nothing escaped, not even the Catholic part, and I did my best to suppress that. Not that it would make a particle of difference with her for it won't, but it will with some of the other relatives." His Uncle Dan, in particular, had a "terrible phobia" about Catholics, he warned Marion, and the prejudices harbored by some of his other uncles and aunts were "so strong that it might be better if we let them discover gradually that you weren't a good Presbyterian." She shouldn't worry about religion insofar as his immediate family was concerned, however, he assured her. "Your being a Catholic won't worry them nearly as much as does my having a philosophy all my own."

What kind of a ceremony would they have? John, Jr. asked Marion. "Whether we have a Catholic, Jewish, or even Russian ceremony, I care not—a civil one by a J.P. would suit me best of all—but as I know you prefer a Catholic one, I have a suggestion to make: Suppose we have first of all a Catholic ceremony early in the day—and strictly private except for two witnesses. Then later in the day we could have a standard Protestant ceremony to which all the relatives could be invited. If you have few or no Catholic friends and relatives, then the Protestant service could cause no comment, while I can assure you that the Catholic one for me would cause no end of talk and even hard feeling in our family."

One of Marion's letters to my father in Minneapolis was opened in error by John, Sr.'s male secretary. In a subsequent letter, John, Jr. begged: "**I implore** of you, please, please, when you are writing to me put the Jr. **after the** MacMillan. One of your letters was forwarded to me from Montana, and it did not have the Jr. on it. Of course it went into Father's secretary, and I rather imagine he received something of a shock when he opened it. . . . It was the one which started: 'Dearest: Our engagement is all over town.'"

The whole family called him Junior to distinguish him from the other Johns, he continued. "I hate it, but you may have to do the same thing." If it wasn't for the fact "that Tommy (the secretary, Thomas Totushek) doesn't talk," news of their engagement would be all over the office. "I am going to do my best not to have it generally known about town until after I have had a chance to tell Mother. She lands in N.Y. on April 26th or 27th."

Another of Marion's letters apparently mentioned that she still had a cough and was thinking of giving up smoking. "I could bless you if you did, altho I couldn't love you any more than I do now," John, Jr. replied. "I had no intention of asking you to quit, except not to smoke around my father. I well remember when the Dr. made me give it up how I suffered, and unless you were better off for it, I wouldn't ask you to do so. Do try to give up the inhaling tho even if you don't quit. That's what causes the cough. . . . You'll begin to think you are marrying into an awfully queer family, with our tobacco and religious prejudices. Really, we aren't very queer though—just Scotch."

Monday, April 11, was a "big day" for John, Jr. "First I received a wonderful letter from you saying your cold was better; then I had letters from both Aunt Emma and Uncle Fred telling me how perfect they thought you were, which naturally made me very happy. On top of all this I received an awfully nice note from your father. He must be a dandy."

In his first letter to his prospective son-in-law, Frank Dickson had written: "Marion appears to be very happy. Her happiness comes first with us. She has a good Scotch head on her shoulders. Her mother and I feel quite sure she has made a wise selection. We shall be very happy indeed to meet you."

Despite my father's efforts to keep his engagement quiet, word of it naturally leaked out. It amused him to learn that "Janie Stewart told Helen Hawley that the MacDonalds had it by mail from the Cliffords," he wrote Marion. Many of his friends heard it indirectly from Mrs. Bennett, he said, "who gave you a perfectly splendid send-off." Marion was the "talk of the town," he gushed; "News of you has created a distinct sensation." He hoped they would be able to be married May 21, but everything hinged on business, which was very involved at the moment.

His next several letters came from the Hotel La Salle in Chicago, where "we succeeded in leasing an Elevator from the Armour Grain Co., one on which we have had our eyes for a long time. It is a small one located at Milwaukee, but very modern (6 months old) and ideal for our requirements. We had to abandon the idea yesterday of taking over the officers and business of Armour, to my great disappointment. I feel awfully sorry for the two Armour boys. They are behaving like men."

While waiting to close on that deal, he and the Cargill men with him "all went through the big elevator here, the largest and finest in the world. It was a great treat, but very exhausting as it seems to cover acres, and is 150 feet high. It can hold about the equal of 150 trainloads of grain of 50 cars each. We all want to take it on, and hope when Father arrives that he can get the rental down to a reasonable figure. They want a thousand dollars a day for it. Which is about twice too much as I see it."

Over dinner one evening in Chicago, John, Jr. discussed Marion with his father's brothers Dan and Will MacMillan. Dan, whom he described to Marion as "such a dear but with many eccentricities," was traveling with him as acting head of the business in John, Sr.'s absence. "Uncle Will," he explained, "is professor of mathematical astronomy at the University of Chicago, and is my favorite uncle, as we have very much in common intellectually. We vacation together quite frequently. He was quite crushed when I told him I was going to be married. I think he felt as I did when I married cousin George [Cargill] the other day.

"Then he wanted to know all the gory details, and finally said he would fix it with Father so that Father would appreciate just how fortunate he was to have you come into the family. Your being of Highland extraction covers a multitude of sins, and justifies everything. Had you been in jail, been divorced four times and had ten children it would still be all right with that side of the family."

John, Jr. was finding from talking to his relatives in Chicago that "the idea of marriage after an acquaintance of only a week seems to others almost scandalous, and certainly gives an impression of recklessness. It's hard in a way for me to understand this for it seems not only natural for me to marry you, but the very thought that you might by hook or crook get away from me inspires in me a feeling of the utmost terror. Never have I had anything frighten me as does that.

"However, with the family this is very different, and I know that it will be particularly so with Mother & Father for they are conventional in a high degree,

Marion Dickson Ehrhorn

and Father is extremely deliberate in his decisions. He never could understand my decision methods, and always mistrusts any decisions of mine which seem to him to lack the proper amount of deliberation."

Writing to Marion on Sunday, April 17, John, Jr. claimed to have had "an awfully good and much needed rest today" after being gone since Tuesday. "I played 14 holes of golf with Cargill this morning. I started out with par for the first five holes, but quickly tired and my score at the 14th was simply wretched.

"I chewed the rag with Jack Hawley [a close friend with whom he formed a company called Hawley Inventions, John, Jr. being president] all afternoon. We discussed everything under the sun. About suppertime (we have supper on Sunday evening) his wife went off for a picnic, whereupon we had a swell libation, which was so powerful that I had to dispense with supper.

"In your letter you said you had been very extravagant. I don't want you to worry for an instant about being extravagant. While we will have to live very modestly after we are married, at the same time I can take care of every reasonable wish now, and if there is *anything* you want which you feel you can't afford I want you to let me know *at once*."

His mother had written that she and John, Sr. would be arriving in New York the following week, he added. "I plan to leave here not later than Thursday night. I expect to be in Buffalo Saturday and Sunday, and New York Monday, and perhaps Tuesday. However, plan to write me in Minneapolis thereafter."

The next day, Monday, John, Jr. received both a letter and telegram from Marion. Replying first to the letter, "a wonderful one too, for in it you accepted my suggestion of the two ceremonies," he queried her: "We will say nothing of the Catholic one to any except the immediate family though? Do you agree with me?"

Concerning the telegram: "I am so delighted that you like [the ring], but you are to feel that you can change the setting for anything you want when you get here in Minneapolis. Cargill was quite childishly pleased over your telegram too, for he helped me order that setting made. It's absurd I know but you can't know how pleased and thrilled I am at the thought that mine is the only ring you are now wearing."

One of the last of my father's surviving letters to Marion—Vol. I, No. 25—was written April 22 in Milwaukee, where he was overseeing the takeover of the newly acquired Armour elevator. "I had dinner last night with Howard and Mabel [McMillan]," he recounted in a buoyant mood. "Howard you know is the cousin of my own age, whom I've known so very intimately all my life. I am awfully fond of him. This was the first chance they had really had to quiz me about you, and they managed to find out about everything I know about you myself. They were delighted beyond words, and particularly Howard because we have been drifting apart since his marriage.

John H. MacMillan, Jr.

"Cargill was much worried because I haven't a picture of you to show Mother. I told him I had no real need of a picture of you, as everything about you stood out far more vividly in my mind than it could in a picture, but he thought I should have one to show her, so if you have a snapshot or anything please send it along to Mpls. As for Aunt Emma's picture of me, tear it up. I never had a picture taken which resembled me in the slightest."

He hadn't written her the day before—the first day he had missed doing so since leaving her, he explained, because "I was snowed under from the time I got up until I got on the train at 10:45," and this next day had been almost as hectic: "Spent all morning and most of the afternoon out at the new elevator, and I am weary and dirty. It's a fine plant, but the dust is so suffocating

Marion Hamilton Dickson Ehrhorn
MacMillan on her wedding day

that I can still scarcely breathe. They have been weighing up all the grain in the house, so we can take it over, and dust arises in great clouds from every belt and spout. It is inches deep on the floor. I leave in an hour for Buffalo via Chicago."

If his parents tried to dissuade him about marrying so quickly, almost on the spur of the moment, there is no evidence of it in the family papers. My parents' whirlwind courtship culminated in California where it had begun two months earlier. The two were joined in marriage on May 21 at Fred and Emma Hanchette's residence at 440 South Hill Avenue in Pasadena. John, Jr. had taken the train to California May 9, and his parents had followed him there a week later. Clergyman Calvin P. Erdman of the local First Presbyterian Church read the afternoon service. The official witness was my father's boyhood chum Paul F. Clifford, who had grown up next door to him in Minneapolis.

Marion always fibbed about her age, and my father may have never known how old she really was. For their wedding license, she gave her age as thirty. Born July 14, 1892, she was actually less than two months away from her thirty-fifth birthday. Twelve years earlier, when marrying Adolph Ehrhorn, she had said that she was twenty-one. This also was incorrect, but only by a year.

In the world outside the immediate MacMillan sphere, John, Jr. and Marion's wedding was upstaged by another Minnesotan. The day before, Captain Charles A. Lindbergh had left Roosevelt Field in New York alone in his *Spirit of St. Louis* on the first solo nonstop transatlantic flight from New York to Paris. Welcomed by a roaring throng of forty thousand spectators, he reached Le Bourget airfield 3,610 miles and 33½ hours later, at 10:21 P.M. on May 21. In California, where it was nine hours earlier, John, Jr. and Marion said their vows less than three hours after Lucky Lindy's touch-down had ushered in a new age.

My parents set up housekeeping in Minneapolis in a double house at 212 W. 22nd Street that faced the side of Cargill and Pauline's Pleasant Avenue apartment across the street. My brother John Hugh III was born there the next year on February 28. Hugh's energy was "limitedless," my father would write to John, Sr. in 1931. "I am beginning to think we will have to have nurses take care of him in relays."

In a biographical article for the Class of 1917's Decennial Record that Yale published in 1928, John, Jr. wrote that after his discharge from the army, he had worked for a year as a broker for the Cargill Elevator Company in the wheat pit at Duluth, Minnesota. Following this he put in "three or four years . . . becoming a hard-boiled logger on the coast of British Columbia about 200 miles northwest of Vancouver in the employ of The Cargill Company of Canada, Ltd."

> Finally, however [he continued], the powers that be decided that the hard-boiling process had continued long enough . . . so I returned to the head office in Minneapolis as an assistant in the wheat department, of which I was put in charge within another year or two. At the moment, in addition to this work, I am striving in spare time to be the Moses to lead the Valier Montana Land & Water Company out of its financial difficulties. This is an irrigation project located in the most desolate part of Montana.

John Hugh MacMillan III

Daniel D. MacMillan, known familiarly at the Minneapolis office as "Uncle Dan." Dan had begun working in the grain business in W.W. Cargill's office in La Crosse when he was fifteen.

Amber Belle as pictured in the St. Louis Post-Dispatch, *1909*

If our family had a skeleton in its closet—and I think it's safe to say we did—her name was Amber Belle. She was Uncle Dan's wife. Uncle Dan was a kind, gentle man who lived his whole life in his brother John, Sr.'s shadow and worked side by side with him at Cargill. After moving to Minneapolis Dan MacMillan had charge of the country line elevators and became an authority on crops. Later, as Cargill's senior vice president, he worked in an advisory capacity in the futures and merchandising branches of the business.

Never lucky in love, Dan was completely smitten by Amber Belle. More than ten years earlier Emma Cargill had set her cap for Dan, but he hadn't responded. So demoralized was he coming out of the Texas debacle that he wouldn't consider the possibility of marrying. When he finally did, his choice was extremely unfortunate. Amber Belle Kidd Hamilton Tourney McDonald, her full name when she married Dan MacMillan in 1909, had a notorious history.

A born schemer, Amber Belle was the daughter of a Methodist minister named Kidd from Wisconsin; orphaned when she was nine, she was raised in England by adoptive parents. At the tender age of seventeen, Amber Belle married Dr. Charles Benjamin Hamilton of London who died soon afterwards. Next she married Alexandre Tourney, a wealthy mine owner, whom she divorced after living with him for just one year.

Her trail disappears for many years after that, but Amber Belle returned to this country and was living in style in Kansas City when she married a wealthy middle-aged Minneapolis lumberman named Mitchell McDonald in May 1908. Having fallen temporarily under her spell, McDonald conveniently forgot that he already had a wife and two children in Minneapolis. When Amber Belle subsequently married Daniel D. MacMillan less than a year later in a Presbyterian ceremony in St. Joseph, Missouri, she was involved in an unsavory bigamy suit.

Unquestionably, there was more to Amber Belle than met the eye. Dan believed the beautiful and vivacious Amber Belle to be the injured party in the bigamy business, but his new bride was no innocent. At age thirty-nine, Amber Belle was a well-traveled woman of the world who cultivated and exploited wealthy friends. A full-page article concerning her nefarious relationship with McDonald appeared in the Sunday magazine section of the *St. Louis Post-Dispatch* in April 1909 (by which time she was already married to Dan); among other things it revealed that she had dabbled in hypnotism.

Dan MacMillan and Amber Belle spent a very short time together as man and wife. Less than a month after they married, Dan was heartsick with doubts about her. While Amber Belle was in Canada, threatening to have McDonald extradited on the bigamy charges, one of her attorneys informed Dan that her cash assets amounted to about fifteen thousand dollars, not sixty thousand as she had told him.

"Amber, isn't there some mistake?" he wrote to her in Toronto. "I cannot believe you had any motive in deceiving me. On this small amount how have you kept your mother? How did you keep your home and servants? I have as much childlike faith in your purity and integrity this moment as when I plighted my troth with you. . . . I can stand the loss of health. I can stand the loss of wealth, but I could never survive loss of confidence in you."

Dan soon realized, however, that he had been gulled. The woman he worshiped had been a phantom of his imagination. After returning shamefaced to his Minneapolis family, McDonald agreed to pay her $110,000 to drop a civil suit against him. In 1912, pregnant with Dan's child, Amber Belle returned to England and gave birth to a son, Donald. The boy was a toddler, and Amber Belle was still married to Dan, when she returned to this country with a newly hatched scheme.

In 1914 the Dayton, Ohio *Herald* announced the arrival of "Mrs. D.D. McMillan," who was visiting the city to meet with "a number of well-known philanthropists." According to the paper, she had been in the United States for four months, going from state to state to raise funds for a proposed children's hospital at Atlantic City; she had already won the support of many prominent men including a Catholic cardinal, two senators, and the Chief Justice of the United States. It appears that Amber Belle had Donald with her on this visit, and that Dan was able to see his son before his mother took him back to England. It would be more than a dozen years before he saw Donald again.

In November 1927, John, Sr. wrote to Secretary of State Frank B. Kellogg in Washington, D.C., requesting a letter of introduction for his brother to the American ambassador in England. Dan had "some family matters of very great importance which require his presence in London," my grandfather explained.

"My brother is senior Vice President of this Company, and in complete charge of its affairs during my absence," he added in reference to his character. "Needless to say, he is a man of the highest integrity and character, and is comfortably fixed financially."

Dan was looking forward with what must have been great anticipation to meeting Donald, who was fifteen. The boy had been raised abroad after Dan and Amber Belle were estranged, and Dan had suffered greatly from having no family of his own. As it turned out, he had to cancel his trip, however, due to poor health. Dan was suffering from repeated attacks of severe stomach pain when he checked into the Mayo Clinic in Rochester, Minnesota, in December. In January he had his gall bladder removed at Presbyterian Hospital in Chicago. Following surgery, he took his doctor's advice and spent three months recuperating at the Pine Crest Inn in Tryon, North Carolina.

When Dan was unable to go to Europe, Amber Belle brought Donald to this country and enrolled him in a private school at Silver Bay on Lake George in New York. Dan saw his son there for the first time since the boy was an infant, and Donald, whom Dan found to be "a refined cultured youth of excellent promise," won his father's affections completely. "I wish I were able to convey to you even some slight appreciation of the satisfaction I experienced upon receiving you back into my life after long years of separation," he wrote to Donald upon returning to Minneapolis.

Dan had provided for Donald in a lump-sum settlement when he and Amber were divorced in 1915, but Amber had gone through the money, leaving Dan with the responsibility for Donald's schooling and living expenses in this country, which proved to be considerable. Donald didn't know the meaning of thrift—one of Dan's guiding principles—but Dan was about to teach him. In December 1928 he sent Donald a check for four hundred dollars to cover an itemized list from Amber Belle that included a tennis racket and records for his portable Victrola, informing him:

"There will be no more large checks. Hereafter you will receive your monthly allowance of $150.00 and no more. Over a period of a year your tuition and board amounts to $87.50 per month, leaving an excess of $62.50, which should be ample to take care of all of your other requirements for the year. I have never known of any boy more thoroughly equipped than you are at the present time. . . . Since the 1st of June I have paid out for you in one way or another just $6,000, or $1,000 a month. There is not any father in the United States who allows his child to spend money at this rate."

Donald made excellent grades at the Silver Bay School, but the next fall, "Mrs. Burgess"—as Amber Belle was now calling herself (whether she had actually remarried in unknown)—transferred Donald to Montclair Academy in Montclair, New Jersey. When Donald needed additional funds in October and again in November, Dan sent him checks for $100 and $150, but told him that "successive calls for money over and above the amount of your allowance must terminate. . . . You are now spending, individually, more than the average family of the United States with between four and five to provide for." Whatever ideas Donald might have concerning his father's affluence were highly exaggerated, Dan told him. "My circumstances are exceedingly modest."

That seemed to settle the matter. Donald's requests ceased, and his father was satisfied that he was budgeting his allowance. At Christmas time Dan went to New York to see Donald and became even more enamored with his son. "It is a great satisfaction to know that you enjoyed our reunion," he wrote Donald in January. "It was an outstanding occasion for me. I was fully in accord with your selections for our theatrical entertainment. And when we were alone your company was no less enjoyable for your conversation showed breadth and catholicity of taste in intellectual pursuits."

Further surprises awaited the enthusiastic father, however. In April Dan was dumbfounded to receive a telegram from Montclair Academy stating that Donald had been suspended because his account was $1,150 in arrears. The school would readmit Donald if Dan paid the bill in full within ten days, it advised. "DONALD HERE AWAITING YOUR REPLY." Sending his check the next day, Dan explained that he was completely unaware of the delinquency. "His mother evidently takes charge of his allowance, which is her legal right . . . but has evidently applied it otherwise than on his education." In the future Dan promised, he would "personally take charge of the financial side of [Donald's] education."

Donald entered Princeton in the fall of 1930, and after his first year, he traveled west to get acquainted with his MacMillan relatives. Dan met his train in Chicago, and Uncle Will took the two of them to the planetarium and to lunch at the University Club. Donald also spent two weeks with his Aunt Mary Rowles in La Crosse, where he had "the time of his life," Dan wrote his brother Will. Mary's husband Dr. John Rowles had died after a lengthy illness the previous September. "Mary seemed to be better than I have seen her for years and more like her old self," Dan remarked.

Dan soon rewrote his will to provide for Donald's future, and he had Donald with him again during the following summer of 1932. This time they both visited Mary Rowles and enjoyed "many lovely automobile drives" in the Mississippi Valley around La Crosse. In Minneapolis Dan introduced Donald to the family business on visits to the Cargill headquarters. When it came time for Donald to motor back to Princeton, Dan wrote to a Cargill official in Albany, New York, "The route he is taking lies through Albany and I should very much like to have him obtain a birdseye view of the plant." Dan especially wanted Donald to see the new Cargill elevator at Albany on his trip back east.

In September 1931, going out on a limb, John H. MacMillan, Jr. had signed an agreement with the Albany Port District Commission for the construction of the world's largest terminal elevator, built to Cargill company specifications, which the Port Commission then leased to the Cargill Grain Company. This plant became a cornerstone of the rapidly expanding Cargill enterprises, of vital importance for imports and exports as well as domestic business.

During the 1920s Cargill had gone from being a regional firm to a national and international organization. Cargill opened its first non-U.S. office in Montreal in 1928; four years later it also had offices in Genoa, Italy; Winnipeg, Canada; Rotterdam, Holland; Buenos Aires, Argentina; and London. After posting record earnings of $1,236,000 for the 1929-1930 crop year, it topped this figure the very next year with profits of $1,302,000.

At age sixty one, his business career at its apogee, John, Sr. began building the home in which he would spend the rest of his life. As a young married

Three generations of MacMillans: Cargill, Jr., John, Sr., and Cargill

man, my grandfather had built houses in Fort Worth, Texas, and Pine Bluff, Arkansas, only to have to leave them after short occupancies. For the past thirty years he and Edna had lived in rented houses. The site he selected on Lake Minnetonka for what would become a family compound was ideal. It also had a picturesque history.

Until the Dakota Indians surrendered their Minnesota homelands west of the Mississippi for pennies an acre in 1851, Lake Minnetonka with its winding, wooded shoreline remained one of the region's best-kept secrets. Embracing a tangled welter of bays, coves, islands, and peninsulas, the lake and its environs teemed with fish and wild game, wild rice, edible roots and berries, barks for medicines, and maple sugar trees. When the Indians put their marks on the treaties at Mendota, they asked that the lake be included in their reservation. Instead the area was opened to white settlers who sectioned it off, cut down the trees, and plowed up the deep rich soil.

On Lake Minnetonka's north shore where Orono developed, the reedy, swampy ground that edged Brown's Bay and Smith Bay was a duck hunter's dream—a major flyway for black ducks, bluebills, mallards, pintails, wood ducks, and coots. Between the two bays stretches a narrow-necked peninsula identified on old maps as Promontory Point or Starvation Point. In 1880 former Minneapolis mayor George Brackett purchased Starvation Point from pioneer Nathan Stubbs to build a summer home and renamed it Orono Point after his boyhood home in Maine. Joseph Orono was a heroic Penobscot chief who had pledged his tribe to the patriots' cause in the Revolutionary War. Orono Point has since become known as Brackett's Point, but the Indian name stuck to the township, formed in 1889.

By that time Lake Minnetonka was one of this country's most popular summer resorts. Wealthy Southerners came from St. Louis and Kansas City, some of them accompanied by their household staffs. In 1882 former President Ulysses S. Grant presided at the grand opening of railroad tycoon James J. Hill's turreted Queen Anne-style Hotel Lafayette, the most opulent of a number of glittering late-nineteenth-century hotels at Minnetonka. Hill's steamboat *Belle of Minnetonka*, one of more than a dozen such vessels plying the lake, carried twenty-five hundred pleasure-seeking passengers.

Thousands of Minneapolitans rode the trains (some of which also belonged to J. J. Hill) to the summer communities of Wayzata and Excelsior on Lake Minnetonka for a day of picnicking or a week's vacation at a favorite boarding house. Many well-to-do Minneapolis businessmen—men named Gale, Burton, Phelps, Bovey, Sidle, Carpenter, Pillsbury, Bell, and Dunwoody—built elegant summer "cottages" at the lake. With the advent of automobile travel and better roads, people like my grandfather who worked in Minneapolis could live at Lake Minnetonka year round. Like many of their neighbors, John and Edna MacMillan found the lake an attractive alternative to remaining in Loring Park, where the downtown business district had literally advanced to their Clifton Avenue doorstep.

After renting a cottage belonging to banker George Orde at Lake Minnetonka for two seasons, John and Edna purchased the property as well as the adjoining Harvey Leighton farm, giving them a total of eighty acres. The Orde property had formerly belonged to one of George Brackett's sons. The Leightons were pioneer farmers in what is now the city of Orono; Harvey Leighton's father had owned the property before him. According to the *Minnetonka Herald*, the residence John, Sr. was building was second in size only to a sixty-room edifice being put up on 240 acres at Gray's Bay by Wayzata Mayor Rufus R. Rand—the chateau-like structure that now houses Cargill's world headquarters.

"Slept in old house [Orde cottage] last time," John, Sr. wrote in his diary on Wednesday, August 13, 1930. The next day workmen began "destroying old house, moving garage and barn." On August 20, after returning from a trip with John, Jr. to Omaha (where Cargill's archetypal large-bin terminal, the brainchild of John, Jr., was running day and night to accommodate the new crop), he

My grandmother Edna Cargill
MacMillan

noted: "Slept in Leighton Cottage Wednesday night for first time. Leightons moved out night previous."

My grandfather's house would cost him seventy-five thousand dollars. The architect who drew the plans for the three-story, brick and half-timbered residence with a prominent round tower set into its front facade was Ernest Kennedy, a Minneapolitan who had studied at the Sorbonne and also designed houses for Howard I. McMillan in Minneapolis, and Howard's father John D. McMillan and Charles D. Velie at Lake Minnetonka. The building contractor was H. O. Berklund from nearby Long Lake.

The Foothills Hotel in Ojai, California, where John, Sr. and Edna wintered in February and March 1931

"Foundation completed at new house," John, Sr. noted on September 30. Carl Bolander and Sons from Minneapolis used trucks and power shovels to excavate for the basement and a team of horses to help haul dirt out of the area. Nurserymen Kelley and Kelley from Long Lake laid out roads and drives, graded the property with teams of horses, and planted elms and maples.

In late fall, before the onset of winter, my grandparents returned to Minneapolis; their new house would not be ready until the following summer. They had given up their longtime home at 317 Clifton Avenue a year earlier, so they were lodging temporarily in a new luxury apartment hotel at 510 Groveland, which remains one of the city's most prestigious addresses. After Christmas, for the third year in a row, John, Sr. and Edna went to southern California for an extended vacation with friends from Minneapolis. Their destination was the Foothills Hotel in Ojai near Santa Barbara, which they used as a home away from home while taking side trips and visiting the Hanchettes in southern California. Prior to leaving Minneapolis, John, Sr. had ordered a "new Big 1931 model Packard sedan" to be delivered upon their return.

Keeping an eye on their new house for them in their absence, John, Jr. reported on February 2: "The plastering in the house seems to be about finished. The walls in the library are in, but not plastered, and it is . . . going to be a very beautiful room indeed and will not suffer by having such thick walls."

His brother Cargill had just signed a contract to build a Colonial-style house, also designed by Ernest Kennedy, on a portion of the Orde-Leighton property for his growing family—which now included sons Cargill, Jr. and Whitney. Cargill was ecstatic about the property, particularly with regard to the wildlife. He wrote to his parents: "Pauline went snow-shoeing on Saturday morning and said that all the pheasants in the country seemed to be located in that tamarack swamp She said that literally at least several hundred birds got

The house Cargill MacMillan built in the family compound at Orono in 1931. This residence was razed in 1991 to make room for his son Whitney MacMillan's new home.

210

My mother Marion with my brother Hugh and me. I was named William Duncan MacMillan II for my father's Uncle Will, the astronomer. As a child, I was sometimes called Willie.

Hugh and me at 1785 Emerson

out of the swamp. . . . They have obviously gone in there for food and Pauline thought that I ought to make arrangements to feed them. If they begin to die off I will of course see that some food is put out so that we will keep some birds."

John, Jr. was building at the lake as well, adding a wing to the former Leighton cottage, where his parents had spent the previous summer. He and Marion also now had two sons; I had been born at Hill Crest Surgical Hospital in Minneapolis on July 5, 1930. Until my parents built their own house at the lake a few years later, we spent summers in the revamped Leighton house. From October to May for three years, we rented a white frame Colonial-style house in Minneapolis at 1785 Emerson Avenue. My earliest memories are of sitting or playing on the back step of this house. The step was white and went up into the kitchen area.

MacMillan Lake, or "Rudolph's Pond"
as the family referred to it early on for
the hired man charged with filling it.
"Rudolph's pond is a complete and
dismal failure," Cargill wrote to his
parents in January 1932. "His dam
does not hold the water long enough
for it to freeze and he keeps flooding
and flooding to no avail." By April,
however, Rudolph had mastered the
problem. "Cargill tells me the lake is
up another inch this morning on the
strength of eight hours pumping
by Rudolph," John, Jr. informed his
father. "Cargill measured the lake and
estimates that it is between three and
four acres in area."

While the work on my grandparents' house continued, John, Sr. saved each and every one of the several hundred invoices he incurred—bills itemizing seven water closets (toilets); eight antique gilt-and-tortoise-shell brackets for the library; a crystal-trimmed chandelier for the dining room; a terrazzo floor in the glazed porch; and a "Botticino" marble mantel. C.H. Klein Brick Company in Chaska, Minnesota, supplied "kiln run" brick at twelve dollars per thousand. Cut stone came from Jones and Hartley in Minneapolis.

Unskilled workers employed by the general contractor were paid as little as forty cents an hour; plumbers received $1.70, and plumbers' helpers, $1.00. The Ray Roofing Company of St. Paul charged $2,500 to put on the "No. 1 clear Albion slate" roof. This was the same Ray family from La Crosse into which Austen Cargill had married.

Before he had finished reshaping the property to fit his idea of a proper country estate, my grandfather also created MacMillan Lake. In May 1932, when his electric meter showed a whopping 3,036 kilowatt hours consumed during April, up from an average 200 kilowatt hours monthly, the Minneapolis General Electric Company thought that there must be some mistake and billed him a minimal charge until it could check out the meter. John, Sr. replied that the figure in question was no doubt correct, explaining, "We have been running our pump constantly for the purpose of filling an artificial lake on the property."

Margaret Mount Cargill

Longridge with John H. MacMillan, Sr. in front doorway about 1935

Edna had charge of the decorating, of course, and she followed the example of her extravagant mother. My grandmother wanted a French Empire look, which her maiden cousin Margaret Mount Cargill, an interior designer in New York, helped her achieve for something under twenty-five thousand dollars, not including the service wing. To complement the French-style furniture, some of it antique, Margaret selected wallpapers, rugs, curtains, upholstery fabrics, lamps, vases, even French prints. Margaret Mount Cargill was the only child of James (Jim) Flett Cargill, whose nervous breakdown in 1903 had made room for my grandfather in Cargill's Minneapolis office.

While Edna was in California during the winter that the house was under construction, she also ordered furniture through Minerva Barry Dickson, my maternal grandmother. Mrs. Dickson had been widowed shortly after my parents were married in 1927 and had a decorating business in San Francisco. One invoice for furniture from the F. H. Harder Manufacturing Company included two walnut Louis XV beds (for the master bedroom), $240; four Louis XV cane seat and back chairs, $180; two walnut dressers, $350; a chaise lounge in "stock white," $54; and two chairs upholstered in sateen, one blue, $50, one gold, $55.

Nine busy months after breaking ground, John, Sr. and Edna moved out to the grand new house they called Longridge on a Thursday, June 11, 1931. It was a warm day, with the temperature reaching eighty-two degrees, but unpleasantly wet. "Heavy rains and our roads are muddy. No furniture downstairs, very little upstairs," John, Sr. noted in his diary.

The next day in a letter to Minerva Dickson in California, he wrote: "We slept in the house last night for the first time but I presume it will really be about the first of July before we will be really living there. I think we have a cook coming today and our old house-maid is coming next Monday and I suppose we will slowly get settled. It is a great satisfaction to have John and Marion

The more private, south-facing side of Longridge

so near us. We see the babies every day now."

Into this idyllic picture crept reality. It had been almost nineteen months since the stock market crashed in October 1929, and the MacMillans were not nearly so insulated from the ensuing Depression as they might seem to have been. In the immediate future, it would take a terrible toll on John, Sr.'s health and well-being.

Cargill was one of the largest users of bank credit in the United States, and with the economy sagging, lenders were tightening their credit requirements. John, Sr. made the rounds of the banks in several cities, and in early January 1932 he and Edna went to New York where he met with bankers. He wrote in his diary that he also had a "long visit" concerning "our Mexican matters" with H. A. Basham of Mexico City and "found him rather hopeful." (After the Mexican Claims Act was passed in 1941, the Cargill Securities Company finally received $300,000 in compensation for timber lands expropriated by the Mexican government.)

John H. MacMillan, Sr. in his library at Longridge

This trip completely debilitated John, Sr., who was never any too robust to begin with. Exhausted and not at all well, he was too weak to return to Minneapolis. From New York my grandparents went directly to Baltimore where he was hospitalized for almost a month at Johns Hopkins Hospital. My grandfather was having difficulty voiding, but the attending physicians, Drs. J. A. C. Colston and Leslie M. Gay, discovered something more serious. "Found my heart in bad shape," John, Sr. noted. In fact, he had suffered a heart attack.

On January 8 Dr. Colston described John, Sr. as being "extremely tired and showing what must be considered a beginning myocardial break with hypertension and moderate arteriosclerosis. The heart is definitely enlarged." His past medical history included a broken arm as a child; adult typhoid at thirty-three (when he was in Pine Bluff), also malaria; several nervous breakdowns from overwork; no periods of depression; one or two cups of coffee every day; no tobacco, tea, drugs, or alcohol. He measured five feet, ten-and-a-half inches tall, and his average weight was 176 pounds.

Dr. Colston ordered bed rest in the hospital for my grandfather, two weeks later performing an operation on his enlarged prostate. John, Sr. was discharged from the hospital and returned to Minneapolis after two weeks, but he once again had trouble voiding. After several trips to Swedish Hospital to use a catheter, he returned to Baltimore to see Dr. Colston. In Baltimore, however, the obstruction difficulty disappeared without treatment. John, Sr. was far from up to par, however, and my grandparents decided to go south to Thomasville, Georgia, for an extended vacation.

Keeping his parents posted on what was happening at home, Cargill filled them in on this bit of local news on March 7: "We are having a very important election at Orono tomorrow. It seems that the [incumbent township supervisor] is the man who tried to get the dance pavilion put through down on the [Lake Minnetonka] shore in front of us. He is a bad actor from all accounts and is supposed to be connected with the bootleg ring around Stubbs Bay. A more respectable element have gotten Bill Kelley [of Kelley and Kelley, the firm that landscaped Longridge] to run against him and it is hoped that Bill can defeat him."

My grandfather was still weak as a kitten when he and Edna returned to Minneapolis in the spring. "I have been gaining slowly but steadily," he wrote to Dr. Gay on May 13. "I did not come to our office until about ten days after I got back, and then tried the two hour limit at my desk, which you suggested, but I found that was a little more than I could stand at the start. However this week I have been able to put in two hours without difficulty and I feel very much stronger physically." Despite pronouncing himself cured, John, Sr. from this time forward curtailed his activities at the office. In August Cargill's board of directors elected John, Jr. its new general manager.

Both of John and Edna's daughters-in-law were pregnant that summer. In

Dan MacMillan with his grandnephew John Hugh MacMillan III at Longridge about 1930

Pauline MacMillan with Whitney,
Cargill, Jr., and baby Alice

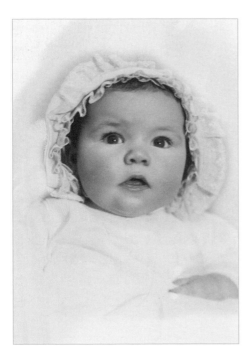

My sister Marion Hamilton MacMillan

July, my Aunt Pauline Whitney MacMillan gave birth to a daughter named Alice Whitney MacMillan. This was indeed cause for celebration! Extending "hearty congratulations" to the Cargill MacMillans, the editor of the company publication *Cargill News* remarked, "It is the first time in nearly fifty years that a daughter has been born in the MacMillan family." Three months later, finishing out our family and giving my grandparents a second baby granddaughter, my mother gave birth to my sister Marion Hamilton MacMillan on October 17.

"Our long expected daughter arrived last night," John, Jr. wrote his Uncle Will the next morning. "The baby weighed six pounds and six ounces and resembles very much her brothers at that age. We plan to call her Marion Hamilton, which is Marion's name and was her grandmother's."

On Thanksgiving Day, all the MacMillans motored to St. Cloud for dinner at Mrs. Whitney's house—John and Edna, and the John, Jr. and Cargill MacMillan families, never expecting the tragedy that awaited them. The terse entry in my grandfather's diary for that day, November 24, reads: "About 3 P.M. Dr. Arey telephoned Pauline that Baby Alice was dead—a frightful shock to us all and we all at once started home."

Two days later, John, Sr. wrote sadly: "Funeral of Little Alice at home. Dr. Wm. H. Boddy officiated. Just family and relatives." According to her death certificate, four-month-old Alice Whitney MacMillan suffocated from an upper respiratory infection.

ROOSEVELT AND RECOVERY

John, Jr. and Marion at home in the 1930s

Just adorable: my brother Hugh and me

America was in the worst of the Depression when my father John H. MacMillan, Jr. was elected vice president and general manager of the Cargill companies in August 1932. The promotion could not have come at a more inopportune time for the nervous young heir to the Cargill empire. The economy was at its lowest ebb; one of the most popular songs that year was "Brother, Can You Spare a Dime?"

President Hoover could talk endlessly predicting economic recovery, but the business slump following the 1929 stock market crash had careered out of control. Hoover was a mining engineer and a humanitarian who had organized Belgian relief during World War I, rescuing from starvation ten million people. But he had become a laughing stock. To "hoover" once meant to help. Now makeshift shanty towns called "Hoovervilles" had sprung up on the outskirts and even in the hearts of cities (there was one in Central Park). The wandering jobless carried their tattered belongings in "Hoover bags." Thirteen million men were out of work, the unemployment rate hovered at twenty-four percent, and the bread lines that formed in the cities cut across all walks of life.

In California, Cargill Chairman and President John H. MacMillan, Sr. lay convalescing after a permanently debilitating heart attack brought on by overwork and worry, exacerbated by several years' struggle with Hoover's Farm Board. Created to stabilize prices by establishing cooperatives to buy and sell farm surpluses, the Farm Board eventually proved monumentally ill-conceived, but not before it had engendered enormous antagonism between farmers and grain dealers. "Unfortunately," wrote John, Sr. in defense of the grain industry,

217

"it has been a popular pastime to chase the grain trade and yet they have been, and still are, the best friends the farmer has ever had."

In the 1990s fewer than two percent of Americans live on farms, but sixty years ago more than a quarter of the population was trying to make a living farming. Many of them failed. "Agricultural prices hadn't been so low since the reign of Queen Elizabeth," wrote historian William Manchester. Bumper crops in the wheat states sent wheat prices plummeting from $1.03 in 1929 to thirty-some cents per bushel in 1932, and the price for a bushel of corn fell to seven cents, making it cheaper to burn corn for fuel than to sell it and buy coal. Farmers fought foreclosure—sometimes arming themselves and holding off law officers at the gates to their farms—but many of them ended up renting from banks the very fields that had been in their families for generations.

Hoover euphemistically termed the disastrous economic tailspin a "depression," to avoid calling it a "panic" or "crisis." "Depression" had been the standard word for an economic slowdown since the early nineteenth century, indicating a *chronic* condition, while a "panic" denotes an *acute* economic illness. A "panic" is the sudden reversal of a market trend on extraordinarily high volume. A seller's panic on Wall Street has often marked the onset of a depression but is not the same thing. It is interesting that in 1937, when the economy that had been slowly climbing out of the pit reached in 1933 suddenly slumped again, no one knew what to call it. The country was already in a depression, after all. So the economists, probably delighted to have a problem they could actually solve, coined the term "recession." Ever since, the word "depression"—now usually spelled with a capital—has referred specifically to the 1930s, and economic downturns are now always called recessions.

At the onset of the Depression, the Cargill enterprises had prospered. Cargill earnings topped the million-dollar mark for the first time since 1916–1917 in both 1930 and 1931. However, earnings were off for the 1931–1932 crop year, dropping to a still respectable $482,000. Even before the figures were out, John, Sr. took remedial action.

In April 1932, emulating President Hoover who had reduced his personal salary of $75,000 by twenty percent and persuaded his vice president and nine cabinet members to take similar cuts, John, Sr. announced a twenty percent pay reduction for Cargill employees from the top down. At the bottom of the pay scale, clerks who had been making $60 per month would see their pay drop to $48. Explaining this "first general cut in salaries in the history of the Cargill Companies," John, Sr. blamed "the crop failure in our Northwestern growing states" and "continued political interference with the grain business."

Prior to the cutback, John, Sr. had been making a comfortable $50,000 per year, which had enabled him to build his large country home on Lake Minnetonka; John, Jr., his father's heir apparent, $18,000; and Vice President

My mother Marion with Hugh and me

218

John, Sr. with Marnie on his lap in the electric cart he drove to get around Longridge. Our cousin Paula (Whitney and Cargill, Jr.'s sister) is sitting beside him. I'm on the floor with Mickey, our Sealyham terrier. The other dog—an English sheepdog named Jackie—belonged to the Cargill MacMillans.

Dan MacMillan, $15,000. Turning down an invitation to visit a nephew in Illinois over the Decoration Day holiday that year in May, Dan MacMillan wrote: "I must confide to you the fact that I am thinking in terms of pennies these days rather than in terms of dollars."

Though groomed since boyhood to one day take charge of the family business, John, Jr. had ahead of him one of the most difficult years of his career. President Hoover faced almost certain defeat in the November election, but the grain trade also feared the Democratic candidate, New York Governor Franklin Roosevelt. "As far as I can make out he is very much the same type as Mr. Hoover, and I am afraid equally dangerous," wrote John, Sr. Where Hoover had tried to cure farm ills by subsidizing exports from surplus domestic crops, Roosevelt favored a voluntary allotment plan to reduce production. In Cargill's immediate future loomed both growing federal regulation and increasingly tight credit that threatened to strangle the sixty-seven-year-old company.

People who knew my father considered him to be a genius. High-strung and quirky, he was a handsome man with thinning brown hair, a brush mustache, and penetrating dark eyes. Thirty-seven years old in 1932, he had helped shape Cargill policy for the past ten years, and John, Sr. had come to rely more and more on his son's creative thinking. My father was responsible for innovations that would have far-reaching implications for the Cargill Company. Early on, for instance, he had espoused the concept of an "endless belt," by which Cargill would control the movement of grain from the farmer to the final buyer by managing transportation and insurance in addition to handling and storage. The firm later extended this endless belt theory to grain processing.

My father and grandfather were quite different in their approaches to the business. John, Sr. had learned through adversity to maintain a conservative stance, but his son enjoyed risk-taking and would thrive in a risk-filled business. Their contrasting personalities also resulted in different management styles. John, Sr. would insist on having all the facts, but he was willing to delegate authority. John, Jr., on the other hand, had more of a "take charge" attitude and favored retaining centralized control over the firm's every activity.

Already John, Jr. had put his stamp on Cargill's accounting and office procedures, consolidated its grain marketing operations, and reorganized the company's transportation facilities. In 1930, going out on a limb with his father's blessing and technical help from colleague Frank Neilson, he built a radically new type of large-bin elevator with a suspended roof. The Omaha installation revolutionized grain elevator construction.

The very next year, hearing that the Albany Port Commission was planning to build a new export grain terminal and lease it to a Canadian syndicate, John, Jr. rushed to New York. Albany was 143 miles from the ocean, but it was destined to become a seaport by the dredging of the upper reaches of the

Hudson River. An alternative deep-water port to Montreal, Albany could also supply foreign trade while Montreal was closed in winter.

Meeting with Port Commission chairman Peter G. Ten Eyck, John, Jr. learned that the city was willing to spend $1.5 million for a grain storage facility with a capacity of $3^{1}/_{2}$ million bushels. Doing some on-the-spot calculating, and citing the recently built Omaha elevator, he told Ten Eyck that, for the same $1.5 million, Cargill could instead build a gigantic 12-million-bushel terminal. Because it was the largest shipper from the Great Lakes (except for Canadian Wheat Pool shipments), Cargill could each fall fill a large elevator at Albany to supply its foreign trade while the Port of Montreal was closed.

Notorious for acting independently, John, Jr. concluded the deal without seeking or getting approval from anyone back in Minneapolis. Ten Eyck canceled negotiations with the Canadians, and Cargill began construction immediately. Governor Roosevelt was among the dignitaries attending the dedication of the Port of Albany in June 1932, and within a few weeks workers were unloading and loading grain at the world's largest terminal elevator. Owned by the Port Commission and leased to Cargill, it had ended up being a $13^{1}/_{2}$-million-bushel facility.

John, Jr.'s new elevators worried the banking community. "There has been considerable gossip in the grain circles about these elevators," an officer of the First National Bank of Chicago warned John, Sr. in July 1932. "Some of our friends think that there is considerable potential danger in loading up bins with 750,000 bushels, particularly if there be a wet harvest." John, Sr. didn't agree. Standing behind John, Jr., he replied: "We have found that by using the proper precautions (Cargill had also developed new methods of measuring temperature and turning grain) this large type of bin is even safer than the old type." In the days and months ahead, bankers would have a lot more to worry about than the configuration of Cargill's elevators.

Nineteen thirty-two was a watershed year in American history. On November 8, disillusioned with Hoover and his ineffectual attempts at mending the economy, Americans elected fifty-year-old Franklin Delano Roosevelt president in a Democratic landslide that carried all but seven states. Promising citizens a "New Deal," Roosevelt's party platform embodied an aggressive program of relief, recovery, and reform measures that would repeal Prohibition, provide unemployment assistance, lower tariffs, subsidize farmers, rehabilitate railroads, safeguard consumers and investors, and slash government spending.

During the extended "lame duck" period between Roosevelt's election and his inauguration on March 4, 1933 (the Twentieth Amendment to the Constitution that year would change inauguration day to January 20), the economic situation in the country continued to deteriorate and bankers became particularly pessimistic. John, Sr. and John, Jr. spent the week following the election in New York meeting with and reassuring nervous lenders. "Called at

220

My grandmother Minerva Barry Dickson with me, Marnie, and Hugh

John, Jr. on vacation

Guaranty Trust, New York Trust, Goldman, Sachs, Chase National Bank, Manufacturers Trust," John, Sr. wrote in his diary on Monday, November 14.

As he often did, John, Sr. managed to mix business with pleasure, traveling home from New York via Chicago where he visited Will and Janet and his sister Mary, who happened to be there as well. Stopping in La Crosse, where he also had relatives, he arranged with officials of the Chicago, Milwaukee and St Paul Railroad to exchange the La Crosse and Southeastern Railway for a twenty-five years' lease of Milwaukee Elevator B.

Christmas that year was a happy affair, with the whole family and Dan and Donald and the Whitneys from St. Cloud at John, Sr.'s new house. "The children ate in that back dining room and, judging from the noise, they had a wonderful time," he wrote in a thank-you note (for a desk set that included a scissors, paper knife, and magnifying glass) to Emma Hanchette.

On Christmas night, leaving their brood in the care of Marion's mother Minerva Dickson, my parents departed for New York to take a much-needed vacation cruise to the Panama Canal. "This is one of the finest rests I ever remember," John, Jr. wrote in a long letter to his parents on January 5 from a United Fruit Company steamer. "Marion (who had given birth to my sister Marnie in October) is much much better, and seems to be quite her old self again. . . . The boat is practically deserted. All the passengers except a handful got off at Havana. The weather has been absolutely perfect."

Even at this distance, however, John, Jr. had a lot more than vacationing on his mind. Bothered by broader concerns back home, he went on in his letter to lament the recent death of Ex-President Calvin Coolidge. "It is a great loss to the country, as he was almost the only possible prospective leader for the Republican party." Addressing business issues including inflation and a proposed domestic allotment program that worried him, he finally concluded, "I know we came away to forget business but it's pretty hard to do so in trying times like these."

My father and mother arrived back in New York on a Monday, January 16. John, Sr. and Edna met them there the next day at the Barclay Hotel. John, Sr. wanted to brief his son before he and Edna set sail the following Saturday for their winter vacation in California by way of the Panama Canal. While his parents were away, John, Jr. kept in close touch by letter with his father concerning Cargill's increasingly precarious credit arrangements.

One of the nation's largest users of bank credit, Cargill had $12,750,000 in notes payable to nineteen different banks in January 1933. Ever since John, Sr. had disentangled the company from its creditors in 1916, Cargill had been able to borrow money on unsecured notes payable, essentially on John, Sr.'s signature, but all this was changing. Now bankers were requesting "bankers' acceptances," drafts backed by inventory and "accepted" or guaranteed by the bank,

221

which could be resold in financial markets. Acceptance borrowing was regulated by the Federal Reserve Board, and grain used as collateral had to be stored in federal- or state-licensed warehouses.

"I had a very strenuous time in New York," John, Jr. informed his father on January 31, "as after we had the Produce Exchange all lined up to handle our receipts as we wanted them, the Federal Reserve Board refused to pass the arrangement as satisfactory . . . so we had to start all over again. It finally develops that we have only two alternatives: One is to license our houses under the Federal Warehouse Act, and the other is to make use of the services of a field warehouse company, as have General Mills."

From New York, my father had gone to Washington. "I spent a day . . . with the warehouse people and the Federal Reserve Board and it is clearly going to take some time to work out what we require. I returned to New York and at the suggestions of . . . the Guaranty we are putting in applications to license our houses under Federal regulation, and just as soon as we can issue collateral I will return to New York and complete our arrangement."

On his return trip home to Minneapolis, John, Jr. called on the Continental Bank in Chicago and the First Wisconsin in Milwaukee. The bankers in both cities were pleasant enough, but noncommittal. The First Wisconsin "definitely did not want to do business with us until after our next June statement is out. . . . I am morally certain that the trouble with both the Continental and the First in Wisconsin reflects a combination of competitors' insinuations [running down a competitor was not unheard of in the industry] as well as reflecting the general strain in the banking world."

The next week the Continental sent a Mr. Overlook up to Minneapolis to go over Cargill's books. "He understood the grain business from start to finish [and] I really rather enjoyed the three days [he spent here]," John, Jr. wrote to his father on February 7.

"He made the most comprehensive study of our business ever made by an outsider and . . . had there been anything wrong he would have found it. [He] was unable to make a single constructive suggestion or criticize our position in any way, although he did state that our business was not conducted in what the Chicago banks considered an orthodox manner. . . . I am very certain that his recommendation will be that the business is sound, well managed, etc., etc., but that . . . the borrowings should probably be on a secured basis. In fact his last recommendation to me was that we transfer our borrowing to a secured basis as quickly as possible."

Despite Overlook's vote of approval, Cargill's credit situation deteriorated day by day. "There is no question that conditions are exceedingly critical and we are doing everything we can to liquidate," John, Jr. continued. "I think you can definitely count out all our Western banks as sources of credit, except for our local Northwestern banks." If bank credit was going to be impeded, Cargill would have to liquidate grain stocks held in storage at its various locations.

"I have not heard from the First National here," John, Jr. advised his father on February 14. "I discussed liquidating at some length with [their man] Wakefield last week and he agreed with me that we should not liquidate if we could arrange our acceptance credit, but otherwise he felt it was necessary. . . . In view of the complete crop failure in the Southwest you must well understand our reluctance to sell anything out of Omaha. At the recent rate of our sales in the East we estimate that everything there can be liquidated by the 1st of July but that it would be decidedly to our advantage not to liquidate certain substantial portions. However, we are selling as though everything had to go."

Bankers in the Middle West were "absolutely hysterical," John, Jr. wrote. "They are interested in nothing except paper which can be discounted instantly into cash. . . . In Michigan the Governor has declared an eight day banking holiday this morning, and I understand that in Wisconsin banks are failing at the rate of sixty a week."

It was an absurd and perilous atmosphere in which to do business. On February 28 John, Jr. advised his father that he was "seriously considering moving about a million dollars of cash up to the Royal Bank [in Canada] until this crisis blows over." The tension in the banking world was increasing daily, and he foresaw a general banking moratorium that would close down the Board of Trade and make it very difficult for Cargill to fulfill its various foreign commitments without some outside source of cash. Uncle Dan agreed with him, my father reported.

John, Jr. knew whereof he spoke. Nearly five thousand banks with deposits in excess of three billion dollars had failed since 1929, and the governors of twenty-two states would close their banks before Franklin Roosevelt took office on March 4. One of Cargill's lenders, Northwestern Bank, when ordered to close in Wisconsin, wired John, Jr. on March 3:

NORTHWEST BANC CORPN BANKS LOCATED IN WISCONSIN OPENED FOR BUSINESS AS USUAL THIS MORNING ACCORDING TO E. W. DECKER, PRESIDENT, DESPITE THE MANDATORY ORDER ISSUED BY GOV. SCHMEDEMANN FOR A TWO WEEK BANK HOLIDAY. MR. DECKER ADDED THAT THE BANKS IN HIS GROUP WOULD NOT CLOSE UNTIL HE WAS ASSURED THAT THE GOVERNOR HAD AUTHORITY TO ENFORCE SUCH AN ORDER.

But the panic was on. At 4:30 on the morning of March 4, New York's Governor Lehman ordered a bank holiday, and Governor Horner of Illinois followed suit. When Roosevelt was sworn in later that day, the general situation was calamitous. Paraphrasing Thoreau in his inaugural address, Roosevelt told Americans:

FORWARD WITH ROOSEVELT

223

First of all, let me assert my firm belief that the only thing we have to fear is fear itself—nameless, unreasoning, unjustified terror which paralyzes needed efforts to convert retreat into advance. . . . This nation asks for action, and action now!

Americans across the country cheered. "America hasn't been as happy in three years as they are today," wrote Will Rogers in his column the next day. "No money, no banks, no work, no nothing, but they know they got a man in there who is wise to Congress, wise to our so-called big men. The whole country is with him."

Calling a special session of Congress on Sunday, March 5, President Roosevelt proclaimed a national bank holiday while he drafted his Emergency Banking Act. On Monday, the New York Stock Exchange opened long enough for its president, Richard Whitney, to announce that it was closing, and the Chicago Board of Trade locked its doors for the first time since 1848.

"To say that we are worried about these matters would put it mildly," John, Jr. wrote his father on March 6. "We have discontinued business everywhere except in Canada. . . . This, to me, is a hurricane far worse than that which prevailed in 1893 or 1907, and it will be a long time before we can resume business as usual."

The next day found John, Jr. more hopeful. Three days earlier, on inauguration day, he had written letters to twenty-some creditor banks to propose a new acceptance policy for loans once the grain exchanges reopened. Advising the banks that Cargill might need more money in a hurry to finance a probable advance "of 25% or perhaps 50% shortly after [the market] reopens," he had included a statement listing Cargill's Bills Payable ($12,349,500), Cash and Collectables ($2,525,000), and Value of Inventory ($14,025,000). Now he was hearing back from the bankers, and "the reaction from this letter has been uniformly favorable," he informed John, Sr.

"In every case they expressed appreciation at our frankness in stating the possibilities in the situation, and I am sure it did a great deal of good." Two bankers had called him from New York, he reported, "about our possibly needing more money, and their tone was so friendly and helpful . . . that I have an entirely different feeling than I have previously had. . . . I really feel that this particular crisis is going to go a long way in establishing confidence in the grain trade, and ourselves in particular."

Two days later on Thursday, March 9, in a record eight hours, Congress passed President Roosevelt's Emergency Banking Bill, which amounted to a bailout of the banks by the government. That same day Cargill and Pauline MacMillan landed in New York following more than two months in Europe, where Cargill had been attending to company business in Rotterdam, Genoa, and London. Since the banks (though not the grain markets) would reopen on Monday, John, Jr. asked

A photo of me with "Willie" penciled on the back

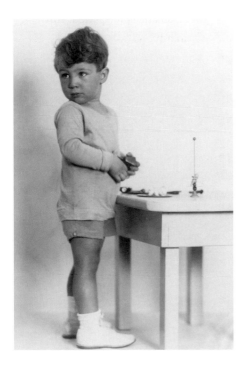

My brother Hugh had a penchant for getting into trouble

his brother to stay in New York as the Cargill liaison.

Breathing easier once he believed Cargill's credit problems to be over, John, Jr. was immediately full of new plans that he outlined in a letter to his father dated March 10. Having learned that there were docks with warehouses available which had not been rented for years in Portland, he was thinking of buying an ocean boat in an effort to "embarrass" the railroads into giving Cargill better rates out of Albany. For starters, he knew of a boat in good running condition that would carry 175,000 bushels and could probably be purchased for $7,500.

"Our idea is to buy such a boat, equip it with pneumatic machinery costing perhaps $2,000 or $2,500, which would enable us to load into trucks over the rail. . . . We would then fill the boat with grain at Albany, send it to Portland, discharge the crew, and peddle our grain by truck. Whenever the boat was empty we would pick up a crew at Portland for a round trip to Albany and back, and be ready again for business in a week." Glad once more to be able to concentrate on operating plans, he concluded, "I am very sure that not only the country's crisis but our own is very definitely a matter of the past. . . . I am taking the children to the circus this afternoon as Marion is laid up with a bad cold."

By Monday, March 13, any euphoria my father may have felt had vanished. "Cargill called on the New York Trust Company this morning and the bankers told him that they were functioning as usual but interest rates were sky high and would probably be around 5%," he wrote to his father. "So apparently credit is opening up in a thoroughly normal fashion." There was a problem, however.

"We had a request from the Irving for specific information about our position, which indicates that they are uneasy about us, so I am going to New York at once to give them the information they want in person. It is also probable that if they are uneasy the other New York banks are also, and they certainly should be called upon before the markets open."

At home, John, Jr. said, he and my mother had had quite a scare the previous Saturday night when "just as we were going out to dinner, Hugh started the washing machine by himself and ran his right arm through the wringer. Fortunately, Madeline [one of the maids] was able to stop it just as it reached his shoulder and get his arm out. He was terribly bruised but no bones were broken and Doctor Anderson says he will be quite all right in a few days."

He hadn't said so to his father, but the Irving Trust letter had severely shaken John, Jr. Dan MacMillan wrote to his brother John, Sr. the next day that "Junior" had left for New York and that it was probably the wise thing to do. "In any event I think it was a good thing for him to get away from the office for he was cracking under the strain. . . . The fact that he had to face the Irving Trust Company and go over the situation in general with them seemed to unnerve him and he went to pieces badly. He retched and vomited greatly for a few moments. . . .

"It is unfortunate that Junior has these tailspins occasionally, but if I am around to reassure him he straightens right out. . . . As you know, he has a tendency to keep himself under high tension all the time, and these vomiting spells are merely warnings to him that he has been overdoing the situation." My father could always count on his queasy stomach to betray him in a pinch, but once in New York he held up well.

As it turned out, John, Jr. wouldn't be returning home anytime soon. John, Sr. and Edna joined their sons there on Monday, March 20. "Rained all day. Called at Guaranty," John, Sr. noted that day in his diary. Eventually father and sons were party to a plan that put together a consortium of banks headed by the Chase to handle their large-scale revolving credit.

In the meantime, writing to Marion on March 26 from the Biltmore where he and his family were staying, my father confessed to missing her terribly. "I'd have given most anything to have been home all day on my upstairs sun porch, and to have had you come in from time to time just to keep me from concentrating on anything. The rest today was really most welcome, but it wasn't like being home. . . .

"Our luncheon yesterday was really a treat with a flock of distinguished guests who were chuck full of interesting side lights on the political situation. Their sympathies were all with us on the farm bill, but as they were bankers and public utility people they were having their legislative troubles too. They all had nothing but praise for Roosevelt though. . . .

"Please tell me what exactly you have done to your hair. I don't like all these changes. Please grow a great big chignon, just like you used to have."

On March 30, when he was still in New York and even more anxious to go home, John, Jr. explained: "The whole trouble is that our banks can't agree among themselves as to our correct manner of borrowing, and Father & I really are sitting around twirling our thumbs while our banks are squabbling. Their own jealousies are simply terrific, and would ordinarily amuse, were it not that I want to get home to you and the children."

Rubbing noses: My mother Marion and Marnie

Craigbank, the French chateau my father built at Orono with MacMillan Lake in the foreground

T he 1933 bank crisis instilled in John, Jr. a healthy respect for credit that he would never forget. Many years later in 1949 he commented: "My Great-uncle, Sam Cargill, had a saying that 'credit is as delicate as the pupil of your eye.' From my own experience I know this to be true."

Early 1933 had been a desperate time that Cargill, Inc. survived because of intrinsic strengths, but my father could take some of the credit too. It was his first year at the helm, and the company went on to post profits of more than $1 million for the 1932-1933 crop year. Moreover, its net worth reached an all-time high of $6,977,000. John, Jr. considered "it the most successful year in the history of the business."

A rear view of Craigbank from the air about 1935

Hugh and Duncan in a sailboat on MacMillan Lake. This catboat was built by a local boatworks; the sail came from a boat my mother had as a girl on San Francisco Bay.

With so much on his mind, he had put off building a family home which he now began on the site of the former Leighton cottage in Orono. My grandparents had lived in the Leighton cottage while building their house at the lake, and we had spent the past several summers there. The site overlooked man-made Lake MacMillan, which my grandfather had pumped full of water and which is still a very pretty lake. My father patterned the house after country chateaus he had seen in France during World War I. My mother named it Craigbank for the Dickson family home in Campbeltown, Scotland. It was a solid but not especially extravagant house that would be their home for the rest of their lives.

"We went out to our house yesterday afternoon and the progress they have made while we were gone seemed very wonderful indeed," John, Jr. wrote in January 1934 to his father in California. "The house looks even better on the ground than it did on the drawings." My parents had just returned from their usual end-of-the-year vacation. This was their first trip to Jamaica, which would become their favorite vacation destination. Right from the start my father was sold on the island, explaining that it helped him unwind and recuperate from stress-related health problems.

That same winter John, Sr. and Edna took an extended trip to the Orient with friends from Minneapolis on the S.S. *Lurline*. In a letter that caught up with them abroad, John, Jr. reported in February: "Our house is making rapid strides. They are now putting on the slate roof and putting in the windows. The plumbers and electricians have the house all torn up. Berklund [the contractor] still insists we will get in in the middle of May."

John, Jr.'s letter also contained news of a sinister nature. "The town is frightfully excited over the kidnapping menace and the gossip is that two important groups of underworld characters have moved into Minneapolis during the past few months and it is believed that they are making their headquarters in the Lake Minnetonka district," he informed his father.

At any rate a protective committee [has] been formed, with the various local authorities cooperating together and with some of our leading citizens on the committee. Dick Gale received numerous threatening letters and an attempt was made to hold him up. Consequently he is traveling around with a bodyguard. Mrs. [James Ford] Bell had a terrifying experience in which she was apparently saved from an attempted kidnapping only on the part of quick action by her chauffeur. It is certainly mighty consoling to know that we are not worth while being molested and I am also thankful that we have avoided publicity. I think there is no doubt that Dick Gale's trouble dates back to his equestrian activities being chronicled by every newspaper daily.

During the early 1930s the Twin Cities had become a haven for hoodlums. After Prohibition was repealed and bootlegging profits dwindled, mobsters increasingly turned to robbery and kidnapping. The Lindbergh baby kidnapping and killing in 1932 was followed by kidnappings in Minnesota. In June 1933 the Barker-Karpis gang kidnapped St. Paul brewer William Hamm, Jr., who was released four days later after his family paid one hundred thousand dollars ransom. In January 1934 this same gang seized St. Paul banker Edward Bremer and this time demanded and got *two* hundred thousand dollars.

The possibility that my brother and sister and I might be kidnapped when we were children curtailed our activities. We didn't go to camp, and we were under constant surveillance, if not by our parents, then by the household staff. For a time, we couldn't go anywhere, but we had our cousins Cargill, Jr., Whitney, and Paula next door, and other children came over. We never lacked for playmates.

For three summers from the time I was about eight, our good friend Mr. Charlie Bell arranged for a young man named Bob to entertain and supervise several boys including me. The group included David Bell (who was my best friend when we were growing up and in college), Brewster Atwater, Steve Krogness, Johnny Winton, Richard Crawford, and Denny Webb. We'd spend a day at each house. Sometimes we played indoors, sometimes we played in the woods, sometimes we went sailing.

I remember the first time these boys came over; I didn't want any part of it. My mother told me, "You're going to play for the day, and you're going to like it, and they're going to be fun to be with." I wanted to go to camp, but that was out, and she said that I should go down to the warming cabin we had on our lake and do the best I could.

So I went down there and I picked up one of Uncle Will's cigars and stuck it in my mouth and lit it. When the boys came looking for me, I swaggered around the corner with the cigar in my face. Nobody said a thing. Now every

Watching tennis at Craigbank. "These two tennis courts have worked out marvelously and have given us a life and activity which we never had in Orono before," John, Jr. wrote to his brother Gee in 1935. Edna and John, Sr. are pictured with their granddaughters Paula and Marnie. Cargill, Jr. is behind them on the hill.

once in a while, one of my friends will remind me that the first time he ever saw me, I had a cigar in my mouth.

In 1927 John, Sr. had written about Cargill's business, "We have never engaged in the export trade, and do not expect to do so at present," but John, Jr. found the possibilities of both export and import trading exciting. He had posted the first Cargill employee abroad in 1929, opening an office in Genoa, and by 1932 also had representatives in Rotterdam and London. In late fall 1933, after the bank crisis abated, Cargill was importing large quantities of rye from Hungary, Argentina, and Poland. "We are buying [rye cargoes] at such a price that we can move them to Chicago via Montreal and still make five cents per bushel profit," John, Jr. wrote to his father.

Profits for the 1933–34 crop year were, in fact, spectacular, largely because of rye. Cargill ended up trading wheat at a net loss that year, but heavy trading in rye and corn accounted for overall earnings just shy of $2 million, setting a new record. Any rejoicing was shortlived, however. The drought that had been forecast in early 1934 was by this time causing widespread devastation, turning formerly productive farm lands from Texas to the Dakotas into one giant "dust bowl."

The dry death scorched pastures and corn fields and turned plowed land into sand dunes," wrote historian William Leuchtenburg. "Farmers watched helplessly as cattle fell in their tracks and died. In Vinita, Oklahoma . . . the sun topped 100 degrees for thirty-five straight days; on the thirty-sixth, it climbed to 117 degrees." Droves of ruined farmers and their families took to the road in old trucks and cars. These were the "Okies" portrayed in John Steinbeck's *The Grapes of Wrath*. To help combat drought in the future, the newly-established Soil Conservation Service in 1935 recommended planting shelterbelts in the Plains region to prevent wind erosion, an innovative concept that was ridiculed by some people.

Cargill, Inc. was meanwhile incorporating companies in Argentina, England, and Holland. Laying out his instructions to the man he sent to Argentina, John, Jr. wrote in June 1934: "The first principle of our firm is that we decline positively to do business by bribery or any other irregular means, and as in Latin countries most business is done this way you will be at a most distinct handicap, which however cannot be helped. . . . The people with whom you will deal in general are high grade and exceedingly courteous in every respect. However, their standards of business conduct are substantially different from ours and they have not the same respect for faithful performance of contract that we have."

From Europe, John, Jr. was informed that summer by Ed Grimes, a Cargill employee who had been sent abroad to open new offices: "Switzerland, Holland, Belgium and France and, of course, Italy are tightening up regulations on trade day by day. . . . A responsible organization that can handle a two-way traffic . . . stands a grand chance of making orderly progress in all of this present disorder." In the case of Germany, the disorder was being fanned by Adolph Hitler. "Saw a lot of Hitler demonstrations," Grimes wrote. "Hitler is determined to reduce imports . . . has this 'self-sufficiency' idea in mind. . . . The young people of Germany are undoubtedly behind [him]. You can see them in great groups marching and singing—along highways and in the streets. . . . The people in Italy, Germany and even [here in France] with its slogan 'Vivre libre ou mourir' (live free or die) seem to be surrendering their freedom and liberty to a group of politicians."

Adolph Hitler, the son of an obscure Austrian official, was forty-three when he became Chancellor of Germany in January 1933. Like Roosevelt he would lead his country for the next twelve years. Establishing a one-party Nazi regime, Hitler assumed dictatorial powers, outlawing freedom of the press, labor unions, and opposition political parties. Taking Germany out of the League of Nations, he began illegally rearming for expansion, and his Gestapo hunted down and jailed or shot enemies of the state.

My father was not ready to take Hitler seriously, however. "The war scare in Europe has had us all anxious, but I personally cannot see any possibility of serious trouble," he wrote to his father in March 1935. "It seems to me that Germany is in such a weak position that she would be forced to give in on any act of a strong stand on the part of France alone. . . . Hitler has overplayed his hand . . . the French will probably insist upon his retirement."

John, Jr. went to South America to see Brazil and Argentina for himself in January 1935, sailing with Marion on a luxury Prince liner. "To say that my enthusiasm over the Argentine and its commercial and economic future is limitless would be putting it mildly," he wrote in February to his parents, who were now on the S.S. *Empress of Japan*, sailing from British Columbia to the Orient.

John, Sr. and Edna in India. "We are due at Singapore late this afternoon," John, Sr. wrote to Bess Wheeler on March 3, 1935. "Our weather is . . . the real tropical sort that you read about. . . . The Vanderbilts had the cabin next to ours but we saw nothing of them as Mrs. Vanderbilt was ill all the way to Monaco and on the advice of their doctor they left the ship there."

In an economic sense the country is where the U.S. was in 1880, and Canada about 1905. Its acreage under the plow has doubled since 1921, and in my opinion it will double again in the next thirteen years. Its natural fertility is beyond belief. I went to Rosario (on the hottest day in the history of the country) and saw a sight such as I never dreamed could be. Rosario is in the center of the corn belt, and the country was just like Iowa, except that to the corn fields stretching as far as you could see in every direction you had added orchards of oranges, peaches, pears, plums, apricots, palm trees, with occasional fields of vegetables, alfalfa or flax. On much of the land they get two crops, first of flax, then of corn. They cut alfalfa the year around with yields that make you dizzy. This year the Argentine will export about 600 million bushels of grain, nearly half of it corn—and the crop is only a fair crop, as the heat cooked it before the rain came.

Uncle Will with Hugh and me at Craigbank

Marion and John, Jr. in Jamaica

At home, times remained very difficult; the 1935 wheat crop was hardly better than the previous drought year, and Cargill, Inc. finished the crop year with a net loss of nearly one million dollars. On the plus side, 1935 was the first year that Cargill purchased and stored soybeans. Originally used in the United States as a forage crop, soybeans have turned out to be the most versatile plant known to science. Soybean oil is used for cooking oils, soaps, cleaning compounds, paints, linoleum, inks and stains, pharmaceuticals, and plastics; the residue soybean meal is a high-protein animal feed. The new kid on the block in 1935, soybeans that year were the fifth-ranking grain in farm value after corn, wheat, oats, and barley.

This was also the same year, incidentally, that Uncle Will MacMillan was quoted in *The New York Times* on December 21 as saying that there was no scientific basis for the Star of Bethlehem. Talk about the grinch who stole Christmas! Will had been a mathematical astronomer at the University of Chicago for thirty years and despite his Presbyterian upbringing was a self-proclaimed atheist. "It is the theme for a beautiful religious legend," he said, "but astronomy agrees the star never existed. [Furthermore] it is impossible for anyone to follow a star to a given spot. Take for example two men in different cities following the same star. After an hour's traveling both could look up and each say the star was directly above him, yet they would be many miles apart."

In December 1936 my father was named president of Cargill, Inc. John, Sr. was still in poor health and had suffered another setback that led to his resignation, although he retained his position as chairman of the board. As vice president and general manager, John, Jr. had made most of the policy

decisions for a number of years, but now his position was official. "The fact that Junior was made President of Cargill, Incorporated was merely a recognition of what has been an actual fact for a long time," John, Sr. informed a colleague. "There is really no change in the situation, although I do think it will make it a lot easier for me to have him have the title as well as the responsibility."

My father and mother celebrated his promotion with a six weeks' trip to Jamaica. "There is something about the monotony of the climate and the warmth which seems to be wonderful for heart trouble and blood pressure," John, Jr. wrote to Uncle Dan in March 1937. "Incidentally, you can live in Jamaica for about a fourth of what you can at home. . . . Unfortunately I added a few more pounds, bringing me up to a comfortable 200."

My parents flew home from Kingston that year, and although my father still considered air travel unsafe in the United States, he loved it. "I am very certain that we will never go to Jamaica again except by air," he wrote to John, Sr. The airplane ride "was unquestionably the highest spot in my travels I ever experienced. In all the flights I took in France I never saw anything which for beauty could compete with what we saw on this flight. . . . There was not a cloud in the sky as we flew over Jamaica."

Never one to back off from his principles, John, Jr. made headlines in 1937 when he clashed with the Chicago Board of Trade. In one of the most bitter fights in grain trade history, Cargill, Inc. stood accused by Secretary of Agriculture Henry Wallace and the Chicago Board of Trade (CBOT) of attempting to corner the September corn futures market.

Corn had been a scarce commodity in the fall of 1937, due in part to the crop failure the year before, and Cargill, Inc. had been buying heavily in corn futures for September. When the traders who had sold corn futures to Cargill couldn't deliver, the CBOT ordered Cargill to sell a million bushels of corn to relieve the "squeeze." Cargill refused, maintaining that to do so would demoralize prices and cost Cargill two million dollars. A contemporary saying moralized about this phenomenon, "He who sells what isn't hissen, *buys it back* or goes to prison."

The fat was in the fire. Three days before trading would have halted automatically, the CBOT suspended dealings, ordered the "shorts" to pay Cargill the going price, and expelled Cargill from the exchange for trying to corner September corn. Cargill retaliated with charges that the CBOT was favoring short sellers at Cargill's expense and took its grievances to the Commodity Exchange Authority (CEA). Siding with the CBOT, Secretary Henry Wallace cited Cargill for price manipulation and violation of the Commodity Exchange Act.

I was seven years old when this affair began, and my father was continually attending hearings out of town. It used to upset me terribly to see him go

Appearing before the Commodity Exchange Authority in Chicago on December 1, 1937, my father began: "Mr. Chairman, my name is John H. MacMillan, Jr. I live in Wayzata, Minnesota. I am president of Cargill, Inc. of Minneapolis, Minnesota, and am testifying here on its behalf."

Me, about seven years old

Marnie at breakfast about 1935

up to the attic and come down carrying his suitcase. I would say, "Why do you have to go? Can't you just send somebody else? Can't you, can't you . . . ? To me the "office" was doing this to him, and I thought it was very unfair.

The Wallace action was finally settled by stipulation in 1940. Cargill, Inc. was allowed to plead not guilty, but Cargill Grain Company of Illinois and John H. MacMillan, Jr. were denied trading privileges on all contract grain and commodity markets. Everyone knew that my father never traded personally, however, and the Cargill Grain Company of Illinois was being liquidated.

Cargill's split with the CBOT turned out to be a real boon for the company. Although barred from trading on the exchange, Cargill remained in the Chicago market, where it was able to outbid member firms bound by regulation to bid through commission men who received a one percent commission on cash grain coming into the city.

Flying to Jamaica: Hugh and Marnie

The Constant Spring Hotel near Kingston. "Marnie is a regular water rat," John, Jr. wrote to his parents. "She . . . jumps in from a height of 12 to 14 [feet]. The spectators all shout to her not to jump, and everyone gasps when she does, whereupon she comes to the surface laughing uproariously."

"Things have been going so well with us this week (it was a week ago today that we were expelled from the Chicago Board)," my father wrote John, Sr. on April 1, 1938, "that the boys are all talking about having got rid of our hoodoo."

That winter my parents took my brother and sister and me and our governess with them on vacation to Jamaica. We flew from Miami to Kingston, where we checked into the Constant Spring Hotel. Soon afterwards my father found a house to rent on Old Hope Road near downtown Kingston for the rest of our stay. We swam in the pool at the Constant Spring and counted ourselves some of the luckiest children anywhere.

Duncan and Hugh with a Jamaican worker

235

During the 1930s another family drama, this one again involving Dan and his son Donald, was also being played out. Had it not been for Donald, it now appears that Uncle Dan MacMillan might one day have settled down with a woman named Isabel ("Belle") Trow Servis who considered herself his second wife. Women whose names included "Belle" seemed to have had a special attraction for Uncle Dan.

Dan and Mrs. Servis's astonishing relationship is revealed in a letter she wrote to Edna MacMillan dated June 1, 1933, in which she claimed that she and Dan had been married fifteen years earlier in September 1918. "The marriage was secret and unconventional," she wrote, "but that it was not legal, I did not know until much later."

Mrs. Servis, a widowed insurance saleswoman from La Crosse, said that she had stuck by Dan all these long years, mindful of the pain Amber Belle had inflicted upon him, until she now realized that he would never admit to their relationship. She wanted John and Edna to judge whether or not Dan should "be held to some measure of accountability." John and Edna apparently did not intervene, and Dan never legitimized this marriage, but he and Mrs. Servis remained lifelong friends. She was often included in family gatherings.

With Dan's son Donald on the scene, however, Mrs. Servis increasingly took a back seat to the youth in his father's affections. For many years, Dan and Belle Servis had maintained separate apartments at the old Leamington Hotel in Minneapolis, but after Donald graduated from Princeton in 1935, Dan leased an upper duplex for himself and his son at 660 Summit Avenue in St. Paul.

Donald brought incredible vigor to his father's life. Suddenly Dan had a son and heir with whom he could make long-term plans. In 1936, when he was sixty-three, Dan purchased an aging river cottage northeast of the Twin Cities at Marine-on-St. Croix. It was the first house he had ever owned.

"The cottage still stands by the river and cries out for occupants from time to time," Dan wrote to his sister Mary Rowles in La Crosse that summer. "I have been over there once or twice lately [and] the countryside was lovely. One night . . . there was a soft haze in the atmosphere just as the moon was rising full. I don't think I ever imagined anything more beautiful in my life than the scene presented. I wished at the time that you could have seen it."

Dan wanted to teach Donald the grain business from the ground up, but Donald's temperament was unsuited for a commercial career. He had studied languages at Princeton, and his real forte would turn out to be interior design. In the meantime, Donald enrolled in law school at Harvard in the fall of 1936. Dan spent Christmas that year with Will and Janet at their apartment in Chicago.

"The presents were distributed in the afternoon and the festivity was soon over," Dan wrote to Cargill's wife Pauline (whom he and almost everyone else in the family called "Paul"). "There was no tree or other outward insignia of

Uncle Dan's son Donald MacMillan

Christmas. Three old people are not apt to cavort about much especially when one is somewhat valitudinarian (*sic*)."

The word Dan was looking for was valetudinarian, which means one whose chief concern is his invalidism. Dan's heart had not been normal since he contracted typhoid fever in Texas when he was eighteen, and he had recently been hospitalized for recurring heart pains at Billings Memorial Hospital Clinic at the University of Chicago. Following the holidays, he was going south to convalesce, he told Pauline. "I dread both the trip and the sojourn for it will be both desolate and lonely."

In late March, John, Jr. received a letter from Dan at the Hotel Monteleone in New Orleans. The previous evening Dan had suffered "a rather mean attack . . . which lasted perhaps about three quarters of an hour," he said, but he was "really more worried at the present moment about my arthritis than I am of the heart." His doctors subsequently put him in a cervical brace to see if it would help his arthritis and, indirectly, his angina. Despite his poor health, Dan was back in harness in June, when he traveled to Kansas and Nebraska to check out reports of black rust in the wheat fields.

On his riverfront property, Dan was now planning to build a larger house. Writing to Donald in Cambridge in November, he discussed the pros and cons of a "modernistic" versus a "farm house type" structure. Dan favored the farm house plan, he told Donald, "as it would be considerably more commodious in taking care of large parties. Furthermore, the living room and sun-room together would make a very splendid ballroom. . . . I wish you would never have to hire space in town." In the meantime, doing his share for the cabin for Christmas, Dan had purchased "the andirons and metal basket, also the Minton ware . . . and some other dishes . . . at Mrs. Alice Best Rogers place."

Dan had excellent taste in home furnishings—an expertise he passed on to his son—and he liked to prowl antique shops. "It is quite an education, especially in the matter of elevating one's standards in furniture, bric-a-brac etc.," he wrote Donald. Cautioning Donald against buying antiques in New York, where his son was spending Christmas in 1937 with McCrea family relatives, Dan told him that "any nice antique in New York will be a full 25% above Chicago."

Dan spent Christmas again that year with Will and Janet and their sister Mary Rowles, and the four of them afterwards rented a house in New Orleans for the winter. Dan played the invalid as well as his nervous nature allowed, attempting to get enough rest to forestall any major difficulties, but by spring he was back in the hospital in Chicago.

"We just got news that you had a hemorrhage in your eye," Cargill MacMillan wrote Uncle Dan from Minneapolis on April 21, 1938. "Father and mother got back night before last after a very satisfactory trip [a three-month vacation by ship through the Panama Canal to South America]," and John, Sr. was very anxious to know "just what your condition is."

Business had been very poor so far that year, Cargill advised Dan, but "at the present moment the prospects are good for next year, which is a condition that we have not seen for several years. It is, of course, too early to tell anything about Spring Wheat but soil conditions on the whole are better than they have been at this time for several years."

Dan's health continued to deteriorate, but he medicated himself with nitro-glycerin and pressed ahead with plans for the new house. "Yesterday I took Mr. [Edwin] Lundie [a prominent St. Paul architect] over to the cabin," he wrote to Donald in June. "I told him that I wanted a very modest little home," Dan continued, "and he seemed delighted with the spot. Said it was a very unconventional situation and should lend itself to the imagination very properly. . . . His idea is to use the cabin as a base." Dan suggested to Lundie that he go see a motion picture playing in St. Paul called *Bringing Up Baby* with Cary Grant and Katherine Hepburn because it contained a cottage with a stone interior that Dan thought in good taste.

Donald, too, wanted a small house, writing to Dan that "on every score a small home is the safest thing for me," and "when I have the upkeep myself in the future there is no assurance that I will be able to keep up a large establishment." In the East and elsewhere, Donald said, everyone was moving to the country and into cottages. "The antique shops in Boston are jammed with priceless pieces being sold because the owners of large homes are breaking them up."

In another of the many letters that were exchanged between father and son during this period, Dan turned down a suggestion from Donald about windows he thought would be too expensive: "I understand your liking for part circular windows such as you have incorporated in the dining room and living room, but . . . all my life I have understood that such type of construction is virtually prohibitive to a person of ordinary means. . . . In any event I do not want more than $8,000 or $10,000 in the place."

Just how much the "cottage" eventually cost Dan we don't know, but the large three-story turreted stone house he ended up building at the river's edge is still known locally as "the castle." After he began construction during the summer of 1938, there is no further mention of the house in his extant letters. When Dan wrote to Donald on June 15, it was to inform him of Emma Hanchette's death:

> I do not know the exact particulars but I think her condition was dropsical [related to edema]. Aunt Edna had been out there for two weeks and had just returned this morning. Austen is flying out by plane tonight or tomorrow morning. Aunt Mary has been up for the past few days and returned yesterday to La Crosse. Mrs. Servis went with her. Uncle Will is visiting with Uncle John. . . . I am wiring Aunt Budley a message of condolence.

Dan, whom Emma had once hoped to marry, now had less than a year to live himself. He returned to New Orleans after Christmas but was stricken ill soon after arriving, and the attending physician rushed him back to his doctors in Chicago. "If anything comes up, will you get in touch with me and I will try and straighten the matter out, if I can," Donald wrote to his father's secretary Leo Sheehan in Minneapolis on January 22. "His heart is in such a precarious state these last two weeks that on no account can he have any shocks, such as government correspondence on that tax he is protesting."

When he learned that Dan would have to remain in the hospital for at least four months, Donald moved into Uncle Will's apartment in Chicago to be close to him. Actually, the doctors gave Dan very little chance of ever being able to leave the hospital, Donald informed Leo Sheehan.

The house at Marine-on-St. Croix was still unfinished when Dan died in the hospital at age sixty-six in late March 1939. His sister Bess Wheeler, who had arrived in time to say goodbye, wrote to her daughter Katherine: "I am glad Uncle John [John, Sr.] is still in Pasadena because the distance will help soften the blow for him. Uncle Will is all to pieces over it and it is almost harder for him than for Donald." John, Sr.'s own health prevented him from returning home for his brother's funeral in La Crosse.

Edwin Lundie's drawing for Dan MacMillan's residence at Marine-on-St. Croix

Dan apparently left no will, as none could be found, and Donald notified Uncle Will that his father's funds "were instantly tied up at the time of his death. This means naturally that the April checks going to Aunt Mary and Aunt Janet cannot be sent out. . . . You will of course have to take such measures as you see fit to tell them about this and to help them out if you feel you can."

Donald never lived in the stone cottage Dan intended for him. Instead he wanted a career in New York and went on to graduate from the Parsons School of Design, eventually becoming one of the country's outstanding authorities on early Americana. Donald worked as a design consultant to the Henry Francis duPont Winterthur Museum at Wilmington, Delaware, and wrote two books, *Good Taste in Home Decoration* and *Great Furniture Styles: 1660-1830*. The new house at Marine was used instead by Uncle Will who gladly summered there.

Years later in 1947 my father was advised by a Minneapolis moving and storage company that it had some of Donald's furniture--choice items that Dan had picked out including a settee and eight chairs upholstered in red brocade. Donald had put the items in storage and then quit paying his account despite "both persuasion and threats," the firm said. "It is a bit too elegant for the trade we have in our used furniture department, and it has occurred to us that you might be interested in it." John, Jr. had no use for the furniture either.

John H. MacMillan, Sr. with his four grandsons, Cargill, Jr., Hugh, Duncan, and Whitney

My aunt Pauline with my cousins Paula and Whitney, sailing for Jamaica, 1940

"This invasion of Norway of course has raised havoc with all our foreign trades," John, Sr. wrote to his son Cargill, who was vacationing in Jamaica, on April 12, 1940. "We have about 800,000 bushels sold to Norway and Denmark, which I imagine will have to be cancelled."

Seven months earlier on September 1, 1939, the infamous day now considered the beginning of World War II, Adolph Hitler had launched a blitzkrieg on Poland. Fourteen hundred *Luftwaffe* dive bombers crippled Polish airfields, while five powerful armies in fourteen panzer divisions smashed across the country's frontiers. Two days later, Great Britain and France declared war on Germany.

In April 1940, German troops moved into Denmark, a neutral nation that had recently concluded a non-aggression pact with Hitler, and then into Norway. Denmark fell in a single day, but the Norwegians and an Allied expeditionary force put up a stubborn fight before Norway capitulated in June. In the meantime, grain shipments to the Scandinavian countries were suspended, and Cargill, Inc. recalled its agent in Copenhagen. During the frantic days that followed, Cargill also closed its office in Rotterdam when Nazi armies invaded Belgium and Holland. By mid-June, the Germans occupied Paris.

In England, Winston Churchill vowed to fight to the bloody end and looked to America for help. In this country, while wanting to see Hitler defeated, the vast majority of people did not want to fight another war in Europe. Adopting a bold "short of war" policy that would sharply divide American opinion, President Roosevelt, in an address to the graduating class at the University of Virginia on

June 10, 1940, announced: "We will extend to the opponents of force the material resources of this nation."

My grandfather John MacMillan, Sr. (although he disagreed vehemently with much of Roosevelt's domestic policy and hoped for a Republican victory in the fall presidential race) applauded the president's courage. "I am glad to note that we are doing everything possible for England," he wrote to Minnesota Senator Henrik Shipstead.

> This menace of Nazi-ism [sic] and Fascism to a Democracy to me is beyond words, and as long as there is nothing in International Law that prevents us from selling supplies to England, I think by all means we should do everything in our power.
>
> It may interest you to know that one of our staff, Greenman, has just returned from Copenhagen where he had been for some time before permission was granted to him to return to this country by the Germans. . . . Mr. Greenman cannot speak in strong enough terms about the danger to this country of the Fifth Column.

Echoing John, Sr.'s concerns, *Cargill News* editorialized in its July 1940 issue: "A new Europe is being created by force and conquest. Age old traditions are being swept aside, customs changed, and living conditions upset. . . . We, as a people, have escaped hardships and suffering so far, but sooner or later we will have to face . . . facts firmly and squarely. Fifth columnists will be in our midst, and everything of a vital nature should be guarded carefully, especially around elevators and warehouses, as well as in offices, stores and buildings."

John, Jr. was among the minority of Americans who believed that this country should take an active and leading role in the war. He did not mince

The whole family: Marnie, Hugh, Marion, John, Jr., and Duncan. My father took this picture by dashing back to the couch after setting up the camera.

My mother Marion with our Packard. Except when she played tennis, my mother always wore high-heeled pumps.

words on the subject. In September 1940, when President Roosevelt agreed to lend Great Britain fifty old destroyers in exchange for long-term leases on British naval and air bases in the Caribbean and Newfoundland, my father wrote his friend newspaperman John Cowles:

> Under normal conditions I would endorse whole-heartedly your efforts to force the President to work through Congress. However, with conditions as they are I think the Republican leaders are making a great mistake in endeavoring to hamper the President in any way. . . . Everyone knows that Congressional debate is interminable and that delay might well have been fatal to our English friends. . . . It seems very plain to me that if the English are defeated we are next on the list and it is also plain to me that the only hope for security for ourselves and our children is through having the world policed jointly by England and the United States.

As for Japan, which had been fighting in China since 1937, John, Jr. told Cowles: "I personally would like nothing better than to see the President immediately ban all exports of anything which might conceivably have any war value to Japan, including cotton, oil and copper. Such a move would be very apt to drive the Japanese into the Dutch East Indies in an effort to secure their supplies there by force. To prevent this I believe it is the duty of the President, as Commander-in-Chief of the Navy, at once to order the fleet to Singapore. Such a course . . . not only would not mean war but would force an immediate settlement of the Oriental situation by round-table discussion. Failure to take such a step means that the Japanese swallow at their leisure Hong Kong, Singapore and the Dutch East Indies, which would make the task of dislodging them later ten-fold greater than would be the case if they were prevented from doing so by our fleet at Singapore."

My father's opinions jibed with those of some of this country's leading authorities on the Orient and were exactly right, of course. In December 1941, Hong Kong would be attacked at the same time as Pearl Harbor, Malaya, and the Philippines. A month later, the Japanese would invade the Dutch East Indies; in February 1942, Yamashita, the "Tiger of Malaya," would defeat the British on Singapore.

Earlier in 1940, while staying at the Constant Spring Hotel in Jamaica, my parents had gotten a close-up look at the war. "Now that we are away we can write of the war," John, Jr. had written on March 10 to his father, who was wintering with my grandmother at the Huntington Hotel in Pasadena.

"Jamaica is the headquarters for much of their [British] naval activity, hence the rigid censorship. Warships were coming and going all the time, and we met many of the officers. We were even invited aboard one, the Assiniboine, for tea. The day of the tea, the Germans picked for the dash of those freighters (formerly loaded with Bunge wheat) from Aruba, so everything available put to sea on short notice including the Assiniboine."

My father planned to build a winter home that year on a small plantation called Mount Lebanon that he had purchased outside of Kingston. He had recorded the property in my mother's name ("I wish to take no chances of anyone's being able to claim that I have established a residence in Jamaica"), and put in stakes where he wanted the house located. Part of this acreage, which was wonderfully scenic and looked down to the sea, was producing pimento and coffee in 1940, and my father planted two hundred orange and grapefruit trees.

In April he had sent copies of his rough plans to contractor Emmanuel Henriques in Jamaica, asking him to prepare detailed plans and cost estimates so that the actual building could begin in July "should conditions seem to warrant it." To George Green, a Jamaican man he had hired to look after Mount Lebanon in his absence, John, Jr. wrote: "I note what you say about building a road, but I very much prefer to lay out such a road myself as highway location and engineering is one of my hobbies and I was looking forward to doing this myself next winter."

The drawings Henriques sent John, Jr. in June "very much pleased" my father, he replied. "With very few exceptions they reflect fully the notes as I sent them to you." However, given the current situation, he decided to delay construction. "Events in Europe are moving so rapidly at the moment that I think you can understand my reluctance to proceed at this particular moment." By mid-September, when he had given up any hope of building that season, my father wrote to his friend Captain Allan Phillips at the Liguanea Club in Jamaica:

I know you will be interested in the changing sentiment in the United States. Whereas six months ago everyone was anti-German, today they are rapidly

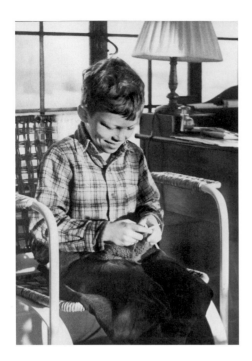

Me with my knitting

becoming Pro-English, and I am very hopeful that it is only a matter of a few months before public opinion will bring about active participation in the war itself. . . . Messrs. Roosevelt and Hitler permitting, we will see you in January.

I was ten years old that year and in fifth grade at Wayzata Grade School. In October, I fell from the roof of my grandfather's goose house, a distance of seven or eight feet, and ruptured my spleen. John, Sr. kept geese and swans on the lake in the summer, and the pen he had for them was ordinarily covered with wire mesh fencing. We used to run down the hill towards the pen, onto and off the roof of the goose house, and land spread-eagle on the wire. This time the fencing wasn't there, and I landed on a metal tub on the bottom of the pen. My cousin Whitney was with me, and he said I was all right, but I was unable to ride my bike and had to push it all the way home.

"Little Duncan had a very serious accident a few days ago," John Sr. wrote a few days later to his nephew Donald MacMillan (in whom he had taken a paternal interest since Dan's death). "Junior and Marion were at the Minneapolis Club for dinner preparatory to going to the football game. Fortunately the maid knew enough to get hold of Dr. Arey immediately and he got to the house in very short order. He telephoned Junior and Marion to meet him at the hospital in half an hour. . . . Fortunately, by ten o'clock at night . . . the [internal] bleeding had stopped, so that an operation was unnecessary, but the poor little chap will have to lie in bed in the hospital with three nurses to watch him to see that he does not move for an indefinite period of time."

I came home from the hospital after two weeks, but I had developed a severe case of anemia. During long periods that winter I was confined to the house. To entertain me, my grandmother Dickson taught me how to knit. After Christmas, my father, who was rundown and needing a vacation himself, took

The de Cordoba house on Old Hope Road near Kingston, which my father rented for our vacation in Jamaica

Marion, on the right, with friends at the beach in Jamaica

Marnie, me, and Hugh on the front gate of the de Cordoba house in Jamaica

my mother, the three of us children, and a nurse to Jamaica, where the tropical climate worked its usual magic.

"First of all you will be relieved to know that I am feeling ever so much better," my father wrote to John, Sr. at his office at the Chamber of Commerce in early January 1941. "In fact, I expect to be playing tennis by the end of this week. The children are entirely different, especially Duncan. The improvement in their looks and energy is beyond belief, and they eat like horses.

One day we were invited to tea at King's House by Governor Sir Arthur Richards and his wife. "They have three children just the age of our own and we were the only ones for tea," my father wrote to John, Sr. "Afterward they gave a tennis party of eight, while the children swam and rode horse-back. It was extremely interesting and very pleasant. The Governor . . . had just returned from England and was full of his experiences."

John D. McMillan

John Hugh MacMillan III. "We had quite an experience last Saturday night with Marion giving a dinner dance in honor of Hughie's birthday," my father wrote to his parents on March 4, 1942. "The party was a huge success—the damage to the house being much less than anticipated. . . . Hughie's contemporaries are a singularly attractive group of youngsters with simply inexhaustible energy."

We were still in Jamaica in February when my grandfather suffered a serious heart attack at the Huntington Hotel in California. "My best guess is that he will recover," my father reassured his brother "Gee" (Cargill MacMillan), who had immediately flown out to California from Minneapolis. "You know that if you survive the first 24 hours with a coronary thrombosis . . . you almost invariably recover, assuming complete rest."

My grandfather spent the next ten weeks confined to bed in California. During his convalescence, his cousin John D. McMillan died in March at the age of eighty-one in Minneapolis. Fifty-two years earlier in 1888, John D. had given my grandfather his first job in the grain business. He was a founding partner of the Osborne-McMillan Elevator Company and chairman of the board of directors of the Minneapolis firm at the time of his death. Widowed seven years earlier, John D. McMillan was survived by three children, John Russell, Howard (one of my father's best friends), and Mrs. Frank (Katherine) Shepard of New York. He was buried at La Crosse.

In 1941 my father decided to move forward with the plans for a house in Jamaica near Kingston. Workmen removed an existing house on the property and had begun excavating for the foundation while we were there. In March, my father sent a new set of plans to a second contractor in Port Antonio. (Henriques "tried to play us for a sucker," he explained to his father.) When the new estimate far exceeded my father's expectations, he asked the contractor to quote him for labor only. He would send the materials from the United States, he said, "as I happen to be in preferred position [and] and can get lower quotations on [practically] everything." This scheme quickly proved impractical, however, and my father decided to postpone building until after the war.

That winter he had made arrangements for us to spend our vacation in Ocho Rios at the Shaw Park Hotel, one of Uncle Cargill and Aunt Pauline's favorite resorts. There was some uncertainty about whether we would be able to go to Jamaica or not, though, since my father's passport had been collected at Miami coming home on our last trip. Finally, the State Department wrote, instructing him to send duplicate photographs of the five of us who were planning to travel on his passport. He mailed them off on December 5. Two days later, the Japanese bombed Pearl Harbor.

Citing "the present international situation," the State Department subsequently refused passports to all Americans traveling for pleasure. My parents ended up going to Key West alone that year. We children stayed behind in Orono with Grandmother Dickson. Key West did not agree with my parents. "John says it is the deadest place they have ever seen but as that is the place he was looking for to start with he ought to be well satisfied," John, Sr. wrote his brother Will in January 1942.

My father arrived home in Minneapolis feeling less than par that year.

"We have great excitement at the house as Marion bought a bicycle for her own use," John, Jr. wrote to his parents at the Huntington Hotel in California in April 1942. "Nearly everyone at the Lake seems to be buying bicycles. Our private advisories on the tire situation are terrible and they are now talking about allowing only one car to a family and seizing all spare tires. . . . I would not be at all surprised to see all our friends lose their station wagons."

"John is not in good shape and I do not know what to do about it," Cargill wrote to their parents in California in March. "He throws up regularly every morning after he comes into the office, and unless he leaves the office right after lunch he is sick again. When he is not troubled with this nervous nausea he is in splendid shape and does not feel tired nor anything else."

My father had come back from World War I with a nervous constitution, but his health was increasingly an issue. The previous year, after experiencing chest pains in Jamaica, he had seen Dr. Marx White in Minneapolis for a thorough physical. Dr. White found him to be in excellent condition with no damage to his heart or arteries, but his blood pressure was too high at 210, and the doctor prescribed shorter hours and more rest.

In 1942 his doctors insisted he take more time off. "I am back at my desk today for the first time in three months, the doctors having had me in their clutches for that period," John, Jr. wrote in July to former Yale classmate Maurice Smith. Smith had reentered the service and was serving as a major at the Air Gunnery School in Las Vegas.

"I cannot tell you how we all envy your being able to get back in the service," my father told him. "As you know, I enjoyed the army immensely." But my father was making his own contribution to the war effort in Minnesota, and in truth he would not have changed places with Smith for the world. Doing what he liked to do best, John, Jr. was building boats, telling Smith with obvious pride, "Our ship building is coming as well as can be expected, meaning that we are held up for lack of steel, but we should be going full blast in a few more weeks."

Boats, which had been my father's passion as a child, held the same fascination for him as an adult, and his talent for design begot Cargill's shipbuilding division. In the late 1930s, following a long series of experiments by John, Jr. and Frank Neilson on Lake Minnetonka, Cargill, Inc. designed and built a wholly new type of articulated barge at Albany, New York. Shorter than traditional units and having square ends, the new barges were a huge success, able to carry twice the tonnage at one half the capital cost of the largest other single-locking units on the New York Barge Canal.

The time was also ripe for Cargill to develop its own ocean transportation. Prior to 1920 the company did no exporting, limiting its business to country elevators and terminal elevators at western Great Lakes ports. After that time, Cargill had opened offices along the Atlantic seaboard in the East and abroad. Now, to compete with larger grain companies for export trade, Cargill began building its own specially equipped ocean vessels, incorporating machinery the company had already developed for self-loading and unloading grain.

One of these was launched in the spring of 1941 by a party of dignitaries that included Cargill President and General Manager J. H. MacMillan, Jr., Vice President Austen S. Cargill, and the mayors of Albany and Rensselaer, New York.

Cargill, Inc.'s pride, the M/V (Motor Vessel) Victoria, *which carried 500,00 bushels of grain or 105,000 barrels of liquid*

Eleven-year-old Marnie MacMillan christening the towboat Cartaska, *launched at the Dingle Boat Works in St. Paul in September 1944. Developed jointly by Cargill, Inc. and the Chrysler Corporation, the* Cartaska *was designed to propel barges assembled at the Cargill shipyard at Chaska, Minnesota. The other girls are Paula MacMillan and Elizabeth Fullerton.*

The startlingly innovative *Victoria* was a pioneering vessel. First, an ocean-going ship had never been built that far up the Hudson—150 miles from New York City at Albany. Secondly, the boat's giant hull was launched broadside when partly complete, making unnecessary the erection of a huge shipway; its all-metal superstructure was installed in sections by a crane.

Because of the great need for tankers during wartime, the *Victoria*, originally christened the *Carlantic*, was finished for use as either a tanker or grain carrier. She was sold to an Argentine firm to carry oil to Buenos Aires and linseed from Buenos Aires to New York. On her maiden trip from Argentina to the United States in April 1942, loaded with flaxseed, the *Victoria* was torpedoed twice. The crew abandoned ship and was picked up after thirty-six hours in lifeboats on the Atlantic Ocean. Despite severe damage, however, the *Victoria* was later discovered still afloat. Her crew returned to her, and thanks to her all-welded construction, the ship reached New York under her own power.

During World War II, Cargill, Inc. built eighteen ocean-going tankers for the navy and four river towboats for the army at Port Cargill on the Minnesota River. "As soon as the steel mills can produce the material, Cargill, Inc., ship-building division, Savage, Minn., will lay keels for six medium tankers for use in shuttling vital supplies to the United Nations," the *Minneapolis Star Journal* announced in June 1942.

Two thousand miles from the sea, Port Cargill occupied the former site of the International Stock Farm, where owner Will Savage built a track and Mosque-like stable for his beloved mahogany-colored stallion Dan Patch. When this world-class pacer died in July 1916, Savage suffered inconsolable grief and died himself the next day. Twin funerals were held at the same hour for the horse and owner.

Arthur Loring Wheeler, born in 1883 in Brattleboro, Vermont. He traced his ancestry to George Wheeler, a native of England who settled in Concord, Massachusetts, in the early 1600s.

John H. MacMillan, Sr. and John H. MacMillan, Jr. officiating, hats in hand, at keel-laying ceremonies for the first two oil tankers built at Port Cargill, the Agawam *and the* Elkhorn. *With them at the left of the platform on Labor Day, September 7, 1942, is shipbuilder and plant superintendent Chris Jensen.*

To provide access to the Mississippi River for tankers built at Port Cargill, army engineers dredged a nine-foot channel in the Minnesota River. John, Jr. bought controlling interest in the Minnesota Western Railway to service the plant. Chris Jensen, nicknamed the "wild Dane," a mechanical wizard who had built Cargill's first barges at Albany (working outdoors with a handful of men during the unusually severe winter of 1937–1938) and later supervised the building of the *Victoria*, came on as general superintendent at Port Cargill. The position of purchasing agent went to Arthur Wheeler, John, Sr.'s brother-in-law, who was glad to have a job.

In 1940 Wheeler, married to my grandfather's youngest sister Bess MacMillan, had been edged out as general manager of the Eberhard division of the Eastern Malleable Iron Company in Cleveland. This came as an enormous blow to Arthur, who had started work as a sales representative for the Eberhard Manufacturing Company twenty-six years earlier and worked his way up to company president. After Eberhard merged with the Eastern Malleable Iron Company in 1936, Arthur Wheeler was named managing director of the Eberhard Division. Even then, however, the Wheelers were just scraping by.

When Bess and Arthur's daughter Mary Elizabeth, a student at Wheaton College in Norton, Massachusetts, wanted to go to Europe with friends in 1936, her father wrote to her that he simply didn't have the money. In a sad letter, by turns wistful and morose, he blamed himself for their meager circumstances:

> In the first place I should never have got married because I did not have any money saved up. Your mother and I did marry however and have been very, very happy. . . . I do not blame you at all for expecting these things. I have been through it and have cussed the day I ever heard of Harvard . . . because I could not do what my friends could. I have no friends at all now practically and that is partly the reason. It made me bitter and I withdrew from keeping up contacts which I could not go along with from a money stand-point.

There was "possibly one bright spot in the picture," Arthur surmised. "For six years I have been in mortal terror that I would be out of a job and in the bread line. That terror is past possibly for a short time (10 years maybe if I can keep well) provided we can make money for the new combination." Less than four years later, however, Arthur Wheeler was replaced and out of work.

Letters flew back and forth between John, Sr. and Arthur, Arthur outlining his options, and my grandfather giving him practical advice. At one point, when Arthur wanted to borrow twenty-five thousand dollars to buy into the Bissett Steel Company, John, Sr. sent his son Cargill to Ohio to help Arthur assess matters. Cargill had a good head for business, John, Sr. told Arthur, but both Cargill and Arthur were apparently taken in by the steel man.

A month after sending Arthur the money, John, Sr. wrote to him in December 1940: "I agree with you in feeling the utmost contempt for Mr. Bissett. This has struck me all in a heap and I do not know what to suggest [but] with all this war work going on, I am inclined to believe you can make a new contact."

Arthur remained optimistic about his prospects, but he could not get back on his feet. John, Sr. loaned him a smaller amount of money in 1941 to help finance a sales agency. When that foundered, my grandfather brought Arthur to Minnesota in the spring of 1942 as general purchasing agent for Cargill's new shipyards. Arthur rented rooms at the Windsor Apartment Hotel at Third Avenue South and Franklin in Minneapolis, where Bess joined him.

"Well on April 6th I arrived here and the shipyard was only a 300 acre farm," Arthur wrote to his daughter Mary Elizabeth in late May. "Now there is a flag-pole and a flag flying and [an] office building 322 ft. long by 58 ft. wide 3/4 completed. Two miles of railroad with tracks layed (*sic*). A panel shop started. A welding building up. Piles and ways being assembled. Quite a start. . . . We are still using the farm house with its trap door to go downstairs to a 1/2 toilet but progress is being made."

He and Bess would be spending most of their weekends at "Uncle John's," Arthur wrote. "I shall accept as I had one go with Aunt Edna about not staying there all the time until Mother came and no more for me. Just the same your Aunt Edna is one fine person even if as she says the MacMillans did take her in."

There were also idyllic weekends at Uncle Will's wilderness retreat at Marine-on-St. Croix. "Father got a canoe Sunday afternoon," Bess wrote to Mary

"Watching workman lower keel in place." This photograph of Duncan, John, Jr., Hugh, and Marnie MacMillan with worker Burt Blaeser appeared in the Minneapolis paper following the keel-laying ceremonies for the tankers Agawam *and* Elkhorn *in September 1942.*

*Uncle Will, Aunt Bess, and Arthur
Wheeler at Marine-on-St. Croix, "out
for a lovely paddle"*

Elizabeth on Tuesday, October 20. "He and I walked up for it and took Aunt Nette [her older sister Janet] out for a lovely paddle. It was one of October's perfect days, warm in the sun, cool in the shade, crisp air in the golden sunshine. I have never seen the river so quiet so that the swish of water on the paddle was like music to me. . . it was like a place of magic."

The next weekend, the last one of the season before Will closed the house and headed south to the ranch in Lubbock, ended tragically. On Sunday morning, October 25, fifty-eight-year-old Arthur Wheeler suddenly keeled over and died of a heart attack in Uncle Will's kitchen. Aunt Janet, who could be a very difficult person, was at the cabin and had been on a tirade the night before. Neither Arthur nor Bess had been able to sleep, their younger daughter Katherine later recalled. Arthur's body was cremated and his funeral held in Stillwater. Afterwards, Aunt Bess stayed on with John, Sr. and Edna in Orono.

John, Sr. helped his sister with the tangle of lawyers and insurance. "Uncle John read the will and said it was just what he expected from father—that it was perfect," Bess wrote Mary Elizabeth on November 10. "Aunt Edna" was playing bridge that afternoon with three of her friends, Bess said. "Mrs. Lane I have known for many years and Mrs. Langdon is the mother of Mabel who married Howard McMillan. . . . The other one is a Mrs. Loring. . . . They all think Uncle John perfect and it warms my heart."

Bess returned to Cleveland Heights and sold her house in April 1943, but she was back in Orono in time for the launching of Cargill's fourth Navy tanker, the U.S.S. *Genesee* at Port Cargill on September 25. "The family were all present," she wrote Mary Elizabeth two days later. "Aunt Mary, Uncle Will, Malcolm and Oradelle [Rowles]. . . . They included me in the sponsor's party of 8 or 10 so I was up on the platform [and] they took a picture of the whole group. . . . I have never been at anything where there was such a big thrill packed into so short a time."

The launching of the Genesee *at Port Cargill in September 1943. If you look closely, you can see Hugh and Cargill, Jr. and me hanging onto the ship's railing.*

In January, when John, Sr. and Edna traveled to the Huntington Hotel in California for the winter, Bess went with them. Edna was glad for her company. "Aunt Bess is the loveliest thing that ever was," she wrote Pauline in March. "She looks so beautiful and loves everything and everybody (meaning our friends). We couldn't have gotten on without her."

In April 1944, Edna Cargill MacMillan officiated at the launching of the U.S.S. *Chehalis* at Port Cargill. "It was a real thrill to be able to do my small part in sending that huge ship on its way," she told a reporter. If my grandmother had had her druthers, however, she wouldn't have been up on the platform at all.

When the Secretary of the Navy had contacted her at the Huntington in Pasadena and invited her to sponsor the launching, Edna had implored her son Cargill in Minneapolis: "You just must get me out of it. . . . Say I am lame and can't climb the steps or that I am subject to colds and the weather is sure to make me ill. . . . I'll do something for you someday."

Prodded by her husband, who was bursting with pride over their sons' accomplishments at Port Cargill, Edna nonetheless ended up doing the honors and christened the ship with a bottle of Chehalis River water. Minneapolis columnist and radio commentator Cedric Adams officiated at the event, which was recorded and broadcast later the same day on Cargill's regular radio program over WCCO.

Two months later in June, John, Jr., his brother Cargill, and their uncle Austen Cargill sailed the new tanker U.S.S. *Elkhorn* down the Mississippi to be formally delivered to the navy in New Orleans.

"Our trip down was a huge success," my father wrote home to Hugh and me. "Our running time was 38 hours, and we averaged better than 16 miles per hour, although we never used more than two of her four engines. . . .

"We had 93 people on board, 50 of them being from the Navy. The whole 50 of them were in the way—and did no work. We even had to have our painters do the handling of lines while the Navy looked on and laughed. The next boat we bring down we will bar the Navy entirely.

"We had great praise from everyone on the quality of our workmanship, especially on the welding. The Navy told us there was only one yard in the U.S. which did as good work (in quality) as we are doing. That one is at Manitowoc, Wisc. . . .

"The weather was perfect, clear, light winds, and temp. about 50 degrees. We all got slightly wind and sunburned. We also inspected our new Ottawa, Ill. elevator, which is small but perfect.

"On the way back we saw a sign over a small grocery store. We are recommending it . . . as a slogan for our financial division. *In God We Trust. All others cash*. We also learned of a new slogan for achieving success in the Navy. *Shoot the bull. Pass the buck. Make seven copies of everything*.

"That may work in the Navy, but it doesn't when you're with Cargill." The letter was signed, "Affectionately, Daddy."

After my grandparents returned home to Minneapolis from California in the spring of 1944, John, Sr. declined rapidly. In early September, he was hospitalized with a severe heart attack, followed by a second attack two weeks later. "Everyone, including the doctors, are exceedingly pessimistic about his pulling through," my father wrote on September 20 to Hugh, who had started his second year at Taft in Connecticut. "He is in an oxygen tent and his voice was vigorous and he wanted to know all about you and your trip East, but his blood pressure has simply gone out of sight."

My grandfather was comatose most of the next month and died on Friday night, October 20, at Abbott Hospital in Minneapolis. Seventy-five years old, John H. MacMillan, Sr. was chairman of the board of Cargill, Inc., the firm he had headed for thirty-five years since Will Cargill's death in 1909.

"I don't see how I can carry on," Edna wrote Bess, thanking her for sending flowers. "It is so empty and all gone." Many, many people had to be turned away from the funeral which was held at Westminster Presbyterian Church in "our new chapel," she said. "I was so glad Will and Janet could be here but we did so long for you. . . . I am missing you so much that I don't know what to do." My grandfather's body was taken home to La Crosse and buried in his father Duncan D. McMillan's plot at Oak Grove Cemetery.

"I regret exceedingly that I had not written you some time ago to tell you of Father's death last October," John, Jr. wrote to Dr. Leslie Gay in Baltimore in July 1944. "You will be interested to know however that his mind was clear up to the very last.

Edna Cargill MacMillan and John H. MacMillan, Sr. at the launching of the U.S.S. Chehalis *at Port Cargill in April 1944*

John H. MacMillan, Sr. Oil painting
by Edward V. Brewer

"If I remember correctly it was in 1933 that you warned both Father and myself of the precarious state of his health, and I know that you yourself at the time were very dubious of the chances for more than a very few months.

"We have, therefore, been exceedingly thankful for the twelve years that he lasted. During that period, of course, he did very little of a physical nature, but nevertheless contributed heavily to the continued progress of the company, so that they should be looked upon as an exceedingly valuable and useful period in his life.

"This leaves only his brother, Will, the professor of Mathematical Astronomy at the University of Chicago, as the only survivor of three brothers. He is, I am happy to state, in excellent health, but of course we all know that astronomers are the longest lived of any occupation."

RAIN MAKES GRAIN

John, Jr. was a big fan of Uncle Will's and greatly influenced by him to the point that my father became one of the outstanding *amateur* meteorologists of his time. John, Jr.'s studies were more than a hobby; for him they were serious business. By better understanding the mysteries of the earth's atmosphere, he hoped to be able to forecast rainfall, droughts, and other weather phenomena affecting Cargill, Inc. and the grain industry.

In 1942, after twenty years of studying and charting weather patterns, he completed the first draft of a book about his weather theories while he was home sick with a case of the grippe (influenza) in February. "I now find that it is possible to predict exactly the changes in climate, as well as the weather," he had written to his parents in California.

> From this it follows that Turkestan was at its driest 700 years ago and at its wettest 7200 years ago, while Mesopotamia was at its wettest 6000 years ago, Egypt 5500 years ago, and North Africa 4500 years ago. The United States, including the Great Plains, is increasing in wetness, which will not culminate for another 2000 years. China is also increasing, while Europe is decreasing.
>
> We are now exactly in the midst of an inter-glacial period and the only reason why Greenland has remained ice covered is that the Northern Hemisphere maximum of precipitation and minimum of temperature happens to fall over the mountains of Greenland.

A month earlier, while he and my mother were vacationing in Florida, he had predicted that a hurricane or at least high-velocity winds would strike the area twelve or fourteen days hence. The commanding officer at a nearby navy

John H. MacMillan, Jr. in his library at home

air base politely heard him out but ignored his warning to batten down the installation. After the storm arrived on schedule and caused heavy destruction, John, Jr. was invited to speak before the heads of the Weather Bureau and weather experts for the army and navy in Washington.

"My lecture was extremely well received," my father informed Uncle Will. Retired U.S. Navy Commander F.W. Reichelderfer, chief of the Weather Bureau, wrote thanking John, Jr. for the public-spirited interest which had prompted him to share the results of his work with the government: "The improvement and extension of weather forecasting technique is extremely important for peace-time activities as well as for war operations and we desire to explore fully every possibility which may lead to further development."

By January 1944 John, Jr.'s continuing weather studies had "produced some perfectly amazing results with extremely far-reaching implications in the fields of astronomy, geology and climatology," he apprised Uncle Will. "What we call weather, as distinguished from climate, is almost wholly a tidal phenomenon, and I have finally unravelled the mechanism by which it works. . . . I have, however, learned so darn much that . . . it is going to take another couple of years before [my book] is ready for the printer."

My father also surmised that there was possibly a tenth planet—he called it Hellangone—a theory that had greatly intrigued John, Sr. "I have thought about your 10th planet a great deal," my grandfather had written from the Huntington in Pasadena in February 1944. "You might . . . check up and see what the net result would be of a $10,000 donation to a university to check your result."

Earlier my father had secured patents for innovative construction techniques he developed to build the Omaha elevator (1937) and an improved cigarette package (1938). Now he wrote asking Minneapolis attorneys Paul, Paul and Moore if it was possible to patent his method of long-range weather forecasting. No, the firm replied, but he should copyright his book once it was printed. John, Jr. would later obtain patents for a watercraft hull tunnel and propeller arrangement in 1957 and, posthumously, a method of erecting air-supported structures—in his case, grain elevators—in 1963.

My father never did publish his book, but neither did he abandon his research. In early 1953 the armed services asked for his help with weather forecasting during the Korean War. "I am beginning a lecture course at home," he confided in a letter to my brother Hugh.

In the meantime, as World War II wound down, the *Minneapolis Journal* announced in September 1944 that Cargill, Inc. had purchased the Rufus Rand estate called Still Pond on Lake Minnetonka for its executive offices. Overlooking Gray's Bay on more than two hundred acres, the sprawling, steep-roofed chateau-like house had cost the Minneapolis businessman an estimated half million dollars in 1931.

Cargill, Inc. moved its headquarters to the former Rand mansion in 1946.

Rufus R. Rand was the last surviving member of the Lafayette Escadrille when he died in 1971. The Rand Tower he built in downtown Minneapolis is now the Dain Tower.

Patterned after French country houses that Rand had seen abroad as a fighter pilot with the famed Lafayette Escadrille during World War I, Still Pond contained sixty rooms and sixteen baths. Rufus Rand owned the Minneapolis Gas Company (his grandfather had founded the Minneapolis Gas Light Company), and he and his wife and six daughters had lived at Still Pond a brief ten years, during which time the Depression ate away at the family's wealth. When Rand returned to Europe during World War II (he served as an executive officer at a bomber base in England and accompanied the invasion force into North Africa), his wife and daughters moved back to Minneapolis. Still Pond was put up for sale and stood empty for several years, falling into disrepair. Watching from the sidelines, John, Jr. knew that he had within his grasp an opportunity that would not repeat itself.

After Cargill, Inc. took possession of the residence, remodeling was delayed until late 1945 due to wartime shortages. While it remained unoccupied, the house was used to store lifeboats built for the armed services by the Minnetonka Boat Works. The boats were equipped with full emergency gas tanks, and certain members of our family, then teenagers, occasionally lifted a little gas now and then to augment their ration card allotments.

One hundred twenty-five Cargill officials and supporting staff people moved to Minnetonka in the summer of 1946. "It was Shangri La, a little bit like a dream," remembered Cargill Vice President Lou Crosby. Parlors, kitchens, bedrooms, servants' quarters, bathrooms, even the second-floor infirmary, were given a new lease on life as offices. Cargill, Inc.'s board of directors today meets in what used to be the second-floor master bedroom, furnished with French provincial-style furniture.

Not everybody at the time thought the move was a good decision. The company was bucking conventional business wisdom by leaving the thriving downtown commercial district, and the stately country house bore little resemblance to a modern office building. But President John H. MacMillan, Jr. was content to let people gossip. His seemingly rash decision to move Cargill headquarters to the countryside was part of a well-planned strategy that would help propel the company into the international arena.

Remote from the hubbub and frenzied atmosphere of the downtown Grain Exchange, the secluded Rand property provided a think-tank type of environment that would motivate top officers to work more creatively and efficiently. The concept was a romantic one that had its genesis overseas, where John, Jr. had watched General Pershing direct American field operations from a French chateau during World War I.

Business Week highlighted Cargill's new headquarters in an article titled "Moving to Mansions—a Trend" that mentioned similar moves by a handful of large companies. The editor of the *Northwestern Miller* roundly applauded the Cargill move in a long editorial. "We distinctly approve of it," wrote Robert E. Sterling. "The consensus of the dinner table was that too much high-priced and high-powered executive ability . . . is frittered away by the attrition of office details."

Nineteen forty-five turned out to be one of the best years and one of the worst years in the history of mankind; it marked the end of one era and the beginning of another. In April President Roosevelt suffered a fatal stroke at his winter White House in Warm Springs, Georgia. (His last words were "I have a terrible headache.") Days later Adolph Hitler committed suicide in a bunker in Berlin. After almost six years of war, the Germans surrendered unconditionally to the Allies in May. In August the United States dropped the first atomic bombs on Hiroshima and Nagasaki, bringing World War II to its ghastly conclusion.

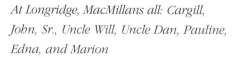

At Longridge, MacMillans all: Cargill, John, Sr., Uncle Will, Uncle Dan, Pauline, Edna, and Marion

John, Jr. playing tennis with Mrs. John S. "Juty" Pillsbury at Craigbank

John, Jr., on the right, with his golfing buddies at Woodhill Country Club in Wayzata. Standing, left to right, are DeWalt Ankeny, Totten Heffelfinger, John Snyder, Howard McMillan, Harrison R. "Jimmy" Johnston; front row: Harold Tearse, Lucian Strong, and Crawford Johnson.

In the war's aftermath, America remained prosperous. People had money to spend, saved from the days when nothing could be bought, and there was a tremendous demand for consumer goods including the first new cars. "Life here . . . is rapidly returning to normal and we are told by the first of the year we shall even have tires and all the shoes and butter we want," John, Jr. wrote in October 1945 to Charles Bolles Rogers, a longtime friend with the American Red Cross in New York.

Still overweight and wrestling with high blood pressure, my father turned fifty in December that year. "What a birthday!" he wrote in his journal.

"Your mother doubtless told you about the birthday party she gave me, which was quite the finest party I ever had," he wrote to my brother Hugh at Taft. "We had 42 guests for a dinner dance, and no-one went home until about half past one, so I know they all had a good time. Mr. Strong read a poem which was very funny and Mr. Tearse put on an even funnier imitation of me, complete with gestures. He used all my favorite adjectives and expressions and kept it up for nearly a half hour. Everyone was immensely amused."

His friends knew John, Jr. as a fast-talking, fast-moving man who always had a smile on his face. He loved life in all its complexities. At age fifty, with a beautiful wife and three teenage children, my father was president of Cargill, Inc., vice president of the still-struggling Valier Montana Land and Water Company, and a director of the First National Bank of Minneapolis. He also sat on the boards of two railroads, the Chicago and Northwestern, and the Chicago, St. Paul, Minneapolis and Omaha, which serviced Cargill, Inc.'s grain business.

His favorite sport and pastime was golf, and he took his game seriously. On the third day of the President's Cup tournament at the Woodhill Country Club in Wayzata in August 1945, winding up with a 77, he wrote in his journal: "Played

Marnie, Duncan, John, Jr., and Hugh on the beach at the Hillsboro Club in Florida, 1949. The Hillsboro was a home away from home for us where we spent our spring break each year.

with H. R. Johnston, Clarence Hill and Weaver Dobson. We tied for 1st in sweep. Note: Probably best round of golf I have ever had. Could easily have been a 71 or 2 if putts were falling." One of my father's close friends and frequent golf partners at Woodhill, Harrison R. (Jimmy) Johnston was Minnesota's first big-time golfer. In 1929 Johnston had won the National Amateur competition, coming home from Pebble Beach to a ticker-tape parade in downtown St. Paul.

As much as John, Jr. was enjoying life in 1946, he was at the same time in poor health and suffering from frequent fatigue, nausea, and headaches. If he continued at his current pace, he would be dead in a year, his doctors warned him; he should think about giving up work and retiring somewhere out of the United States where he could get away from the stress of business. Abandoning Cargill was not an option my father would ever have considered. Instead he put himself on an austere diet that literally changed and saved his life.

We were at the Hillsboro Club in Florida when my father ran into an old friend, Harvey Smith, walking along the beach. Smith had earlier been at death's door, he told my father; now, thanks to Dr. Walter Kempner's rice diet, he was restored to excellent health. Kempner was engaged in research and practiced at Duke University Hospital in Durham, North Carolina.

My father already knew of Kempner and his revolutionary rice diet for reducing high blood pressure. "This is in line with the well known fact that high blood pressure is rarely found among the Oriental people whose diet consists largely of rice," he had written to our family physician Dr. Reid in 1944.

Copying his friend Smith's diet, my father began limiting himself each day to two ounces of rice cooked without salt, one double orange juice, two cooked fruits, two raw fruits, one baked potato, and one small lamb chop. No salt, no water. The first month he lost six pounds, bringing his weight down to 180 pounds, but his blood pressure was still too high at 196/108. On April 28, shortly after returning home to Minnesota, he noted in his journal: "STARTED STRICT RICE DIET i.e. cut out carrots, lettuce, celery, baked potato and the chop."

In June, John, Jr. checked into Duke University Hospital and put himself in Dr. Kempner's hands. Upon examination he was found to have hypertensive cardiovascular renal disease, and he was started on the basic rice diet: fruit and fruit juices, sugar or dextrose, and boiled rice, supplemented by vitamins A, B, D, and iron. To allow his damaged kidney cells to heal, he was to have no coffee, tea, milk, or beer, and, especially, no water. The results were almost miraculous.

"I am literally a new man," he wrote to former Yale classmate Dr. Dickenson Richards (who had been class valedictorian) in July. "It may interest you to know that less than three months on the rice diet brought my blood pressure down from 240 over 140 to 140 over 84." He now weighed 169 pounds and would continue to lose weight.

Dr. Kempner was doing experimental work on cholesterol in the 1940s that was light years ahead of its time. Born and educated in Germany, where both his parents were prominent physicians, Walter Kempner was a graduate of the University of Heidelberg. In 1934 his brilliant research in Berlin on cellular metabolism attracted the attention of Dr. Frederick M. Hanes, chairman of the medical school at Duke University. Recognizing the importance of Kempner's work, Hanes (a member of the hosiery family) went to Europe and persuaded Kempner to come to Duke.

My mother celebrated my father's homecoming from Duke with a cocktail party for seventy friends and neighbors on the third of July. On the Fourth, the whole party moved to Woodhill for dinner and dancing. It was the height of what someone in my parents' crowd dubbed "the silly season" (roughly the entire summer), when there was a party at someone's house or at Woodhill almost every night. Everybody drank too much in those days—mother loved her martinis—but nobody considered it a problem.

My father was driving a new Cadillac that summer; it cost him "$2445 without the radio." He sold the Packard we had used since December 1941 for $1525, $200 more than he had paid for it. In August he also took delivery of a second car, a black Studebaker, which he described as "rather tiny and no back seat."

The week John, Jr. came home from Durham, Cargill, Inc. moved into its new world headquarters at Lake Minnetonka. He was thrilled; the offices were

Dr. Walter Kempner. Believing that Kempner's work was "unquestionably the most important discovery to date in geriatrics," John, Jr. was one of the founders of the Walter Kempner Foundation and served as its president from the time it was incorporated in 1949 until his death eleven years later.

John, Jr. took this photo of himself in the mirror in my mother's bedroom. "I have become greatly interested in photography after a lapse of twenty-five years," he had written to his uncle Dan MacMillan in 1937. "As you know, I had a small Zeiss Vest-Pocket Camera given me which takes pictures 1³/₄ by 2¹/₄ inches. I have also ordered an enlarger . . . and I find that by enlarging them by 4.5 diameters, which would correspond to increasing the focal range of the camera from 3¹/₈ to 15 inches, that the pictures become stereoscopic if you merely close one eye. The results are startling and pleasing beyond words and I have had an immense amount of fun with it. I recommend it to you as a very pleasant diversion."

"wonderful," he wrote in his diary. But he was very weak physically, and he took time off from work that month on Dr. Kempner's instructions. "Played golf," he wrote wearily on July 13. "Very tired afterwards. Dinner at Hawks. Nothing for me to eat. Very clear and very hot. *Golf is not for me.*"

Although he was "leading a wholly normal life," he simply did not have the stamina for golf, he wrote Dr. Kempner. The tomato a day that Kempner had added to his diet to alleviate dizziness had "helped tremendously, but . . . I am still distinctly lackadaisical and without much ambition for activity, either mental or physical." He had begun taking long walks, and he occasionally spent whole days that summer just watching my mother play tennis at Woodhill.

So sold was he on the rice diet, however, that he also started his mother on it. My grandmother had been having trouble with her memory since before John, Sr. died, and my father hoped the diet would clean out clogged arteries in her brain. "I am very worried lest she have the same difficulty that Grandpa Stowell had," John, Jr. wrote to his cousin William Cargill.

In early August, when he was still not feeling "up to par," John, Jr. flew back to Durham. "American took care of me. My first ride in new DC4s," he noted. A week later on the fourteenth, with some small adjustments to his diet, his blood pressure was down to 128/72, his lowest reading yet. The next day he had "Steak! for dinner." Writing to his mother, he told her that she must stick to her diet religiously. "I have seen more miracles here than I ever expected to see and my own is too wonderful to be true. . . . The doctor even thinks that next summer I will be able to play tennis again.

"There remains no doubt in my mind but that your arthritis and also loss of memory will be permanently cured [but] it takes weeks to undo the harm done for instance by eating a single roll. The three most devastating things are salt, butter and protein."

With her husband at Duke, Marion binged on tennis. "I had the best day of the summer on Friday which I might add, I couldn't have done, had you been home [probably meaning that she couldn't have stayed so long at the club]," she wrote to my father on Sunday, August 18. "I played eleven sets that day with the temperature over 95. . . . In years I have never played such good tennis and those men who usually hate mixed doubles said they thoroughly enjoyed themselves. . . . I got home at 7:15, had a hot bath, a gin fizz, a sandwich and bed—absolutely divine."

There was a polio scare that summer that was making my mother "decidedly nervous," she added. "The polio keeps a steady pace—one child opposite the Hamms got it yesterday."

My parents had a good and loving relationship and held each other in high regard. In a letter to his mother-in-law Mrs. Dickson about this time, John, Jr. wrote enthusiastically: "You have no idea what an outstanding woman she is, not only as a wife and Mother but her position in the community is something which has rarely been achieved by women coming from out-of-town at her age." My father's devotion to my mother rather limited his objectivity. However, she was well known for her ability to organize all sorts of social events.

When my father came home from Durham at the end of the month, there was high excitement again on the home front. Looking back, it was almost as if John, Jr. had won the lottery that summer. The new Cargill offices had pleased him enormously. Now, waiting for him at Port Cargill was the first in a series of boats that would be named *Carmac*. Built in 1929 by George Lawley and Sons as the *Wanderer,* the 115-foot yacht had been requisitioned by the U.S. Navy during World War II to chase submarines in the North Sea. Cargill, Inc. purchased it from the War Shipping Administration for $16,150 and spent another $36,000 renovating it.

"Our annual cost of operation will be around $40,000, which means that our branch managers will have to sell three or four million more bushels of grain as a result of buying it than they would otherwise," John, Jr. had advised Austen Cargill.

The company would use this new "inspection vessel"—which carried ten passengers and a crew of fifteen—for inspection trips of its plants and elevators, and the boat would also be available to the MacMillan and Cargill families for vacation cruises. Soon after his return from North Carolina, my father took our family on a sentimental five-day journey downriver aboard the *Carmac* to La Crosse.

The Carmac *at anchor in British Columbia*

Duke University Hospital in the 1940s. "The Duke campus is very beautiful and I suggest you follow along the road past the hospital through the pine forest to the chapel, which is wonderfully beautiful," John, Jr. wrote to his mother after she entered the hospital in September 1946.

Edna Cargill MacMillan

"Visited Cargill home, Cemetery and Grandad Bluff. Spent an hour at Elevator. . . . Beautiful day," he noted. Coming home on Sunday, September 1, "Children swam in Lake Pepin." We were indeed having an idyllic summer, and my father had even managed to inspect an elevator.

The next week, still worried about his mother's health, John, Jr. put her on the train to Duke University with her cook and companion Marcella Thilgen. "I must warn you," he informed Dr. Kempner, "that when she is either very tired or very confused she has an obsession that she is desperately poor and no amount of reasoning will do any good. The facts are of course that while I would not describe her as rich she most certainly is not poor." Writing to his mother, he told her to "be sure to go for walks in the Duke Gardens [as they] are much too beautiful to miss."

Edna took an immediate liking to the hospital. "My Dearest Junior," she wrote after settling into her room: "I am going to learn to say 'John' instead of Junior (if I can). . . . Everything has gone perfectly, everyone so nice and efficient without end. . . . Dr. Kempner . . . did nothing all the time during our conversation but tell how wonderful you were, your wonderful mind and all. . . . I have a perfect room and Marcella is having a grand time with the woman who shares her room. . . . Truth to tell I am going to have a good time."

Back home, Hugh and I were packing up to fly east for our first year (1946) at Berkshire School in Sheffield, Massachusetts. My father had originally planned to send both Hugh and me to Phillips Academy at Andover where he had gone to school, but Phillips turned down Hugh's application after seeing his Blake transcripts. So Hugh had entered Taft School in Connecticut where he had gotten off to a rocky start.

Again, my father's loyalty clouded his objectivity: "The intensely gregarious side to his nature is, I am certain, the cause of his scholastic difficulties," he wrote to Headmaster Paul Cruikshank in December 1944. "On the other hand, knowing the immense value in life of leadership and personal popularity, I am reluctant to ask you to invoke too much discipline in behalf of his studies."

After the following summer John, Jr. was writing again on Hugh's behalf, this time to Taft's Director of Studies Daniel Fenton:

"Mathematics was my forte in school and my engineering work has forced me to keep it up, so the last few days of Hughie's vacation I tutored him for a few periods myself and came to the conclusion that he would certainly fail his examination. . . . May I therefore request that you allow him to continue with the Middle Algebra, and consider this letter as authority to have him tutored at the first sign that he is not keeping up.

"Hugh also recalled to me the fact that I had been at Yale when you were there . . . you were the proctor in Pierson Hall during the year 1913–14, my Freshman year, and I remember you very well indeed. We must have tried your patience sorely for [the students] at Pierson Hall were by no means the most orderly or law-abiding members of the class."

My father's diplomacy helped keep Hugh in Taft, and I was set to join him there in the fall of 1945. "Both [Hugh's] mother and I are so pleased with your handling of Hugh, who is admittedly a very difficult youngster, that we would like to turn Duncan over to you," my father wrote Headmaster Cruikshank that year in May. "The boy lost a year because of bad health but has been continuously on the honor roll this year."

Ultimately, I never went to Taft because the doctors were still concerned about my health and Hugh and Taft had officially parted ways. It was decided that we would both enroll at Berkshire. "[Duncan's] physician is still extremely reluctant to consent to his going East [and] the only type of school we dare choose for him would be a very small one [where] he would be under extremely close and constant supervision," my father informed Taft. "They both leave by plane on Monday morning and Duncan is going to Boston to see a distinguished blood specialist, Dr. [George] Minot," John, Jr. wrote to his mother at Duke in

Berkshire School in Sheffield, Massachusetts

265

mid-September. "The wing in Duke Hospital named 'Minot' [in which Edna was housed] is in his honor." Dr. Minot is credited with discovering vitamin B-12.

In Pittsfield Hugh took the train to Sheffield, and I continued on the plane to Boston. My father had given me explicit, typed instructions:

"You are due in Boston at 9:40 Standard or Railroad time. This is 10:40 Boston, or daylight saving time and your appointment with Dr. Minot is for 11:30 so you will have very little time to waste. Breakfast on the train.

"The first thing on arrival, go to a phone booth, look in the phone book for the number of our Boston office listed under Cargill, Inc. or possibly under the name of our manager Mr. Eddie Donahue. Ask him to wire me of your safe arrival, and tell him you will get in touch with him after leaving Dr. Minot, if you possibly have time and still can catch your train.

"You should really have checked your bag at the parcel room before phoning Mr. Donahue. After phoning take a taxicab to Dr. George R. Minot's office. If your train was late then phone him from the station the first thing (phone number Kenmore 8600) and ask him when and where he will see you. Office is at 311 Beacon Street.

"Take a bottle of Dimol in your pocket to show him. Be sure to ask him about liver shots and exercise and ask him to write Mr. DeWindt at Berkshire school copy to me.

"When you finish with Dr. Minot take a taxicab back to the South Station. Then phone Mr. Donahue and ask him again to wire me a brief summary of what Dr. Minot had to say.

"Then get luncheon and take the next train back to Pittsfield. You have a first class ticket so buy at the window a seat in the parlor car, or one in a Pullman car. Of course if there are none available you will have to ride in a day coach, but if there are any pullman cars on the train at all the chances are that you will be able to persuade the Pullman conductor to sell you one. The cost will be around $1 or perhaps $1.50."

Dr. Minot diagnosed me as having chronic hemolytic jaundice. "The evidence for this is that he has abnormal fragility of his red blood cells; they break up . . . much more easily than normal," he informed my father. "This disease is one with which the individual is usually born, and many times one never knows anything about it until some episode occurs at the age of about ten years. Anemia may then increase and then decrease.

"I have to suppose that it will be wise to have your boy's spleen removed. . . . I would advise that it be done by one of the highly competent men we have here in Boston. There are, of course, many others. They take spleens out very well, for instance, at the Mayo Clinic."

For the time being, my parents decided to delay my splenectomy, and I started at Berkshire. Located at the foot of Mount Everett, the school was everything I could have hoped for. I loved the beautiful mountain setting and size of the school—with fewer than 150 students we all got to know each other. After so many difficult years of uncertainty about my health and enforced bed rest, I remember the support and nurturing of the faculty with gratitude. Berkshire provided me an environment in which I was able to thrive and pursue a number of different interests. Years later I would be a trustee at Berkshire from 1979–1984.

"I certainly hated to see you leave on the plane this morning," my father wrote to me on September 16. "The house is going to seem very empty without you and Hugh around and I am sure it is going to be very monotonous not having the feeling that trouble of some kind is just around the corner."

At the end of the month he sent each of us a check for fifty dollars with directions to deposit the money "immediately with the school, making sure that they keep separate accounts for each of you." This was to be the amount of our monthly allowance, he wrote, out of which we were to pay for everything we needed except tuition. "You will . . . have to buy all of your clothes, and the only items I will pay for will be railroad fare and pullman. You will even have to buy your own meals and pay your own tips out of your allowance."

Fifty dollars went a lot farther then than it would today. The average weekly wage for workers in 1946 ranged from sixty dollars in the auto industry to twenty-five dollars in the retail trade. (In 1949 the Truman administration would pass a minimum wage law of seventy-five cents an hour.) A typical single-family house cost less than eight thousand dollars. You could buy a hamburger for a dime and a six-pack of Pepsi for a quarter.

In December my father returned to Duke, where Dr. Kempner fine-tuned his diet, and he brought my grandmother and Marcella Thilgen home with him. Edna was still very foggy; she sometimes had long periods when her memory seemed completely normal, which my father attributed to the rice diet, but she never really recovered. Marcella, who was extraordinarily fond of milk and had arrived at Duke weighing 250 pounds, returned fifty pounds lighter. Hugh and I flew home from school for the holidays, and Grandmother Dickson joined us from California.

My father couldn't have been happier. Sitting at his desk on New Year's Eve—after working all day on his weather charts before going to the Lashers for cocktails and Woodhill for dinner—John, Jr. wrote from his heart:

"So ends a wonderful year! Health restored. All well & children developing beautifully. The most prosperous year in history of business. Our new lake offices & the Carmac. If only father were alive!"

My parents traveled to Jamaica in style aboard the new *Carmac* that winter. They still hoped to build their long-awaited winter home there, but it would have to wait until construction materials became easier to obtain. Interviewed

*William Duncan MacMillan II
(my school photo in 1949)*

upon their arrival by a reporter for the island *Gleaner*, John, Jr. said that it was unfortunate that Jamaica was not enjoying the post-war prosperity it should. He blamed politicians for shortages of items like flour and sugar, explaining that labor policies in both the U.K. and U.S.A. were handicapping producing areas. "There is no getting away from it," my father said. "If prices were higher for the primary producer, the labouring man would be better off, for the reason that he would make more."

While our parents were away, Hugh, who had been doing poorly at Berkshire, quit school, and they returned home to find him there. "He left school on his own volition but I am quite certain he would have been asked to leave within a day or two if he had not done so voluntarily," my father wrote to his brother Gee. "His marks were just incredibly bad. We are still debating whether to put him in West High or put him to work." Hugh opted to complete high school and made his own arrangements to finish the year at West High in Minneapolis.

My father was once again having health problems. He thought that he had developed ulcers in Jamaica, but the real trouble turned out to be diverticulitis. Dr. Kempner advised him to cut down on fruit and increase the amount of rice in his diet. John, Jr. had been eating salt-free canned foods prepared for infants and invalids by the H. J. Heinz Company, and he now wrote to the company asking if it would consider putting up salt-free boiled rice in ten-ounce cans:

> I am quite satisfied that eventually there will be a very large demand for such a product. Within a very few years there will almost certainly be several million people on the rice diet as it seems to be a complete cure for all diseases of the circulatory system. . . . I would be very glad right now to give you an order for a dozen cases.

In November 1948, I was in my senior year at Berkshire when Uncle Will died at the age of seventy-seven of cardiac failure at the old Miller Hospital in St. Paul. He was the last of the three MacMillan brothers who had set off for Texas in 1891 to make their fortunes in the grain business. Instead, Will had become a leading astronomer. Primarily concerned with the formation of the planets and stars, Will spent his entire career teaching at the University of Chicago, where he had graduated *summa cum laude* with a Ph.D. in mathematics and astronomy in 1908.

Uncle Will's research attracted worldwide attention. "MACMILLAN CALLS UNIVERSE ENDLESS," *The New York Times* declared in 1932. "A universe containing millions of worlds, some of them dead and others inhabited by beings as far superior to mankind as men are to single cells, is visioned by Dr. William D. MacMillan . . . in a new theory of cosmogony announced by him today at the University of Chicago. The next year the *Times* reported that Professor MacMillan had been using infra-red rays at the University's Yerkes Observatory in Williams

John, Jr., on the rice diet for three years when he was photographed on the beach at Hillsboro with friend Ambi Grey in 1949

*The Housatonic Valley League champions.
That's me on the left end, front row, in my
senior year at Berkshire.*

*William D. MacMillan at Marine-on-
St. Croix. Uncle Will was named for his
mother's brother William McCrea, who
died in Andersonville prison during the
Civil War, and his father Duncan D.
McMillan. John, Jr. had a special affinity
for his Uncle Will—they both had keenly
scientific minds—and he no doubt hoped
that I would exhibit this same propensity
when he named me William Duncan
MacMillan II.*

Bay, Wisconsin, in an attempt to answer the question of whether or not there was life on Venus.

Will knew Albert Einstein and on three occasions participated in debates with the German-American physicist about the then-revolutionary theory of relativity. One time out of the three, Uncle Will won the debate. Another time, when his brother Dan and John, Jr. and Cargill took the train to Chicago and walked in late, right in the middle of the debate, Uncle Will was so startled at seeing his relatives that he lost his train of thought—and the debate. The family had a saying, "If Uncle Will had just beaten Einstein twice instead of once, we probably would have hired him back."

There was a woman in Uncle Will's life, someone in Texas, but he never married. After retiring from the University of Chicago he divided his time between the ranch in Lubbock and the house Dan built at Marine-on-St. Croix. Their spinster sister Janet spent her summers there with him.

Will's religious beliefs were not shared by the rest of the family. Brought up Presbyterian, he had gone through theological school and emerged a complete atheist. He delighted in discussions on almost any topic, but he would start conversations in front of the grandchildren by saying, "There is no God, there is no God." My grandmother Edna hated this and would shoo us children out of the room.

All the MacMillan men—Grandfather, Uncle Will, Uncle Cargill, and Dad— loved to get into lively discussions. Typically, one of them would bone up on a controversial subject and bring it up in conversation before luncheon or dinner, which then became quite animated. Often they could have settled a point in one minute flat by looking up something in the dictionary or encyclopedia, but they never did. They would argue for hours.

269

*Uncle Will's three sisters at Marine-on-
St. Croix in the 1940s: Mary Rowles,
Bess Wheeler, and Janet MacMillan.
Aunt Mary, who had moved to Jacksonville,
Florida, died suddenly at age eighty-one
while visiting Janet in Chicago in April
1949. Aunt Janet died at age eighty-five
in a Chicago nursing home in May 1966.
Aunt Bess lived to be ninety-one, dying in
Princeton, New Jersey, in August 1975.*

Much of what I remember about Uncle Will clashes with his professional image. He always wore a dark blue suit, but he was bowlegged and walked with a horseman's gait; he looked like a typical rancher. Hugh and I persuaded him to teach us how to shoot a long-barreled horse pistol on the front lawn at my grandparents' house. He had a very long watch chain that he liked to swing around, he smoked cigars (to which he introduced me at a tender age as I mentioned earlier), and he had a voracious appetite.

Uncle Will's table manners did not reflect his upbringing. One night at my grandparents' house when we had asparagus for dinner, he took all of it. My grandmother said, "You put that back. It's for everybody." When he ate peas, he

*Marnie receiving a silver bracelet as
Queen of Berkshire's 1949 House Party*

270

would put his napkin up to his neck and take the peas with a knife and just shovel them in. At Marine-on-St. Croix, he ate his breakfast cereal out of a flower bowl. He would cook the cereal in the evening and put it on a shelf overnight so that it would be ready in the morning.

In the last letter I received from Uncle Will at Berkshire, he told me how pleased he was that I was showing some literary skill. I was editor-in-chief of the school paper, *The Green and Gray,* the year he died. I was also on the Student Council, sang in the Glee Club, and lettered in soccer, hockey, and tennis. The senior class voted me "Biggest drag with the faculty," meaning that I had many friends among the teachers. My sister Marnie was chosen Queen of Berkshire's 1949 House Party in February that year. "You can be very proud of 'la petite soeur,'" I wrote home to our parents. Marnie was sweet sixteen and in her first year at Westover School in Middlebury, Connecticut.

That spring my father appeared on the cover of the April 16 issue of *Business Week.* John, Jr. normally eschewed publicity, but his growing international reputation made it virtually impossible to avoid press coverage altogether. Marking his sixteenth year as president of "the largest private handler of farm products in the U.S.," the magazine reported that John, Jr. was steering the company into soybean processing, letting contracts for an extraction plant that could handle seven hundred tons of soybeans daily. The plant was in Chicago on the Calumet River, alongside the company's terminal elevators.

Prior to World War II, Cargill had ranked among the top three or four firms in the global grain trade, the others being foreign-owned. As much as sixty percent of Cargill's business had one end outside of the United States. After the war shut off this trade, Cargill had begun diversifying in feeds, seeds, vegetable oils, and farm supplies. In 1945 Cargill bought Nutrena Mills to become a leading competitor in the animal and poultry feed business. The next year the company was operating a flaxseed crushing plant at Port Cargill, filling a great demand for linseed oil, particularly in paint.

Cargill, Inc. employed three thousand workers, and the company ran its own management training program for college graduates, recruiting talent from midwestern universities and prominent liberal arts institutions. John, Jr. was initially especially enthusiastic about Yale "because of the intense competitive spirit which is peculiarly developed at Yale [and] which is all too often lacking in small universities." But when neither of his sons went to Yale, he later changed his mind about the school, writing to a former Yale classmate: "Our experience with Yale men has been a disappointment, and I think our best ones today are coming from Williams, Princeton and Brown. . . . I am greatly distressed over the trend of things at Yale. . . . My overall enthusiasm has waned considerably."

Writing to me at Berkshire in March 1947, my father explained his rather idiosyncratic preference for eastern schools: "I think I have told you many times that half of your success in life will depend on controlling your emotions. In fact that is the great advantage which the graduates of Eastern schools have over the Western schools. Eight years in the East teaches you to control yourself and the result is that these men in the business world are much sought after because they simply do not quarrel with people around them."

Explaining his unique philosophy of recruiting further in a letter to a college professor, John, Jr. stated that "we must limit ourselves to one type of man. He must first be of a background which would furnish him with excellent manners. This is because in his future role as a co-ordinator he will have to get along with other men. He must also possess iron self-discipline to the end that when irritated he will not show his irritation. We can only find this type in men of excellent family. This does not mean a family of wealth. It means a family of culture and the sons of educators, ministers, etc., are just as welcome as are the sons of wealthy fathers."

In 1957 my father would write to the director of admissions at Phillips Academy:

> My company has had a program for the past 28 years of hiring from 12 to 50 university graduates each year and then putting them through an intensive training course. . . . The most important single factor in leadership of the type we are seeking is manners, and this, in turn, is found only in youngsters from certain backgrounds—mainly a background of education and culture.
>
> We are having extreme difficulty . . . in staffing our important posts in foreign countries and at home where this is a prerequisite. It is true that a certain amount of culture can be acquired after these youngsters enter school and college, but there is no substitute for the family background.

As I try to understand my father's insistence on this single attribute, I believe that his experience at Yale influenced him to prefer the veneer of eastern manners over what he perceived to be the less polished culture of the Midwest and West. This prejudice is ironic in view of the fact that his own roots were deeply planted in the Midwest, and that Cargill's management has included many fine, talented, and well-mannered individuals from the Upper Midwest.

In a college recruitment brochure that he wrote for Cargill, Inc., which remains one of the most comprehensive statements of Cargill culture ever circulated, John, Jr. listed the ten attributes that he considered most responsible for the company's success:

> *Owner management.*
> *Very conservative dividend policy.*
> *No public pressure on management.*

The integration of the businesses.
Fact that all activities are germane to the grain field.
The vital and fundamental nature of the commodities and
products dealt in. Man, beast and bird must eat!
Heavy commercial borrowings mean that its management
must be conservative if credit is to be maintained.
The companies do not speculate.
The care taken in the selection and training of prospective executives.
An enviable record for fair dealing and of integrity both as
to contracts and the quality of its products and merchandise.

The Cargill corporate culture bred a group of highly-motivated executives, most of whom were inordinately loyal to family management. Family members through several generations have also maintained close ties among themselves.

Following my graduation from Berkshire, my father, Uncle Cargill, and Austen Cargill put together a two-week trip aboard the *Carmac* for my cousins Cargill, Jr. and Whitney, and Hugh and me to inspect Cargill lumber operations in British Columbia. For the three older men who had logged there almost three decades earlier, it was a trip back in time.

We left Minneapolis by train on the *Empire Builder* on a Saturday evening and were met thirty-six hours later in Seattle by Captain Fluitt with the *Carmac*. The next morning we dropped anchor at Port Angeles in the Strait of Juan de Fuca. Austen had arranged for us to tour the Rayonier wood cellulose plant, where the manager was Harry Sprague, one of his boyhood friends. "They make the highest grade of purified wood cellulose," Uncle Cargill wrote in a notebook journal he kept of the trip. "It takes roughly 1000 board feet of logs (they use hemlock logs) to make a ton of the finished product which looks and feels like very white blotting paper. . . .

"Mr. and Mrs. Sprague came aboard for luncheon and then we went thru the Crown Zellerbach newsprint plant," Cargill, Sr. continued. "Here about 425 tons is produced daily with a little over 600 men. . . . This operation was largely mechanical as contrasted with the chemical one we saw in the morning. About 80% of the wood used is ground up against carborundum wheels into dust and only 20% is made into chips and then into sulphite. The paper making rolls ran at about 1200 feet a minute. While we were watching the paper strips broke twice. This causes great commotion."

We arrived in Vancouver on Wednesday, and Austen and Uncle Cargill and Cargill, Jr. went into town to see Eustace Smith who had sold W. W. Cargill our timber tract at Big Creek more than forty years earlier about 1905. Now Cargill, Inc. was reselling the property, and the old gentleman was once again handling the sale. "The cruise made by Eustace Smith showed 225 million feet which was about 80% of Lacy's 1911 cruise and much more than we expected," Uncle Cargill noted. "This made the sale price $356,000."

They also had time for shopping. "Cargill, Jr. and I . . . took in the Hudson Bay Co's store and Birk's," my uncle wrote. "I couldn't get any china for Pauline but got a jacket on sale. Cargill Jr. got a pair of flannel trousers [and] a fine woolen plaid shirt."

In the meantime John, Jr. had toured one of the Harbor Commission elevators. It turned out there was storage space for three million bushels that had not been used for three years. My father hoped to lease the space at a cut rate by agreeing to store only American grain.

We then sailed northward up the scenic Inside Passageway, through Seymour Narrows as far as the head of Knight Inlet, to inspect our Bonanza Lake Tract at Beaver Cove. "What we saw made us sick," Uncle Cargill wrote. "Logging methods have improved very little in 25 years. . . . The terrible waste of 25 years ago is still going on. They are leaving more wood behind than they are taking out."

One evening, anchored in Cypress Harbor, everyone except Uncle Cargill (who wasn't feeling well) rode over in the launch to see Broughton Lagoon. My father wanted to see the place where he and Cargill had become caught in a riptide twenty-eight years earlier and thought their end had come. When we had not returned from our excursion by dark, Uncle Cargill got worried and sent the captain out to look for us in the outboard.

The place was still bad luck. We had hit a submerged log, knocking out the propeller, and were paddling for all we were worth in five-minute shifts, bucking the tide, when Captain Fluitt found us and took us in tow. Uncle Austen had fallen in during the excitement of hitting the log, but he was all admiration for the paddling job we had done. Another hour probably would have gotten us in. "I was certainly relieved when they got back safe, sound, and excited," Cargill wrote.

Another day we inspected our Tom Brown Lake Tract at Glendale Cove. "I have heard that this . . . is the last great cedar show on good accessible ground," Cargill, Sr. wrote. "We were very much impressed with one gadget they had. It consisted of a very sturdy little steel boat, nearly round, which was used for booming logs. The fellow that ran it seemed to be able to do the work of several boom men.

"After seeing the logging, we went across the Cove and went thru the Cannery where they are packing as much as 40,000 salmon, which average 5 lbs, per day. We then weighed anchor, passed our 2 Knight Inlet Limits . . . and reached our old Camp 3 about 5:45. . . . It was amazing how the 2nd growth had come up. We had trouble finding our old road, but finally located it and climbed up it nearly to the end. The planks and ties had pretty well rotted out

Knight Inlet, British Columbia: Hugh, Duncan, Cargill, Jr., Whitney, and Cargill, Sr. on the deck of the Carmac. "I've been around quite a bit but question if I have ever seen so much grand beauty," Uncle Cargill wrote. "It was a field day for picture taking. We stopped for a few minutes at the place where a Glacier comes down nearly to the water which is a milky blue from the rock flour made by the ice. This is great grizzly bear country."

Cargill, Sr. and Duncan MacMillan surveying logging waste at our Bonanza Lake tract, Beaver Cove

but the grade was still in good shape so the climbing was not too bad. . . . I counted my paces coming down. They amounted to 2843. The average grade, John Jr said, was about 16%."

Everyone had a good time on this trip, and it was one of the best I have ever taken. One night Cargill, Jr. and I went salmon spearing with a couple of the loggers from our Port Neville Logging Camp. Cargill, Sr. and Cargill, Jr. did a lot of fishing for salmon and trout (rainbows and cutthroats), and we came back with gorgeous photographs of British Columbia. I also came home knowing a lot more about our family's logging history. This kind of information later stood me in good stead when I became president of the Cargill Lumber Company. In the meantime, I was headed for college, and Yale did not want me.

My father's snapshot of Marnie and me being towed home after winning a race on Lake Minnetonka. The name of our "C" boat was the Waterloo.

John, Jr. in Jamaica

"I don't feel, Mr. MacMillan, that we have any right to push Duncan's candidacy for Yale more than we have," Berkshire's headmaster Delano DeWindt wrote to my father in June 1949. "Had Duncan distinguished himself the latter part of this year, I would have been willing to go to bat for him at Yale strenuously, but while he gave us indications of real capacity he never delivered."

During the summer after graduating from Berkshire, I had been working in a job that I liked in the insurance department at Cargill. Colgate, Hamilton, and Bowdoin had accepted me for the fall, but I was more motivated by the work at Cargill than going to college immediately.

My father had other ideas, of course, and during our trip to British Columbia he encouraged me to choose a suitable school, which according to him did not include the three colleges that had accepted me. In a search for a school that appealed to me and that would also meet with my father's approval, Brown University seemed a good choice, although I had no thought of being

A photo by John, Jr. of downtown Kingston in the British Crown colony. Jamaica became an independent dominion within the British Commonwealth in 1962.

The guest cottage my parents built and occupied at Green Castle

accepted for the fall since it was already August. However, with the assistance of Cargill's Vice President John G. Peterson, Class of 1917 at Brown, and the recommendation of my Latin teacher at Berkshire, I found myself at Brown one week before classes started. Little did I realize then that the next four years would be the beginning of a lifelong relationship with the school and one of the most important commitments of my life.

While I was away at school that year, my father bid on a plantation in Jamaica. "It is nearly a thousand acres, mostly in coconuts, but with some bananas and some sugar, and is about 35 miles from Kingston on the North shore of the island," John, Jr. wrote to his children in February.

This was the old estate of Green Castle at Annotto Bay in St. Mary's parish. At its peak as a sugar plantation it boasted four hundred black slaves. The 1784 probate inventory for John Ellis gave their name, age, occupation, condition, and value. In addition to field hands of both sexes, there were carpenters, sawyers, coopers, blacksmiths, masons, cattle keepers, mule boys, sheep boys, fowl keepers, ropemakers, gardeners, and a midwife.

Most of the slaves were described as "able," but others were "sickly," "elderly but well," "ill disposed," or "a runaway." A few were "useless" due to old age and infirmities. Twenty-one slaves including "house wenches," pastry cooks, a butler, and a stableman worked at the "Great House," which, according to the inventory, was furnished with upholstered sofas, twelve mahogany chairs with "hair bottoms," two large dining tables, two card tables, a Pembroke table, a round tea table, oil cloth carpet, pictures, a barometer and thermometer, and a fender and fire apparatus for the fireplace. Seven bedrooms were outfitted with bedsteads, feather beds, lawn mosquito netting, bedside carpets, oil cloth floor coverings, looking glasses, chamber chairs, and other chairs.

Ninety miles south of Cuba in the Caribbean Sea, the island of Jamaica was "discovered" and claimed for Spain by Columbus on his second voyage in 1494. The first Spanish settlers arrived in 1510, enslaved the native Arawak Indians, and imported black slaves from Africa. In 1660, after being soundly defeated by the English at Rio Nuevo, the Spanish ceded Jamaica to the English Crown.

By the 1930s Green Castle was owned by the Banana Company of Jamaica, Ltd., which cultivated bananas and raised quality Indian cattle on the estate. The banana company sold Green Castle to one of its employees, J. Roy Johnson, and Johnson sold it to my father. They closed the deal in June 1950.

"The new guest cottage is a dream," John, Jr. wrote in his diary in January 1952. In addition to this one-story dwelling, which my parents occupied, there survived an early twentieth-century "great house," which was given to the new manager. My father then set about becoming a farmer and cattle rancher.

"I would like to underplant the pimento and coconuts with sugar cane to be fed to the cattle, so we can gradually build up our herd," he wrote to my brother Hugh in January 1955. "We now have 204 head and they are beautiful animals." These were the high-humped Brahmin variety of cattle, which we still raise at Green Castle.

Since my father's day, Green Castle has grown to about 1,400 acres and become my responsibility. We have been one of the largest growers of papaya, shipping to England, France, Switzerland, Holland, and the United States, and we have also had considerable success with bananas, coconuts, cocoa, plantain, pimento, and vegetables for the local market. Unfortunately, the auspicious and profitable beginning we had with papaya turned to disappointment in 1996 when the crop was struck with a virus. Whether sufficiently resistant strains will be developed is still a question. It should not surprise a Cargill family member that farming never stops presenting tough challenges. My father certainly experienced this, but he would have marveled at the excitement of seeing the Green Castle office functioning with telephones, computers, and FAX machines.

We launched another entrepreneurial venture in the late 1990s—growing dendrobium orchids for export to the cut flower retail market. This project is now underway, and our research indicates a high probability of success. Although orchids are an entirely new direction for Green Castle, they have been a lifelong passion for me. I have grown and shown orchids at home in Minnesota for many years.

John, Jr. inspecting coconuts at Green Castle. In a letter to Hugh in August 1953, my father complained: "I am terribly discouraged about Jamaica. The government flatly refuses to let me grow Robusta coffee and it looks very much to me as though I have acquired a fine winter residence and that is all."

That I would one day manage Green Castle never crossed my mind when I was in college, but I grew up knowing that I would one day enter the family grain business. Following my freshman year at Brown, I worked as an assistant corn merchant for Cargill in Minneapolis. In a progress report to my father in July, Executive Vice President H. Terry Morrison told him that I was following through with my assigned mission "in a very creditable manner. He appears to be anxious to learn more and more about the Grain Division operations and what they are all about."

> Erv [Kelm, who was head of the grain division] tells me he has a grand sense of humor, and that his associates kid him a lot. That indicates to me that he is popular with his fellow workers and is not riding on your coat tail. I think his attitude is splendid. Kelm wound up by saying, "Duncan is a d— good boy."

It was an eventful summer. Outside of my work responsibilities I found time to sail. Sailing was an important part of my life all through the 1940s and my college years. My father had started us off early with an "X" boat and sailing lessons at the Minnetonka Yacht Club. My cousin Whitney, Hugh, and I sailed together and were able to compete with considerable success. "David Bell took me in motor boat to photograph Duncan winning 'C' boat race [on Lake Minnetonka]," my father noted in his journal on August 16, 1950.

Trips to Inland Lakes regattas in Neenah and Lake Geneva, Wisconsin, were adventures with a limited budget. We drove my grandmother Edna MacMillan's old Packard pulling our "C" boat, the *Waterloo*, on a second-hand trailer that swayed at high speeds. We pumped gas for the car at grandmother's house and carried it in five-gallon drums in the bottom of the boat. Our housekeeper Martha Norris made us sandwiches for four or five days, and we took our own tent to camp.

In August 1950, two days after Hugh and I returned from the Inland Lakes regatta in Madison (we placed third in one race), my father took me to Abbott Hospital in Minneapolis, where Drs. O. J. Campbell and Nate Plimpton removed my spleen, an operation which has improved my health enormously. After many years of visiting the Mayo Clinic, Boston Children's Hospital, and the University of Minnesota, it had been finally determined that I had spherocytosis or chronic hemolytic anemia, which is characterized by spherocytic red blood cells. In this disorder—which has been inherited by my four daughters and their children—the system produces numerous hard red blood cells instead of soft cells. These hard cells become trapped in the spleen as though they were dead, when, in fact, they are actually alive. The spleen kills them off, resulting in anemia. The only treatment is to remove the spleen. Fortunately, we were able to profit from this knowledge with my children, who had their spleens removed when they were still very young.

Marnie with father and mother at her debut at the Woodhill Country Club, December 22, 1950. Marnie was home following her first term at Vassar.

Another John, Jr. photo, this one of Marion, John Hugh IV "the tiger", Alex the dog, and Susie MacMillan, May 1953. John Hugh IV, born in July 1952, was my parents' first grandchild. "He can now stand on his own feet and it is just a matter of a week or two I think before he will actually be walking," my father wrote. "He has several teeth coming in and is a most promising youngster. I am wildly enthusiastic about him."

When I returned to Brown in the fall of 1950 for my sophomore year, the United States was once again at war. In late June, after only five years of peace, President Truman ordered U.S. forces to the aid of South Korea when it was attacked by North Korean troops crossing the 38th parallel. I was advised that my draft category was 1–A and instructed to report for active duty at the Providence military base. The fact that I still had an impressive looking splenectomy wound gave the draft board pause, however, and I never did end up in military service.

My father had not seen the war coming. In a letter to a colleague in July he had predicted that the "Korean scare" would be over in two weeks. "The Russians do not want a general war at this time as the crop in the Ukraine was in 10 days ago and they would need every day of dry weather until the Autumn rains come to move their armies around. . . . The Russians will intervene for peace." But the war escalated quickly after the Chinese Communists joined the fighting on the side of the North Koreans in late 1950.

With the outbreak of war, grain prices rose as production decreased. Cargill, Inc. posted record profits for the crop year 1950–51 of $5.9 million and was continually acquiring new elevators to keep up with the surge of business. In a column in *Cargill News,* John, Jr. assured Cargill employees going to war that they could expect to return to their old or similar positions when they came home. In their absence the company would make up the difference between their military pay and their salaries at Cargill.

My father was disappointed that I was unable to go into the service, but Hugh did his stint. He volunteered for the army in early February 1952, leaving behind his bride of six months, Susie Velie, who was pregnant with their son John Hugh IV. Hugh reported at Fort Sheridan in Illinois.

"I have looked up Fort Sheridan on the map and note it is right next to Lake Forest, which of course is a lovely town," my father wrote Hugh. "We want to hear all about your experiences—what parts of it you find you like and what parts you do not like. I myself feel you are having a marvelous opportunity. You are competing against all the other men of your age and I really envy you very much the opportunity."

John, Jr. doubted that he would know any of Hugh's superior officers: "The army officers I knew in World War I are nearly all dead or retired. You may remember I was exceedingly precocious and really circulated in rather exalted circles, age considered. I had very few friends other than our Minneapolis crowd who were not Field Officers and practically all World War I Field Officers are now retired."

My parents celebrated their twenty-fifth anniversary on May 21, 1952. John, Jr. "gave M. M. diamond pin selected by Betty Fullerton," he wrote in his diary. Aunt Pauline held a "beautiful" party for a dozen couples at which their friends presented them with a silver soup tureen. "Your mother seemed delighted over the pin," my father wrote Marnie at Vassar the next day. "It is about time I bought her something as it is the first bit of jewelry I have given her since you were born." In a letter to me at Brown the same day, he outlined the upcoming inspection trip he and I were taking to South America and suggested that I begin supplementing my studies "with a little reading about Brazil."

In 1948 Cargill, Inc. had entered into an agreement with the International Basic Economy Corporation of New York (IBEC) headed by Nelson Rockefeller to establish a merchandising company for handling grain and related products in Brazil. Rockefeller had approached John, Jr., explaining that he wanted to demonstrate that a for-profit enterprise could benefit while upgrading the economies of underdeveloped countries. Capitalized by Brazilian interests as well as IBEC and Cargill, Inc., the new company was known as Cargill Agricola e Commercial, S.A.

Father and I flew from New York on June 16 to Caracas, Venezuela, then took a chartered plane along the coast to view coffee, rice, sesame, potato, and corn plantations. "I never dreamed so many coffee trees were in existence," my father wrote. From Trinidad, we flew to Sao Paulo, where we had our office. Father called on bankers and our prize customer, Corn Products.

"To date it has been a perfectly beautiful trip but very very strenuous," my father wrote to my mother on June 24 from the Hotel Comodoro in Sao Paulo. "I am thriving under it, but Duncan is on the ropes. . . . I have had practically all meals in my room, Duncan below. Duncan lives so well, what with food, drink & cigars that he is rather an expensive courier. I see now why he is always broke."

The next day we flew by DC6 from Sao Paulo across Brazil and Bolivia to Guayaquil, Ecuador—an eleven-and-a-half hour flight at 275 miles per hour. "We have a plane chartered tomorrow morning to fly us over the valley," my father wrote mother. "I am wildly enthusiastic about agricultural possibilities in Venezuela; Ecuador I understand offers just as great. . . . Duncan has been wonderful company, and I am really proud to be able to introduce him as my son. . . .

"Your chocolate was a flop. It melted in Trinidad, ruining Duncan's shirts. Everything else has been wonderful tho. Today for the first time I run out of bread. . . . please phone Leo [Sheehan] to ask Mrs. Kuhn to resume shipments of bread to arrive [in Jamaica] by July 14th."

Coming home by way of Panama, Jamaica, and Cuba, we celebrated my twenty-second birthday on July 5 at Green Castle. Father was suffering from diverticulitis, but he rarely let something like that incapacitate him. "The bananas are beautiful, but rather low in quality due to last year's drought," he wrote home. "They are taking 12 to 15 months to make the 1st crop—not the 10

My mother Marion in front of her portrait in our living room at Craigbank on the night of Hugh's bridal dinner, August 1951. With her is my father's cousin Howard McMillan.

months represented to me a year ago. The subsequent crops will be 10 months though." He instructed the overseer to plant additional bananas as well as rice and coffee.

My father called it "a wonderful trip," writing in his diary when we arrived home on July 12 that "we flew 17,000 miles and saw things which could not be seen any other way." He came home to find Marion "over-tennised," he added.

John, Jr. did not have a spare moment when he returned to the office. "Our business is improving considerably and I am not nearly so worried as I was a few months ago," he advised Hugh and Susie on August 22, 1952. "The Minnesota Western is doing a tremendous business, running several special trains every week. The new elevator at Blomkest [Minnesota] has worked out admirably and will prove to be one of our largest points."

His assurance about business to Hugh notwithstanding, Cargill was facing serious challenges at that time. Profits for the 1951-1952 crop year reached only $673,000, a record low for the postwar years. During that twelve-month period, Cargill was also under fire from the government. In September 1951 the government accused Cargill of violating the federal Seed Act by adulterating its high-grade Montana alfalfa seed with lower-grade Arizona alfalfa and selling it under false pretenses. Much to John, Jr.'s chagrin, the charges were true; the fault lay with four lower-level management employees who had taken matters into their own hands.

Shortly before the hearings in March 1953, Cargill, Inc. decided to withdraw completely from field seed production, citing the "loss of prestige that has certainly attended this . . . very unfortunate and unhappy matter." District Court Judge Gunnar Nordbye noted that he was "satisfied that none of the . . . officers or directors [of Cargill, Inc.], were aware of what was going on," and fined the company five hundred dollars on each of ten counts.

Cargill, Inc. was also in hot water in 1952 with the Commodity Credit Corporation (CCC) and the Commodity Exchange Authority (CEA). At issue in the first instance was CCC surplus grain that had been stored overlong in Cargill elevators. "The government loaded out a few cargoes and then stopped," Cargill, Sr. explained in a letter to Cargill, Jr. in October. "The corn sat in the elevator for months and months and then began to get out of condition. We informed the gov't. of the state of affairs, but they did nothing. Finally we got Washington to take a hand and eventually the corn was shipped, but by this time hundreds of thousands of bushels graded sample grade and, of course, the Gov't took an awful licking." This case escalated to the point that the government filed criminal charges against Cargill's superintendent at Albany and another Cargill employee, but a jury two years hence would completely exonerate them and Cargill, Inc.

As for the Commodity Exchange Administration, "[they have] been harassing us on our futures operations in Winnipeg and [have] had us in a constant state of turmoil," my father informed my brother in September 1952. Cargill, Inc. was doing a land-office business that fall, he confided: "On one day alone we sold seven cargoes of Winter Wheat. This amounted to about $5,000,000 worth of wheat and was sold to every conceivable place. Yesterday we bought 12 million oats in two trades from the Wheat Board in Canada for shipment in October." He didn't "mind the strain incidental to that sort of thing," he said, "but I certainly hate to spend all my time with the lawyers."

When General Dwight Eisenhower won the presidential election that fall, John, Jr. was elated. It was the first time the Republicans had been in power in twenty years. "The election of course was magnificent news," he wrote to me at Brown.

> I myself feel that it gives us four more years of relief of having conditions deteriorate. I am under no illusions though. In a scheme of government such as ours where the "have nots" are in position to spend the savings of the thrifty, it is just a short time until there will not be any savings left. The moment the Left Wingers get in control again—which I fear very much will be four years from now—we will see things begin to disintegrate in a hurry. The moral, of course, is to get your house in order to be able to resist the disintegration.

The "relief" John, Jr. anticipated did nothing to mitigate Cargill's current problems, however, and by Christmas the government was pursuing Cargill, Inc. again. "We have certainly had a plague of government charges against us and as far as I can make out they are purely for political reasons with the government more interested with the publicity they receive because of the seriousness of the charges than they are whether the charges be true or not," my father wrote Hugh on December 26. "We were indicted a week ago at Syracuse on 54 criminal counts, but as yet we have not even received a copy of the charges. . . .

"We also are about to be charged on the oats indictment." [The CEA was citing violations in connection with the importation of large quantities of Canadian oats.] This one however will require many years of litigation before it can be brought to a decision. . . .

"I am inclined to think that the government has rendered us a very great service however because it has pinpointed the places in our organization where the controls were not adequate. We are in the process of fixing these up but it does take time."

With the company under siege, morale at the office suffered. Employees needed to know the truth; they needed to be reassured. In an article in *Cargill News*, Austen Cargill, who had been chairman of the board since August 1950, stated: "At no time in the 87 years of Cargill's history has there been any just reason to question the company's honesty and integrity."

There is none now. I can tell you without reservation that no difficulties which we now face are the result of any management policies encouraging or condoning unlawful or unscrupulous actions. Our policy is just the opposite.

I want you to know that Cargill has not willfully violated any laws or contracts. It would be ridiculous to say that we have made no mistakes in our long business lifetime. We have made many. More will probably be made in spite of all precautions and controls. That by no means indicates, however, that by intention or design we either flout the law or short-change the customer.

We are a large company and an aggressive one. We live in a goldfish bowl. We are a natural target for those who are suspicious of largeness and for those who find in progressive companies a threat to their personal interests . . . there is always a temptation to make political hay by loudly attacking such businesses. Remember that these unproven attacks reach the front pages while later refutation usually is given little or no prominence.

We intend to continue our growth and do so by being aggressive. Only in that way are we sure that we can protect our job and yours. Rest assured, however, that in the process we will take no steps which will impair, let alone destroy, our good name. Without it Cargill could not have lived since 1865 as a successful and respected citizen of the business community.

At the John H. MacMillan, Jr. home in Orono, whatever the trials and tribulations at the office, life went on, usually quite pleasantly. I came home from Brown for Christmas in 1952, arriving ahead of Sally Stevens, to whom I was about to propose. On the evening of December 26, after writing earlier in the day to Hugh about the "plague of government charges against us," my father wrote in his diary: "Duncan's Sally arrived. What a girl!" I thought so, too.

David Bell, my best friend when we were growing up as well as in college

Duncan MacMillan and Sally Stevens, front and center, at a Psi Upsilon fraternity party at Brown. Behind them are David Bell and Alice Russell, who was Sally's college roommate at Wheaton. My sister Marnie is also in this photo.

Sally and I had met at Brown a year and a half earlier on a blind date arranged by my buddy David Bell, who followed me to Brown. Sally was from Nashua, New Hampshire, where her father was president of the Maine Manufacturing Company, a family-owned firm that had built "White Mountain" ice refrigerators before entering the steel kitchen cabinet and school equipment field.

My first meeting with her parents was nearly a disaster. I appeared in Nashua after being rained out on a ski trip to Mount Washington. I hadn't shaved for several days and was looking very scruffy. Her parents were entertaining friends at a bridge party when I arrived. They took one look at me and suggested that I should go upstairs and get cleaned up. They were visibly relieved when I came down dressed in a jacket and tie.

The previous October my parents had invited Sally to spend a weekend with us aboard the *Carmac* on the Hudson River. Instead, Sally ended up in the hospital with appendicitis. On the day after Christmas when Sally came to Minneapolis, arriving from Boston at the old Wold-Chamberlain airport, she still had not met my parents. Finding no one there to meet her, Sally wondered if she had made a mistake in coming.

"I got to the airport in my little gray flannel suit and gloves and hat and no Duncan to meet me," she remembered. "The airport was very small and there was no flight back to Boston and I didn't know what to do. Finally, Duncan sailed in with David Bell and Steve Krogness. One of Duncan's former girlfriends was getting married, and they whisked me off to the wedding in my travel clothes."

The 115-foot yacht Carmac, *which piled up on reefs near Watch Hill Passage, Rhode Island, on September 18, 1953*

My bride Sarah Marian Stevens MacMillan with her parents Marian Sarah and Philip Ellis Stevens

That evening at home, my mother, in her imperious way, inspected Sally thoroughly. She was cordial, but no doubt disappointed not to have selected someone from Minneapolis for me herself. She was also astonished to find that I had brought home a beautiful bride without her counsel. My father never had any reservations, however. "This is the happiest day of my life," he told Sally. "I just want you to know how pleased I am."

I gave Sally an engagement ring on New Year's Eve, and we set a wedding date for the following September. My father was pleased with my last term's performance at Brown, he wrote to Hugh: "He has 3 B's and a C for his mid-term, which in the history of our branch of the MacMillan family is something unparalleled. I understand I am to receive letters of commendation from the Vice-President and Dean of the University."

Following graduation in the spring, I went to work for Cargill while Sally traveled to Europe with her parents for the coronation of Queen Elizabeth. The trip had been planned for a year. It was a unique coronation, as both the queen mother and the dowager queen were still living, so royal flags for all three queens were flying at the same time. A year and a half earlier, traveling on the Cunard liner *Queen Mary*, Cargill and Pauline MacMillan had gone to England for King George's funeral in February 1952.

Our wedding on September 26, 1953, was marred by calamity. The week before the ceremony, the motor vessel *Carmac*, which was to have been the scene of our bridal dinner, slammed into reefs while traveling up the East Coast. I was having lunch with Sally in Nashua when her uncle walked in the door and said, "I just heard on the news that a yacht called the *Carmac* has gone aground."

The accident happened at two o'clock in the morning, and John G. Peterson and his wife, the only two passengers aboard, narrowly escaped drowning when high seas caught the lifeboat in which they had been lowered and smashed it against the side of the *Carmac*. Peterson, who had recently taken Austen Cargill's place as chairman of the board, was tossed unconscious onto the deck, and Mrs. Peterson was thrown into the water. Luckily, she was a strong swimmer; Mrs. Peterson survived thirty minutes in the dark water before the ship's captain reached her with a life raft.

The Petersons and the *Carmac*'s thirteen crew members were rescued by the Coast Guard, and a waiting ambulance took the Petersons to the hospital. Mr. Peterson suffered back injuries, and his wife had a broken collarbone. But the *Carmac* was done for; the boat was still clinging to the rocks a year later when she was finished off by a hurricane.

As everything for the bridal dinner was lost in the accident, the party was held at the country club in Nashua. Sally and I were married in the First Unitarian Church, where both her father and grandfather had been active. Sally had six bridesmaids (including my sister Marnie) and three junior bridesmaids.

W. Duncan MacMillan on his wedding day with parents John, Jr. and Marion MacMillan

Marnie with father on graduation day at Vassar, June 1954

The reception following the ceremony was held at Sally's parents' two-story brick home on Berkeley Street.

It was a point of pride with my father that he never drank in public. When the photographer came around, he would slip his drink under his coat. He did manage to escape being photographed with a drink in his hand, but a movie camera captured him pulling the drink out from its hiding place.

Our wedding trip to Europe was a gift from my parents. We sailed on the Holland American liner *New Amsterdam*. To impress Sally, I had written to the steamship company and obtained a brochure of the boat so that I would know my way around. I memorized where everything was in relation to our room.

As we were boarding, a steward informed us that our room had been changed. "What do you mean it's been changed?" I demanded. "This is my wedding trip." The man smiled and explained, "You're going to be in the bridal suite." I protested that I couldn't afford the bridal suite, but it had all been arranged at no extra cost to us by John Peterson, who did extensive business through the banks with Holland American.

My brother and sister and I were all married in the space of three years. My brother Hugh had married Susan Velie in August 1951, and in August 1954 Marnie married Kimberly-Clark heir Bill Kimberly. Sadly, her marriage was in trouble from the start and ended in annulment.

None of us had suspected that Bill Kimberly was a prospective suitor when Marnie brought him home in the fall of 1954. "We have had an awfully attractive boy staying with us for the last day or two—one of Marnie's friends," father wrote to Hugh and Susie in September. "His father is the President of Kimberly-Clark and they live at Neenah. I do not think Marnie has the slightest interest in him except that he is good company. He is not as large . . . as Duncan, and Marnie has never had anyone yet around her who is not at least six feet two."

But by the time Marnie graduated from Vassar in June, she and Bill were engaged. Wedding plans were being made when she and our cousin Paula (Cargill, Sr.'s daughter) accompanied father to Jamaica on the *Carmac II* in June. At this point, the wedding was suddenly in question as Marnie was not comfortable with Bill's unexpected announcement that he intended to become a minister.

"Marnie flatly states (and I commend her position) that she will not be the wife of a churchman," my father informed my mother from *Carmac II* on June 23. "At the moment . . . the odds seem against any wedding on Aug. 20th, but you can't tell. . . . I think you should go ahead with all your wedding plans, but do not (I suggest) let any invitations go out until we return home on the 14th [of July]. Also, don't think of expense. Our children's happiness is always foremost." Bill soon capitulated to Marnie's ultimatum that he choose between her and the church, but Marnie was still uncertain. In fact my parents pressured her strongly to proceed in spite of her reservations.

"Marnie seems very very happy, but simply terrified at the thought of marriage—nothing to do with Bill, it's just fear of the unknown," my father wrote to my mother on July 10 before leaving Jamaica. He could not conceive of Marnie not being happy with Bill, he said.

My mother was now in full swing with the wedding preparations, and Marnie was swept along, whatever her fears. "Your mother is a total wreck from the wedding preparations, while Marnie positively blooms the more she does," father wrote Hugh in the army on August 17. "She seems to have the constitution of an ox and I never saw a youngster more happy."

The bridal dinner at Woodhill on Thursday evening, August 19, 1954, "was the finest bridal dinner I ever attended," John, Jr. wrote. The wedding the next day at Westminster Presbyterian Church in Minneapolis was a grand affair. Paula MacMillan was Marnie's maid of honor, and my sister's eight bridesmaids included Sally. Hugh and I were ushers. At the reception at my parents' home, reminiscing with Bill's father, John, Jr. learned that "as far as I can make out that part of Wisconsin which was not logged by my grandfathers [was] logged by his, which made for a rather interesting situation."

Father was very fond of Bill and wanted to bring him into the Cargill training program. "I know he would be a fine addition to the Cargill team," father wrote to Hugh a year later in August 1955.

But weeks after that letter, the marriage was over. "Marnie is home, as you know, and very tired and somewhat listless," John, Jr. wrote to Hugh and Susie in October. "I suspected for a while that she might have some other romantic interest but I am positive this is not the case. I think Bill is just too immature for her. At any rate we were all terribly distressed over the separation and there is nothing whatever one can do about it and it is one of those things which simply cannot be criticized."

Four months after Marnie's marriage to Bill Kimberly, my boyhood friend David Bell married Bill's sister Jo Kimberly Smith, a young widow with a baby son. Six months to the day that he was married, Marine Lieutenant David Bell crashed in the fog while flying a fighter jet over the Sea of Japan. His wife Jo was pregnant and on her way to Japan when the accident happened. She was met at the plane with the news that David had been lost. His parents Charles H. and Lucy Winton Bell established the David Winton Bell Foundation in Minneapolis in his memory.

The loss of David was enormous for me. I will always remember and cherish his friendship, along with his energy, drive, curiosity, and irrepressible love of life. I spent many hours in his home when I was growing up. His family became like a second family to me. I treasure those happy memories and their continuing friendship, particularly that of his father, Charles H. Bell, who recently celebrated his ninetieth birthday.

The family ready to sail for Europe on the Queen Elizabeth *in May 1956. Left to right are Cargill MacMillan, Sr., his wife Pauline, Marion, Marnie, their friend Mrs. Hill, John, Jr., and another friend, Mrs. Hawkes. John, Jr. did not sail with the others, but flew instead to London where they joined him on the* Carmac III.

The post-war 1950s were a time of gutsy growth for Cargill, Inc. Expanding its export operations to all four coasts, the company built, bought, leased, and enlarged its elevators at key ports. In Portland, Oregon, Cargill acquired the terminal elevator facilities of Kerr, Gifford & Company.

"Last Saturday I went out to Portland with John Peterson on the Empire Builder where we spent Monday inspecting our properties and getting to know the organization," my father wrote in November to Sally and me on our honeymoon. "They really have a tremendous operation there, operating three terminal elevators and a dock which handles general cargo for the public. We are going to add five million bushels of space to one of the elevators . . .

"The Kerr-Gifford organization is extremely high-grade and you can see what old Mr. Peter Kerr was like through his organization. His two sons-in-law took us out to his house for tea. The old gentleman is 92 years and he has a perfectly glorious home a few miles out of the city with a garden that is almost unique. He makes walking sticks for a hobby and as a mark of great honor he presented Mr. Peterson and myself each with one. They are made of holly and really beautiful affairs. . . .

"We are under terrific pressure from all directions," my father continued. "Baton Rouge wants to build us an elevator. The Pennsylvania railroad wants to build us one at Norfolk, and we are under pressure for another one on the St. Lawrence River. Naturally we cannot do all these things at once but they are all highly desirable projects and it is rather distressing to have to push these people aside knowing that they might be able to interest some of our competitors.

"I am also going over to Stillwater tomorrow to address the Country Division on what we expect of them in the next few years. We are making a determined effort to buy more and more grain in the country and less and less on the trading floors in Minneapolis and Duluth, and up-to-date we have done pretty well. When I came into the business we had some 200 country elevators in the four Northwestern states. Today we are down to 34, and on the 34 we purchased more than twice the largest amount we ever purchased with 200. I call this progress. We usually buy about a hundred million bushels of grain in these four states and we are already buying nearly 60 million through our branch offices and country elevators and direct by truck at Port Cargill and Duluth.

"I look for great things from our transportation division. We are already bringing large amounts of coal and molasses up the river and have just contracted to bring some peanuts, and are working on a deal which will enable us to bring China Clay from Georgia to Wisconsin and sugar from New Orleans to Chicago. It is all very exciting and very interesting."

My official entry into the grain business dates to the spring of 1954 when I was admitted to membership on the Minneapolis Grain Exchange. Identifying me as "a fifth-line descendant of the Cargill and MacMillan families," the Minneapolis paper reported:

"'Dunc,' as he is called on the trading floor . . . got his first taste in the grain trade at 17, when he spent the summer vacation in Cargill's grain sampling room. Since then, he has trained at country and terminal elevators. Now married and 23, Duncan will be an assistant to Clyde C. Cook, Sr., who is in charge of spring wheat merchandising for Cargill at Minneapolis. . . . His cousin, Cargill MacMillan, Jr., also a fifth-line descendant to enter the grain business, was a member of the Minneapolis exchange in 1952. Currently, he is at the firm's New York offices."

> Records of the Minneapolis exchange [the newspaper continued] show that the first member of the family to become a member of the exchange was William A. Stowell, who was admitted Aug. 5, 1885. Next in line came W. W. Cargill, son-in-law of Stowell, who also was admitted early in the '80s. On Oct. 20, 1903, John H. MacMillan, son-in-law of W.W. Cargill, stepped into the ranks, later to be followed by his son, John H. MacMillan, Jr., who became a member Nov. 18, 1921, and finally "Dunc."

I was working on the trading floor about a month later when my father showed up unexpectedly. It was the first time he had been on the trading floor in several years, and many of the men didn't recognize him at first.

> It is hard to realize it [my father wrote to Hugh] but I am now one of the Senior Members of the active grain trade, and I could see from the way they all looked at

me they thought that Methuselah himself had appeared. In fact it is not too much to say that my appearance created something of a sensation. I had to introduce myself to the doorman, but after all I had lost 67 pounds since I worked on the floor.

Sally and I set up housekeeping in a rented guest cottage in Ferndale, which was near my parents' home in Orono. It was freezing in the winter and hot in the summer, but Sally thought it was charming. Nine and a half months after we were married, our daughter Sarah was born in July 1954. She was only six weeks old when she had a hemolytic crisis that required a blood transfusion, so we knew that she had inherited my condition. Doctors at Boston Children's Hospital removed her spleen a year later, on her first birthday.

"I am thrilled that Sarah is coming along so well and your letter telling about this condition being mistaken for malaria was most illuminating," my father wrote following her surgery. "I have no doubt whatever that my Father was the carrier and I think it very likely that we have other members of the family with mysterious life-long ailments, like Aunt Janet [who] may have had the same condition."

By then Sally and I were living in Montreal. In September 1954 Peter Brees, a Belgian who was the first foreign Cargill trainee hired as an overseas manager, had started up "Kerrgill" (later Tradax, Canada, Ltd.) to handle Cargill's international operations. As Erv Kelm had decided that I would benefit from a

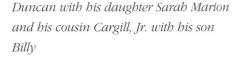

Duncan with his daughter Sarah Marion and his cousin Cargill, Jr. with his son Billy

A white frame tract house Sally and I rented in Pointe Claire outside Montreal

year's experience there, seeing an entire crop through, Sally and I moved in April 1955.

I have vivid memories of the day our second daughter Kitty (Katherine Wells) was born. When Sally telephoned me at the office that she needed to go to the hospital, a snowstorm turned a thirty-minute trip home into two and a half hours. We then had to fight our way back to Montreal with a detour into a ditch. I pushed the car back on the road with Sally at the wheel. Although we made it to the hospital on time, Kitty was born with what now seemed to be the inevitable blood condition. She soon had her spleen removed.

For a young and inexperienced person, my assignment in Montreal was difficult. I was sent there as a merchant, but in addition, my father and Erv Kelm had charged me with the responsibility of keeping them informed about the new venture's activities. The role of sleuth was not comfortable to me. However, I enjoyed what independence I had, and the challenge of the new experience. Sally and I liked Montreal and made lifelong friends there.

We were no sooner settled in Canada, however, than my father was making plans to move us abroad. "My own thinking," he wrote on May 31, 1955, "is that we should rush the transfer of our headquarters to Europe, leaving in Montreal just a forwarding office for Canadian grain and domestic sales in Canada. I thought for a long time we would need a big layout there as this would be the North American headquarters of Cargill International, but I am inclined more and more to thinking that it will be unnecessary if we have our headquarters in Geneva as Cargill International could then use our Canadian and American companies as their North American agents, just as we are agents for others in Europe."

The next year in May we all went to Europe. Packed for a month abroad, my parents and Marnie took the Burlington *Zephyr* train from Minneapolis to Chicago and changed trains for New York. My mother and Marnie, joined by

Cargill and Pauline MacMillan, sailed the next day on the *Queen Elizabeth* for Southhampton. After seeing them safely off, my father took an evening train to Durham, North Carolina, for two days of routine lab tests at Duke. "Seems I am not to blame for Duncan's hemolytic anemia," he scribbled in his diary.

My father weighed only 133 pounds, but Dr. Kempner wanted him to lose five more pounds. He was advised to increase his potatoes intake to eight ounces daily and eat eight ounces of steak each week, and he could have an additional twelve ounces of meat weekly that had been boiled five times to render it salt-free. Dr. Kempner also recommended that he "SLOW UP," my father wrote.

John, Jr. didn't know the meaning of the words. His mind occupied with expansive plans for Cargill, Inc., he returned to New York, where he cooked his own lunch and dinner at the Statler Hotel before taking a bus to the airport for a PanAm flight to London.

"Perfect flight except . . . went to MEN's room & on way back FAINTED in Aisle," he scrawled. "Also regurgitated while out. What a MESS." Blaming his "syncope" on the "very large dinner" he had prepared, he wrote Dr. Kempner, "The moral of course is that 'gluttony must be avoided at all hazards.'"

Arriving in London on a Sunday morning, John, Jr. boarded the new *Carmac III* at St. Catherine's Dock to wait for his family. (The *Carmac II*, which Cargill, Inc. had purchased in 1955, had turned out to have too many problems.) Still not well but maintaining his exercise routine, John, Jr. took a two-hour stroll through Wapping that evening. "FELT LIKE HELL," he wrote in his diary. I arrived the next day from Montreal by plane, and was on hand when reporters caught up with my father in the early evening.

Publicity was of no value to him in his business, John, Jr. told the *Daily Mail*, but he was always eager to spread the gospel of good health. The next day's paper carried a jaunty picture of him taking his constitutional that accompanied an article headlined "HOW I KEEP ALIVE, MILLIONAIRE MUST NEVER TAKE SALT":

> A tanned and smiling millionaire stood in a shabby dockland street beside the Thames last night and talked about—salt. "I should have died ten years ago," said 60-year-old John H. MacMillan. "But I have kept going because I never touch salt. Not a single grain of the stuff."
>
> Mr. MacMillan is in dockland to keep away from salt. For this lean, publicity-shunning American grain magnate is staying here, on his white-hulled 243-ton motor yacht rather than risk salt-tainted food in an hotel. . . . Of the price of bread, the grey-haired millionaire would not talk at all. "I am just here to help some friends who have transportation difficulties," he remarked.

Actually, my father had designed a huge, fully rigged sailing barge that he felt certain would reduce the costs of ocean transportation, and he was looking

The world's largest liner, the R.M.S. Queen Elizabeth. *In 1947, responding to an emergency order from the British Ministry of Food, the* Queen Elizabeth *had transported eight thousand bushels of Cargill Crystal Brand seed flax to England in time for spring planting.*

for the right firm to build several of them. A month before he had written Hugh: "As matters stand now, we will have somewhere between 70 and 75,000 square feet of sail area and probably about 1200 HP in the kicker. I hope to get by with a crew of not over 18 and we will make it self-unloading, so we should never have to spend more than two days in port."

The *Queen Elizabeth* arrived a day late, on Tuesday, and father and I met mother and Marnie and Cargill and Pauline at the boat train. London was the first leg of a whirlwind European study and inspection trip aboard the *Carmac*; we wined and dined our foreign agents in London, Kiel, Copenhagen, Helsingborg, and Hamburg. "It's been lots of fun, but it's been a terrific schedule," Marnie wrote on May 20 to Hugh and Susie. Hugh, now out of the army, was working for Cargill, Inc. in Baton Rouge as a grain merchant and assistant buyer.

"[In Hamburg] we took a cooks tour [the correct spelling is "Cooke's," for British travel agent Thomas Cooke and Sons] around the shipyards and the No. and So. Elbe in the freezing rain [she continued]. We were out in an open top launch for two hours looking at big boats, little boats, big grain elevators, little elevators. We did have fun that night though [when] the whole group went to a typically German beer hall. Most of us drank beer out of beer steins and 'prosted' each other. The high point of the evening was when Ma and Dad and Aunt Pauline and the rest of us got up on the table, linked arms and sang with the crowd. . . . The same thing happened with the press as London. Huge picture of the boat and an article on Mr. MacMillan and Mr. Cargill [Cargill MacMillan], millionaires cruising the world."

John, Jr. on board the Carmac III *in Hamburg, 1956. "Bachman came aboard and took us to office," he wrote in his diary on May 17. "His wife also joined us for luncheon. . . . [In the evening] Marnie, Duncan & Bachman went to* Moulin Rouge, *rest of us to bed."*

However, my father and Uncle Cargill had more on their minds than a pleasure cruise, of course. They had taken the *Carmac* into the North Sea and the Baltic to analyze grain importing opportunities in northern Europe. John, Jr.'s notes indicate that by May 18 he had concluded that Cargill, Inc. should build storage and handling facilities in Rotterdam, Antwerp, Hamburg, and Liverpool, and he wanted to build twenty large ocean-going vessels at a total cost of forty million dollars to carry on the trade. We had also gone to Europe that spring to open our new overseas office in Geneva at 1 Rue Massot (which my father described as "beautiful, but in my opinion a trifle small").

Marnie and I would be staying in Geneva. "Sally arrived by plane from the U.S.", my father noted on May 25. "In p.m. inspected Mother's purchase of two houses one for $142,000 and the other for $72,000. Both beautiful." After a year in Montreal, I had a new assignment trading feed grains overseas. Marnie, whose marriage to Bill Kimberly had broken up, was going to work as a secretary for Walter Gage, the new head of the Geneva office. Sally and I rented the smaller of the two houses purchased with Grandmother's funds (she had never actually seen them), and Walter Gage leased the other.

My father was "wildly enthusiastic" over Geneva. He had fallen in love

Le Manon, *which Sally and I rented from my grandmother*

Duncan and Sally on the Carmac III, *April 1957. We had come aboard in Nice and sailed with my parents on a business trip to Athens and the Greek islands. My father took pride in the fact that the* Carmac III *was the largest American yacht on the seas.*

with the city as a boy during a six-month stay with his mother. "I can think of no more wonderful place to settle," he wrote to Sally and me after arriving home in Minnesota. "I only hope that you can learn to love it as much as I do. One thing is certain you can count on frequent visits from me."

The house Sally and I rented had a beautiful view of the city and Lake Geneva. "The garden looks very good and the best ever since we have been here," I wrote to my father in July 1960. "We have enough flowers to fill every room daily." I also grew corn and other vegetables from seed. Europeans have never had the enthusiasm for sweet corn that Americans do.

Geneva was an old world culture that was responding to and changing rapidly with the influx of American companies and modern communications. The challenge of building the new business and seeing the development of the international grain trade in this environment was tremendously exciting.

Outside the business of Cargill, Geneva was a marvelous place to live for a young American family. There was all the fun and pleasure of enjoying its beautiful setting—Sally and I spent many pleasant evenings on the lake in a small motorboat anchored outside the hotels sipping coffee and watching the lights turn Geneva into a bejeweled city—and it was well situated for travel to all of Europe. We all learned French and made wonderful friends.

And my appetite for sports was more than satisfied. I water-skied, played squash and tennis and golf, and joined a hockey team in Geneva. My great joy was skiing. Every weekend in Geneva we would attack the slopes at Megeve, Val d'Isere, Avoriaz, or Chamonix. For several years we rented chalets at Schonreid near Gstaad where we skied with friends from Canada and Minneapolis.

Our personal physician in Geneva was Dr. Jacques Lagier, and beginning in 1964 he and I with several others took yearly week-long ski trips through the heart of the Alpine arc on the Haute Route (high road), probably the world's most challenging sustained ski tour. These ski trips on which we traversed the

Duncan with Kitty and Sarah on Mont Saléve in France

tops of the mountains between Mont Blanc (15,772 feet) and Monte Rosa (15,199 feet) were the true highlight of my athletic life. I loved everything about them— the planning, preparations, getting in shape, reaching the top and skiing down, even returning home sunburned and blistered. My friendship with Jacques Lagier was a significant factor in these adventures. He was a wonderful man on whose insights and advice I relied.

We had some close scrapes together. One time Jacques and I got caught in a whiteout. Jacques dropped into a hole. My tracks disappeared behind me, and I didn't dare move, afraid I would go into the same hole. He finally climbed out, forty-five minutes later, in the blinding blizzard. We bivouacked that night in a shepherd's hut. The next day was beautiful with a foot of powder.

A photograph taken in Switzerland in 1958 when I was twenty-eight. In a birthday letter to me in July, my father had written: "It seems hard for me to believe that it was 28 years ago next Saturday when I watched Bobby Jones sink that 40-foot putt on the 18th green at Interlachen—so you see I had two great thrills on that day!"

296

In April 1957 Austen Cargill died while on a fishing trip near Needles, California. Austen was sixty-nine and had stepped down as chairman of Cargill's board of directors four years earlier (when his place was taken by financial officer John Peterson). He was survived by his wife Anne Ray Cargill and two adopted children, Margaret Anne Cargill of Pasadena and James Ray Cargill of Minneapolis. The son of founder W. W. Cargill, Austen had been part of the Cargill organization since 1909 and was still a member of the board at the time of his death.

"Austen was of course a part of my earliest recollection and we used to play together in La Crosse," Aunt Bess MacMillan Wheeler wrote to my father following Austen's death. "I remember especially Sunday evenings when the two families went to church and we children were under the watchful eye of Aunt Tassie. As I recall 'battle' was our favorite—consisting of rolled up newspapers for weapons. The fact that I was four years older enabled me to compete in what sounds like a boy's game."

In an earlier era, Cargill, Inc. had been run by a triumvirate consisting of John H. MacMillan, Sr., his brother Dan McMillan, and Austen Cargill. When the next generation of MacMillans—my father and his brother Cargill MacMillan—came into leadership roles in the company, Austen again represented the Cargill family. Austen had been party to the failed plot to oust John H. MacMillan, Sr. in 1925, but the families had gotten past this, and Austen and my father and Uncle Cargill worked well together. His death was a great loss to the company and actually prefigured the end of the "John, Jr. years." Within a few years my father would also be gone and his brother Cargill incapacitated.

The New York Times announced in August 1957 that John H. MacMillan, Jr. had been named chairman and chief operating officer of Cargill, Inc. His brother Cargill succeeded him as president. Keeping in touch with his cousin William Cargill, his childhood playmate from La Crosse, John, Jr. wrote to him after Christmas on December 27: "Marion and I are off for Jamaica tonight, so I thought before I left I would write just to bring you up-to-date on some of the family gossip . . .

Austen Stowell Cargill, in an oil painting by Edward V. Brewer

Mother . . . is now 86 years old, but in remarkably vigorous health except for her memory. Cargill has been sick with what was probably pneumonia for nearly all of December but turned up at the office today for the first time and seems well on the mend. . . .Cargill Junior is our Regional Manager with headquarters in Chicago and is doing extremely well, while Whitney is one of our senior merchants here in Minneapolis and also doing very well. He has quite a genius knack for merchandising.

Of my own three, Hugh is here with me in charge of our trucking operations, which have developed to a rather large volume. He is showing good promise and is a driver with great originality. Duncan and Marnie are both in Geneva, where Duncan is

Hugh, Marnie, Marion, John Hugh IV,
and Duncan at Craigbank

also a merchant, and Marnie is studying . . . at the University of Geneva. She is taking post-graduate work in languages [to qualify] as a secretarial interpreter.

The rest of us are all well, although I have a feeling (as always just before vacation) of being pushed around a bit.

Marnie and Hubert Sontheim at
Craigbank, 1958

Our family was growing by leaps and bounds in those years; already my parents had five grandchildren. In addition to our two little girls, Hugh and Susie had three children: John Hugh IV, who was five; David Deere, three, and a new daughter, Kate Bovey, born in July.

In 1958 my sister Marnie married a Swiss lawyer, Hubert Sontheim, who worked in our Geneva office. After visiting all of us in Switzerland that spring, my father wrote Marnie in May, "I cannot tell you how I enjoyed my stay in Geneva and I am especially happy over your choice of Hubert. He is going to prove a valuable addition to the family and I look forward to working with him with pleasurable anticipation." Marnie and Hubert were married at Craigbank in Orono in August.

Cargill, Inc. was also growing exponentially. Earlier that year, in anticipation of the opening of the St. Lawrence Seaway, the company had begun construction of a twelve-million-bushel storage and export facility at Baie Comeau in Quebec. This would be my father's last and grandest pet project, but it was plagued with problems.

"We had a real blow today as it develops we cannot possibly get Baie Comeau ready to ship grain before December 1st, and a more realistic date probably is January 1st," John, Jr. wrote to his brother Cargill in April 1958. "The trouble came in the foundation problem on the shipping pier. This pier will take eight months to build instead of the two and a half."

January 1 came and went, and the plant was still a long way from operational. "We are trying to untangle the Baie Comeau mess, but still do not know enough to make any intelligent comments," John, Jr. wrote to John Peterson. "It now turns out that . . . they won't be able to lay the floor in the first big bin until the frost is completely out of the ground, which is usually the first part of June. In late December, Cargill's man on the site wired Minneapolis: "Already too late, with continually below freezing weather, to pour thin slab on ground already frozen, considering that this area is mostly solid rock and rock fill . . . also on a slope."

The next spring there was a fire at Baie Comeau. "That plant seems to be hoodoo'ed," my father wrote to me in Geneva on March 18, 1960, "but I am still hoping we will [be] shipping by the 1st of June and receiving by the 1st of May." Three days later Uncle Cargill suffered a stroke. My father wrote to Marnie and me in Switzerland:

Cargill MacMillan, 1952. Uncle Cargill either read pocket thrillers or geology, archeology, and history texts. "There is nothing in the middle—it's one extreme or the other," he told a reporter in 1957.

The doctor says now that he has had an embolism, a blood clot has broken loose from some part of his body and lodged in his brain, shutting off the circulation in part of the brain. This has resulted in almost total paralysis . . . and the two halves of his body for several days were different in color. . . . His speech . . . is seriously affected [but] his mind seems to be quite clear.

Uncle Cargill was still in the hospital and only slightly improved six weeks later when his mother Edna experienced a severe cerebral hemorrhage. Writing to Marnie and me with updates on their conditions in May 1960, my father exhorted us to watch our own health:

I am enclosing a clipping which I want you to read very carefully. In our family all three factors of which [the writer] speaks are present. We all have a tendency of high blood pressure, we all die of heart disease, and we all have high blood cholesterol due to our liking and craving rich foods. These are three things I want you to be mindful of. They should be watched very carefully.

I am especially concerned over your smoking as that is a serious strain on the heart, and I think undoubtedly the only thing that saved my life was the fact that for practical purposes I stopped smoking at age 24.

Uncle Cargill's absence from the office increased my father's workload, and business was continuing at a good clip, he added. Hugh was "very excited over his towboat [the *Austen S. Cargill*] as the builders are going all-out and making very rapid progress." My father was also "very much elated" by some recent statistics: "We have unquestionably moved into No. 1 place on American grain exports. We are doing about 28.6% of the total, against Continental's 25.4, with Dreyfus and Bunge far behind at 17 and 10, respectively."

The next month John, Jr. had no misgivings about selling all of Cargill, Inc.'s West Coast timber holdings. "I am glad we have cleaned up the timber," he wrote on June 10. "We were badly in need of [cash] as we had to raise $850,000 to pay the inheritance tax on Uncle Austen's estate."

He had just returned from his first trip to Duluth in several years, he said: "I flew up in the morning and back in the afternoon . . . to inspect the new elevators we bought from Norris. . . . It is far and away the best truck location at the head of the lakes and is served by all railroads."

In Switzerland, I had put together our first bulk cement cargo. "The vessel loads June 18 in Antwerp and I think I will go up to take a look," I wrote to my father on June 10. "The whole freight world is watching this business closely as it will entirely alter the nature of the international cement biz. I compare this as an equivalent to the first bulk grain cargo." I was also trading canned goods and frozen chickens, and we were gearing up for the

California peach crop and Argentine pears in the fall.

The next day, I reminded my father, I was representing him in his capacity as president of the Havana Company, one of our subsidiaries, at the launching of the 73,000-ton tanker *J. Paul Getty* at Dunkerque. The president of the Ateliers Chantier de France shipyard was doing the honors, and I would ride down from Paris on his private train.

"Paul Getty, as you may know, is an old classmate of mine at Emerson School," my father wrote back on June 17, "and he certainly has outdistanced the rest of us—in the business world at least." On the by-now-sore subject of Cargill's mammoth Canadian grain elevator, he commented: "Baie Comeau is supposed to receive its first grain tomorrow and I certainly hope everything goes off as planned. That miserable thing has dragged as we never had anything drag before."

All was in readiness on July 27, however, when representatives of the federal and provincial governments and press toured the huge waterside Baie Comeau elevator and joined officials of Cargill Grain Company, Ltd. to witness its consecration in Catholic Quebec.

"I was greatly impressed with the French speaking Bishop Couturier, who blessed the house," my father wrote. "He is only 47 years old and does not look 40 and . . . has a keen commercial instinct. He wanted to know the arithmetic of everything connected with the elevator, which we of course were happy to give him."

In his remarks, my father told visitors that the Baie Comeau project had necessitated the largest capital expenditure in the history of his family firm. In fact, he disclosed, the multi-million dollar structure represented ten percent of the net worth of Cargill, Inc. and was without a doubt one of the most daring investments the corporation had ever made.

The opening of the St. Lawrence Seaway commenced a new age in ocean shipping from North America. Cargill's elevator at Baie Comeau enabled the company to stockpile American and Canadian grain during the Great Lakes summer shipping season for export during the winter when Duluth and other lake ports were frozen. "The only trouble with the new plant is that it simply is not big enough," my father wrote. "The eleven or twelve million bushels of space is only about one-third what we need right now."

With Baie Comeau launched and "off to a wonderful start," Cargill, Inc. was taking on two new businesses in this country, my father informed me on August 9. "One is a program at Port Cargill, where we plan to feed 15,000 steers in partnership with Armour & Company. The other is . . . we are building an egg factory near Memphis in conjunction with a large chain of super markets. Both should be of great help to Nutrena who is urgently in need of this kind of assistance."

To keep tabs on our foreign operations, he and mother were coming abroad in early November. They would fly to Glasgow and there board the

John, Jr., on the right, at the consecration of his grandest pet project, the Baie Comeau elevator in Quebec

Carmac, stopping in Amsterdam and Dunkerque before reaching London, and from there fly to Geneva. "About my provisions," my father wrote in September, "I will need rice, some Matzos, and I am planning to bring with me enough puffed rice to get me back to the Carmac. I will also need about 250 grams of meat [and] fresh vegetables. . . . I am drinking very little if at all. . . . Your mother would like some sherry, a bottle of French vermouth and some Gordon's gin and a modest amount will last her a long time."

This was John, Jr.'s last trip overseas. I recall that while he was in London, he and Erv Kelm and my cousin Whitney went to the top of a grain elevator or flour mill owned by Ranks. A violent gust of wind literally picked my father up off the ground. He was actually sailing when a bystander grabbed him by the coat and saved him from going over.

During the week my parents spent with us in Geneva, my father and I found time to discuss, among other things, canned goods, which we both felt represented a good opportunity for Cargill, Inc. "All in all I feel that we had an extremely valuable trip to Europe, which we should repeat at an early opportunity," he wrote upon returning home. "I am still very anxious to cover the Southern half of the Irish Sea which we were unable to do, but I am even more interested in getting rolling immediately on our tinned goods technique."

The last letter I received from my father is dated November 22. "Dear Duncan," he wrote. "Both Kelm and I have had repeated meetings, and . . . you can rest assured you will receive the utmost of support from here. . . . I am satisfied that this canned goods business of yours is going to furnish us a complete answer to distribution of grain to outports of Europe, besides showing us a profit in, as, of and by itself. The potential is staggeringly great.

"Hughie's christening date [for the *Austen S. Cargill*] is definitely set for December 8th. . . . I hope you will squeeze in a tour with us." Built in St. Louis, the 6,630 horsepower unit was the largest towboat ever built for a non-public inland waterways firm and would routinely handle up to thirty-two fully loaded jumbo barges carrying in excess of forty thousand tons. My father planned to be aboard for its first work trip carrying grain downriver to Baton Rouge immediately following the ceremony. "I am quite excited over the prospects for the trip, and really looking forward to it," he wrote.

"I have been hoping to get a cable from you as to the arrival of the baby [Sally and I were expecting our third child] but no word so far. Our love to Sally. Affectionately, Father."

One day after writing this letter, on Wednesday, November 23, the day before Thanksgiving, my father became faint, or had a stroke, at his dining room table. He had finished dinner and was waiting for dessert. Our housekeeper Martha Norris remembered that she had prepared a persimmon, one of his favorite fruits, but he told her, "Martha I'm sorry. I cannot eat my dessert." My mother and Martha got him upstairs and into bed and called the doctor, who put him in the hospital. I flew home from Geneva the following day, but my father was never himself again.

It was a hectic time. In Geneva, the day after I left for Minneapolis, Sally gave birth to our third daughter, Lucy Caroline. In Minneapolis my father underwent an operation at Methodist Hospital to relieve pressure caused by internal bleeding in his brain. The result was that he developed horrible epileptic-like seizures; three men could not hold him down.

"Mr. MacMillan seemed in rather good spirits on leaving the office the morning of the 23rd," his secretary Leo Sheehan wrote to friends of my parents in Jamaica. "However I might say that his cousin Howard McMillan (about John and Cargill's age) passed away suddenly the evening before of a heart attack and this naturally was a source of considerable grief to him."

My father had actually been doubly upset by his cousin Howard's death because there were hard feelings between the two men. In 1956 Howard had sold Cargill common stock he owned back to the company for what he felt was an unfair price. Thereafter, although the two men (and their families) remained close, their relationship was never what it had been. Upon learning that Howard had died, my father was devastated; he would now never be able to make amends to his lifelong friend.

Following three brain operations in Minneapolis, my father, unconscious and with a tube in his brain, was flown in a navy plane to Durham, North Carolina. It was too late to do anything for him, and he died at Duke University Medical Center on December 23. The next day's *New York Times* noted that Cargill, Inc. had more than tripled in size under John, Jr.'s management over the

The towboat Austen S. Cargill, *christened on schedule at the Market Street dock in St. Louis on December 8, 1960, while John, Jr., laid unconscious in a Minneapolis hospital. Austen's daughter Margaret Anne Cargill did the honors.*

past twenty-some years. "Its annual sales volume is more than a billion dollars, making it the nation's largest grain-handling company."

A memorial service was held at Westminister Presbyterian Church in Minneapolis, and my father's ashes were placed in the sundial at Craigbank. After my mother's death in 1980, his remains and hers were buried at Lakewood Cemetery in Minneapolis.

My father had reached Cargill, Inc.'s mandatory retirement age of sixty-five on December 1 while he lay in a coma at Duke University. However, he had not intended to withdraw altogether from the company. Instead, John, Jr. had planned to head up Cargill's foreign operations from Geneva—the city with which he had become smitten as an eleven-year-old boy and that he still loved above all others.

With the death of my father, the management of Cargill, Inc. passed, for the first time, out of the family. His death, then, marked the end of an era. When I think about my father, the characteristic which has left the strongest impression me, and which, I believe, most defined him, was his ceaselessly questing mind. He was an enormously restless person, who was constantly inventing and creating. Under his leadership many aspects of the grain business were completely restructured. He was continuously trying to introduce improvements and innovations to every area of Cargill's business activities.

A quintessential maverick, he clung to certain rigid notions, while at the same time espousing the most forward thinking and pioneering ideas. He understood the dangers of salt, cholesterol, overweight, and smoking long before they were widely recognized. Certain proof of his eccentricity (and frugality) was the sight of my father wearing a red handkerchief in the style of a pirate on the golf course. He explained to his family and friends that laundering a cotton handkerchief was less expensive than dry cleaning a golf hat.

For my father the corporation came first, even before family. He admitted that he was negligent as a father, and I believe that all of his children suffered from his absence. However, he passed to me a love of the history of the family and a devotion to the company that have been significant constants in my life.

John H. MacMillan, Jr., in an oil painting by Edward V. Brewer

EPILOGUE

The history of Cargill, Incorporated is to a large extent the history of the American grain business. But that business, especially in the last four decades, can only be understood in global terms and against the backdrop of its earlier history.

Cargill was founded in 1865, just as the Civil War ended and the titanic energies unleashed by that conflict were turning towards the conquest of the West. The company grew rapidly from the start. The nation's railroads expanded explosively in the last decades of the nineteenth century, and the number of miles of track, a mere 35,000 miles in 1865, increased to more than 250,000 by 1890. Much of this railroad building took place in the Great Plains, making possible the settlement and development of millions of acres of some of the finest grain-growing land in the world.

The railroads also efficiently linked these new agricultural areas to the growing markets of the rapidly industrializing East and to the wharves of the Atlantic ports. Grain dealers like Cargill became a second but equally vital link between the western farmers who grew the grain and the eastern cities that consumed it in ever-increasing quantities. Bringing buyers and sellers together, after all, is precisely what a broker does.

American grain production soared. In 1870 there had been only 2,660,000 farms in the United States. A mere thirty years later, in 1900, there were 5,740,000, while the nation's total acreage devoted to crops more than doubled as well. Even more dramatic was the acreage devoted to grain production. In 1866, the year after Cargill was founded, the nation raised corn on 30,017,000 acres. By 1900 American farmers were planting 94,852,000 acres of corn. Wheat acreage, too, more than tripled from 15,408,000 to 49,203,000.

While the growth of corn, wheat, and other traditional grain crops would continue in the twentieth century—due more to increased yield than to increased acreage—another major crop joined them, one almost unknown in the nineteenth century.

Although widely grown in eastern Asia since antiquity, the soybean remained little more than a botanical curiosity in the West until the late-nineteenth century. In 1900 no more than two thousand acres were planted to soybeans in the entire country. By the 1960s, however, the United States was producing about sixty percent of the world's supply. By 1991 soybeans were being grown on fifty-eight million acres (an area more than twice the size of New York State), exceeding the total land devoted to wheat.

There are several reasons for this extraordinary growth. The soybean is remarkably versatile. A bushel of soybeans produces about eleven gallons of oil that is useful in both food products and numerous industrial applications. The same bushel also yields about forty-seven pounds of soybean cake, essential for a wide variety of animal feeds as well as human food supplements. Soybean plants also make excellent forage and green manure.

This was the swiftly changing agricultural and commercial world into which Cargill was born and in which it flourished. In the first ninety years of its existence, Cargill grew to be one of the country's leading grain dealers. Remarkably, this took place under the leadership of only three chief executives: the founder, W. W. Cargill; his son-in-law John MacMillan, Sr.; and the latter's son, John MacMillan, Jr. Each brought to the role qualities needed for success in his time, and these qualities were different, just as the times were different.

W. W. Cargill was a classic nineteenth-century entrepreneur: a risk-taker and a visionary with a boundless faith in the promise of the country. John MacMillan, Sr., on the other hand, was perfectly suited to reshape the company in the troubled times after W. W.'s death, when what was needed were caution, organization, and financial and accounting sophistication. John MacMillan, Jr., in turn, expanded his father's circumspect midwestern outlook into an international perspective. This was vital to the success of Cargill, Incorporated in the rapidly integrating global economy of the post-World War II era.

The sudden death of John MacMillan, Jr. on December 23, 1960, marked a profound time of transition for Cargill. Two other members of the family management team had also recently left the scene, adding to the air of uncertainty. Austen Cargill, the company president, had died in 1957, and Cargill MacMillan, who replaced him in that office, suffered a massive stroke early in 1960 and could no longer take an active role in company affairs.

The loss of these three men in so short a time was a great blow to Cargill. They had been extraordinarily effective as a team, each supplying strengths that the other two lacked. To somewhat oversimplify three complex personalities, John MacMillan, Jr. had been the idea man, the corporate visionary with a gift for anticipating trends in the market and the economy as a whole and for devising profitable ways to exploit those trends. Cargill MacMillan was the numbers man, the bean-counter, who helped keep his brother's ideas from getting out of hand. Austen Cargill was the one with the common touch. His intuitive understanding of business politics and public relations greatly helped the development of company plans and policies.

Although a number of younger members of the family were coming up in the company, none of them had yet acquired general management experience, and none held a seat on the company board. For the first time, Cargill, Incorporated was faced with the necessity of turning to non-family members for senior management expertise.

Five of these young heirs, Whitney MacMillan and his brother Cargill, Jr., their first cousins, Hugh and Duncan MacMillan, and Austen Cargill's son James, met several times in 1961. All in their thirties and each holding a junior position in the company management, they developed a list of what they considered the most important family objectives to be.

Three of these objectives were deemed to be of great importance. First, control of the company should remain with the family. Second, the policy of spurring capital growth by retaining earnings within the company should continue. And third, the company's long tradition of responsibility towards its employees should be carried forward.

But their overriding objective was to assure that "best management to the top" should always be the company's policy, rather than accommodating the interests of individual family members. John MacMillan, Jr., for instance, had wanted one of these younger heirs to be elected to the board, favoring James Cargill. But the group put its own interests aside, informing the board: "It is our strongest belief that the Board must be made up of the best men available. . . . Under no circumstances do we want you to consider John's promise . . . to be a command to you." And, indeed, the board decided to elect Sumner B. Young, a Cargill lawyer, to the vacant seat.

Erwin E. Kelm, who had replaced Cargill MacMillan as president, now headed the management team running Cargill. He was the first non-family member to do so in the nearly century-long history of the company. Erwin Kelm had graduated from the University of Minnesota in 1933 as a marketing major. The country was mired in the depths of the Great Depression, but he received two job offers, one from Montgomery Ward and the other from Cargill. He chose Cargill and remained with the company for his entire career.

Kelm soon proved himself a more than capable grain trader. He loved the hurly-burly of the game and possessed that deep drive to win which is crucial for long-term success. By the end of World War II, he was vice president in charge of the Grain Division. In 1954 he became operations manager of the company and a year later was elected to the board of directors. Kelm remained the head of the company until 1977, serving as chairman of the board after 1968. By the time Kelm retired, after seventeen years, the company had changed greatly from what it had been only two decades earlier, as had the world in which it operated and the corporate culture of Cargill itself.

Like John MacMillan, Jr. before him, Erwin Kelm felt that the management of Cargill required more than one hand at the helm. He soon appointed two executive vice presidents, Fred Seed and Bob Diercks. Seed had graduated from the University of Minnesota the year before Kelm, in 1932, and like Kelm had immediately gone to work for Cargill. He started as a grain merchant, but broadened his experience by working subsequently for the feed and transportation divisions. In 1946 he was named head of the Vegetable Oil Division and became the youngest man to take a seat on the board of directors. He ultimately replaced Kelm as president when Kelm became chairman of the board.

Bob Diercks was also a graduate of the University of Minnesota, earning his degree in 1937. Going to work first in the export department of the Grain Division, he later became a branch and then merchandising manager. In 1954 he was appointed vice president in charge of the Grain Division; five years later he was elected to the board.

This new team proved quite as effective as the old family team under John MacMillan, Jr. The fact that such talent was available is a tribute to the longstanding company policy, begun in the late twenties, of recruiting managerial candidates right out of college and training them within the company for positions of greater responsibility commensurate with their growing experience. This policy, adopted decades before other large companies began to use it, is no small part of the reason that Cargill has flourished.

A related policy of almost equal importance was the company's time-honored practice of promoting from within. Rather than hiring executives from outside the company, Cargill had a tradition of meeting increased management needs in a division by seeking out talent in other divisions and transferring and retraining as necessary. This policy has given Cargill two great advantages. First, it produced a cadre of management with diverse experience in the ever-widening range of Cargill's activities. Second, it fostered an intense company loyalty among its management employees.

Three short years after John, Jr.'s death, 1963 would turn out to be a watershed year for Cargill owing to three major events—one internal, two external. In a decisive break with the past, Cargill arranged for a thorough review of its methods and practices by a team from Chase Manhattan Bank. Chase Manhattan had been the company's banker for decades, but this study marked a new development in the relationship. The review was prompted by the decline in profits the company had experienced since 1960. While company earnings had averaged $5.5 million during John, Jr.'s final six years, in 1962 they stood at $3.5 million.

The Chase Manhattan study of Cargill's operations, business practices, and organization marked the opening up of a company that had always been very private, both in its ownership and in its culture. Up to this point it had not even had an outside director. John MacMillan, Jr. had liked the idea of a board that could assemble "on five minutes' notice," and dismissed the value of an independent voice.

But the Chase Manhattan study, although many of its recommendations were slow to be accepted, or even rejected outright, shook up the company and its management in many positive ways. There was a dramatic improvement in company profits. In the fiscal year 1965–66, profits soared to a record $16.7 million. While by no means all of that improvement can be attributed to Chase Manhattan's recommendations, they did provide the basis for justifying changes to corporate operations and decision making. The study greatly strengthened the company by preparing it for the economic revolution that was sweeping the business world.

Ironically, during the same year that the Chase Manhattan team showed Cargill ways to meet the future, the company became deeply enmeshed in an episode that today, only thirty-five years later, reads like ancient history. But it remains one of Wall Street's more famous moments, the so-called salad-oil scandal.

Anthony "Tino" De Angelis, an oil trader and speculator, attempted to corner the market in both soybean and cottonseed oil that year. To do this, he bought vast quantities of both commodities on the spot and futures markets and claimed to be storing them in the tank farm he owned in Bayonne, New Jersey, just across upper New York Bay from lower Manhattan.

To finance his continuing purchases and trades in the futures market, he sold warehouse receipts for this oil, mostly to a subsidiary of American Express called the American Express Field Warehousing Company. When American Express tried, in turn, to sell this paper transaction, it needed an audit to certify that the oil was indeed where the warehouse receipts said it was and in the quantities specified. The ensuing inspection of De Angelis's tanks revealed that they were mostly empty.

The results were spectacular. On November 19, 1963, De Angelis's Allied Crude Vegetable Oil Refining Company filed for bankruptcy. But the disaster did not stop there. Two major Wall Street brokerage houses, Ira Haupt and Co. and Williston and Beane, had been deeply involved in De Angelis's speculations, and with his failure their own was imminent. They were both suspended from trading on Wednesday, November 20, and the threat of panic gripped Wall Street.

In those days securities held in "street name" and cash balances on deposit with brokers were not insured as they are today. That meant that if these two firms went under, their thirty thousand customers might find their assets tied up for years in bankruptcy proceedings. They and customers of other brokers' houses began demanding delivery of securities and cash balances. It was the Wall Street equivalent of a run on the bank, with sound institutions threatened as much as weak ones. Williston and Beane was reinstated when Merrill Lynch offered it a half-million-dollar loan to meet capital requirements and announced it was prepared to take the firm over if necessary (which, in the end, it did). There was no saving Ira Haupt, however, and the New York Stock Exchange, for the first time in its history, arranged the orderly liquidation of a member firm in order to assure calm on Wall Street.

This Wall Street drama was carried out within the far larger drama surrounding the Kennedy assassination, which took place that Friday, November 22, causing instant panic on the Exchange until the Board of Governors was able to meet and order it closed.

Cargill never had any financial dealings with De Angelis himself, who went to jail, or the brokerage houses that fell with him. But the company was seriously affected because it was in the vegetable oil business and in the futures market for vegetable oils during the ordinary course of its affairs. Many other oil dealers and processors who had depended on the De Angelis operation of storage facilities found themselves caught up as well.

Oil prices plummeted in the wake of the scandal, while meal—a byproduct of soybean oil production—soared. Cargill initially took a write-off of $1,488,000 on its Allied loss, no small sum when company profits in 1964 were $7,737,000.

American Express, although under no legal obligation to do so, assumed responsibility for its subsidiary's obligations, allowing Cargill to recoup part of its losses. Still, it was an expensive lesson in the hazards of the marketplace. Cargill's Oil Division learned those lessons quickly. "We view the past year," said its annual report for 1963–64, "as a sort of arduous shakedown cruise, testing our organization and policies of past years." That was putting things mildly.

The third challenge to Cargill was the beginning of a fundamental shift in the global grain trade, which caused an equally significant change in the company outlook. The international market in grain began a period of growth such as it had not known since the late-nineteenth century. The Soviet Union and other countries in the Communist Bloc played a large part in this development.

Imperial Russia had been a major player in that nineteenth-century grain market. In the favorable years before World War I it had, in fact, been the world's leading exporter of grain. But the war crippled Russian exports, and after the war Communism and Stalin's forced collectivization devastated Soviet production. With Stalin's death in 1953 and a loosening of the terror with which he had ruled, the situation began to change. Under Stalin public opinion, for all intents and purposes, did not exist. But by the early 1960s the Soviet government began to curry domestic popular favor, making the steady improvement of living standards state policy. Soviet agriculture, however, still hobbled by Communist doctrine, could not increase the food supply. So Nikita Khrushchev made a momentous decision. Swallowing its pride, the Soviet Union would buy what it needed abroad.

In September 1963 Canada announced that it would sell $500 million worth of wheat to the Soviet Union. This was the largest single international grain sale in history up to that point, and its effects on the commodity markets were profound and long-term. Rumors raced through the market that the Soviet Union was looking to buy much more wheat from other grain-producing countries. When these rumors turned out to be correct, the United States, the largest grain-grower of all, was presented with a great dilemma.

American farmers, supported by subsidies devised in the terrible years of the 1930s, grew far more grain than the domestic market could absorb. A great new overseas market was a heaven-sent solution to the chronic surpluses of American agriculture. But selling grain to the Soviet Union, it was thought, might only strengthen our primary political adversary. Both the Democratic and Republican parties were sharply divided on the issue. Many labor unions objected, including even the Longshoremen's Union, which stood to gain significantly in jobs from any large grain sale to Russia. But President Kennedy, who had the power to make the final decision, agreed to the sale, arguing that it was a sign that "a more peaceful world is both possible and beneficial to us all." Early in 1964 Cargill, Incorporated signed an agreement with the Soviet Union to supply it with 700,000 tons of wheat.

Other eastern-bloc countries also wanted to buy American grain. Cargill was the first to make a major sale, 100,000 tons of wheat to Hungary that soon swelled to 220,000 tons. Fortuitously, Cargill had a Geneva-based subsidiary, Tradax, which was in closer touch with European grain markets than was possible in North America. This office was well positioned to strike a deal quickly.

The impact of these sales both on Cargill's bottom line and the management's confidence was considerable. In 1962–63, the company had earned $4.3 million. The following year, it earned $7.7 million, an increase of fully seventy-nine percent. Earnings would have been even higher, had not the salad-oil scandal cut deeply into profits that year. Yet profits still amounted to forty percent of sales in 1963–64, up from twenty-five percent the year before.

These numbers assured the new management that it was heading the company in the right direction. Erwin Kelm wrote in the first "Cargill Annual Report" that "There is no question in my mind that we have all the resources—the personnel, the will, the programs—to make next year, Cargill's 100th year, the greatest in its history." (As a privately held company, Cargill was not obliged to issue a public report; this report was for internal use and for banks and brokerage houses.)

The second half of the 1960s was relatively calm, at least compared to the time of the first Soviet grain sales and the years to come in the next decade. Erwin Kelm was determined to double the company's net worth in ten years. He accomplished the goal in only seven, when it reached $141,021,000 in 1968.

In the agricultural world, famine in India required the shipment of millions of tons of grains to the subcontinent, and Cargill had a major share of that business. But by far the biggest development in agriculture was the so-called Green Revolution. New varieties of grains and new techniques of husbandry greatly improved the yields in third-world countries and helped solve chronic problems of hunger and poverty. It was in India, the country most threatened by famine in these years, that the potential of these new developments had their strongest showing.

India imported new rice varieties for the first time in 1964, but only enough to plant 200 acres. A scant two years later, at the height of the famine, this new seed was planted on 2,195,000 acres. New dwarf varieties of wheat showed similar figures. The effect on Indian production was pronounced. In 1966–67 India produced 74,230,000 tons of grains. The following year, thanks in large measure to the new seed varieties, production rose to 95,050,000 tons, an increase of twenty-eight percent. India has not been seriously threatened with famine since.

The increasing self-sufficiency of third-world countries in grain production as a result of the Green Revolution would contribute significantly to the relative stagnation of the world grain grade during the next two decades. Cargill, Incorporated would begin diversifying by moving into numerous related and unrelated ventures. The early 1970s, however, also brought about changes in the nature of the Cold War and American foreign policy that permitted massive grain sales to the Soviet Union.

In June 1971, when President Richard Nixon made world headlines by ending the trade embargo with China that had been in place since 1950, he also removed two Cold War restraints on foreign trade: the need for special export licenses for goods sold to the Soviet Union, and the requirement imposed by President Kennedy that fifty percent of all grain sales to Communist countries be carried in U.S.-flagged vessels.

American vessels, because of unions and numerous governmental regulations, were much more expensive to operate than vessels registered in other countries, especially such "flags of convenience" as Panama and Liberia. The Kennedy stricture had greatly complicated the Russian grain sales of 1964, and its removal increased the chances of developing a continuing commercial relationship with the Soviet Union.

Since 1964 the Soviet Union had preferred to buy its grain from other countries, such as Australia, Argentina, and Canada. But the unusually cold winter of 1971–72 resulted in staggering Soviet crop setbacks. Secretary of Agriculture Earl Butz visited Moscow in the spring of 1972 and met privately for ninety minutes with Leonid Brezhnev, the Soviet leader. It was the first time that a senior American official had met with Brezhnev since Nikita Khrushchev fell from power in 1964 and inspired numerous speculations about new American grain sales.

Such sales were indeed in the offing. When the deals were concluded, their size astonished everyone inside and outside the grain business. On July 8 President Nixon announced that the Soviets had agreed to buy no less than $750 million in American grain over the next three years. The Soviets could choose what mix of grain they wanted, but Secretary Butz said that if they chose to take it all in corn—which was hardly likely—then they would have to buy a total of 550 million bushels, fully ten percent of the massive 1971 corn crop.

The trade press began talking about "unprecedented" sales of as much as 2,750,000 metric tons of grain that year. But when the Russians had completed their first round of buying, they had bought no less than 4.5 million metric tons of wheat and more than four million tons of corn. And they were soon back for more. In July and August they bought an incredible 19,250,000 metric tons of American grain. The Russians handled these massive purchases with great trading skill and without setting off a buying panic in the grain exchanges, a remarkable accomplishment for Communists not supposed to be conversant with market economics.

When the market woke up, however, the effect was enormous. In early July, the December spring wheat futures price was at 153⅝. By August 11 it had risen to 187½. By the time trading on December futures had ended on December 18, the price stood at 260¾. Needless to say, exports and price rises of such magnitude in a basic commodity had a major influence on the American economy as a whole. They were bound to affect not only the price of food, but thousands of other prices as well.

These economic developments generated much public debate and some misunderstanding. George McGovern, a senator from the major wheat state of South Dakota and the Democratic nominee for president that year, accused Nixon of seeking to exploit American farmers by giving the major grain companies a windfall profit from "secret" sales to the Russians. Anyone who understood the grain markets (or, indeed, free markets in general) knew that this strained the facts. But a knowledge of the complexities of free markets is sometimes in short supply on Capitol Hill, and Cargill broke with its usual practice of maintaining a low profile in the press and issued a statement. It was the only major grain company to do so.

The press release called the allegations of collusion "unfounded, uninformed, in many cases patently absurd and, overall, extremely damaging to the open, competitive U.S. marketing system, which serves every element of the agricultural community so well." Cargill stated that at no time during the negotiations was the company "so fortunate to obtain nor were the Soviets so foolish to offer information relating to the total amount of wheat, the classes of wheat involved or the prices the Soviets were willing to pay. To this date, Cargill does not know the total quantity of wheat, the dates of delivery, the classes of wheat involved or the prices at which it was sold."

In 1973, in the wake of these vast Soviet grain purchases, the market for soybeans began to heat up as well. Again, Soviet purchases drove the escalating prices. During the first week in February, prices reached a historic high of more than five dollars a bushel; in the following month they rose to more than seven dollars; and by June they topped twelve dollars. The Nixon administration, badly burned politically by the turmoil in the commodities markets in 1972, acted decisively to prevent a recurrence. On June 27 it banned the export of soybeans and soybean products. Even more punishing for grain traders, the ban was retroactive to June 13. Thus any contracts made with foreign buyers in the previous two weeks were null and void.

The reaction was swift and ferocious. Foreign countries, especially Japan and the Soviet Union, complained that they had been double-crossed, which, indeed, they had. Cargill was both a winner and a loser in the crisis in the soybean markets. As a major crusher in its own right, it stood to gain. As a trader, however, it was much more likely to lose.

While the total embargo lasted only a week, the subsequent licensing requirements were so complex that Cargill was obliged to keep an expert in Washington to deal with them. Further, foreign countries decided to reduce their reliance on the United States for soybeans. Japan, especially, began to increase its orders in Brazil and elsewhere. Cargill, with its very large foreign operations, which included Brazil, was positioned to exploit this trend. Far more interested in long-term relationships than short-term profits, Cargill also made every effort to accommodate its customers in this highly regulatory environment, even offering a "deferred delivery privilege," whereby foreign buyers could take a later shipment rather than accept a timely one that fell short of their needs.

The crises in the grain markets in the early 1970s were a symptom of an unprecedented economic upheaval in the United States and around the world. Inflation, which had been minimal in the 1950s and early 1960s, began to take off. In 1972 it increased more than eight percent. In 1973, despite a less-than-robust economy, it was even worse. The consumer price index, the most common measure of inflation, rose 12.2 percent that year, higher than it had ever risen in a single year except in time of war and its

immediate aftermath. The wholesale price index, a measure of future inflation, rose an astounding 15.5 percent.

The run-up in food prices following the Russian grain sales in 1972 was
a major factor in these grim figures, as food is a major part of any nation's
economy. Equally important was the sharp rise in oil prices in the wake of
the Arab-Israeli war of that year and the subsequent Arab oil embargo.

Cargill, Incorporated not only survived these economically troubled
times, it expanded and prospered. At the end of the Erwin Kelm era in 1977,
Cargill was a fundamentally different company than it had been at the death
of John MacMillan, Jr. in 1960. Under MacMillan, Cargill was a private company in the fullest sense, operating in a freewheeling manner without releas-
ing information about its structure, operations, or finances beyond what was
required by law. Erwin Kelm initiated enormous changes. To be sure, the
company continued to utilize the advantages of being a private rather than
a publicly held company. At the same time, it began to act more like a public company. The management, including family members, was now professional from top to bottom. The company's public relations operation had
been greatly expanded and become more sophisticated. Its interest in and
attention to "stakeholders," such as farmers and employees, increased.

Perhaps most significantly, Cargill, Incorporated was a much larger and
more powerful company in 1977 than it had been in 1960. In 1961 Cargill's
net earnings were $5,088,000 and its net worth was $70,716,000. In 1977, not
a particularly good year for the company, profits were $110,132,000 and its
net worth had climbed to $1,074,132,000.

Part of those increases can be attributed to the soaring inflation that the
world economy experienced in the late 1960s and 1970s. But a large portion
of that growth was actual. When Erwin Kelm became president of Cargill, the
company was only one of several major American grain businesses. When he
stepped down, Cargill was unequivocally the country's largest privately held
corporation and one of the largest grain companies in the world.

It had also diversified considerably. At the beginning of the Kelm era,
grain trading still dominated Cargill's corporate decisions. Under Kelm the
company moved into flour milling and began trading in peanuts, cotton, and
even metals. It emerged as a major player in the cattle feeding business, and
it ventured into economic areas that were completely outside its traditional
core business. Some of these, such as a Holiday Inn in Belgium, a coal mining venture, and solid-waste management were short-lived. Others, such as
steel minimills, became major company operations.

When Erwin Kelm decided to retire in 1977, there was no question
who would succeed him as CEO of Cargill, Incorporated. Whitney MacMillan
took the reins of Cargill back into family hands. MacMillan graduated from

Yale in 1951 and, like so many who have reached senior management level at Cargill, spent his entire career with the company. He continues today as a director emeritus. Beginning as a general trainee, he worked as a vegetable oil merchant in Minneapolis, San Francisco, and the Philippines. After five years he was transferred to the grain division, was made assistant to the president in 1961, and joined the board of directors in 1966. After becoming a vice president and then one of two executive vice presidents, he replaced the retiring Fred Seed as president of the company in 1975.

Following earlier family role models, MacMillan, throughout his years as head of what has become the largest privately held company in the world, has maintained an extremely private and understated lifestyle. Conservative and taciturn by nature, he prefers modest cars which he drives himself and has never indulged in the excesses of power or luxury.

As an executive, however, Whitney MacMillan garnered considerable attention and recognition. As *Fortune* magazine described him, "MacMillan engages in a devil's advocacy style of management. He stakes out deliberately provocative positions and invites lieutenants to prove him wrong—a tactic that sometimes drives them nuts." Further, MacMillan demonstrated the crucial talent of delegating matters to the right people.

Like Erwin Kelm and his uncle John MacMillan, Jr. before him, Whitney MacMillan assembled a first-rate team around him. His inner circle included Pete McVay, who would succeed him as president and chief operating officer. Often described in news stories as "hard-driving," McVay would be the first Cargill president to come out of the processing side as opposed to the trading side of the business—a clear indication of the growing importance of processing to Cargill's operations. Other members of MacMillan's cabinet—all chosen from within the company—were Barney Saunders, Jim Spicola, and Heinz Hutter.

MacMillan, like his predecessors, insisted on the highest standard of integrity, which he believed to be an ethical imperative and, in addition, good business sense. In 1975, as the political fallout from the Russian grain sales (including hearings in Congress) continued, MacMillan, then president but not yet CEO, sent out a memo to every employee, articulating the company ethical standards:

> Our corporate goals and objectives state: Continue to make certain that all employees of the Cargill Companies recognize and adhere to the principles of integrity which have always been basic to our philosophy and upon which the Cargill Companies' reputation is founded.
>
> 1) This means we have a deep responsibility to conduct ourselves and our business under the highest standards of ethics, integrity, and in compliance with the

laws of all countries and communities in which we have been granted the opportunity to perform our services.

2) This means should there be a question concerning a particular practice, open discussion will surely resolve the issue. If a practice cannot be discussed openly, it must be wrong.

3) This means business secured by means other than legal, open, honest competition is wrong.

4) This means if a transaction cannot be properly recorded in the company books, subject to an independent audit, it must be wrong.

5) This means that Cargill does not want to profit on any practice which is immoral or unethical. Should we discover our business being done in any other than an absolutely proper manner, disciplinary action will be taken.

A company with a good reputation is a good place to work. Cargill has enjoyed 110 years of a fine reputation built on integrity. We must maintain our honor and self-respect as a basis of our continued growth and pride in the Cargill Companies.

Today these standards continue to be a cornerstone of Cargill's culture. Even in countries where bribery and under-the-table dealing are common practice, businessmen have come to respect Cargill's policies. They know they can trust the company to play fair, and that is worth a lot in today's business climate.

As CEO after 1977, Whitney MacMillan faced two overriding concerns. The first was the technological revolution that was rapidly reshaping the world and the world's markets. Since the introduction of the microprocessor—essentially a miniature computer that can be cheaply massproduced—in 1971, the world has been undergoing a rate of change unprecedented since the steam engine initiated the industrial revolution two centuries ago. We have by no means seen the end of this new revolution, but it has already profoundly affected our world, including its political and economic spheres.

One of the clearest illustrations of this technological revolution is the rise in overseas phone calls. In the years since 1950, the population of the United States has roughly doubled, while the mail volume handled by the postal service has quadrupled. The number of overseas telephone calls originating in the United States, however, swelled from about a million in 1950 to more than twenty-five million twenty years later. In 1995, the year Whitney MacMillan retired, the number was a staggering 2,821,000,000.

To put it another way, for every overseas call made in 1950, more than twenty-five hundred are made today. Most of these calls are data transmissions, not voice calls, an indication of just how fast information now unites markets around the world. Further, the Internet, which did not even exist in 1970, today handles an unquantifiable but undoubtedly vast number of additional international communications.

This new reality has had enormous consequences in the world economy. Markets that were once fragmented by the high cost—in dollars and time—of communicating coalesced into single worldwide markets beyond the control of national governments. The international currency market, for instance, which now handles about five trillion dollars a day, has replaced the old nineteenth-century gold standard as the means of keeping the monetary policies of national governments in check. As the international currency market emerged in the early 1980s, inflation began to recede.

Further, the world has learned the lessons of the interwar years, when higher and higher trade barriers greatly worsened the Depression of the 1930s. After World War II, the United States pushed relentlessly, through such organizations as GATT (the General Agreement on Tariffs and Trade) and the World Trade Organization, to lower barriers to trade among all countries. The result has been a fifteen hundred percent explosion in global trading.

Much of this incredible increase in trade has been in industrial goods and, especially in later years, services. The world's grain trade peaked in 1979 at 240 million metric tons. In that year the Soviet Union invaded Afghanistan and President Jimmy Carter, seeking to put pressure on the Soviets to withdraw, placed an embargo on American grain sales to Russia. It was one of the more disastrous foreign policy decisions of the Cold War era. What the United States refused to sell, other grain-exporting countries were only too happy to supply. Thus much of the Russian grain trade that the United States had built up during the 1970s was lost, never to return.

Cargill, however, continued to diversify and expand in other agricultural fields. The company moved increasingly up the "value chain" into processing and manufacturing. In the last two decades, Cargill has become one of the largest crushers and processors of oil seeds and corn in the world, the leading manufacturer of animal feed, and, with the acquisition of numerous flour mills, one of the largest flour producers in North America.

Not all of the company's food processing is in grain. In the mid-1970s Cargill made its entry into the meat-packing business through the acquisition and expansion of Excel, a beef processing and packing company in Wichita, Kansas. It has since become one of the top three beef packers in the U.S. and the number one packer in Canada. In 1989 Cargill opened a state-of-the-art beef-packing plant near Calgary, Alberta, which processes 1,700 carcasses a day.

Cargill has an international seed corn business and trades in sugar, coffee, crude oil, hemp, and rubber. It trades and processes cocoa, rice, orange juice, molasses, and cotton. In addition, Cargill mines mineral fertilizer and salt. As it expanded its foreign operations, Cargill became a major player in all of its agricultural activities.

By the end of the Whitney MacMillan era, Cargill product lines were selling in 66 countries, while it continued to trade commodities in no fewer than 161. In the early 1990s fully forty percent of the company's assets were located overseas. Cargill had become, in every sense of the word, a global company. Worldwide Cargill employment tripled between 1977 and 1995 to 73,000. Sales exceeded $50 billion.

A major factor of Cargill's success has been its near legendary worldwide communications systems. Since the days when the Rothschilds used carrier pigeons to learn the news ahead of others in the marketplace, information has always been gold. In the era before the microprocessor, Cargill had the finest telex network available, and more than once the company was ahead even of the U.S. government in gathering information. Today, while any teenager with a personal computer can communicate across the globe in real time, Cargill still manages to lead the way in the business community. One means by which it achieves that is by conducting business in thirty-nine languages.

The company's private status, so long cherished by the two families that owned it, became the second major concern of the Whitney MacMillan era at Cargill. In order to support the corporation's drive to expand, serious consideration had been given during the Kelm era to public ownership. But the long recognized advantages of private ownership still held sway. Private companies enjoy freedom from the dictates of Wall Street. The volatility of an agricultural business such as Cargill would mean a volatile share price on Wall Street, perhaps even dropping below book value in a depressed year. Finally, pride of ownership is deeply ingrained in the corporate culture of Cargill.

On the other side of the issue, there was a demand for liquidity from stockholders not involved in the business as well as from the next generation of family members. Public ownership could provide the capital necessary to meet their needs. Because of the company policy of retaining earnings and paying out only a small percentage of the profits as dividends (in recent years Cargill has paid out only about five percent of its earnings), income to the shareholders has been very limited. As the number of heirs has grown over time (now about eighty), the pressure to unlock these assets has increased. However, the older generation remained extremely reluctant to make so fundamental a shift as going public would have represented.

The solution to these conflicting interests was an Employee Stock Ownership Plan, or ESOP, which took place in 1992. In an ESOP, a block of stock is set aside in trusteeship and employees become beneficiaries, usually as part of their pension benefits. All Cargill stockholders were allowed to tender up to thirty percent of their stock to the plan.

The actual response of the stockholders was surprising. The heirs as a whole opted to sell only seventeen percent of the stock (for a total of $730 million) they held to the trust. Many family members sold no stock. There were numerous and individual reasons for this. Among the strongest of these was the company's performance in recent decades. An illiquid, low-dividend-paying stock in a company whose net worth was compounding at 12.2 percent annually—thus doubling in value every six years for more than fifty years—is not a bad place to keep one's money. The somewhat unexpected outcome of the ESOP offer represented a strong endorsement of the stewardships of Erwin Kelm and Whitney MacMillan.

Like his cousin Whitney, Duncan MacMillan rose from the ranks at Cargill. His work there began even earlier than Whitney's with summer jobs at Grain Elevator T, where he performed such tasks as sweeping grain and cleaning generators. After graduating from Brown University in 1953, Duncan went to work for Cargill full time in the way so many of his forebears had begun their careers, as a grain trader. He was admitted to membership in the Minneapolis Grain Exchange the following spring.

Cargill began to operate overseas at this time, and Duncan was transferred to Montreal and then to Geneva, where he worked for Tradax, Cargill's European trading operation. Geneva had been chosen for Tradax headquarters because of its central position in Europe, because the city and its communications system—vital to a company whose business was trading commodities—had not been damaged during World War II, and because Switzerland was politically and financially stable. Both John, Jr. and Cargill MacMillan also harbored fond memories of Geneva dating back to their childhoods.

Duncan MacMillan spent eight years in Geneva, while Cargill's international reach expanded as never before. "I cut my teeth on international trading in grains and commodities, including steel, in Geneva," he remembered forty years later. The opportunity to live abroad in a French-speaking city was an enriching experience for the whole family, he recalled, but he and his wife chose to raise their four daughters in this country.

When the family returned to Minnesota in 1964, Duncan took over the operation of Cargill Securities Company, which was renamed Waycrosse, Inc. the following year. Waycrosse handles the assets of the Cargill and MacMillan families outside of Cargill, Incorporated. Ironically, its origins lay in a family disaster.

Will S. Cargill, son of the founder, W. W. Cargill, had proved himself a spendthrift, and his cavalier financial habits after his father's death nearly caused the bankruptcy of the company. Cargill Securities Company was set up as a trust to guarantee payment of certain debts and to keep them off the books of the company itself. These debts were paid in 1916, and Cargill Securities, now unconnected to Cargill, Incorporated except through family ties, continued to hold numerous investments made by W. W. Cargill, including timber land in Canada, Montana, and Mexico. Many of these proved unprofitable and required considerable time on the part of John MacMillan, Sr. and his son.

When Duncan MacMillan took over what would soon be Waycrosse, it was a dormant personal holding company, albeit the biggest shareholder in Cargill, Incorporated. His charge was to acquire a sufficient number of businesses to remove it from the status of a personal holding company. He had the full support of family members of his generation, including Whitney MacMillan, Cargill MacMillan, Jr., and James Cargill, who participated in the management of Waycrosse. While Duncan MacMillan was president of Waycrosse, the organization invested in a number of businesses and bought several companies outright: Henderson Manufacturing, Willmar Manufacturing, and Silent Knight Security Systems. He also introduced Cargill to the steel business.

In 1974, during some of the darkest days in the history of the American steel industry, MacMillan saw opportunity in minimills. These are mills that use electric furnaces and scrap steel. They are much more efficient than the old-fashioned giant mills that had symbolized industrial power in the early years of the century. In later decades the original mills had become technologically obsolete and thus uncompetitive.

Duncan noticed that the new technology of minimills neatly coincided with Minneapolis's plentiful supply of scrap steel and shortage of bar rods—the basic form of steel from which such products as reenforcing bars, rods, and angles are made. He encouraged the company to invest in North Star, a recently successful minimill plant built in St. Paul by a Canadian group in which Waycrosse had already acquired a substantial interest. In its first year, North Star posted profits of $10.4 million, a return on net worth of 56.3 percent. On the basis of this very successful performance, Cargill continued to develop a national presence in the minimill arena. By the end of the 1970s the company's annual steel production exceeded one million tons. In the 1990s Cargill emerged as the nation's eighth largest steel company.

Duncan MacMillan became a director of Cargill, Incorporated in 1966 and remained on the board until he reached the mandatory retirement age of sixty-five in 1997. Today he is a director emeritus and still attends and participates in board meetings.

Apart from his key responsibilities at Cargill and Waycrosse, Duncan has been engaged in many major outside commitments. Among the most important of these is a long and mutually rewarding relationship with Brown University.

Most of Duncan's family had gone to Yale, but illness caused him to postpone college for a year, and his father suggested he look into other possible institutions. Brown University attracted MacMillan for its academic reputation, its metropolitan location, and its Division I hockey team. Brown, in turn, learned that MacMillan was very good at sight-reading Latin and not at all bad at scoring hockey goals. The result has been a forty-five-year association that has benefited both Brown and MacMillan. Duncan graduated in 1953 with a B.A. in classics. He was fluent in Latin and conversant in ancient Greek, Spanish, and French. His relationship with nationally renowned classicist John Rowe Workman grew into a close friendship that MacMillan came to regard as one of the most important positive influences in his life.

In an effort to return to Brown what he gained there, MacMillan has served on the Board of Trustees for a total of twenty-five years, working tirelessly to raise funds for the university. Each Christmas he returns to the school as a reader in Brown's Latin carol service, and he continues to give generously to a wide variety of Brown activities and needs.

To help assure a continuation of the university's strong teaching tradition, MacMillan endowed a chair in the Classics Department in 1984 (John Rowe Workman was the first recipient) and a chair in the Humanities Department in 1993. He also endowed a reading room in the John Carter Brown Library, and on February 10, 1995, Brown University announced his gift of ten million dollars for a new undergraduate science center. Wrote one professor, "The new facility will make teaching and learning within the undergraduate labs more *fun* as well as more effective."

"Philanthropy," said MacMillan at the ground-breaking ceremony in 1995, "is investing money to make a better life for people. . . . Philanthrophy is also very personal. Supporting Brown over the years has provided me with enormous satisfaction and pride. I have watched with great delight over this period of time as Brown has become one of our nation's leading universities. Investing in Brown is an investment not only in our university—it is an investment in the future of our nation and our world."

Duncan MacMillan also continues the long nautical tradition of his Cargill ancestors. Some of his happiest memories are of racing "C" scows on Lake Minnetonka near his childhood home with his brother Hugh and his cousin Whitney MacMillan. The first Cargill family pleasure craft, dating from the later years of the nineteenth century, was a houseboat pushed around the Mississippi and other rivers by a towboat. The houseboat's successor was a sternwheeler built in 1904 at La Crosse, Wisconsin, and named the *Ellen* after Duncan's great-grandmother. President William Howard Taft used this vessel for a trip on the Mississippi. (The *Ellen* was chosen because of its unusually large bathtub, to accommodate the unusually large president.)

Cargill, Incorporated also has a long tradition in water transport. Captain William Dick Cargill was owner and master of several ships in the mid-nineteenth century, and the Cargill company began shipping grain in its own vessels in the early twentieth. Cargill has over the years built and owned a variety of barges, towboats (which actually usually push rather than pull barges), lakers, and ocean-going ships. In 1940 Cargill built the world's first all-welded ship. The all-welded technique was quickly adopted by Henry J. Kaiser for the famous liberty ships that proved crucial to winning the Battle of the Atlantic against the German U-boats.

Many of the facilities for shipping grain in the Midwest were, until recent times, more accessible by water than by land. After World War II, Cargill purchased the motor vessel that became the first CARMAC for inspection trips to company facilities and for customer entertainment. CARMAC II and CARMAC III were acquired by the company for the same purposes. Cargill used them on both the East and West Coasts, in the Gulf of Mexico, and on the lower Mississippi River.

After John MacMillan, Jr.'s death, the company sold CARMAC III, and the four boats of that name that have succeeded her have been owned by Duncan and Hugh MacMillan as charter vessels. The latest of these vessels, CARMAC VII, was delivered to the family in 1991. Built in the Netherlands, she has been called, with justification, "the finest charter motor yacht in the world." Equipped with state-of-the-art navigation tools and communications equipment and possessing a range of five thousand miles, CARMAC VII is capable of any ocean passage.

Duncan MacMillan's numerous other interests include hunting, skiing, racquet sports, scuba diving, raising orchids, and, foremost of all, golf. Characteristically, he has managed to find in his love of golf a business opportunity. With partners and by himself, he has developed golf courses in places as diverse as Las Vegas and his native Minneapolis. His Rush Creek Golf Club, located in the Minneapolis suburb of Maple Grove, recently hosted a major LPGA event.

Duncan MacMillan was also the driving force behind the creation of company archives, first at Waycrosse and then at Cargill itself. These archives enabled Wayne G. Broehl, Jr., professor emeritus at the Amos Tuck School of Business at Dartmouth, to write his multi-volume history of Cargill. These archives also proved helpful when MacMillan privately published a two-volume history of his family titled *MacGhillemhaoil* (Gaelic for MacMillan), which led to the present volume.

MacMillan's interest in history extends well beyond his family. In 1993 he founded the Afton Historical Society Press to publish books that explore and celebrate Minnesota's cultural heritage. One of its first books was *Seth Eastman: A Portfolio of North American Indians* (1995), which showcases fifty-some watercolors of Indian life in Minnesota in the 1840s. The Eastman watercolors had been purchased around the turn of the century by railroad magnate James J. Hill and housed for many decades at the James J. Hill Reference Library in St. Paul, which kept them under wraps. When the library decided to deaccession its Eastman paintings, MacMillan saved them from being dispersed at auction by purchasing the entire collection and making them available for museum exhibitions.

In sum, Duncan MacMillan has turned his energy and creativity to an extraordinary range of activities both inside and outside the umbrella of Cargill operations. In many ways he exemplifies the typical Cargill employee he described in a recent speech:

"Many of our people have been with the company for their entire career," he said. "In my opinion, we are a collection of people united by more than a set of common job skills. We share a similar philosophy and sense of purpose, built around some old-fashioned Midwestern values. Things like hard work, integrity, patience, and dedication to what we believe in. In our case, we attract people who genuinely want to be not just successful but the best in whatever they do—people who believe that by doing our job well, we can make a real difference in the quality of life for the people we serve. It's an old-fashioned idea, really, and to many of today's cynics it probably sounds idealistic. But maybe that's what sets Cargill apart. We have people who don't think it's idealistic. They think it's not just possible, but worthwhile."

This brand of pragmatic idealism has persisted through five generations of Cargill leadership. It goes far in explaining why the remarkable MacMillan family and the equally remarkable company they helped to create has flourished for more than one hundred and thirty years. Cargill is the largest American company to remain so long in family hands.

John Steele Gordon

SELECTED BIBLIOGRAPHY

MACMILLAN: The American Grain Family relies principally on primary sources including family letters, diaries, vital records, oral history interviews, and newspaper and magazine articles contained in our family archives. The following books and reference materials were used to help augment our family story and place it in the context of its times.

Allen, George H., et al. *The Great War.* Five volumes. Philadelphia: George Barrie's Sons, 1915-1921.

Barnett, Correlli. *The Great War.* New York: G.P. Putnam's Sons, 1980.

Bergamini, John D. *The Hundreth Year.* New York: G.P. Putnam's Sons, 1976.

Biographical History of La Crosse, Trempealeau and Buffalo Counties, Wisconsin. Chicago: Lewis Publishing Company, 1892.

Broehl, Wayne G., Jr. *Cargill: Trading the World's Grain.* Hanover: Dartmouth/University Press of New England, 1992.

Broehl, Wayne G., Jr. *Cargill: Going Global.* Hanover: Dartmouth/University Press of New England, 1998.

Bryant, Benjamin F., ed. *Memoirs of La Crosse County.* Madison, Wisconsin: Western Historical Assocation, 1907.

Bumstead, J.M. *The People's Clearance, 1770-1815.* Winnipeg: University of Manitoba Press, 1982.

Burt, Alfred Leroy. *A Short History of Canada for Americans.* Second edition. Minneapolis: University of Minnesota Press, 1944.

Campbell, R.B., and Douglas McDermid. *The Kennedys-MacDiarmids-McDermids-Munros and Other Glengarry-Stormont Pioneers.* Belleville, Ontario: Mika Publishing Company, 1986.

Carr, Rev. Spencer. *A Brief Sketch of La Crosse, Wisc'n.* La Crosse: W.C. Rogers, Printer, Democrat Office, 1854.

Carruth, Gorton, and associates, ed. *The Encyclopedia of American Facts and Dates.* Sixth edition. New York: Thomas Y. Crowell Company, 1972.

Cowan, Helen I. *British Emigration to North America: The First Hundred Years.* Toronto: University of Toronto Press, 1961.

Crutwell, C.R.M.F. *A History of the Great War 1914-1918.* Second edition. Oxford: Clarendon Press, 1961.

Current, Richard Nelson. *Wisconsin: A Bicentennial History.* New York: W.W. Norton & Company, Inc., 1977.

Dos Passos, John. *Mr. Wilson's War.* Garden City, New York: Doubleday & Company, 1962.

Durant, Will and Ariel. *The Age of Napoleon.* New York: Simon and Schuster, 1975.

Edgar, William C., and Loring M. Staples. *The Minneapolis Club.* The Minneapolis Club, 1974.

Foner, Eric, and John A. Garraty, eds. *The Reader's Companion to American History.* Boston: Houghton Mifflin, 1991.

Galbraith, John Kenneth. *The Scotch. A wryly affectionate account of growing up in Canada.* Second edition. Boston: Houghton Mifflin Company, 1985.

Gies, Joseph. *Franklin D. Roosevelt, Portrait of a President.* Garden City, New York: Doubleday & Company, Inc., 1971.

Gilbert, Martin. *First World War Atlas.* New York: The MacMillan Company, 1970.

Grant, I.F. *Highland Folk Ways.* London: Routledge & Kegan Paul, 1961.

Grant, I.F., and Hugh Cheape. *Periods in Highland History.* London: Shepheard-Walwyn, 1987.

Harkness, John Graham. *Stormont, Dundas and Glengarry: A History, 1784-1945.* Privately printed, 1946.

Harper, J.R. *The Fraser Highlanders.* Montreal: The Society of the Montreal Military & Maritime Museum, 1979.

Heminway, J. Callender, ed. *1917: Twenty Years After.* New Haven: Quinnipiack Press, 1938.

Historical Reminiscences of Lake Minnetonka. The Lake Minnetonka Garden Club, 1945.

History of Cargill, Incorporated, 1865-1945. Privately printed, 1945.

Holbrook, Franklin F., and Livia Appel. *Minnesota in the War with Germany*. St. Paul: Minnesota Historical Society, 1928.

Howison, John. *Sketches of Upper Canada*. Edinbugh: Oliver & Boyd, 1825.

Jones, Thelma. *Once Upon a Lake*. Enlarged edition. Minneapolis: Ross and Haines, Inc., 1969.

Katz, Myer. *Echoes of Our Past: Vignettes of Historic La Crosse*. La Crosse: The La Crosse Foundation and the Washburn Foundation, 1985.

Keegan, John, ed. *Encyclopedia of World War II*. Reprint edition. New York: Gallery Books, 1990.

Kilgour, Wm. T. *Lochaber in War and Peace*. Paisley, Scotland: Alexander Gardner, 1908.

Knox, John. *The Siege of Quebec*. Mississauga, Ontario, Canada: Pendragon House of Mississauga, 1980.

Kunz, Virginia Brainard. *St. Paul: Saga of an American City*. Woodland Hills, California: Windsor Publications, Inc., 1977.

Larson, Don W. *Land of the Giants: A History of Minnesota Business*. Minneapolis: Dorn Books, 1979.

Leuchtenburg, William. *Franklin D. Roosevelt and the New Deal, 1932-1940*. New York: Harper & Row, 1963.

Lewis, Samuel. *Topographical Dictionary of Scotland*. London: S. Lewis and Company, 1846.

Logan, James. *McIan's Costumes of the Clans of Scotland*. Reprint edition. Glasgow: David Bryce and Son, 1899.

Lower, Arthur R. M. *The North American Assault on the Canadian Forest*. Toronto: The Ryerson Press, 1938.

——. *Great Britain's Woodyard: British America and the Timber Trade, 1763-1867*. Montreal: McGill-Queen's University Press, 1973.

McCabe, James D. *The Centennial History of the United States*. Philadelphia: The National Publishing Company, 1874.

——. *The Illustrated History of the Centennial Exhibition*. Philadelpia: The National Publishing Company, 1876.

MacDonald, Mairi. *Fort William and Nether Lochaber*. Oban, Scotland: West Highland Publications, 1985.

MacMillan, Somerled. *Bygone Lochaber*. Glasgow: Privately printed, 1971.

——. *Emigration of Lochaber MacMillans to Canada in 1802*. Scotland: Privately printed, 1958.

——. *The MacMillans and Their Septs*. Glasgow: Privately printed, 1952.

MacMillan, W. Duncan. *MacGhillemhaoil*. Volumes 1 and 2. Wayzata, Minnesota: Privately printed, 1990, 1992.

Manchester, William. *The Glory and the Dream*. Boston: Little, Brown and Company, 1973-1974.

Miller, Russell. *The House of Getty*. New York: Henry Holt and Company, 1985.

Morgan, Dan. *Merchants of Grain*. New York: The Viking Press, 1979.

Morison, Samuel Eliot. *The Oxford History of the American People*. New York: Oxford University Press, 1965.

——, ed. *The Parkman Reader*. From the works of Francis Parkman. Boston: Little, Brown and Company, 1955.

Munro, R.W. *Highland Clans and Tartans*. Reprint edition. New York: Crescent Books, 1987.

Murray, Norman. *The Scottish Hand Loom Weavers, 1790-1850: A Social History*. Edinburgh: John Donald Publishers Ltd., 1978.

Nader, Ralph, and William Taylor. *The Big Boys: Power & Position in American Business*. New York: Pantheon Books, 1986.

New Statistical Account of Scotland, Vol. XIV (Inverness—Ross and Cromarty). Edinburgh: William Blackwood and Sons, 1845.

Orel, Harold, Henry L. Snyder, and Marilyn Stokstad, eds. *The Scottish World.* New York: Harrison House/Harry N. Abrams, Inc., 1986.

Pariser, Harry. *Guide to Jamaica.* Chico, California: Moon Publications, 1986.

Parker, Gilbert, and Claude G. Bryan. *Old Quebec: The Fortress of New France.* New York: The MacMillan Company, 1904.

Pershing, John J. *My Experiences in the World War.* New York: Frederick A. Stokes Company, 1931.

Pioneer History of Finch Township. Compiled by the teachers of Finch Township, 1957.

Prebble, John. *Culloden.* London: Secker & Warburg, 1961.

——. *The Highland Clearances.* London: Secker & Warburg, 1963.

——. *The Lion in the North.* New York: Coward, McCann & Geoghegan, Inc., 1971.

Reflections in Loring Pond. Citizens For A Loring Park Community, Wesley United Methodist Church and the Loring-Nicollet Community Council, 1986.

Russell, A. J. *Brief Glimpses of Unfamiliar Loring Park Aspects.* Minneapolis: Leonard H. Wells, 1919.

Sanford, Albert H., and H.J. Hirschheimer. *A History of La Crosse, Wisconsin, 1841-1900.* Reprint edition. La Crosse: La Crosse County Historical Society, 1951.

Sasse, Fred A. *Rookie Days of a Soldier.* St. Paul: W. G. Greene, 1924.

Shachtman, Tom. *Edith & Woodrow: A Presidential Romance.* New York: G. P. Putnam's Sons, 1981.

Sherman, Benjamin M. *The Blake School 1907-1974: A Chronological History.* Minneapolis: The Colwell Press, 1975.

Shutter, Rev. Marion Daniel, ed. *History of Minneapolis: Gateway to the Northwest.* Chicago-Minneapolis: The S. J. Clarke Publishing Company, 1923.

Sinclair, Sir John, ed. *The Statistical Account of Scotland, 1791-1799, Volume XVII* (Inverness-shire, Ross and Cromarty). EP Publishing Limited, 1981.

Stewart, Rev. Alexander. *Nether Lochaber.* Edinbugh: William Paterson, 1883.

Stipanovich, Joseph. *City of Lakes: An Illustrated History of Minneapolis.* Woodland Hills, California: Windsor Publications, Inc., 1982.

Surface, Frank M. *The Grain Trade During the World War.* New York: The MacMillan Company, 1928.

Tebbel, John, ed. *The Battle for North America.* From the works of Francis Parkman. Garden City, New York: Doubleday & Company, Inc., 1948.

Tindall, George Brown. *America: A Narrative History.* New York: Simon & Schuster, Inc., 1981.

Tomasson, Katherine, and Francis Buist. *Battles of the '45.* New York: The MacMillan Company, 1962.

Waugh, W.T. *James Wolfe, Man and Soldier.* Montreal: Louis Carrier & Co., 1928.

Winter, J. M. *The Experience of World War I.* New York: Oxford University Press, 1989.

Work, John. *Cargill Beginnings.* Minneapolis: Cargill, Inc., 1965.

INDEX

ILLUSTRATION CREDITS

Most of the family photographs included in this book are contained in our family archives. Other photos and illustrations on the pages listed are used courtesy of the following individuals and institutions:

2. The Stewart Museum at the Fort, Montreal
10. Charles J. Johnston
11. Charles J. Johnston
15. Scottish Tartan Society
17. Charles J. Johnston
18. National Archives of Canada/C2146
19. National Maritime Museum, Greenwich
23. National Archives of Canada/ C-73702
25t. Archives of Ontario
25l. Charles J. Johnston
26. Charles J. Johnston
27. National Archives of Canada/ C-40331
28. State Historical Society of Wisconsin
29. State Historical Society of Wisconsin
30. La Crosse County Historical Society
31. State Historical Society of Wisconsin
32b. Ann McMillan
33. La Crosse County Historical Society
37t. Duncan Rowles, Jr.
38t. Duncan Rowles, Jr.
39. Murphy Library, University of Wisconsin-La Crosse
40. Murphy Library, University of Wisconsin-La Crosse
41. Marjorie MacMillan Powers
42b. Murphy Library, University of Wisconsin-La Crosse
43. Murphy Library, University of Wisconsin-La Crosse
49t. Lee Taft Johnson
49b. Murphy Library, University of Wisconsin-La Crosse
52. Duncan Rowles, Jr.
54t. Murphy Library, University of Wisconsin-La Crosse

54l. Duncan Rowles, Jr.
55l. Mary Elizabeth Wheeler
55b. Mary Elizabeth Wheeler
56. Mary Elizabeth Wheeler
57. Mary Elizabeth Wheeler
58t. La Crosse County Historical Society
58b. Murphy Library, University of Wisconsin-La Crosse
64b. Minnesota Historical Society (MHS)
65. Murphy Library, University of Wisconsin-La Crosse
66. MHS
67. Marjorie MacMillan Powers
68b. Marjorie MacMillan Powers
70b. Murphy Library, University of Wisconsin-La Crosse
72l. MHS
72r. MHS
74b. Archives Division, Texas State Library
75. Fort Worth Public Library
77t. Lee Taft Johnson
87. Duncan Rowles, Jr.
88. Duncan Rowles, Jr.
89. Lee Taft Johnson
90b. Mary MacMillan Mackey
91. Charles J. Johnston
92. Duncan Rowles, Jr.
101t. MHS
102. Photo by Sweet, MHS
103. MHS
108. San Francisco Archives
110t. MHS
113b. Hennepin History Museum, Minneapolis
120. Cargill Corporate Archives
125t. Murphy Library, University of Wisconsin-La Crosse
125l. Minneapolis Public Library
126. MHS
128. Hennepin History Museum, Minneapolis
129t. MHS
138. The Peabody Museum of Salem
142. Yale University Library
145b. MHS
146b. MHS
147. MHS

148. MHS
151. *Our Sons at Camp Dodge*, DES MOINES REGISTER
152t. *Our Sons at Camp Dodge*, DES MOINES REGISTER
152b. Wheelock Whitney, Jr.
153. Fort Sill Museum
154t. Chrysler Historical Collection
155t. Margaret Harder Shepard
156t. *Our Sons at Camp Dodge*, DES MOINES REGISTER
159. MHS
161. Du Puy-de-Dome Archives Departementales, Clermont-Ferrand
164. MHS
166. MHS
169. MHS
171t. MHS
171l. Du Puy-de-Dome Archives Departementales, Clermont-Ferrand
172. National Maritime Museum, Greenwich
174l. Photo by C. J. Hibbard, MHS
176t. Photo by C. P. Gibson, MHS
176l. CARGILL NEWS
183. Mary MacMillan Mackey
186. Mary MacMillan Mackey
187. Murphy Library, University of Wisconsin-La Crosse
188. Photo by Myron Hall, Stearns County Historical Society
191b. MHS
192. Lee Taft Johnson
223. MHS
233. Minneapolis Public Library
248t. Cargill Corporate Archives
248b. CARGILL NEWS
249. Photo by ST. PAUL PIONEER PRESS, MHS
250. Minneapolis Collection, Minneapolis Public Library
251. Mary Elizabeth Wheeler
252. MHS
257l. Minneapolis Public Library
259b. Woodhill Country Club
261. Duke University
264. Duke University
265. The Berkshire School Archives
303. Public Affairs, Cargill, Inc.